ANGLER PROFILES

*"This dish of meat is too good for any but anglers, or very honest men;
and I trust you will prove both, and therefore I have trusted you with this secret."*

Izaak Walton, *The Compleat Angler*, 1665

ANGLER PROFILES

A COLLECTION OF SOME LEGENDARY ANGLERS' FAVORITE FLIES, FOODS, RODS & WATERS

RUSSELL A. HOPPER

[signature]

ART BY CHRISTOPHER ATKINS & DAVID HALL
REVIEWS BY TED LEESON & GWENN PERKINS

THE HOPE GROUP, INC.
510 Fairmont Avenue
P. O. Box 62
Bowling Green, Kentucky 42102-0062

Published by The Hope Group, Inc.
510 Fairmont Avenue, P. O. Box 62
Bowling Green, Kentucky 42102-0062

Manufactured in the
United States of America.

10 9 8 7 6 5 4 3 2 1

Library of Congress Catalog Card Number:
99-96500

International Standard Book Number:
0-9675262-0-5

QUANTITY PURCHASES

This book is available at a special discount when purchased in large quantities for business, special markets, sales promotional use, fund-raising, or educational use. For information, please contact The Hope Group, Inc., 510 Fairmont Avenue, P. O. Box 62, Bowling Green, Kentucky 42102-0062.

Individuals may order single copies by payment of $24.95 plus $3.25 shipping and handling at the same address. Make checks payable to The Hope Group, Inc. Individuals may use the Order Form in the back of this book.

CREDITS

Angler Profiles was produced by
JM Press
Nashville, Tennessee
http://www.publishyourbook.com

Cover art from
the original oil painting *Bahia Honda*
by Christopher Atkins
atkinscj@aol.com

Pen and ink illustrations provided by
David Hall

SORRY WE MISSED YOU!

Over 2,000 requests were mailed to solicit contributions to this book. If you were omitted, or didn't receive a request, please forgive us.

Your *Angler Profile* may be included in subsequent volumes by providing a personal quote, a listing of your accomplishments, and your favorite food recipe. Also, please provide the number of years you have been fly fishing, your favorite rod weight and length, the number of rods you own, your favorite flies (dry, wet, nymph, streamer, and terrestrial), flies you have invented, and your favorite waters (U.S. river, home river, favorite stream, and home stream).

DEDICATED TO

This book is dedicated to my parents, J. C. and Elsie, for my being and my early value system; my children, Kim and Warren, for their acceptance of me in spite of my shortcomings; my wife's children, Getta and Angela; my wife, Susan, who says that I'm a keeper; and the fellowship that helped to restore my life and give it meaning.

And I present this book to the fly fishing community in memory of Lee Wulff, my first fly fishing hero, and Charles Kuralt, who influenced me to want to see the exotic places of this country where fly fishing is performed.

PROCEEDS TO

A portion of the proceeds from the sale of this book is earmarked for the following nonprofit organizations:

The American Museum of Fly Fishing
P. O. Box 42 - Seminary Avenue
Manchester, Vermont 05254
802-362-3300

Catskill Fly Fishing Center & Museum
P. O. Box 1295 - Old Route 17
Livingston Manor, New York 12758
914-439-4810

Federation of Fly Fishers
P. O. Box 1595
Bozeman, Montana 59771
406-585-7592

Trout Unlimited
1500 Wilson Boulevard, Suite 310
Arlington, Virginia 22209-2404
703-522-0200

A SPECIAL THANKS TO

A special thanks to all the fly fishers who honored me by responding to my unrelenting requests for angler profiles and favorite flies, foods, rods and waters.

I am especially grateful to fellow anglers Gwenn Perkins and Ted Leeson, who were most generous with their reviews; and to Christopher Atkins and David Hall, who provided the art for the cover and interior design.

Alan Anderson's helpful suggestions, our weekly luncheons, his sage wisdom, and his enthusiasm for love and life provided me the encouragement to complete this work.

My fishing companions Ed Craft, Ken Glenn, John Linden, Rick Matthews, Todd Matthews, and Bob Richards provided the much-needed fellowship on the stream during my breaks from the isolation that comes with writing—a communion that can only take place in the mystical world of solitude.

Contents

Ted Leeson Review xi
Gwenn Perkins Review xi

Introduction xiii

Abel, Steve 1, 290
Achor, Kathleen 2
Adams, Leslie 3, 290
Allen, Farrow 4, 290
Amato, Frank W. 5
Ames, Dave 6
Apte, Stuart C. 7, 290
Aroner, Marc 8
Atkins, Christopher 9, 290
Atkinson, R. Valentine 10

Babb, James R. 11
Battles, Bill 13
Beatty, Al 14, 291
Beatty, Gretchen 15, 291
Beck, Barry 16, 291
Beck, Cathy 17, 291
Behnke, Robert 18, 291
Benoit, Benjamin L., III 19
Best, A. K. 20
Betters, Francis E. 21, 292
Birkholm, Deanna Lee 22, 292
Blanton, Dan 23, 292
Borger, Gary A. 24, 292
Borger, Jason 25, 292
Borski, Tim 26, 293
Briscoe, Harry J. 27
Brown, Mac 28, 293

Bruun, Paul M. 29
Bryan, Denver 30
Buchenroth, Buck 31
Burr, Dan 32
Bush, George Herbert Walker 33
Butler, James 34, 293

Cañada, Paul A. 35, 293
Carter, James Earl, Jr. 36
Casada, Jim 37, 293
Casey, Harold 38, 294
Catherwood, William W. 39, 294
Caucci, Al 40, 294
Cave, Jon B. 42, 294
CdeBaca, Conrad 43, 294
Chandler, J. Leon 44, 295
Chavez, Abe 45
Clarke, C. D. 46
Clouser, Bob 47, 295
Cole, Charles 48
Corbin, Peter 49, 295
Coykendall, Ralf 50
Craft, Ed 51, 295
Crawford, Byron Garrison 52, 295
Crockett, Mike 53, 296
Crum, Denny 54
Cruwys, Roger 55, 296
Cutter, Ralph 56, 296

Dahlberg, Larry 57, 296
Davis, Corbett, Jr. 58, 296
Dennis, Jack 59, 297
Dennis, Jerry 60

Dick, Lenox 61
Dietrich, Kirk 62
Doty, John 63
Earnhardt, Tomas W. 64, 297
Edvalds, Jeff 65, 297
Elliott, Charles 66
Ellis, Ray 67, 297
Engerbretson, Dave 68
Engle, Ed 70

Fernandez, J. M. "Chico" 71
Fightmaster, Rob 72, 297
Fisher, Jon 73, 298
Fling, Paul N. 74
Fong, Christine 75
Fong, Michael 76
Forrester, Nick C. 77, 298
Foster, David C. 79, 298
Foster, Ron 80
Fraser, Craig S. 81
Frazier, Luke 82, 298
Fromm, Peter 83, 298
Fullum, Jay "Fishy" 84, 299
Furminsky, Ben 85, 299

Gapen, Dan, Sr. 86, 299
Gardner, Hugh 87, 299
Gates, Rusty 88, 299
Genova, Phil 89, 300
Gibbs, Jerry 90
Gilkes, Cooper A. 91
Glenn, Ken 92, 300

CONTENTS

Goddard, D. L. 94
Gorman, Robert 95
Grobarek, Joseph V. 96, 300
Gunn, Terry 97
Gunn, Wendy Hanvold 98

Hall, David C. 99, 300
Hanson, Carl O. 100
Hanyok, Philip 101
Hardie, Eldridge 102, 300
Harvey, George W. 103, 301
Hawthorne, Tom 104, 301
Helm, Christopher 105, 301
Henley, Bob 106
Hipps, Anthony 107, 301
Hoffman, Henry 108, 301
Holt, Bruce 109, 302
Hommell, George 111
Hopper, Russell 112, 302
Hopper, Susan 113, 302
Hughes, David 114
Humphreys, Joe 115, 302

Izmirian, Richard 116, 302

Jacobs, Jimmy 117
Jacobus, Dann 118
Jindra, Tom 119
Johnson, Tom 120, 303

Karas, Nick 121
Karavolos, Kerry 122
Kaufmann, Randall 124, 303

Keeley, Kim 126
Klausmeyer, David 127
Knopp, Malcolm 128, 303
Koch, Ed 129
Kreh, Bernard "Lefty" 130
Krieger, Fanny B. 131
Krieger, Mel 132
Kulick, Douglas F. 133, 303
Kustich, Rick 134
Kyte, Al 135, 303

LaFontaine, Gary 136
Lawrence, H. Lea 137, 304
Lee, Art 138, 304
Libby, Matt 139, 304
Linden, John 140, 304
Linehan, Tim 141, 304
Livingston, A. D. 143
Loomis, Gary 144, 305

Mahoney, Ivan L. 145
Maler, Tracie 146, 305
Marlowe, Al 147, 305
Marriner, Paul 148
Marriott, Bob 149, 305
Martin, Craig 150
Martin, Darrel 152, 305
Mathews, Craig 153, 306
Matthews, Rick L. 154, 306
Matthews, Todd 155, 306
McDaniel, Gerald E. 156
McGuane, Thomas 157
McIntosh, Ann 158

McManus, Patrick F. 159, 306
Medling, Kenny 160, 306
Merriman, Maggie 161, 307
Meyer, Deke 162, 307
Michalak, Mike 163, 307
Miller, Jack E. 164, 307
Minicucci, Anna 165, 307
Montgomery, M. R. 166
Moore, Winston 167
Morris, Skip 168, 308
Morrow, Laurie 169, 308
Murphy, Lori-Ann 172
Murphy, Nick 173
Murray, Harry W. 174, 308
Murray, John 175

Nauheim, Bob 176, 308
Newman, Bob 177, 308
Norman, Seth Michael 178

O'Keefe, Brian 179, 309
Olsen, Chad 180
Ondaatje, David 181
Owen, Tom 182, 309

Page, Margot 183, 309
Pallot, Diane B. 184, 309
Pallot, Flip 185, 309
Paquette, Ernie 186
Parker, Jon W. 187, 310
Parker, R. M. "Pete" 188, 310
Pate, Billy 189, 310
Pate, Jodi 190, 310

CONTENTS

Patterson, Howard E. 191, 310
Perkins, Leigh H. 192
Pfeiffer, C. Boyd 193, 311
Pfister, Fredrick 194
Phinny, Stephen D. 195
Piccolo, Tom 196, 311
Pobst, Dick 197, 311
Powell, Press 198
Price, Steven D. 199
Probasco, Steve 200, 311
Proper, Datus C. 201, 311
Prosek, James 202, 312
Puckett, James 203, 312

Quinnett, Paul 204, 312

Rafle, Peter 205
Raines, Howell 206, 312
Rajeff, Steve 207, 312
Raymond, Steve 208
Reiger, George W. 209, 313
Richards, Bob 210, 313
Richards, Bruce W. 211
Richards, Carl 212
Robinson, Chuck 213
Rodgers, Bob 214, 313
Rogers, Craig 215, 313
Rogers, Neal & Linda 216, 313
Rosenbauer, Tom 217
Rowinski, Jim 218
Ruimveld, David 219
Ruoff, Rick 220, 314
Ryall, Jim 221

Ryan, Will 222
Ryon, Bob 223

Samson, Jack 224, 314
Schollmeyer, Jim 225, 314
Schramm, Dorothy 226, 314
Schroeder, Don 227
Shenk, Ed 228, 314
Sherman, Marty 229, 315
Shewey, John 230
Shultz, Paul T., III 232
Sigler, Cam 233, 315
Slone, Harry Lee 234, 315
Sosin, Mark 235
Soucie, Gary 236, 315
Spartas, Dale C. 237
Stalcup, Shane 238
Stearns, Bob 239
Stewart, Jim 240
Story, Ed 241
Streeks, E. Neale 242, 315
Swisher, Doug 243

Tabory, Lou 244, 316
Talarico, Sam 245, 316
Talleur, Dick 247, 316
Tanner, Gary P. 248
Tapply, William G. 249, 316
Taylor, Howard L. 250
Taylor, Wanda 251, 316
Teeny, Jim 252, 317
Theus, Tom 253
Thomas, E. Donnall, Jr. 254

Thompson, Doc 255
Tisch, Richard 256
Travis, Tom 257
Troth, Al 258, 317
Troy, John R. 259, 317
Trump, Gene 260, 317
Tullis, Larry 261
Turner, Daniel D. 262, 317

Van Gytenbeek, R. P. 263, 318
Van Patten, Mark 264, 318
Van Put, Ed 265
Vincent, James D. 266, 318
Von Strasser, Rudy 267

Waite, John 268
Waller, Lani 269
Warren, Joe J. 270, 318
Waterman, Charles F. 271, 318
Watt, Jim 272, 319
Watt, Kelly 273, 319
Weaver, Craig 274
Webber, Katharine 275
White, Ray J. 276, 319
Whitlock, Dave 277
Whitlock, Emily 278
Whitner, Richard 279
Wiegers, George A. 280
Williams, Edward F. "Ted" 281, 319
Williams, Mark D. 282, 319
Wilson, Hank 283, 320
Witt, Danielle 284
Wixom, Hartt 285

CONTENTS

Wotton, Davy 286, 320
Wright, Leonard M., Jr. 287, 320
Wulff, Joan Salvato 288, 320
Young, Todd O. 289

Angler Photographs . . . . .290 - 320
Recipe Index . . . . .321 - 326
My Angling Friends . . . . .327 - 334
Order Form 335

The passion for fly fishing poses a delightful paradox. For whatever reason, it kindles a fire only in certain, specific souls, yet in the end is remarkably indifferent about who those souls might belong to. It is highly selective (perhaps even elitist as is sometimes charged), but at the same time utterly democratic. The result, as the profiles in this book amply demonstrate, is that the group of people we call "fly fishers" is in fact an astonishingly disparate and eclectic bunch. In these pages, you'll find legendary anglers and luminaries of the sport alongside ex-presidents, CEO's, and captains of industry, as well as writers, guides, photographers, and other barnacles on the ship of state. Some fish for a living, and others live to fish, but from deadbeats to kings, they are unfailingly interesting individuals.

If the truth be told, there is a little voyeur in all of us, a thoroughly human curiosity to peek at the private lives of famous folks and get some glimpse of what they are like. This book rewards that curiosity in a way that fly anglers can truly appreciate, as the people in these pages speak about why and where they fish, the tackle and flies they favor, and what they like to eat. Passion and food—the twin staffs of life—I can think of nothing more elemental, more intimate, or more revealing.

Ted Leeson is a Contributing Editor for *Fly Rod & Reel* magazine, the author of *The Habit of Rivers* and co-author of *The Fly Tier's Benchside Reference to Technique and Dressing Styles.*

In 1981, I cast a fly rod for the very first time. My adult life has been full of fly fishing ever since. But this was not the start of my fishing experiences.

Growing up, my family spent every summer on Lake St. Catherine in Vermont. Jimmy Martin and I were "summertime best friends." We fished for everything, fish included. All bullfrogs, crayfish, and even old bottles at the bottom of the lake were our quarry. But my favorites were the fish. We fished for many kinds of fish: pike, large and smallmouth bass, perch and bluegills, and sometimes even those moody trout that lived in a nearby stream. I especially liked catching the little pesky rock bass that lived under the dock. They would hide behind the iron wheels that allowed the docks to be rolled in and out of the water every spring and fall. They always nibbled on our toes, which scared the daylights out of me, as we put our feet on the iron wheel to climb up on the end of the dock.

In the evening, each member of my family would put a line out in hopes of catching a nocturnal bullhead. We would pierce the slimy, twisting, thick-bodied earthworms with our hooks, fashioning a great big gob. A perfect lob cast would send the gob intact a good distance out. Large chunks of rock rested on the handles

Continued on next page . . .

of our poles lined up on the end of the dock so as to not let the ugly bullhead take off with our priceless tag sale equipment. By morning invariably at the end of yards of snarled monofilament would be at least one fish. After dad cleaned the fish, my mom would cook them for our breakfast. The aroma of bacon and fish simmering in the skillet lingered in the air and still linger in my memories.

I first learned to fly fish while working for the Orvis Company, Inc. in Manchester, Vermont. After many years of learning, honing fly fishing skills and falling in love with the sport, I became immersed with it on a commercial level. Orvis had a preexisting women's fly fishing school and some women's fishing equipment, that was living a small life of its own. But I could see that there was a need to make a more cohesive, well-rounded program. Thus began The Orvis Women's Outdoor Programs. We started more women's fly fishing schools and some trips were added. We started marketing the women's fishing clothing much more aggressively. More and more Orvis dealers held women's fly fishing schools that were a great success. Within the first year of pushing my vision, the women's clothing line sales experienced a profound growth in sales. With high ticket Alaskan fishing trips for women easily filling, we were on the crest of a wave.

Over the years I enjoyed teaching competition equestrians, alpine and telemark skiing. I have always loved teaching, and teaching fly fishing is no exception. In 1996 while still at Orvis, directing the women's fly fishing schools, I started a fly fishing program for women recovering from breast cancer.

Casting for Recovery is now a national 501(c)(3) not-for-profit organization that I devote all my time to. Casting for Recovery holds retreats all across the country.

It has been suggested that the light repetitive casting motion could be beneficial to women experiencing limited mobility from mastectomy. Many cancer patients define their lives as pre-diagnosis, and post-diagnosis. To be learning a new sport as an adult after a diagnosis of cancer can be a tremendously uplifting experience. The emotional benefits of fly fishing for these women are invaluable. I want to point out a few quotes from this book, which portray the benefits. Peter Rafle shares a quote that hits the nail on the head. *"Hip deep in clear, cold water, with fish rising, and bugs hatching, it's awfully hard to worry about anything but the next cast."* Francis E. Betters' favorite quote dovetails in beautifully; *"There's more to fishing than fishing."*

The anglers whose profiles appear in the pages of this book are vast and varied. These anglers are retired policemen, ball-room dance instructors, oil field chemists, orchestra conductors, house husbands, basketball and wrestling coaches just to name a few. A theme pronounced throughout this book from so many anglers is about giving back, giving back to others and to the resources. Many of the quotes in the following pages reflect this philosophy. Former President George Bush writes, *"Each of us can make a difference in the life of another."* Paul Bruun states, *"My favorite task is helping people have a good time and create memories."* Todd Matthews writes, *"I saw a man today with no smile, so I gave him one."* Let's try to embrace these philosophies.

I truly enjoyed sitting down with this book to learn more about the folks between the pages. Russell A. Hopper has compiled a wide variety of angler profiles that I find refreshing to read and I think you will too.

Have you ever wondered what it would be like to hang out with some of your favorite fly fishing heroes? What kind of questions would you ask? Would you want to know about their favorite flies? Which rods they prefer? Oh yes, don't forget about their favorite waters. Would they honestly share a secret so precious?

These and other questions are answered in this *Angler Profiles: A Collection of Some Legendary Anglers' Favorite Flies, Foods, Rods & Waters.* Before casting further through this collection, however, sit back and think about which fly fishers you would invite to spend an evening with you.

Let your imagination run wild like an elusive five-pound brown trout from your *Curtis Creek*. Pretend that you're hosting an intimate gathering of your favorite anglers. Each guest will be asked to bring a favorite fly and there'll be fish stories plenty. It's potluck and each angler will be bringing his or her food favorite.

Assemble your list or your dream may vanish. Will you invite Joan Salvato Wulff? Of course! How about Lefty Kreh or Jack Samson? Perhaps you will invite Cathy and Berry Beck. Don't forget George Harvey, Billy Pate, Ted Williams, A. D. Livingston or Seth Norman. Should you invite Todd, John, Ed, Ken, Rick and Bob, your fishing buddies, to share in this moment? Oh, making a list is no easy task. Maybe you will have to host another gathering soon and invite some other anglers.

With wild anticipation, your special evening has finally arrived. Your dream starts to unfold. Each invited guest chose to honor you with his or her presence. They're gathered around the dining table awaiting your cast.

As you enter the room discreetly, pause for a moment and take a deep breath. Listen quietly and intently as you try to make out the chitchat coming from that vast pool called experience. Capture the laughter, that magical spirit, the smells and the stories as they swirl through the air.

Greet your guests with gusto. Propose a toast to Dame Juliana Berners, Izaak Walton and Theodore Gordon. Raise your glass again for old Joe Brooks, A. J. McClane, Ray Bergman, Arnold Gingrich, Art Flick, Tom McNally, Robert Traver, Sparse Grey Hackle, Lee Wulff, and Ed Zern, too.

Pull up a chair for yourself and get comfortable. Tonight you are dining with your favorite fly fishers; anglers whose lives are as storied as the famed waters they ply.

Tonight there will be no pretense. No need to preach or otherwise dictate what is or is not a healthy meal. Forget about dieting and such nonsense. Some moments were made for indulgence. Moments like intimate conversation with some fellow travelers and a meal prepared from the recipe of some legendary fly fisher.

Pleasant dreams and a full belly as you wander through this evening. Tight lines be damned!

– Russell Hopper

STEVE ABEL

"If you buy a cheap tool, you end up buying it twice." – Steve's Grandmother

Steve Abel is a machinist, reelmaker and rodmaker who resides in Somis, California. He developed what he calls the first modern tackle bag, the world's best putter, the first roll your own cigar system, some mighty dependable reels, a fishing knife, his famous fishing pliers, and now salt water fly rods.

Able took up the sport of fly fishing in his teens and later originated long-range bluewater fly fishing trips out of Southern California. It was Steve's love of fly fishing that eventually took him into the world of manufacturing fly reels.

Steve was a professional diver in the 1970s, helping salvage sunken ships. However, his life changed measurably when he paid $50 for a 1920s-circa screw machine.

For several years, Steve manufactured parts for heart pacemakers, became a parts supplier to the aerospace industry, and set up machining equipment for firearms companies.

At the age of 39 Steve made some fly reels for an associate and in 1988 started his reel business full time. That business is based in Camarillo, California and is known worldwide as Abel Reel.

Years Fly Fishing
Thirty

Favorite Rod
9 wt 9' Graphite

Rods Owned
Sixty

Favorite Flies
Dry – Royal Wulff
Wet – Woolly Bugger
Nymph – Pheasant Tail
Streamer – Woolly Bugger
Terrestrial – Hopper

Fly Invented
Abel Anchovy

Favorite US River
Bitterroot (MT)

Home River
Sespe (CA)

Favorite Stream
Hot Creek (CA)

Home Stream
Sespe (CA)

AMBROSIA

2 Oranges
2 Bananas

Slice bananas. Cut oranges into wedges. Cut meat of orange away from rind. Put sliced bananas in a bowl. Cut orange into bite sized pieces. Add orange to bananas and mix with spoon.
Enjoy!

Serves: 2

"I am an angler. It's possible that nothing I've told you here is true. When fishing, my 'favorite' is not so much a particular rod or fly or even a particular stream, but rather a particular 'moment' – and in that moment, I may or may not be catching fish."

Kathleen Achor is the Editor of *The American Fly Fisher*, the quarterly historical fly fishing journal of the American Museum of Fly Fishing. She is also a freelance editor and lives in Manchester, Vermont.

As a freelancer, Kathleen says her life can be rather hectic. When continually pestered for information to be included in this book, *Angler Profiles*, Ms. Achor said, *"Don't worry about pestering me! I am an editor ... I know all about the need to nag people about deadlines. I just feel quite apologetic that my life is too hectic to get around to things."*

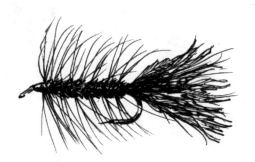

Years Fly Fishing
About Ten
Favorite Rod
5 wt 7' 6" Graphite
Rods Owned
Ten (Mutually)
Favorite Flies
Dry – C.D.C. Caddis
Nymph – Double
Tungsten B. H. Caddis
Streamer – Woolly Bugger
Terrestrial – My
extra one.
Fly Invented
None, yet
Favorite US River
Ausable (NY)
Home River
Battenkill (VT)
Favorite Stream
Mettawee (VT)
Home Stream
Mettawee (VT)

1 ½ Pounds Shrimp
1 Can Tiny Shrimp
1 Pound Smoked Bacon, Fried
1 Large Chopped Onion, Sautéed
1 Large Sweet Red Pepper
2 Cans Black-eyed Peas, with Juice
2 Cans Black Beans
2 Cans Okra (Optional)
3 – 4 Tablespoons Cajun Garlic
2 Tablespoons Gumbo Filet
Pinch of Old Bay Seasoning
Cumin to Taste
Black Pepper to Taste
Brown Rice
Wild Rice

Simmer the bacon, onion, red pepper, black-eyed peas, black beans, okra, and Cajun garlic for 20 minutes. Add the shrimp and simmer for 15 minutes or until shrimp is firm. Add the black pepper, gumbo filet, Old Bay seasoning, and cumin. Add the can of tiny shrimp.

Serve over a brown rice/wild rice mix.

Serves: 5 hungry people

"So wouldn't it be worthwhile if an amateur fly fisherman, like me, could be a 'fly on the wall' in a room where a group of top professionals were having a really in-depth discussion of all kinds of interesting questions about fly fishing?"

Les Adams of Birmingham, Alabama is a book publisher and an attorney. He is the publisher of the multi-volume *Lefty's Little Library of Fly Fishing* and has been fortunate to be able to travel and fly fish extensively all over the world.

The above quote comes from Les's and Lefty Kreh's earlier conversation concerning the need for a high-level meeting to help satisfy, but not cure, the insatiable appetite of the modern day fly fisher. That conversation was responsible for the idea for the *American Masters Fly Fishing Symposium*.

On August 21 and 22, 1991, Les Adams, Lefty Kreh, Dan Blanton, Dave Whitlock, John Randolph, Flip Pallot, Gary Borger and Jim Teeny participated in the *Symposium*.

Years Fly Fishing
Thirty-five

Favorite Rod
8 wt 9' Graphite

Rods Owned
Twenty-two

Favorite Flies
Dry – Black Wulff
Wet – Woolly Bugger
Nymph – Hare's Ear
Streamer – Olive Matuka
Terrestrial – Black Ant

Fly Invented
None, yet

Favorite US River
Goodnews (AK)

Favorite Stream
Hunter River,

South Island,
New Zealand

1 Pound Bacon
1 Large Can of Whole Tomatoes, with Can Liquid
2 Small Cans V-8 Juice
Flour
Worcestershire Sauce
Tabasco Sauce
Salt and Pepper
Grits, Biscuits or Rice

In heavy skillet, fry bacon. Remove and drain. Combine bacon drippings with equal amount of flour. Stir constantly until the roux is dark brown. Lower heat and add tomatoes with can liquid, juices. Add Worcestershire sauce, Tabasco, salt and ground pepper to taste.

"This is an old southern breakfast recipe that originated in north Florida. Once you've served it on grits, you'll need no further proof of the existence of God, because only He could have created this fantastic gravy. If you're out of grits, it's also great on biscuits, or even rice." – Les

FARROW ALLEN

"Tying flies is like preparing your own meals: with the right ingredients and enough time, you can always do it better at home."

Farrow Allen lives in Asheville, North Carolina. He is the Fly Tying and Southeast Regional Editor for *Fly Fish America* magazine. Farrow is an instructor with the Hunter Banks, Co. in Asheville, North Carolina, and presents fly tying seminars for fly shops throughout the south.

Barnes and Noble list eleven books currently available. Farrow has co-authored with Dick Stewart on ten of the books listed as well as three CDs. *Vermont Trout Streams* was co-authored with Peter Shea and Edward Antczak. Allen-Stewart co-authored books include *Flies for Trout, Flies for Saltwater, Flies for Atlantic Salmon, Flies for Bass and Panfish,* and *Flies for Steelhead.*

Prior to his move to North Carolina, Farrow was associated with *American Angler* magazine and lived in Vermont where for twelve years he owned a fly fishing shop.

Years Fly Fishing
A Lot

Favorite Rod
4 wt 9' Scott Powrply

Rods Owned
Twenty to Thirty

Favorite Flies
Dry – Compara Dun
Wet – March Brown
Nymph – Hare's Ear
Streamer – Clouser Minnow
Terrestrial – Letort Hopper

Fly Invented
None, yet

Favorite US River
South Holston (TN)

Home River
Davidson (NC)

Favorite Stream
Beaverdam Creek (TN)

Home Stream
North Mills (NC)

CURRIED RICE SALAD

1 1/3 Cups Cooked Rice
½ Teaspoon Salt and Pepper to Taste
¼ Cup French Dressing
¾ Cup Mayonnaise
1 Tablespoon Minced Onion
½ Cup Chopped Celery
1 Package Frozen Peas, Lightly Cooked
1 Teaspoon Curry Powder, More to Taste
Dash Dry Mustard
Bed of Lettuce

Toss hot cooked rice with French dressing and chill. Mix mayonnaise with curry powder and dry mustard. Mix cooled rice and mayonnaise/curry mixture. Add onion, celery and peas. Salt and pepper.

Serve well chilled on a bed of lettuce.

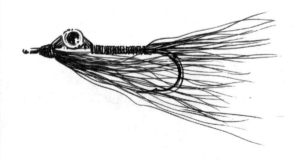

"Do it fast so there is more time to fish."

Frank Amato lives in Portland, Oregon. His company, Frank Amato Publications, Inc., is the publisher of over 100 sport fishing books and two magazines, *Fly Fishing & Tying Journal* and *Salmon Trout Steelhead*. Frank has also written a book, *Fly Casting: Illustrated in Color.* The book was co-authored with the famous Jim Schollmeyer.

Frank's grandparents came from Sicily and so he has always loved pasta dishes. He makes his Pasta Amato with or without meat and adds very little salt. Frank says the dish is a low saturated fat, low salt meal that he eats about six times a week for lunch and supper.

Years Fly Fishing
Forty-one
Favorite Rod
4 wt 9' Graphite
Rods Owned
Thirty
Favorite Flies
Dry – Adams
Wet – Spruce
Nymph – Hare's Ear
Streamer – Mickey Finn
Terrestrial – Hopper
Fly Invented
Night Dancer
Favorite US River
Deschutes (OR)
Home River
Deschutes (OR)
Favorite Stream
Not Provided
Home Stream
Not Provided

© 2000 - Russell A. Hopper

Spaghetti Noodles, Boiled
Hot Chicken Italian Sausage
Olive Oil
Very Little Salt – Cayenne Pepper
Capers
Mushrooms – Garlic – Marjoram
Tomatoes – Broccoli
Green Onions – Zucchini
Pecorino Romano Cheese
Red Wine
Whole Wheat Extra-Sour-Dough Bread

Precook one or two sausages in the microwave. Chop all vegetables, add seasonings, sauté, and briefly simmer in a very large frying pan in a very modest amount of olive oil with water added to help steam-cook the vegetables. You may use a lid to cook them faster. Once the pasta is done, drain and add 3 – 5 tablespoons of cold pressed olive oil. Mix the vegetables, chopped sausage and pasta together.

Serve steaming hot with sharp Pecorino Romano cheese, red wine, and whole-wheat extra-sour-dough bread that has been oven toasted and spread with olive oil and cheese.

DAVE AMES

"No matter where I go, I'm glad I went."

Dave Ames lives in a hidden location in a western state. He says that he is a ne'er do well fishing guide whose greatest accomplishment is that after twenty six years of guiding, he still enjoys fishing on his day off.

When asked about the number of rods he owns, Dave's response was, *"It varies: I buy them in the summer and trade them for food in the winter."*

Dave is the author of *True Love and the Woolly Bugger*, a book consisting of some seven offbeat fishing tales about booze, bartenders, and babes.

As an inventor of fly patterns, Dave says, *"There is nothing new in the world."*

Years Fly Fishing
Twenty-six
Favorite Rod
4 wt 9' Graphite
Rods Owned
See Comments
Favorite Flies
Dry – Parachute Adams
Wet – Jalapeno Maria
Nymph – Prince
Streamer – Rhinestone Cowboy
Terrestrial – Cricket
Fly Invented
See Comments
Favorite US River
Apikuni (MT)
Home River
Willow Spring Creek (MT)
Favorite Stream
Paradise Creek (MT)
Home Stream
Little Flatfoot (MT)

BOURBON SLUSH

Bourbon
Snow
Alpen Glow, if Available
Old Tin Cup

A bourbon slush is best made in an old tin cup, preferably with snow from a cornice that will never melt no matter how hot the summer, because the cornice is on the north side of an alpine ridge that looks out over nothing but mountains as far as the eye can see.

Once you find the proper snow, scrape the surface free of bugs. Then scoop out a heaping white cupful. Add bourbon to taste. If you're not eating well, or if scurvy runs in your family, stir in enough lemonade powder so you won't taste the bugs.

Drink with your feet up on your backpack, your arm around the one you love.

STUART C. APTE

"You don't know, if you don't go."

Stu Apte is a fly fishing legend who has held more than 40 salt water light tackle and fly rod world records, including two longest standing salt water fly rod records. He caught a 58-pound dolphin in 1964 and a 136-pound Pacific sailfish in 1965. Both fish were caught on a 12-pound tippet.

Stu was induced into the *Fishing Hall of Fame* in 1971 and is known in the Florida Keys as Mr. Tarpon.

Before becoming a full time film producer, writer, and consultant, Stu was a fighter pilot in the Navy during the Korean conflict and spent 34 years flying for Pan Am. He began fly fishing in the mid 1940s and began guiding anglers in the mid 1950s in the Florida Keys.

Stu developed the Stu Apte Tarpon Fly and the Stu Apte Improved Blood Knot. His fly has been featured on a US Postage Stamp.

Mr. Tarpon has written numerous fishing articles for magazines and the now-classic book, *Stu Atpe's Fishing in the Florida Keys & Flamingo*. His videos include *Tarpon Country, Saltwater Fly Fishing from A to Z,* and *The Quest for Giant Tarpon*. Stu helped produce the pilot film for ABC Television's *American Sportsman*.

Years Fly Fishing
Fifty-three

Favorite Rod
9 wt 9' Graphite

Rods Owned
Over Forty

Favorite Flies
Dry – Caddis
Wet – Baby Apte Too
Nymph – B.H. Hare's Ear
Streamer – Apte Too # 2 Hook
Terrestrial – Flying Ant

Flies Invented
Apte Tarpon Fly, Apte Too, and Apte Too Plus

Favorite US River
Bighorn (MT) and Missouri (MT) between Wolf Creek and Craig about 45 miles north of Helena, Montana.

Home River
Florida Bay (FL)

Favorite Stream
Gulf Stream (FL)

Home Stream
Everglades (FL)

© 2000 - Russell A. Hopper

BARBECUE SPARE RIBS

Baby Back Ribs
Garlic Powder
Soy Sauce
Teriyaki Sauce
Ginger
Coarse Black Pepper
Thick & Spicy Honey
Barbecue Sauce

Sprinkle garlic powder and pepper liberally on ribs. Sear both sides on grill on high. Baste on mixture of teriyaki sauce, ginger, soy sauce, honey and barbecue sauce, both sides. Grill on low and turn about 15 minutes. Baste again and continue cooking 15 minutes or until done. Set aside extra sauce to serve with ribs.

Serves: 1 rack per person

Stu has appeared with A. J. McClane and Joe Brooks on the *Wide World of Sports*, has been elected *Worldwide Angler of the Year* for lifetime achievement in fishing and conservation, and led the 1989 USA/USSR Atlantic Salmon exploratory expedition to Russia. When not traveling around the world, Stu resides in the Florida Keys.

MARC ARONER

"Larger even than my memories is my anticipation of rivers yet fished." – Charles Kuralt

Marc Aroner is a rodmaker who lives in Conway, Maine.

Years Fly Fishing
Twenty-six

Favorite Rod
4 wt 7' Bamboo

Rods Owned
Six

Favorite Flies
Dry – Cahill
Wet – Not Provided
Nymph – Not Provided
Streamer – Gray Ghost
Terrestrial – Letort Cricket

Fly Invented
None, yet

Favorite US River
Deerfield (MA)

Home River
Not Provided

Favorite Stream
Not Provided

Home Stream
Not Provided

FLAME THROWER BBQ SAUCE

4 Quarts Pineapple Juice
8 – 10 Dried Mexican Chilies
2 Large Onions
½ Cup Chinese Star Anise
½ Cup Soy Sauce
6 Finely Chopped Garlic Cloves
1 Tablespoon Chinese Hot Oil
1 Small Can Tomato Paste
1 Cup Dark Brown Sugar
½ Cup Japanese Rice Vinegar
Salt and Pepper

Add 4 quarts pineapple juice, chilies, star anise and onions. Simmer on low 1 – 2 hours or until reduced ¾ to 7/8s. Strain to remove coarse solids. Add vinegar, soy and brown sugar. Continue to reduce. Add tomato paste, garlic, hot oil, and salt and pepper to taste.

Use fresh or freeze.

"Don't stretch the elastic too much, old chum – it snaps." – David Niven, Cap Ferrat, France (1982)

Christopher Atkins describes himself as a weekend artist. He is a resident of Boston, Massachusetts and spends his summers on Martha's Vineyard Island where he salt water fly fishes and paints.

Christopher's oil painting, *Tarpon – Marquesas Keys*, won an award at the All Island Art exhibit on Martha's Vineyard in the summer of 1996. His art is marketed through his company, Beryl Prints, named after his daughter.

When asked about his art achievements, Christopher responded, *"People buy my art-work."*

Atkins grew up in South America, where in his early days he fished along the Pacific coast of Peru and hunted in the foothills of the Andes. He received his formal education in England and in Canada, and now works out of his studio and office in Cambridge, Massachusetts.

Today, Christopher travels extensively throughout the Florida Keys, where he finds much of the inspiration for his paintings.

Christopher's original oil painting, *Bahia Honda*, was used for the cover of this book, *Angler Profiles*. He may be contacted at his e-mail address: *atkinscj@aol.com* for information about his paintings.

Years Fly Fishing
Thirty

Favorite Rod
9 wt 9' Graphite

Rods Owned
Five

Favorite Flies
Dry – Muddler Minnow
Wet – Sand Eel

Home Waters
Atlantic Ocean

Home Stream
Cape Pogue, Martha's Vineyard (MA)

1 Fresh Bluefish
Container of Louisiana Seafood Magic
Box of Seasoned Breadcrumbs
Box of Bamboo Skewers
1 Block of Butter
Pastry Brush
Charcoal Broiler
Or
Gas Ready Grill

Filet bluefish and cut into rectangular pieces. Mix 50/50 Seafood Magic and breadcrumbs in a bowl. Coat each fish cube in bowl mixture. Fit 4 – 5 pieces of fish on to each bamboo skewer. Melt butter in small pot and have ready with pastry brush on the side. Place fish skewers over charcoal, or gas grill, and rotate as required. Fit fish cubes close together. Keep brushing the Blue Kabobs with the pastry brush and melted butter. Take care not to burn bamboo skewers. Blue Kabobs are done when golden brown. Hand a skewer of Blue Kabobs to each guest.

"Blue Kabobs should be eaten on the fly!" – Christopher

"Truth, adventure, and passion in fly fishing, travel and life."

Val Atkinson resides in San Francisco, California and is an internationally acclaimed and published angling and sports photographer who specializes in Fly Fishing Lifestyles and Travel Imagery. Val's assignments have taken him to over 25 different countries. His work is divided between corporate advertising and editorial. Val's work is often published in magazines such as *Travel and Leisure, The New York Times, Sports Afield, Field & Stream, Gray's Sporting Journal, Fly Fisherman* and many others.

Val has been the staff photographer for Frontiers Travel for over 10 years and is a Contributing Photographer for *Sports Afield* magazine. He operates his own stock photo library as well as being represented by Sharpshooters in Miami and Pacific Press in Tokyo.

In addition to his two books, *Distant Waters: The Greatest Fly Fishing Worldwide* and *Trout and Salmon,* his limited-edition fine art prints, and his other photography, Val says, *"My greatest personal achievement has been in developing a new camera technique on how to photograph myself catching fish."*

Years Fly Fishing
Forty-one

Favorite Rod
6 wt 9' Graphite

Rods Owned
Thirty-five

Favorite Flies
Dry – Coachi – Bondu
Wet – Soft Hackle
Caddis Emerger
Nymph – Bead Head
Anything
Streamer – Mickey Finn
Terrestrial – Beetle

Fly Invented
None, yet

Favorite US River
Henry's Fork (ID)

Home River
Fall River & Hat Creek (CA)

Favorite Stream
Laxa-l-Adaldal (Iceland)

Home Stream
Not Provided

Cheese
Brown Bread
Frying Pan

Take 2 pieces of brown bread and place the cheese of your preference (Swiss, Gouda, or Sharp) in between each slice of bread and place in the frying pan with a plate on top until the cheese is melted, 10 quick minutes.

Let cool and eat.

"This sort of indicates my eating habits. I am a bachelor and a terrible cook! I mostly eat out." – Val

"Fish and visitors smell after three days." – Ben Franklin

James Babb is the Editor and Angling Columnist for *Gray's Sporting Journal*, a former Editor for Lyons & Burford, and a sporting book editor and nautical books consultant for W. W. Norton. He lives in Searsport, Maine.

Jim once fought a 70+ pound giant trevally for almost two hours before landing it on Midway Island. When he cut it open to get the fly out, for the International Game Fish Association, he found he had actually caught an 8-pound rudderfish on his popper and the giant trevally had swallowed the rudderfish, meaning his 16-pound Fly World Record was actually caught on live bait.

Years Fly Fishing
Forty-four

Favorite Rod
5 wt 8' F. E. Thomas Bamboo

Rods Owned
Thirty-eight

Favorite Flies
Dry – Parachute Hare's Ear
Wet – Speck (i.e. soft hackle, wingless irresistible on a heavy hook)
Nymph – Blackburn Tellico
Streamer – B.H. Flashabugger
Terrestrial – McMurray Ant

Fly Invented
The Apprehensive Smelt

Favorite US River
North River (TN)

Home River
Penobscot (ME)

Favorite Stream
Sycamore Creek (TN)

Home Stream
Opeechee (ME)

© 2000 - Russell A. Hopper

---

2 Stocked 8" – 12" Rainbows Per Serving
8 Garlic Cloves, Sliced Thin
½ Cup Lemon Juice
Flat-leaf Parsley
¼ Cup Dry Vermouth
Unsalted Butter
Olive Oil – Chives
Salt and Black Pepper
Dried Red Pepper Pods
Minced Shallots
¼ Cup Strong Chicken or Veal Stock

Dry fish. Rub salt and pepper into skin and cavity. Heat 2 tablespoons olive oil in an iron skillet till smoking. Brown trout quickly on one side 2 – 3 minutes. Turn, then toss into pan ¼ cup butter cut in small chunks, the sliced garlic, and 3 – 4 whole pepper pods. Reduce heat to medium and continue cooking, shaking the pan, until garlic is medium ginger tan. Turn fish and cook 1 more minute, shaking pan continuously. Then remove to warm platter. Add 1 tablespoon minced shallots and cook for 1 minute. Then turn heat to high and add ½ cup fresh lemon juice, ¼ cup dry vermouth and ¼ cup stock.

Continued on next page …

When reduced thick enough to coat the back of a wooden spoon, add ¼ cup more cold unsalted butter cut into bits, the parsley and the fish. Let fish cook slowly about 1 minute on each side to absorb flavors.

Serve with white rice, steamed asparagus or broccoli, French bread, and a vigorous white Graves, Meursault or Cotes du Rhone.

Serves: 2 fish per person

BILL BATTLES

"I fished with a man who knew all the secrets. Fish lay where he said they should lie and took hold as he said they would take, and one remembered and fished it that way for oneself until the knowledge was properly one's own." – Roderick Haig-Brown

Bill Battles is the Editor and Publisher of *Fly Fish America*, the world's second largest fly fishing magazine. Bill lives in North Conway, New Hampshire.

According to Bill, his greatest achievements are his four kids.

Years Fly Fishing
Thirty-six

Favorite Rod
7 wt 9' Graphite

Rods Owned
Fifteen

Favorite Flies
Dry – Compa Dun/Spinner
Wet – Muddler Minnow
Nymph – Small
Black Stonefly
Streamer – Gray Ghost
Terrestrial – Transpar Ant

Fly Invented
Bristol Bay Death Ray

Favorite US River
Alagnak (AK)

Home River
Saco (NH)

Favorite Stream
Beaver Creek (CO)

Home Stream
Not Provided

GRILLED ATLANTIC SALMON

3 – 4 Pound Atlantic Salmon Fillet
(Farm Raised – No Wild Fish!)
¼ Pound Butter
Juice of ¼ Lemon
1 Tablespoon Soy Sauce
¼ Teaspoon Curry Powder
¼ Teaspoon Powdered Ginger
1 Tablespoon Dark Brown Sugar
Wild Rice and Grilled Vegetables

Pull the bones out of the fillet with a pair of needle nose pliers. Spray a large sheet of aluminum foil with Pam or other vegetable oil spray. Melt butter in saucepan and add lemon juice, soy sauce, curry, ginger and brown sugar. Fire up the grill. Place fillet skin side down on the aluminum foil and toss in on the grill. Don't cover the fillet with foil. Splash on the butter mixture. Grill on high, basting fillet every few minutes with the butter mixture. Grill only until the thickest part of the fillet barely flakes when a fork is inserted and twisted. Skin will be crusted black, but the fish will be perfect.

Serve with wild rice and grilled vegetables.

AL BEATTY

"I'm the guy who loves to fly fish, wears glasses, and tends to fall in the water a lot."

Al Beatty is the National Marketing Director for Whiting Farms, producers of Hoffman Hackle. A past President and Secretary of the Federation of Fly Fishers, Al and his wife, Gretchen, own and operate BT's Fly Fishing Products, a mail order fly fishing and fly tying supplier in Delta, Colorado.

Al is a veteran fly tying instructor and demonstrator throughout the world including Fly Fair in Holland, The Chatsworth Angling Fair in England, Fly Days in Norway, Kullagarden in Sweden, and the Danish Fly Festival in Denmark.

A freelance writer, Al is a regular contributor to various fly fishing magazines including *Fly Fish America, The Flyfisher* and the *Angler's Journal*. He and his wife, Gretchen, recently wrote *Tying Hair Wing Flies*. The book is available through the Oregon Council of the Federation of Fly Fishers.

Years Fly Fishing
Forty-one

Favorite Rod
6 wt 9' Graphite

Rods Owned
Twelve

Favorite Flies
Dry – Muddle May
Wet – Coachman
Nymph – B.H. Prince
Streamer – Muddler Minnow
Terrestrial – Henry's
Fork Hopper

Fly Invented
Muddle May

Favorite US River
Bighorn (MT)

Home River
Gunnison (CO)

Favorite Stream
St. Joe (ID)

Home Stream
North Fork Gunnison (CO)

YUMMY LOW FAT MEAT LOAF

1 Pound Very Lean Hamburger (93%)
½ Pound Silky Tofu
¼ Cup Onion, Cubed
2 Egg Whites
½ Cup Cracker Crumbs
Skim Milk as Needed
Salt and Pepper to Taste
1 Can (8 Ounces) Tomato Sauce

Mix all ingredients except the can of tomato sauce. Place in a loaf pan and bake in an oven at 450 degrees for 20 minutes. Reduce the heat to 325 degrees and bake for 50 minutes. Remove the loaf from the oven and pour the can of tomato sauce over the loaf. Return it to the oven for 10 more minutes. Turn off the oven and let the loaf sit in the cooling oven for 10 more minutes.

Serve with your favorite salad, mashed potatoes or vegetables.

Serves: 3 or 4

GRETCHEN BEATTY

"What's the worst that can happen, it can't be 'that' bad!"

Gretchen Beatty says her greatest achievement is in raising great boys. She and her husband, Al, now reside in Delta, Colorado where Gretchen continues to run BT's Fly Fishing Products, a mail order fly fishing and fly tying supplier.

An exceptional fly tyer, she says she still enjoys her husband's company on the river, at the vise, or donating time to the Federation of Fly Fishers. Gretchen is a Tying Co-Editor for the Federation's magazine, *The Flyfisher.*

Years Fly Fishing
Thirty-one
Favorite Rod
5 wt 9' Graphite
Rods Owned
Two plus Al's twelve.
Favorite Flies
Dry – Royal Wulff
Wet – Woolly Bugger
Nymph – B.H. Hare's Ear
Streamer – Spruce
Terrestrial – Beetle
Fly Invented
None, yet
Favorite US River
Yellowstone (MT)
Home River
Gunnison (CO)
Favorite Stream
Lick Creek (ID)
Home Stream
North Fork of Gunnison (CO)

LOW FAT GLAZED CHICKEN*

(*Low Fat Glazed Chicken in Crockpot)

6 Ounces Frozen Orange Juice
Concentrate, Thawed
3 Chicken Breasts, Split
½ Teaspoon Marjoram
1 Dash Ground Nutmeg
1 Dash Garlic Powder (Optional)
¼ Cup Water
2 Tablespoons Cornstarch

Combine thawed orange juice concentrate (not regular orange juice) in a bowl along with marjoram, garlic powder and nutmeg. Split chicken breasts to make 6 servings. Dip each piece into orange juice to coat completely. Place in crockpot. Pour remaining orange juice mixture over chicken.

Cover and cook on low 7 – 9 hours, or cook on high for 4 hours, if you wish. When chicken is done, remove to serving platter.

Pour sauce that remains in crockpot into a saucepan. Mix cornstarch and water and stir into juice in the pan. Cook over medium heat, stirring constantly, until thick and bubbly. Serve sauce over chicken with brown or white rice.

Serves: 6

BARRY BECK

"Fishing memories are wonderful for the soul and I was feeling quite fine."

Barry Beck and his wife, Cathy, are outdoor photographers, writers and guides living in the Fishing Creek Valley of Benton, Pennsylvania. They host fly fishing trips to exciting destinations, are members of the Sage Fly Fishing Team, instruct fly fishing schools, guide and conduct fly fishing presentations. They're also featured Columnists for *Mid-Atlantic Fly Fishing Guide* and Trout Editors for *Fishing World Magazine*.

The Beck's photographs have appeared worldwide and are featured in George Kelly's *Seasons of the Bighorn: Great American Rivers*. Barry is a recipient of *The Charles K. Fox Rising Trout Award*.

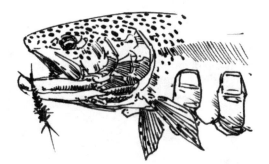

Years Fly Fishing
Forty-one

Favorite Rod
3 wt 8' 9" Graphite

Rods Owned
Over Seventy

Favorite Flies
Dry – Parachute Adams
Wet – Hare's Ear
Nymph – Hare's Ear
Streamer – Woolly Bugger
Terrestrial – Black Ant

Fly Invented
Silly-Legs Bonefish Fly

Favorite US River
Bighorn (MT)

Home River
Susquehanna (PA)

Favorite Stream
Fishing Creek (PA)

Home Stream
Fishing Creek (PA)

OPENING DAY NOODLES

1 ½ – 2 Pounds Ground Beef
1 – 3 Cans Campbell's Beefy
Mushroom Soup
1 Bag Egg Noodles
Salt and Pepper
Browned Mushrooms (Optional)

In a big pot that can later go over the fire, brown the ground beef and drain off any extra fat. Over low heat add the soup. In a separate pot, cook the noodles. Don't overcook or they will get mushy. Slowly add the cooked noodles to the beef and soup mixture. You may need to add a little water to allow for evaporation if it's going to sit on the fire for a long time. Salt and pepper to taste. Browned mushrooms are optional. It's easy to double if the pot is big enough.

Serves: 4 – 6

"Take to the opening day cook-out and enjoy it all day!" – Barry

"Nice fish, but there's a better one just upstream. I'll try him next."

Cathy Beck grew up in a fishing family. She and her husband, Berry Beck, own Raven Creek photography in Benton, Pennsylvania. They are Mid-Atlantic Regional Editors and Contributing Photographers for *Fly Fish America* magazine.

Cathy is the recipient of *The Charles K. Fox Rising Trout Award*. She says her most innovative accomplishment, however, consisted of, *"Landing my husband!"*

In addition to being outstanding photographers, the Becks are writers and guides. Cathy is the author of *Cathy Beck's Fly-Fishing Handbook*.

Concerning her early years, Cathy says, *"I cannot imagine myself fishing as an adult without the endless summers as a child exploring and fishing the ponds on our farm."*

Years Fly Fishing
Twenty-one

Favorite Rod
5 wt 8' 6" Graphite

Rods Owned
Same as Barry

Favorite Flies
Dry – Hendricks or Dun
Wet – Don't have one.
Nymph – Pheasant Tail
Streamer – Mud Head Bugger
Terrestrial – Hopper

Fly Invented
Mud Head Bugger

Favorite US River
Bighorn (MT)

Home River
Susquehanna (PA)

Favorite Stream
Fishing Creek (PA)

Home Stream
Fishing Creek (PA)

© 2000 - Russell A. Hopper

Char Fillets
Doritos Corn Chips

"We don't cook very much at our house, so I'm a little short on recipes. But, one of the best meals I've ever had was Artic Char prepared streamside in Alaska. Our guide was Chuck Kramer and he had quite a reputation for out-of-the-ordinary lunches. In other words, he went to quite a bit of trouble preparing them. This day, however, he forgot the secret "mix" to bread the fish in. He was quite beside himself and didn't know what to do. In the end, he took a bag of Doritos Corn Chips, mashed them into a breading and rolled the char fillets in it. Then, he cooked (or grilled) them over the open fire on aluminum foil. They were delicious! So good that he thought he might use them again! Chuck's clients are always impressed with his cooking skills. On a day that looked like it might be a disaster, he simply out did himself!" – Cathy

Serves: 1 bag + 1 fish = four people

ROBERT BEHNKE

GAZPACHO

"Wild trout and native trout – is there a difference? Why it is important to understand this difference."

Bob Behnke is a Professor of Fisheries Biology with the Department of Fishery and Wildlife of Colorado State University in Fort Collins, Colorado. He has been with Colorado State University since 1966.

Bob says that he attempts to transform scientific stuff for broader audiences. This transformation, an early childhood onset obsession, has led him into studying the diversity of trout, salmon and their relatives. His studies provide the opportunity to travel extensively in Asia, Europe, as well as throughout North America.

As one of America's foremost authorities on wild trout, Bob has kept busy writing Trout Unlimited's *About Trout* column since 1983. He is also the author of *Native Trout of Western North America*.

Years Fly Fishing
Over Fifty

Favorite Rod
3 ¾ wt 8' Graphite

Rods Owned
Over Twenty

Favorite Flies
Dry – Hair Wing
Rio Grande King
Wet – Soft Hackles
Nymph – B.H. Hare's Ear
Streamer – Marabou Muddler
Terrestrial – Adult Damsel

Fly Invented
Unnamed as well as unknown.

Favorite US River
All that still maintain
Native trout.

Home River
Poudre (CO)

Favorite Stream
As with favorite river.

Home Stream
Laramie (CO)

Tomatoes – Onions
Peppers – Cucumbers
Garlic – Olive Oil
Chicken Broth – Tomato Juice
Herbs: Chervil, Parsley, Dill, Chives, Chili Pepper
Amontillado Sherry
Salt – Pepper – Sugar
Croutons – Sour Cream

When the garden is in the height of production, pick roughly equal amounts of tomatoes, onions, peppers and cucumbers. According to amount of vegetables put in blender, add olive oil, chicken broth and tomato juice to cover. This may require several fillings of the blender depending on the crop yield. Some moderate Chile peppers, such as poblano, should be included with sweet peppers. Otherwise add Tabasco. Thoroughly puree and strain. Add salt, sugar and sherry to taste. Serve with croutons and sour cream to which any or all of the following finely chopped herbs are added: chervil, parsley, dill and chives.

Store in refrigerator for several meals as the flavor improves over several days.

"Serves as many as I want. I make 2 – 3 quarts at a time." – Bob

BENJAMIN L. BENOIT III

"After good food, good wines, good friends, and good fishing – what's left in life?"

Ben Benoit resides in Nashville, Tennessee. He is a past President of the Middle Tennessee Fly Fishers, an active member group of the Federation of Fly Fishers.

Ben is the founder of Flyfish @ Youth Camp Fund, a non-profit organization formed to provide scholarships to 12 – 18 year olds so they may attend accredited fly fishing and conservation related programs throughout the U.S. and abroad. He is also the founder-host of Tenn'Clave, an Annual International Fly Fishing Weekend held each October in Bristol, Tennessee, a life member of the Federation of Fly Fishers, and the owner of Pebble Creek Trading Company.

Years Fly Fishing
Over Twenty-five

Favorite Rod
3 wt 7' Graphite

Rods Owned
Fifteen

Favorite Flies
Dry – Sulphur Parachute #16
Wet – Tenn'see Volunteer #14
Nymph – Miller's #8
Streamer – Any of the Carrie Stevens Collection
Terrestrial – Parachute Hopper #2

Flies Invented
Tenn'see Volunteer
Boop's Blue Gill Buster

Favorite US River
Yellowstone (MT)

Home River
South Holston (TN)

Favorite Stream
Pebble Creek (MT)

Home Stream
Mill Creek (TN)

BEN'S TEX-MEX CORNBREAD*

(*Also know as YANKEE BEN'S TEX-MEX CORNBREAD)

2 Eggs, Slightly Beaten
2 Cups Self-rising Yellow Corn Meal Mix
1 Can (15 Ounces) Cream Style Corn
2 Cups Milk
3 Tablespoons Olive Oil
1 ½ Cups Shredded Medium Cheddar Cheese
1 ½ Teaspoons Sugar
2 Tablespoons Chopped Jalapeno Peppers

Preheat oven to 450 degrees. Grease 8" or 6" x 10" Pyrex baking dish or pan. Combine all ingredients and blend well. Pour in dish and bake for 25 to 30 minutes or until top starts to brown. For milder cornbread, substitute chopped green chiles for jalapeno peppers.

Serves: 4 – 6

"Serves four to six people cause you can't only eat one piece!" – Ben

A. K. BEST

GOURMET DINTY MOORE

"Good fishing and good flies are a matter of only two perspectives – yours and the fish's."

A. K. Best is an author, photographer, musician, orchestra conductor, professional fly tier of international stature, designer and an ardent admirer of cane fly rods. He lives in Boulder, Colorado with his wife, Jan. They have three daughters, Sue, Alecia and Elizabeth. A. K. appears regularly in John Gierach's popular fishing adventures.

A. K. has authored *Production Fly Tying: A Collection of Ideas, Notions, Hints and Variations on the Techniques of Fly Tying; Dyeing and Bleaching Natural Fly Tying Materials*; and *A. K.'S Fly Box*. He has written numerous articles for magazines such as *MidAtlantic Fly Fishing Guide*, *Bamboo Fly Rod* and *Fly Rod & Reel*. Video Adventures produced videos featuring A. K. include *Tying Dry Flies, Tying Blue Wing Olives, Tying Caddis & Midges, Tying Callibaetis & Green Drakes, Tying Nymphs & Wets*, and *Tying Terrestrials*.

A. K.'s first trout on a dry fly was caught on a March Brown he tied the night before. He grew up with the idea of keeping big fish and keeping his limit until he caught a 22" 4-pound trout and was encouraged by Kote Winter to release it.

Years Fly Fishing
Thirty
Favorite Rod
5 wt 8' 6" Bamboo
Rods Owned
Lots
Favorite Flies
Dry – Olive Quill Dun
Wet – Not Provided
Nymph – Not Provided
Streamer – Not Provided
Terrestrial – Hoppers
& Ants
Flies Invented
Quill Body Series
of Mayflies
Favorite US River
Frying Pan (CO)
Home River
St. Vrain (CO)
Favorite Stream
Henry's Fork (ID)
Home Stream
Not Provided

---

1 Can Dinty Moore Stew
1 Teaspoon Hickory Salt
1 Teaspoon Garlic Powder

Heat Dinty Moore Stew in can over a Coleman Stove or hot coals. Add hickory salt and garlic powder. As the stew begins to bubble, stir.

When hot, serve on tin plate over 2 slices of whole wheat bread.

Serve with Canadian Club, neat, or with 1 or 2 ice cubes.

Note: Leave lid on can for use as a handle.

"There's more to fishing than fishing."

Fran Betters lives in Wilmington, New York. He is a fly tier, rod builder, fly designer and the author of eleven books.

Fran's fly designs include the Haystack and Mini-Muddler series. He is the originator of the Ausable Wulff, Ausable Caddis, and the Ausable Bomber flies.

Many of Fran's books center around Adirondack themes and include *Adirondack Fish & Game Recipes, Adirondack Tall Tales & Short Stories, Fran Better's Fly Fishing, Fly Tying Pattern Guide* and *A Talk with the Animals of the Adirondacks.* He has two new books coming out soon, one on emergers and the other entitled *Adirondacks – A Fisherman's Paradise.*

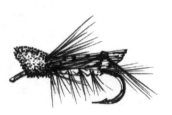

Years Fly Fishing
Fifty-nine

Favorite Rod
4 wt 8' Graphite

Rods Owned
Ten

Favorite Flies
Dry – Ausable Wulff
Wet – Picket Finn
Nymph – Hendrickson
Streamer – Old Fashioned
Bucktail
Terrestrial – Hopper

Flies Invented
See Comments

Favorite US River
West Branch of the Ausable (NY)

Home River
West Branch of the Ausable (NY)

Favorite Stream
Not Provided

Home Stream
Not Provided

1 Box Salted Codfish
¾ Stick Butter
¼ Cup Flour
2 Cups Milk
Salt and Pepper

Pour boiling water over codfish and let sit overnight. Pour off and wash with fresh water. Drain.

Melt butter in pan. Add flour and stir will. Add about 2 cups of milk and bring to a boil, stirring constantly. Add shredded codfish, salt and pepper to taste.

Serve over cooked, cubed potatoes.

Serves: 3 – 4

DEANNA LEE BIRKHOLM

CHOCOLATE SIN CAKE

"Don't show knowledge – share knowledge."
"A steal from Lefty Kreh." – Deanna

Deanna Birkholm is the Publisher and Creator of *Fly Anglers Online*. She learned to fly fish from her grandfather when she was eleven years old. Deanna was the first woman member of Trout Unlimited's Mershon Chapter, Saginaw, Michigan, in 1959 and started the first Federation of Fly Fishers Chapter in Michigan. Over twenty years ago she became the first licensed woman fly fishing guide in Montana where she guided for Dan Bailey.

Deanna was on the Governing Board of Certification for the Federation of Fly Fishers' Casting Instructors and is a Certified Instructor herself.

A member of the Outdoor Writers Association of America, Deanna wrote the widely read fly fishing column for Scripps Howard newspapers and the Associated Press under the name Ladyfisher.

Deanna and her husband, Jim (Castwell) reside in Poulsbo, Washington and teach fly casting twice a month from March through November.

If stranded on a dessert island, the Ladyfisher says she would choose a 6 weight fast rod and lots of bonefish, but her preference is dry fly fishing.

Years Fly Fishing
Fifty-two

Favorite Rod
6 wt 9' Graphite (Gatti)

Rods Owned
Over Twenty

Favorite Flies
Dry – Lady's Fish Finder
Wet – Pink Puff (Bonefish)
Nymph – Do not use.
Streamer – Castwell's
Marble Head (Salt Water)
Terrestrial – Green
Leaf Hopper

Fly Invented
Lady's Fish Finder

Favorite US River
Upper Yellowstone (MT)

Home River
Main Stream Au Sable (MI)

Favorite Stream
Armstrong Spring Creek (MT)

Home Stream
South Branch of the
Au Sable (MI)

© 2000 - Russell A. Hopper

2 Cups Flour
4 Tablespoons Cocoa
2 Teaspoons Soda
1 Cup White Sugar
1 Cup Mayonnaise
1 Cup Strong Cold Coffee
1 Teaspoon Vanilla

Sift together flour, cocoa, soda and sugar. In another bowl, mix mayonnaise, coffee and vanilla. Mix thoroughly. Add liquid mixture slowly to dry ingredients. Beat for 2 minutes. Bake in greased and floured pan at 350 degrees for 25 minutes or until toothpick comes out clean at center of cake. Frost with chocolate frosting.

Serves: 12

DAN BLANTON

"Variety is the spice of life – and fly fishing! Try for every species you can – whenever you can. Life is short, with never enough time for the later."

Dan Blanton has been fly fishing since the age of eleven when his father bought him his first rod. He is one of the most respected fly rod anglers and fly tyers in the world.

Dan is a writer, editor, instructor, photographer, tackle consultant and fly innovator who created the often-imitated salt water fly, the Whistler. He is the former Managing Editor of *Angler* magazine, a Regional Editor for *California Angler*, an Editor-at-Large for *Fly Fishing in Salt Waters* magazine and has contributed to three anthologies: *The Angler's Bible, The Fly Tyer's Almanac* and *Lefty's Little Library*. His current project is his first book, *Fly Fishing With Shooting Heads – Panfish to Billfish*.

In addition to the Whistler Series of flies, Dan originated the Punch Series, Sar-Mul-Mac Series, Sea Arrow Squid and Bay Delta Eelet fly patterns.

Dan is the recipient of the *Arnold Gingrich Memorial Life Membership Award* (1990) and the *Silver King Award* (1995) presented by the Federation of Fly Fishers.

He lives in Morgan Hills, California.

Years Fly Fishing
Forty-six

Favorite Rod
9 wt 9' Graphite

Rods Owned
Twenty

Favorite Flies
Dry – Elk Hair Caddis
Wet – Woolly Worm
Nymph – Prince
Streamer – Fatal Attraction (Fresh Water) and Flashtail Whistler (Salt Water)
Terrestrial – Whitlock Hopper

Flies Invented
See Comments

Favorite US River
Smith (CA)

Home River
Sacramento Delta (CA)

Favorite Stream
East Walker (CA)

Home Salt Chuck
San Francisco Bay and Monterey Bay (CA)

SCOTT LAKE GUMBO

1 – 3 Pounds of White Fish Fillets, Cut into Small Pieces
6 – 8 Small Red Potatoes, Cubed
Oil
1 – 2 Chopped Onions
2 Garlic Cloves
2 Cans Stewed Tomatoes
1 Can Sweet Corn
1 Can Mushrooms, May be Chopped
1 Teaspoon Oregano and Cayenne Pepper
1 Tablespoon Lowry's Seasoned Salt
1 Tablespoon Lemon Pepper

Fry spuds in oil until browned. Drain oil and dry. Fry onions and garlic with potatoes. When onions are half cooked throw all other ingredients into pan. Cook (boil) until fish is cooked (steamed white).

"This is the Scott Lake Gumbo recipe given me by Sean Sloan, my Scott Lake Guide. This is one of several pike recipes he used for shore lunches over the years and is one of my favorites." – Dan

GARY A. BORGER

"The resource must come first."

Gary Borger is one of America's best known fly fishers. He is Professor of Biology at the University of Wisconsin Center in Wausau. Gary has been a fly fisher since 1955, and since 1972 has taught classes and lectured internationally on all aspects of fly fishing for trout and salmon.

A freelance writer, innovative fly tyer, and photographer, Gary is the Midwest Field Editor for *Fly Fisherman* magazine, Fly Fishing Columnist for *North American Fisherman*, and Editor-at-Large for the *Virtual Fly Shop*. He has written five books on fly fishing: *Nymphing, Naturals, The Borger Color System, Designing Trout Flies* and *Presentation*.

Gary pioneered fly fishing videos with his release of *Nymphing* in 1982, and he has produced 22 videos, which have earned him a listing in *Who's Who in Entertainment*. Gary was a consultant on Robert Redford's movie, *A River Runs Through It*.

For his conservation efforts, Gary has been awarded the *Ross Allen Merigold Complete Angler Memorial Award*, the *Charles K. Fox Rising Trout Award* and in 1979, the first *Lew Jewett Memorial Life Member Membership* in the FFF.

Years Fly Fishing
Forty-four

Favorite Rod
See Comments

Rods Owned
One Hundred-Twenty

Favorite Flies
Dry – Loop Wing Dun
Wet – Hair-hackle Hare's Ear
Nymph – Hair Leg
Streamer – Strip Leech
Terrestrial – Foam Beetle

Fly Invented
Braided Butt Damsel and many others.

Favorite US River
Madison (MT)

Home River
Bois Brule (WI)

Favorite Stream
Green Stone (New Zealand)

Home Stream
Prairie (WI)

© 2000 - Russell A. Hopper

HONEY ALMOND BREAD

4 Cups Bread Flour
1 Cup Shaved Almonds
2 Tablespoons No-fat Margarine
2 Tablespoons Honey
½ Heaping Teaspoon Dry Yeast
1 1/3 Cup Lukewarm Water

In bread machine, add dry ingredients first and water last. Bake on medium setting.

Gary is a design consultant for Thomas and Thomas Fly Rod Company and is the designer of the Weinbrenner Ultimate Wading Shoe, the Gary Borger Fly Vest, the Gary Borger Signature Fly Lines by McKinzie Flies, the Gary Borger reel by STH, and many other innovative angling products.

Gary's achievements are recognized in *Who's Who in the Midwest, Who's Who in Science and Engineering, Men of Achievement,* the *Dictionary of International Biography, Who's Who Among America's Teachers, Outstanding People of the 20th Century*, and *Outstanding People of the Millenium*.

Gary's son, Jason, is also well known in the fly fishing community.

When asked about his favorite rod, he replied, *"I have no favorite rod length and line weight."*

JASON BORGER

PROVENÇAL GRILLED BEANS*

"Fly casting is the physical skill of fly fishing. If you can't cast, you can't fish."

Jason Borger caught his first wild trout on a fly rod when he was two and a half years old and spent the summers of his youth fishing many of the world's legendary waters.

Most famous for his role as the *Shadow Caster* in the movie *A River Runs Through It*, one of Jason's most satisfying moments came when he performed the *shadow cast* on a rock only a couple of miles from where he caught his first trout on a fly rod.

Jason is a professional fly fisher, actor, instructor, illustrator, writer, video producer, lecturer and product designer. He collaborated with his father, Gary, on the book, *Presentation,* and his writings have been published in many major sporting journals.

Jason has fished Alaska, Canada, England, New Zealand, Tasmania and throughout the United States. His home is in Wausau, Wisconsin.

Years Fly Fishing
Twenty-seven
Favorite Rod
Depends on conditions.
Rods Owned
About One Hundred-twenty
Favorite Flies
Dry – XD Low Rider Dun
Wet – XD Low Rider Cripple
Nymph – XD Low Rider Nymph
Streamer – Fur-head Version Strip Leech
Terrestrial – One-bunch Beetle
Flies Invented
Low Rider Series and many others.
Favorite US River
Madison (MT)
Home River
Not Provided
Favorite Stream
Dingleburn (New Zealand)
Home Stream
Plover (WI)

(*Provençal Grilled Beans)

Fresh Whole Green Beans
(Kentucky Wonders, etc.)
Cold-pressed, Unfiltered Olive Oil
Herbes De Provence

Fire up the grill! While any grill will do, mesquite is tops. Get the grating hot so the beans sizzle a bit after they're placed on the grating.

Mix approximately ½ cup oil with 1 teaspoon of herbes. Baste the beans on a plate then slap 'em on the grill. Cook for 5 – 7 minutes until just past raw. The beans should char a bit on the grating. Re-baste during cooking once if necessary, and turn the beans so they don't burn too much. Enjoy!

Combine beans, bell peppers, asparagus, and other vegetables, too!

Serves: *"As many as you can get beans for."* – Jason

TIM BORSKI

TIM'S MOM'S NEVER FAIL TUNA

"Pick up the broken pieces and limp on off to the next flat."

Tim Borski is a wildlife artist residing in Islamorada, Florida. His artwork, which is displayed in local galleries throughout the Florida Keys, and his love of the sport of salt water fly fishing, keep Tim on the waters some 250 days each year.

Tim is busy developing a series of fly patterns distributed by the Umpqua Feather Merchants. One of his custom made flies is the Chernobyl Crab, which was designed to attract migrating winter bonefish in the northern Florida Keys.

Borski is a contributor of both artwork and articles to *Fly Fishing in Salt Waters* magazine and other publications. When asked about his achievements, Tim replied, *"Dressing each morning with some semblance of color coordination."*

Prior to his love affair with fly rods and salt water fishing, Tim grew up in Wisconsin fishing for muskie and smallmouth bass. Tim still considers Wisconsin home.

Years Fly Fishing
Thirteen

Favorite Rod
9 wt 9' Graphite

Rods Owned
Ten

Favorite Flies
Dry – Bomber
Wet – Chernobyl Crab
Nymph – Hare's Ear
Streamer – Orange Butt
Tarpon Fly
Terrestrial – Ant

Flies Invented
Chernobyl Crab, Swimming Shrimp, Mangrove Critter, and others.

Favorite US River
Wisconsin (WI)

Home River
Wisconsin (WI)

Favorite Stream
Plover Creek (WI)

Home Stream
Plover Creek (WI)

---

2 Cans Tuna (Chunk Light in Water)
1 Can Cream of Mushroom Soup
½ Soup Can of Milk
1 Can Baby Peas, Drained
1 Bag (6 Ounces) Potato Chips

Mix tuna, soup and milk in casserole dish. Take potatoes chips and crush viciously. Mix with first three ingredients, but save a little to sprinkle on top.

Gently mix in one can of baby peas, drained. Preheat oven to 375 degrees. Bake 15 minutes or until crispy brown and bubbling on top.

Serves: 3

"Say grace. Hi, Mom!" – Tim

HARRY J. BRISCOE

"Fly casting should not be the mechanical operation it has become. Let your rod do the work and you sit back and enjoy!"

Harry Briscoe is the President and owner of Hexagraph Fly Rod Company of Houston, Texas. Harry says the Hexagraph series of rods are the unique fly rods on the market, combining the best of tradition and modern technology. Hexagraphs are built of segmented graphite strips. The rods are solid rather than hollow and behave in a pleasing manner when cast.

The concept of Hexagraph fly rods comes from a master cane rod maker, Walton Powell, who was one of the pioneering synthetic rod makers.

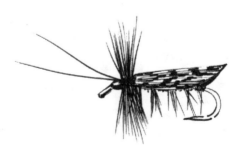

Years Fly Fishing
Forty-one

Favorite Rod
4/5 wt 8' Hexagraph Classic

Rods Owned
Hundreds

Favorite Flies
Dry – Goddard Cadddis # 14
Wet – Rio Grande King # 14
Nymph – Prince # 16
Streamer – Muddler Minnow # 10
Terrestrial – Joe's Hopper # 8

Fly Invented
Roaring River Special

Favorite US River
Upper Colorado (CO)

Home River
South Platte (CO)

Favorite Stream
Gianinetti Spring Creek (CO)

Home Stream
Elk Creek (CO)

ARTICHOKE & CAPER SAUCE*

(*A Pasta Sauce)

2 Tablespoons Butter
2 Tablespoons Olive Oil
2 Medium-sized Onions, Chopped
2 Garlic Cloves, Crushed
3 Tablespoons All Purpose Flour
1 Cup Chicken Broth or Stock
¾ Cup Dry White Wine
1 ½ Cups Peeled, Seeded and Chopped Ripe Tomatoes or 1 Pound Can Italian Tomatoes, Drained and Sliced
1 Can (14 Ounces) Artichoke Hearts, Packed in Water and Drained
2 Teaspoons Dried or 2 Tablespoons Fresh Basil
2 Tablespoons Capers – Salt and Pepper to Taste

In a medium-size skillet, heat the butter and oil over medium heat. Add the onions and garlic. Sauté until pale gold. Stir in flour and cook gently until well blended. Add chicken broth and wine, stirring constantly until the sauce is thickened. Add tomatoes and artichokes and stir into the sauce. Reduce heat to a simmer and add basil and capers. Season with salt and pepper. Simmer for 3 – 5 minutes to allow flavors to blend. Serve over hot pasta and sprinkle with grated Parmesan cheese.

MAC BROWN

"The cast needs to become an extension of one's thought process."

Mac Brown is an Associate Professor of Fly Casting at Western Carolina, a guide and fly fishing instructor and the owner of McLeod's Highland Fly Fishing, Inc. in Bryson City, North Carolina.

The author of *Casting Angles* is also the host of several television programs for Public Television and ESPN. His articles on fly fishing have appeared in *Fly Fisherman* and *Outdoor Life* magazines. He was previously profiled in the May 1998 issue of *Sports Afield*.

Mac is in the process of writing a book about the hatches in the Great Smoky Mountains National Park.

```
    \!/
  <>*#==#.=:-
  /!\   _)
```

Years Fly Fishing
Twenty-eight
Favorite Rod
3 wt 8' 5" Graphite
Rods Owned
Fifty-seven
Favorite Flies
Dry – Parachute Adams
Wet – Partridge and Pheasant
Nymph – Pheasant Tail
Streamer – McLeod's Darter
Terrestrial – Ant
Flies Invented
Many
Favorite US River
The one that I am on presently.
Home River
Nantahala (NC)
Favorite Stream
Deep Creek (NC)
Home Stream
Deep Creek (NC)

LASAGNA

Tomato Sauce
Lot of Noodles
Roccotta Cheese
Cottage Cheese
Mozzarella Cheese
Parmesan Cheese
Meat
Vegetables

Mix cheeses. Build layers. Top off with Parmesan cheese. Cook at 350 degrees for 45 – 50 minutes.

Serves: 12

PAUL M. BRUUN

BAJA SAUTÉ

"My favorite task is helping people have a good time and create memories."

Paul Bruun is a float trip outfitter, Outdoor Columnist for the *Jackson Hole News* and one of the most respected anglers in the fly fishing community.

Growing up fishing in and around Miami's Biscayne Bay, Paul loves fishing the oceans of the world, but lives in Jackson, Wyoming. He is a former Jackson Hole town councilman who is the godfather of the local fly fishing industry—an expert at the business of catching cutthroats.

Paul is responsible for designing the South Fork Skiff Drift Boat and the Patagona SST Jacket. His fly creations include the Mangrove Minnow, Mangrove Midget and the Mangrove Maniac. He's fond of promoting the triple Palomar knot.

Years Fly Fishing
Forty-four
Favorite Rod
7 wt 9' or 10' Graphite
Rods Owned
Twenty-five
Favorite Flies
Dry – Elk Hair Caddis
Wet – Soft Hackle
Nymph – Martinez
Streamer – Muddler Minnow
Terrestrial – Ant
Flies Invented
See Comments
Favorite US River
Snake (WY)
Home River
Snake (WY)
Favorite Stream
Firehole (WY)
Home Stream
Flat Creek (WY)

© 2000 - Russell A. Hopper

Seafood of Choice
Shrimp, Squid Rings, Scallops,
Mussels, Fish or Other Seafood

Sauce Ingredients
Soy Sauce
Chopped Garlic
Rosemary
Finely Chopped Poblano Pepper
Lemon Juice

Other Ingredients
Butter
Blended Rice or Angel Hair Pasta

Mix all sauce ingredients together, depending on your taste. Melt butter in large sauté pan. Add soy sauce mixture. Stir with heat just below bubbling. Add shrimp, squid rings, scallops, mussels, or other seafood. Serve over blended rice or angel hair pasta.

This recipe also works well to sauté Portabella mushrooms, lean pork ribs, small steaks, or with strips of chicken.

DENVER BRYAN

"To offer a man a pole when fly fishing is in his heart is like offering a loaf of bread to one who is dying of thirst." – *"Not my words, just my favorite paraphrase."* – Denver

Denver Bryan is an internationally published photographer whose travels take him around the world in search of nature and fishing. He is head-quartered in Bozeman, Montana. His works have appeared on over 100 magazine covers such as *National Wildlife, Smithsonian, Outdoor Life, Field & Stream*, and *Gray's Sporting Journal*.

Denver is a Contributing Editor for *Gray's Sporting Journal*. He says he is fortunate to be able to happily fish and photograph at the same time.

Kim Leighton and Denver were contributors to the book, *Season's of the Yellowstone: An Angler's Year*. Denver originated the book *Just Horses* and Margot Page wrote the supporting text to augment what is primarily a photography book.

Denver has a new Ducks Unlimited book on Labrador Retrievers entitled *The Life of a Lab* as well as a book on Golden Retrievers entitled *101 Uses for a Golden Retriever*. Signed copies of these books, as well as more about his photography can be found at www.denverbryan.com.

Years Fly Fishing
Eleven

Favorite Rod
5 wt 8' 6" Graphite

Rods Owned
Eight

Favorite Flies
Dry – Elk Hair Caddis
Wet – Bitch Creek
Nymph – G.R. Hare's Ear
Streamer – Woolly Bugger
Terrestrial – Hopper

Fly Invented
None, yet

Favorite US River
Bighorn (MT)

Home River
Yellowstone (MT)

Favorite Stream
East Gallatin (MT)

Home Stream
East Gallatin (MT)

KASKATTAMA GOOSE

Goose or Duck Breasts
½ Cup Olive Oil
½ Cup Soy Sauce
Garlic
Rosemary
Basil

Cut goose or duck breasts into 1" cubes and strips. Marinade goose or duck breasts for 24 hours in a mixture of olive oil and soy sauce seasoned with garlic, rosemary and basil according to taste.

Cook on aluminum foil covered grill until done bleeding.

BUCK BUCHENROTH

CONCH FRITTERS

"If it swims—it is in peril."

Buck Buchenroth is the *1997 World Invitational Bonefish Champion* and invented the Guide Lanyard. Buck resides in Jackson, Wyoming and is a fly fishing guide.

When asked how many rods he owns, Buck replied, *"I'm not telling."*

Years Fly Fishing
Thirty-one

Favorite Rod
4 wt 10' Graphite

Rods Owned
See Comments

Favorite Flies
Dry – Badger Hackled
Red Bellied Humpy # 18
Wet – Western Blue Dun # 14
Nymph – Prince # 14
Streamer – Weighted Lime Kiwi
Muddler # 6
Terrestrial – Mouse Fly #2

Fly Invented
Snake River Jule

Favorite US River
The Upper Snake (WY)

Home River
The Upper Green (WY)

Favorite Stream
North Cotton Wood
Creek (WY)

Home Stream
Fish Creek (WY)

2 Conch
1 Red Pepper, 1 Green Pepper and
1 Yellow Pepper
2 Bottles Bass Ale
1 Large Egg
3 Cups Flour
Pinch of Baking Powder
Seasonings
Cooking Oil
Hot Cocktail Sauce

Free dive to a depth between 30 and 45 feet and gather 2 large conch. Remove body from shell and skin. Dice the conch into small sunflower seed size portions. Dice the peppers into equally small portions. Mix conch, pepper and the egg together in a bowl. Mix in 2 cups of flour, the baking soda, and the seasonings. Further add portions from one of the Bass Ale bottles for consistency. Add remaining cup of flour. Be careful not to over mix as this will cause the cooking fritters not to rise from the batter. Make fritters into ping-pong size balls and drop them into very hot oil. Cook until golden brown. Dip the hot fritter into the cocktail sauce and enjoy them with the remaining Bass Ale.

Serves: 6

DAN BURR

"Like my brother always says, you're either a pretender or a player."

Dan Burr is a sporting artist and illustrator. *Gray's Sporting Journal, Sporting Classics, Field & Stream, The Reader's Digest, Outdoor Life* and other magazines have published his works. He was Wyoming's *Top 40* stamp entrant twice.

After living in Connecticut for five years and earning a living as an illustrator, Dan and his wife, Patti, moved back to his native West. Dan lives in Tetona, Idaho surrounded by the waters that inspired his father and grandfather to love that part of the West.

Some of Dan's works include *The Wooden Boat, Honey Hole* and his *Classic Trout Prints*. His most famous book illustrations are included in the *Magic Attic Club Series*.

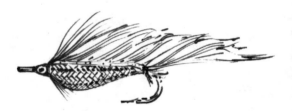

Years Fly Fishing
Twenty-eight

Favorite Rod
3 wt 8' Graphite

Rods Owned
Seven

Favorite Flies
Dry – Pink Cahill
Wet – CDC Emerger
Nymph – B.H. Zebra
Streamer – Zonker
Terrestrial – Schroeder's Hopper

Fly Invented
Nothing Famous

Favorite US River
South Fork of the Snake (ID)

Home River
Teton (ID)

Favorite Stream
Dream Creek, Wind River Mountains (WY)

Home Stream
Spring Creek (ID)

DUTCH OVEN GROUSE

2 Ruffed Grouse
Wild Rice
Apples, Sliced or Wedged
1 Onion, Sliced
Chicken Broth
Butter
Salt and Pepper

Cut up grouse and brown in butter. Add sliced onion, sliced or wedged apples, rice, broth, salt and pepper. Simmer for 1 hour. If needed, add extra water for the rice.

Serves: 4

"You can cook this on a fire or stove top. Just enjoy it because it's delicious." – Dan

GEORGE HERBERT WALKER BUSH

BARBECUED CHICKEN

"Each of us can make a difference in the life of another."

George Bush was the forty-first President of the United States and is an avid fly fisher dividing time between his home in Houston, Texas and his beloved Kennebucport, Maine.

The President hosts an Annual George Bush Bonefish Tournament and raises money for The Everglades Trust, an organization started by the late George Barley to save the Everglades and Florida Bay from pollution and development.

Retired Kuwaiti General Khalid bin Sultan's gratitude for President Bush's role in the Gulf War was expressed when the General had rodmakers Thomas and Thomas build a rod for the former President. Thomas & Thomas rodmaker Tom Dorsey built the rod and Ted Juracsik produced the reel to go with the rod. The rod is the one featured in this Angler Profile.

The President was a second place winner in the October 29, 1998 Fifth Annual George Bush /Cheeca Lodge Bonefish Tournament in Islamorada, Florida when he caught and released a 13-pound bonefish.

Years Fly Fishing
Since 1993
Featured Rod
*9 wt 9' Horizon
HS909S Graphite*
Featured Reel
*444 Engraved Billy
Pate Bonefish Reel*
Rod & Reel Case
Leather D. B. Dunn
Favorite Fly
Eel Fly for Stripers
Bluefish Waters
Atlantic Ocean
Atlantic Salmon River
Adlatok (Labrador)
Other Waters
Islamorada (FL)

1 Three Pound Fryer, Quartered
1 Large Garlic Clove, Crushed
1 Teaspoon Salt
½ Teaspoon Pepper
1 Tablespoon Oil
3 Tablespoons Lemon Juice

Put ingredients in Ziplock bag. Shake to coat well. Refrigerate 24 hours if possible, turning bag several times. When coals are ready, place chicken on grill, skin side up, basting with marinade. Cook until well-browned before turning. If baking in oven, bake at 400 degrees, skin side down first. About 20 minutes before the chicken is done, begin using your favorite barbecue sauce.

"This is First Lady Barbara Bush's recipe and one of the family's most popular." – George

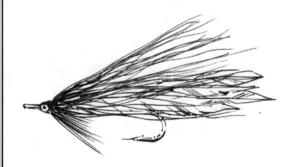

JAMES BUTLER

"I consider myself to be a lucky angler, rather than an accomplished one."

Jim Butler, who resides in Rockland, Maine, has been involved with *Fly Rod & Reel* magazine for twelve years and is the magazine's current Editor-in-Chief. Jim has an angling acquaintance who once hooked a pig on his backcast. *"Now I wish I had done that,"* says Jim.

On Jim's second day on the flats, in Belize, he took a grand slam, bonefish, tarpon and permit on a fly on the same day. He attributes that feat almost entirely to luck and a fine guide, Eddie Hyde, of Turneffe Flats.

When asked to identify flies invented, Jim said, *"None with a career long enough to give it a name."*

Years Fly Fishing
Twenty-five

Favorite Rod
8 wt 9' Graphite

Rods Owned
Fifteen

Favorite Flies
Dry – Parachute Adams
Wet – Any number of
soft hackles.
Nymph – Pheasant Tail
Streamer – Woolly Bugger
Terrestrial – McMurray Ant

Fly Invented
See Comments

Favorite US River
Kennebec (ME)

Home River
Kennebec (ME)

Favorite Stream
An impossible choice.

Home Stream
St. George River (ME)

BUTLER'S BARBECUE MARINADE*

(*Butler's Brilliant Barbecue Marinade)

½ Cup Olive Oil
2 Tablespoons Balsamic Vinegar
2 Tablespoons Soy Sauce
Fresh Cilantro
Black Pepper

Mix half a cup of olive oil and a couple table-spoons each of balsamic vinegar and soy sauce in a glass baking dish or bowl. Drop in a healthy hand-ful of fresh cilantro, chopped (remember to wash it first), and throw in some freshly ground black pepper.

Place meat of your choice (pork chops, chicken breasts, or beef of one cut or another) in the bowl, coat thoroughly with marinade. Let sit for a couple of hours—turning occasionally—or longer if you thought ahead. Then grill to your taste; barely done is better than overdone, in Jim's book.

"This recipe is really just a marinade 'foundation.' I find myself adding a little white pepper or Tabasco sauce to add a kick, sometimes cumin, or sage or thyme for a more subtle flavor. It never comes out the same twice, but it's always good." – Jim

"Foolishly, we have made fly fishing into a sport of the elite. Trout don't care about the skin color or social position of the angler—they focus only on the fly."

Paul Cañada is a full-time freelance writer, photographer, illustrator, Warm Water Editor for *Flyfishing & Tying Journal*, and Columnist (Bass Master Column) for *Southern Sporting Journal* magazines.

Paul is one of the few fly fishing bass anglers that has successfully transferred bass fishing tournament knowledge over to fly angling. He is also one of the very few Hispanic full-time freelance outdoor writers in this country. All four of his grandparents were immigrants from Spain.

An award winning writer, photographer and illustrator, who resides in Fort Worth, Texas, Paul has won an award for outdoor fiction every year he has been writing.

Paul is known for what he calls burning a fly, a quick, hard strip with his arm fully extended away from his body quickly followed by a sweep of the rod tip. The action causes the fly to move 12 to 16 inches, then suddenly jump another 2 to 3 feet, giving the bass no choice but to take the fly.

Years Fly Fishing
Three Seasons

Favorite Rod
9 wt 9' GLX Loomis

Rods Owned
Twenty-three Total
7 Fly Rods

Favorite Flies
Dry – Adams
Wet – Andy Burk's Rattling Jig
Nymph – G.R. Hare's Ear
Streamer – Charlie Cypert's 6" Clouser with Hackle
Terrestrial – Dave Whitlock's Diving Frog

Fly Invented
Spanish Fly Streamer

Favorite US River
East Walker (NV)

Home River
Brazos (TX)

Favorite Stream
Rio Costilla (NM)

Home Stream
Upper Mountain Fork (OK)

---

4 Large Baking Potatoes
4 Eggs
Garlic Salt
Vegetable Cooking Oil

Take 4 baking potatoes, cut them into thin, vertical slices, and gently sprinkle garlic salt over them. Place the potatoes into a large frying pan with cooking oil, frying them until they're brown.

Throw the finished potatoes, less the cooking oil, into a bowl of 3 to 4 beaten eggs and mix. Cover the surface of each potato with egg. Depending on the size of potatoes, you may need to add more egg.

Empty the frying pan of oil, throw the potato/egg mix back into the frying pan, and cook long enough to fry the lower layer of egg. Place a plate over the frying pan and flip the tortilla onto the plate.

Slide the tortilla back into the frying pan, cooked side up, and cook long enough to fry remaining egg. Don't burn the egg. When cooking is complete, again place the plate over the pan and flip the tortilla onto the plate. The end product is what Paul's dad called a tortilla or "potato cake."

Serves: 4 per tortilla

James Earl Carter Jr.

"The trout don't give a darn if you're President of the United States, or a local farmer or a high school kid."

Jimmy Carter was the thirty-ninth President of the United States and a former Governor of the State of Georgia. He and his wife, Rosalynn, reside in Plains, Georgia.

Former President Carter was in attendance when the Federation of Fly Fishers' International Fly Center was dedicated in August 1981. His and Rosalynn's fly fishing fly rods have been donated to the American Museum of Fly Fishing.

During his Presidency, Jimmy Carter moved from amateur to expert status in fly fishing for trout and in fly fishing. He tied flies in the White House and built a drying reel for fly lines on the day after 1980s vote.

In addition to learning how to nymph fish with Joe Humphreys, the President has fished with legends such as Lloyd Riss, Don Daughenbaugh, Thomas Maxwell, George Harvey, Ed Shenk and Eric Leiser.

President Carter's wife, Rosalynn, was the only First Lady to fly fish and she often outfishes the President, to his occasional chagrin.

Years Fly Fishing
Since 1979 while Governor of Georgia

Favorite Rod
5 wt 9' Fenwick (Circa 1988)

Home River
Chattahoochee (GA)

Favorite Stream
Big Hunting Creek (GA)

Rosalynn's Strawberry Cake

1 Package (18 ½ Ounces) Yellow or White Cake Mix
1 Package (3 Ounces) Strawberry Gelatin
¾ Cup Vegetable Oil
1 Cup Chopped Nuts
4 Eggs
2 Tablespoons Flour
1 Package (10 Ounces) Frozen Sliced Sweetened Strawberries, Thawed or
1 Pint Fresh Sliced Strawberries with ½ Cup Sugar
½ Pint Heavy Cream, Whipped
1 Tablespoon Sugar

Preheat oven to 350 degrees. Grease a 10" Angel Food Cake pan or 10" Bundt pan. Combine cake mix, strawberry gelatin, vegetable oil, nuts eggs, flour and strawberries in a large bowl. Beat with an electric mixer at medium—high speed for 3 minutes or until well blended.

Pour batter into pan and bake for 55 – 65 minutes or until a cake tester comes out clean.

Cool for 10 minutes on rack. Turn out of pan to cool completely.

Serve with plain or with sweetened whipped cream.

JIM CASADA

"From a marvelously misspent childhood fly fishing in the Smokies until today, fly fishing for trout has been a bright thread running through the entire fabric of my life."

Jim Casada makes his home in Rock Hill, South Carolina. He is an outdoor writer, retired professor and a seminar speaker.

The recipient of the Federation of Fly Fishers' *Arnold Gingrich Memorial Award* and *Honorary Life Member* of the Federation of Fly Fishers is the author of fifteen books on the outdoors, including the award-winning *Modern Fly Fishing*. Jim has won more than 70 writing and photography awards.

Jim is a past President of the Southeastern Outdoor Press Association and current President-Elect of the Outdoor Writers Association of America.

Casada has authored in excess of 2,500 magazine articles, is the Senior Editor of *Sporting Classics*, Editor-at-Large for *Turkey and Turkey Hunting* and Senior Contributor to *TroutSouth*.

Some of Jim's other books include *The Complete Venison Cookbook, Tales of Whitetails*, and *America's Greatest Game Bird*.

Years Fly Fishing
Fifty-one

Favorite Rod
5 wt 7' 6" Graphite

Rods Owned
Over Fifty

Favorite Flies
Dry – Parachute Adams
Wet – Coachman
Nymph – B.H. Prince
Streamer – Black Matuka
Terrestrial – Japanese Beetle

Fly Invented
None, yet

Favorite US River
Smith (MT)

Home River
Nantahala (NC)

Favorite Stream
Deep Creek (NC)

Home Stream
Deep Creek (NC)

VENISON LOIN STEAK*

(*Venison Loin Steak with Crab & Shrimp Sauce)

1 Pound Loin Steaks, Cut ½" Thick
1 Tablespoon Olive Oil – 1 Tablespoon Margarine

<u>Crab & Shrimp Sauce</u>
2 Tablespoons Olive Oil
½ Pound Fresh Mushrooms, Sliced
2 Cups Whipping Cream
¼ Cup White Zinfandel Wine
¼ Cup Margarine Cut into 12 Pieces
½ Pound Real or Surimi Crabmeat
12 Medium Shrimp, Cooked and Peeled

Heat olive oil and margarine in a large skillet and quickly cook venison loin until medium-rare. Place on a platter and keep warm. It is best to cook the loin after the sauce has started thickening.

For the sauce, heat two tablespoons oil in a large skillet. Add mushrooms to skillet and sauté 5 minutes. Add cream and wine and reduce until thickened, 10 – 12 minutes. Stir in margarine one piece at a time incorporating each piece completely before adding meat. Add crabmeat, shrimp, and heat through, about 1 minute. Pour over venison and serve immediately. Salt and pepper to taste.

Serves: 4

HAROLD CASEY

PINEAPPLE PIE

"I like top water with hair bugs for smallmouth bass. Put everything back."

Harold Casey of Frankfort, Kentucky is retired. He comes highly recommended for this book by his friend Byron Crawford of the *Louisville Courier-Journal* who says Harold is the guru of fly rods in Kentucky and owns some fly rods that were made by the masters.

Harold files the barbs off his hooks and has been known to wear a tie when fishing. Dave Klausmeyer copied one of his F. E. Thomas rods and Harold says, *"It's a master-piece."* Harold has four Thomas rods.

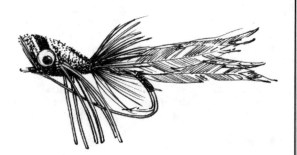

Years Fly Fishing
Sixty-six

Favorite Rod
5 wt 8' Bamboo
A 4 Ounce Payne Model 200

Rods Owned
Twenty-two

Favorite Flies
Dry – Yellow Hair Bug
Wet – Not Provided
Nymph – Not Provided
Streamer – Not Provided
Terrestrial – Crawfish

Fly Invented
None, yet

Favorite US River
Big Hole (MT)

Home River
Fishing Creek (KY)

Favorite Stream
Not Provided

Home Stream
Not Provided

¾ Cup Sugar
¼ Cup Flour
½ Teaspoon Salt
2 ½ Cups (1 Pound) Crushed Pineapple
1 Cup Sour Cream
1 Teaspoon Lemon Juice
2 Beaten Egg Yokes
1 – 8" Baked Crust

Meringue
2 Egg Whites
1 Teaspoon Vanilla
½ Teaspoon Cream of Tartar
4 Tablespoons Sugar

In pan, combine sugar, flour and salt. Stir in pineapple, sour cream and lemon juice. Cook and stir until the mixture thickens and bubbles 2 minutes. Stir small amount into the egg yolks. Return to hot mixture, stirring constantly. Cook and stir for 2 minutes. Spoon into cooled pastry crust.

To make the meringue, beat 2 egg whites with 1-teaspoon vanilla and ½ teaspoon of cream of tartar until stiff. Beat in 4 tablespoons of sugar until the sugar is dissolved.

Spread meringue over the top of the pie and bake at 350 degrees for 12 – 15 minutes.

WILLIAM W. CATHERWOOD

"Any great game fish is worthy of a quality fly tied with respect and skill without considering time or cost."

Bill Catherwood is a legendary fishing tackle designer and manufacturer. Known as the first to tie accurate imitations of the salt water naturals, Bill has been awarded the *Lifetime Achievement Award* by the Federation of Fly Fishers.

Bill's lifelike saltwater patterns were named The Giant Killers in a 1968 Tom McNally article. This series was the first to *"match the hatch"* for salt water species by developing his patterns to imitate baitfish. One of the patterns is called The Mullet.

Strippers and bluefish are Bill's favorite game fish. To imitate these species, Bill keeps specially bred chickens to produce long hackles needed for his six-inch patterns and keeps black-faced sheep used for the hair in many of his flies.

Bill's videos include *Catherwood Mackerals & Mullets, Catherwood Fodder Fish* and *Catherwood Seeker Styles,* which are included in the *Hooked on Fly Tying Series.*

The self trained Ichthyologist (a branch of zoology treating fishes) and his wife, Grace, live in Tewksbury, Massachusetts.

Years Fly Fishing
Sixty-six

Favorite Rod
10 wt 9' Graphite

Rods Owned
Four

Favorite Flies
Dry – Parachute Spider
Wet – Castor Rex
Nymph – Caddis
Streamer – Gray Imposter
Terrestrial – Valley Midge

Flies Invented
The Giant Killer Series, Lobster and Other Crustaceans

Favorite US River
Merrimac (MA)

Home River
Merrimac (MA)

Favorite Stream
Shawsheen (MA)

Home Stream
Shawsheen (MA)

BAKED BONITO

5 ½ or 6 Pound Bonito
Mayonnaise
Dill
Pepper
Lemon Juice

Split the bonito down the back and open it out flat as with a mackerel. Smear the fleshy side of the fish with mayonnaise. Sprinkle pepper and dill liberally and bake the bonito at 375 degrees until browned.

Squirt lemon juice over portions, to taste.

Serves: 5 – 6

AL CAUCCI

WHITE CLAM SAUCE ALA CAUCCI

"Nature provides the trout with keen instincts that enable them to take advantage of the most available food supply in the most efficient manner."

An author, teacher, lecture and fly fishing entrepreneur, Al Caucci resides in Tannersville, Pennsylvania and owns the nationally acclaimed Al Caucci Flyfishing Schools. 1999 marked Al's 15th consecutive year of fly fishing schools and programs on the Delaware River, as well as bonefish schools in the Bahamas and trout programs in the Rockies. He also co-owns the 600 acre Delaware River Club Flyfishing Resort featuring over 2 miles of private access on the famous West Branch of the Delaware.

Al Caucci and Bob Nastasi have co-authored five books: *Comparahatch, Hatches, Fly-Tyer's Color Guide, Instant Mayfly Identification Guide* and *Hatches II*. Al created the famous Comparadun in 1966. As co-creators and developers of the Compara-fly series of patterns, Al and Bob have revolutionized the way trout flies are tied and fished today.

Al has written for most major fly fishing magazines and is currently the Entomology Editor for *Fly Fish America* magazine.

Years Fly Fishing
Thirty-nine

Favorite Rod
5 wt 9' Graphite (Trout)
8 wt 9' Graphite (Bonefish)

Rods Owned
Dozens

Favorite Flies
Dry – Comparadun
Wet – Compara-Emerger
Nymph – Pheasant Tail
Streamer – Black Woolly Bugger
Terrestrial – Flying Ant

Fly Invented
Comparadun

Favorite US River
Missouri below Holter Dam (MT)

Home River
West Branch Delaware (PA)

Favorite Stream
Upper E. B. Delaware (NY)

Home Stream
Beaverkill (NY) & Brodheads (PA)

---

4 Anchovy Fillets, Chopped
2 – 3 Large Cloves Garlic, Pressed
1 Tablespoon Onion, Finely Chopped
3 Tablespoons Fresh Parsley, Finely Chopped
Salt and Pepper to Taste
¼ Teaspoon Ground Red Pepper
¾ Cup Pure Berio or Colavita Olive Oil
½ Teaspoon Italian Seasoning (Optional)
½ Cup Good Dry White Wine
1 Dozen Medium Cherrystone Clams
or 2 Dozen Little Necks
2 Tablespoons Butter
3 Tablespoons Parmesan Cheese, Imported
1 Pound Linguine, Imported from Italy

Clean clams and heat slightly to loosen shell for easier shucking. Don't overheat. Remove clams from the shells reserving separately clams and clam juice (1 cup needed). Add olive oil to medium size saucepan and heat to medium heat. Sauté garlic and onion until amber. Add anchovies, parsley, red pepper, salt, pepper, Italian seasoning, and continue to sauté. Add wine and reduce by ½. If making ahead of time, you can stop at this point. Add 1 cup of the fresh clam juice and reduce by ½.

Boil 4 – 5 quarts of water for pasta. Cut clams into bite size pieces. While pasta is cooking, add clams to sauce and cook briefly until tender.

Continued on next page …

Add butter and cheese to sauce over medium heat for more of a gravy consistency. When pasta is done (al dente), strain into colander and remove all water. Place pasta in a warm serving bowl, add sauce, and toss thoroughly, but rapidly, reserving most clam pieces for the top when serving. Add Parmesan.

"Mangia Bene!" – Al

Jon B. Cave

Key Lime Pie

"For the fly fishing student: Accelerate – stop – drop."

Jon Cave is a writer, former guide, photographer and lecturer who makes his home in Geneva, Florida. Jon has a M.S. degree in Natural Resources, specializing in fisheries. He has been a United States Coast Guard approved salt water guide for over 20 years.

Active in resource management and protection, Jon is an Advisory Council member for the Atlantic States Marine Fisheries Commission.

Jon is the founder (1975) of the oldest fly fishing school in the South, has over 23 years as a professional fly casting instructor, and has fly fished world-wide in both fresh and salt water for bluegill to billfish.

The Greater Indian River Lagoon System, including the Indian River, but mostly into the Lagoon or the Banana River, is Jon's favorite U.S. river.

Jon is a Governor of the Federation of Fly Fishers' Casting Certification Program and a former head of the Federation's Salt Water Committee. He is a Contributing Editor to *Fly Fishing in Salt Water*.

Jon is the Federation of Fly Fishers' 1998 recipient of the *Silver King Award* for extraordinary contributions to the sport of salt water fly fishing over an extended period of time.

Years Fly Fishing
Forty Something
Favorite Rod
8 wt 9' Graphite
Rods Owned
Over Twenty-five
Favorite Flies
Dry – Olive Elk Hair Caddis
Wet – Black Woolly Worm
Nymph – Prince
Streamer – Gold Wobbler
Terrestrial – Dave's Hopper
Flies Invented
Wobbler (Spoon Fly) and Rattlin' Minnow
Favorite US River
Yellowstone (WY)
Home River
See Comments
Favorite Stream
Slough Creek (WY)
Home Stream
St. John's River (FL)

4 Egg Yolks
1 Can Sweetened Milk
4 Ounces Key Lime Juice
Graham Cracker Piecrust
Whipped Cream

Mix 4 egg yolks and 1 can of sweetened milk together. Slowly add 4 ounces of key lime juice. Pour mixture into graham cracker pie crust. Bake for 20 minutes at 350 degrees. Refrigerate for 1 hour and top the edge of the pie with whipped cream.

Serves: 8

"I learned to cast side-arm while kneeling behind a tree."

Conrad CdeBaca is a fabricator living in Nashville, Tennessee. He is a member of the Middle Tennessee Fly Fishers, an active member group of the Federation of Fly Fishers. Conrad served as Vice President, Banquet Chairman and Board Member during 1998.

Years Fly Fishing
Six

Favorite Rod
2 wt 7' 9" Graphite

Rods Owned
Two

Favorite Flies
Dry – My Own
Wet – Dark Watchett
Nymph – Early
Brown Stonefly
Streamer – Muddler Minnow
Terrestrial – Black Ant

Fly Invented
C.S. Dry Fly

Favorite US River
Rio Grande (NM)

Home River
Caney Fork (TN)

Favorite Stream
Laurel Fork (TN)

Home Stream
Laurel Fork (TN)

© 2000 - Russell A. Hopper

1 Pound Hot Sausage
4 Potatoes, Chopped ½" x ½"
5 Eggs
1 Jar Salsa, Medium to Hot
2 Dozen Flour Tortillas
Cup Water
12" Skillet
Optional – Cheese

Brown sausage. Chop potatoes into ½" x ½" cubes and add to the browned sausage. Pour in 1 cup of water. Cook until the potatoes are soft. Push sausage and potatoes to the side. Crack and beat eggs. Pour the eggs into the middle of the pan. Mix with sausage and potatoes. Cook until the eggs are done. Heat tortillas. Scoop mix into the center of tortilla, but not too much or it won't roll up. Shake salsa and pour on the mix. Roll and flip up the bottom.

Serves: 6

J. Leon Chandler

Bluegill Cocktail

"Happiness is watching a trout take a dry fly."

Leon Chandler is widely recognized as America's Ambassador of Fly Fishing. At the age of 19, he joined the Cortland Line Company where he worked for 50 ½ years, until his 1992 retirement.

Chandler served as President of the American Fishing Tackle Manufacturers Association for two years (69—70), served for twenty-two years on the National Board of Directors of Trout Unlimited and as TU's National President for two years (79—80).

Leon has demonstrated fly casting and fly fishing skills before more people than anyone now living has. He has been to Finland, Poland, Hungary, Berlin and Japan where thousands of Japanese fly fishermen are now using techniques first taught by a soft spoken, gentle man, "Chandler-San from America."

Leon resides in Homer, New York. During trout season he can be frequently found, with his motorhome, on his favorite Catskill streams or roaming around Montana, Idaho or Wyoming enjoying the sport that has played such a dominant role in his life for so many years.

Fly Rod & Reel magazine named Leon *Angler of the Year* in 1994. He is one of four members of the Catskill Fly Fishing Museum's *Hall of Fame.*

Years Fly Fishing
Sixty-one

Favorite Rod
5 wt 9' 6" Graphite

Rods Owned
Lots

Favorite Flies
Dry – Parachute Adams
Wet – Soft Hackles
Nymph – B.H. Pheasant Tail
Streamer – Woolly Bugger or
Muddler Minnow
Terrestrial – Hopper

Fly Invented
None, yet

Favorite US River
Missouri (MT)

Home River
Catskills (NY)

Favorite Stream
Catskills (NY)

Home Stream
Catskills (NY)

Bluegill
Slightly Salted Boiling Water
Red Shrimp Cocktail Sauce

With a sharp knife, use the normal procedure for removing the filets. While a bit more tedious than in filleting larger fish like the bass and the walleye, with patience, it is easy to remove two small boneless white filets from each fish. Drop them in slightly salted boiling water for 3 minutes. Place the boiled filets in the refrigerator for a couple of hours to chill. Then crumble the white flaky meat into an appropriately small dish. Cover with red shrimp cocktail sauce and you will have a dish that is as tasty as anything served by a fancy restaurant.

"While I am a strong advocate of the catch and release philosophy for most fish species, I feel less inclined where the bluegill is concerned. Most of the warm water places I fish for panfish are over populated. A body of water will only support so many pounds of fish—perhaps hundreds of big ones, or thousands of small ones. I have no emotional problem with keeping a few panfish for the table." – Leon

ABE CHAVEZ

RED ENCHILADAS

"A good rooster will crow in any chicken house; meaning a good fisherman can catch fish in any stream."

Abe Chavez is the owner of Abe's Motel & Fly Shop in Navajo Dam, New Mexico. He claims to be the best guide to the San Juan River since 1958. Abe's is known around the world and he has personally watched the San Juan fishery develop from day one.

Abe is the inventor of the famed San Juan Worm and the creator of his now famous son, Tim Chavez, who was born 'n' raised on the San Juan.

Years Fly Fishing
Forty-six
Favorite Rod
5 wt 9' Graphite
Rods Owned
Three
Favorite Flies
Dry – Adams
Wet – Not Provided
Nymph – Pheasant Tail
Streamer – Dark
Spruce Matuka
Terrestrial – Hopper
Fly Invented
San Juan Worm
Favorite US River
San Juan (NM)
Home River
San Juan (NM)
Favorite Stream
Not Provided
Home Stream
Not Provided

1 Can Red Chilies
2 Pounds Pork
1 Package Corn Tortillas
1 Package Cheddar Cheese
1 Can Enchilada Sauce
2 Cans Taco Sauce
Lettuce
Diced Tomatoes
1 Onion, Chopped

Brown pork in pan and drain grease. Add taco sauce, enchilada sauce and red chilies; let simmer. Grate cheese, chop onion, and dice tomatoes. Put pork mixture, cheese, onion, lettuce, and tomatoes inside each corn tortilla (frozen type). Put in 13" x 9 ½" cake pan. Put a layer of pork mixture on bottom, and then add cheese, tomatoes and onion on top. Bake in oven at 425 degrees until cheese melts, about 10 minutes.

"I keep praying for the day I can out fish Tim Borski!"

C. D. Clarke is a painter of figurative sporting scenes and landscapes for anglers and hunters around the world in such exotic places as the Caribbean, Scotland, England, Hawaii, the Bahamas, Canada, Alaska, Montana and South America.

Clarke's works have been exhibited widely including the American Museum of Fly Fishing, Easton Waterfowl Festival, Holland and Holland, and the Mirimachi Salmon Museum.

The artist, who lives in Upper Fairmount, Maryland, recently won the Congressional Sportsman's Caucus' coveted *Artist of the Year Award.*

An avid fisherman, Clarke's career highlights include catching a 100-pound tarpon and a 14-pound bonefish.

Years Fly Fishing
Over Thirty

Favorite Rod
Depends on type of fishing.

Rods Owned
Over Twenty

Favorites Flies
All depends on the type of fishing. Tarpon and bonefish are my favorite.

Favorite US River
Blackfoot (MT)

Home River
Chesapeake Bay (MD)

Favorite Stream
Not Provided

Home Stream
Chesapeake Bay (MD)

© 2000 - Russell A. Hopper

Worcestershire Sauce
Lemon Juice
Garlic, Crushed
Orange Marmalade

Take equal parts of Worcestershire Sauce, lemon juice, and orange marmalade. Raspberry or another tart jam can be used as a substitute. Add crushed garlic. Reduce by ½ over medium heat.
Serve hot and enjoy!

"Practice catch and release fishing and you could repeat yesterday's success."

Bob Clouser says he is self-employed in the fly fishing business. That's like saying Babe Ruth was a baseball player.

Striving to get a better minnow imitation, more in action than in looks, Bob Clouser developed the famous Clouser Deep Minnow, a fly the legendary Lefty Kreh says if he had but one salt water fly to use for the rest of his life, it would be this pattern.

First developed in 1985 as a smallmouth bass fly, Kreh was the first person to advocate its use in salt water. Today, the fly is sold in some 16-color variations, the chartreuse-and-white being the most effective.

A fly fisher since the age of 14, Bob opened his fly shop in 1980 after losing his job of 26 years in the meat department when the store closed.

Bob Clouser has received the 1995 *Conservation Award of the Year* presented by the Susquehanna Smallmouth Alliance, the *Warm Water Committee Achievement Award* of the Federation of Fly Fishers, and the *Dr. James Henshall Award* of the Federation of Fly Fishers.

Bob's shop is run by his son, Bob Jr., and his wife, Joan, in Middletown/Royalton, Pennsylvania.

Years Fly Fishing
Forty-six

Favorite Rod
8 wt 9' Graphite

Rods Owned
Eleven

Favorite Flies
Dry – White Fly
Wet – March Brown
Nymph – Clouser
Swimming Nymph
Streamer – Clouser Minnow
Terrestrial – Cricket

Fly Invented
See Comments

Favorite US River
Susquehanna (PA)

Home River
Susquehanna (PA)

Favorite Stream
Penns Creek (PA)

Home Stream
Swatara Creek (PA)

---

1 Pound Venison Tenderloin
1 Small Onion, Sliced
2 Cups Mushrooms, Sliced
1 Can Beef Gravy
Oil

Place oil in a pan. Add onion and mushrooms. Sauté them on low heat for about 5 minutes. Add the venison and enough water to cover the meat. Place a lid on the pan and cook on medium heat until the meat is tender. Drain off any excess water left. Add gravy and stir until well mixed.

Serve over cooked rice to make a delicious meal.

In addition to being a guide, Bob teaches fly fishing, fly casting and fly tying. A frequent lecturer, he gives various slide show presentations, is a freelance outdoor photographer, and writes fly fishing and fly tying articles for a variety of fishing magazines. He developed the Clouser Series of flies including the Deep Minnow, Crayfish, Swimming Nymph, Crippled Minnow, Mad Tom, Hellgrammite, E-Z Popper, Floating Minnow and many others.

CHARLES COLE

CALIFORNIA CASSAROLE

"We need to conserve our natural resources for future generations through education and conservation."

Charlie Cole is a consulting engineer. He is the past President of the Deep Creek Fly Fishers, recipient of the Deep Creek Fly Fishers' *President's Award* and President of the Southwest Council of the Federation of Fly Fishers from which he received the *Don Haiger Award*. Charlie lives in Banning, California.

Years Fly Fishing
Sixty-four

Favorite Rod
2 wt 7' 9" Graphite

Rods Owned
Over Thirty-five

Favorite Flies
Dry – Elk Hair Caddis
Wet – Coachman
Nymph – G.R. Hare's Ear
Streamer – Matuka
Terrestrial – Henry's
Fork Hopper

Fly Invented
Little Golden

Favorite US River
Gallatin (MT)

Home River
Owens (CA)

Favorite Stream
Silver Creek (CA)

Home Stream
Bear Creek (CA)

© 2000 - Russell A. Hopper

½ Cup Mayonnaise
1 Cup Chopped White Onion
Butter
4 Cups Cooked White Rice
2 Cups Sour Cream
1 Cup Cream Style Cottage Cheese
1 Bay Leaf
½ Teaspoon Salt
1/8 Teaspoon Pepper
2 Cups Grated Cheddar Cheese
2 Cups Green Ortega Chilies, Chopped

Sauté onions in butter for 5 minutes. Then add rice, sour cream, cottage cheese, mayonnaise and seasonings. In a glass-baking bowl, alternate in layers the rice, grated cheese, chilies, etc. Bake at 375 degrees for 25 minutes.

This recipe can be made up into the bowl and carried on ice. When coming in from a day of fishing, in a short time dinner is ready and satisfying.

Serves: 4 – 6 healthy appetites

PETER CORBIN

"Take time to see the whole landscape, not just the fish."

Peter Corbin, a Millbrook, New York resident, is a landscape artist who enjoys painting scenes of hunters and fishermen. His sporting art has been featured in *Gray's Sporting Journal, Wildlife Art, Sports Afield, The Atlantic Salmon Journal* and some eight different hunting and fishing books.

Peter's work is in the permanent collections of The National Art Museum of Sport and he did commissioned drawings of The White House under President Carter.

Painting portraits of people and the water they love, showing the human spirit of fly fishing, is one of Peter's goals.

Years Fly Fishing
Forty-seven

Favorite Rod
7 wt 8' 7" Graphite

Rods Owned
Fifteen

Favorite Flies
Dry – The Usual
Wet – Sand Eel
Nymph – Black Stone
or Hare's Ear
Streamer – Glass Minnow
Terrestrial – Hopper

Fly Invented
None, yet

Favorite Water
Lobsterville Beach
on Martha's Vineyard (MA)

Home River
Millbrook (NY)

Favorite Stream
Moise Salmon River (Province
of Quebec Canada)

Home Stream
Turkey Hollow (NY)

STUFFED ATLANTIC SALMON*

(*Atlantic Salmon Stuffed with
Shrimp & Crabmeat)

Farm Raised Salmon Roast or Whole Fish
Small Onion, Chopped
Olive Oil
2 Tablespoons Butter
Thyme
Parsley
1 Cup Shrimp and Crabmeat
1 ½ Cups Breadcrumbs
4 Mushrooms, Sliced
Egg Yoke
½ Cup Red Wine

Sauté chopped onion in olive oil and 2 tablespoons butter until clear. Add 4 sliced mushrooms, parsley and thyme. Continue cooking in skillet for 2 – 3 minutes. Remove from the stove. Add 1 ½ cups breadcrumbs, boiled shrimp, and crabmeat. Bind with egg yoke.

Use farmed salmon (release wild fish) and stuff its cavity. Place in a foil lined dish and add ½ cup red wine.

Bake covered at 375 degrees for 45 minutes. Remove top foil and cook 10 minutes more.

RALF COYKENDALL

SPINACH STUFF ALA COYKENDALL

"Friendship is something you work at!"

Ralf Coykendall is a noted bird and decoy carver, awarding winning artist, and the author of some dozen books on hunting and fishing. His books include *The Golden Age of Fly Fishing: The Best of the Sportsman 1927—1937; You and Your Retriever; Wildfowling at a Glance*; and multiple editions of *Coykendall's Sporting Collectibles Price Guide.*

Coykendall presently writes a monthly sporting collectibles column for *Outdoor Life.*

Ralf has been retriever field trial judge and officer, craft society director, and newspaper editor. His father, Ralf, Sr., served as advertising director of *The Sportsman* magazine through much of its existence.

The author makes his home in Manchester Center, Vermont.

Years Fly Fishing
Fifty-six

Favorite Rod
6' 6" Bamboo

Rods Owned
Four

Favorite Flies
Dry – Royal Coachman
Wet – Coachman
Nymph – Stonefly
Streamer – Gray Ghost
Terrestrial – Ant or Hopper

Favorite US River
Rogue (OR)

Home River
Battenkill (VT)

Favorite Stream
Upper Battenkill in the weeds (VT).

Home Stream
Mettowee (VT)

© 2000 - Russell A. Hopper

2 Packages Frozen Spinach
4 Large Eggs
1 Small – Medium Yellow Onion
Mayonnaise (Must be Miracle Whip!)
Worcestershire Sauce
Salt and Pepper to Taste
Paprika

This is a great spread for crackers and an exciting and unusual salad.

Cook and drain the spinach. Hardboil the eggs and chop fine for a spread or coarse if preparing for a salad. Chop the onion. Mix spinach, eggs and onion. Add enough mayonnaise, Miracle Whip, to thoroughly moisten. Add Worcestershire sauce, salt and pepper, to taste. Mix well. Chill.

Garnish with paprika and watch your guest's eyes light up. They've never enjoyed spinach so much!

"Expect nothing."

Ed (Mr. Natural) Craft, along with Ken Glenn, is a co-creator of a mystical fly fishing haven called Rainbow Bend. In the tradition of Sheridan Anderson's *Curtis Creek Manifesto*, Rainbow Bend can accurately be called *"a delightful, unspoiled stretch of water that you will cherish above all others."* And like Sheridan Anderson, Ed and Ken know there are few Rainbow Bends in this life so they intend to *"keep its secret well."*

Ed resides in Bowling Green, Kentucky with his wife, Tina. Being retired, Ed spends his time in the wilderness whenever possible. When asked about his personal innovations and achievements, Ed quietly says, *"None I know of."* However, Ed is the founder of Uncle Eddie's Bugs & Lures. Three of his flies (*Booby Bug, Bumble Bug* and *Bou-Bug*) were featured in the June/July 1999 issue of *Warmwater Fly Fishing* magazine.

Mr. Natural is one of the six founders and four-term Secretary of the Sons of the Cumberland, a Kentucky non-profit fly fishing fellowship that practices catch and release fly fishing.

Years Fly Fishing
Thirteen
Favorite Rod
6 wt 8' 6" Graphite
Rods Owned
Four
Favorite Flies
Dry – White, Sponge Rubber Spider #10
Wet – Partridge & Orange
Nymph – Don't know any.
Streamer – The Rainbow Bend
Terrestrial – Women
Fly Invented
Corn-head Woolly Bugger
Favorite US River
Green (KY)
Home River
Green (KY)
Favorite Lake
Koontz (IN)
Home Lake
Malone (KY)

1 Cup Cooked Brown Rice
1 Cup Cooked Beans, Any Kind
1 Raw Onion
Hot Sauce
Salt
Whatever You Can Find Left Over in the Refrigerator, Unspoiled
Corn Chips

Put 1 cup of cooked rice and 1 cup of cooked beans in a bowl. Add leftovers (chop if necessary). Put bowl in microwave on high for 3 minutes. Stir and cook for 2 more minutes. Chop ¼ cup raw onion and sprinkle on top. Add hot sauce and salt to taste. Serve with corn chips on the side.

To make LUNCH-IN-A-BOWL SPECIAL #1 to go, add a lid.

Serves: 1, as in Ed

"I'd rather fish all day in a pretty, secluded place, and catch nothing, than fish three hours in a crowded, mistreated stream and catch my limit of smallmouths."

Byron Crawford of Shelbyville, Kentucky is a Columnist for the *Louisville Courier-Journal* newspaper and the host of the *Emmy Award* winning *Kentucky Life* magazine series on the Kentucky Educational Television Network. He is also the author of two books on Kentucky folk life, a humorist and a storyteller.

Byron began fly fishing as a youngster in central Kentucky and still has his old reconditioned bamboo fly rod that he used back then. He's acquired another bamboo rod, a 1930s model, from his friend Harold Casey, one of Kentucky's outstanding fly fishermen, rod makers and collectors.

Years Fly Fishing
Since the age of 12 (40 off and on).

Favorite Rod
8' 5" Bamboo

Rods Owned
Two

Favorite Flies
Dry – Yellow Hairbug
Wet – Woolly Bugger
Nymph – Mayfly
Streamer – Crazy Charlie Crayfish Pattern
Terrestrial – Young Hopper

Fly Invented
Filter Fly (fluffed cigarette filter with cellophane wings)

Favorite US River
Snake (ID), Big South Fork (KY) or Cumberland (KY)

Home River
Dix (KY)

Favorite Stream
Big Hickman Creek (KY)

Home Stream
Hanging Fork of Dix (KY)

1 Head Cabbage
4 Tablespoons Butter
4 Tablespoons Flour
2 Cups Milk
1/3 Cup Breadcrumbs
1 Cup Grated Cheese
Salt, Pepper and Paprika

Shred an average head of cabbage. Cook until just short of being done. Place a layer of cabbage in a baking dish, sprinkle a layer of grated cheese, then pour a layer of the sauce made of 4 tablespoons butter, 4 tablespoons flour and 2 cups milk.

Add second layer of each, seasoning with salt, pepper and paprika. Add breadcrumbs as the top layer and dot with butter. Bake in a 350-degree oven until crumbs are browned.

To make sauce, melt 4 tablespoons of butter in a heavy saucepan, stir in flour and blend well over low heat. Slowly stir in milk, stirring constantly and cook for 2 minutes.

Serves: 6 – 8

MIKE CROCKETT

"Get up every morning and give thanks for another twenty-four hours."

Mike Crockett is a fishing writer, attorney and investor. He lives in Telluride, Colorado.

When asked about his favorite stuff, Mike replied, *"For me, what is interesting and valuable about fly fishing is not the detail and trivia of the bugs and flies and equipment, but the activity itself and the contact with the natural world. So, it would be silly for me to try and pick a favorite rod (I never met one I didn't like) or stream or fly (ditto)."*

Mike and Grant McClintock are co-writers of two books, *Watermark* and *Flywater*, and the *Flywater Interactive* CD-ROM.

~ 53 ~

Years Fly Fishing
Twenty, but days of fishing is a better question.
Favorite Rod
See Comments
Favorite Flies
Whatever Works
Fly Invented
None, yet
Favorite US River
About a hundred.
Home River
San Miguel (CO)

RANCHO LA PUERTA*

(*Chef Bill Wavrin's Grandpa's Pan-fry)

2 Pan-size Brookies, Browns or Whatever You Just Landed, Cleaned
Salt and Pepper to Taste
1 Tablespoon White Flour
2 Tablespoons Corn Meal
1 Tablespoon Butter
1 Tablespoon Corn Oil
1 Large White Onion, Peeled and Sliced
1 Lemon

Place a cast iron skillet over medium high heat with the butter and oil. Season each trout with salt and pepper. Place flour and corn meal in a pie tin and mix to combine. Dredge each seasoned fish in the corn meal mix to coat. Place the coated fish in the hot cast iron skillet with the onions, moving the onions to the side and searing each side of the trout until golden. Then place fish on top of onions until onions are golden. Squeeze lemon over golden fish and onions.

Serve with campfire baked potatoes, butter and corn bread, and honey.

DENNY CRUM

FETTUCCINI ALFREDO

"Fish don't live in ugly places."

Denny Crum makes his home in Louisville, Kentucky where he is Head Basketball Coach for the University of Louisville.

Crum is a member of basketball's *Hall of Fame*, has had his picture snapped six times as a member of NCAA's *Final Four* and his teams have won two of those games.

Years Fly Fishing
Eleven

Favorite Rod
7 wt 9' Graphite

Rods Owned
Twelve

Favorite Flies
Dry – Elk Hair Caddis
Wet – Woolly Bugger
Nymph – Hare's Ear
Streamer – Shad Imitation
Terrestrial – Hopper

Fly Invented
None, yet

Favorite US River
Green (UT)

Home River
Cumberland (KY)

Favorite Stream
Henry's Fork of the Snake (ID)

Home Stream
Len Camp Creek (KY)

4 Quarts Water
¾ Teaspoon Salt
1 Pound Noodles (Homemade, if Available)
¼ Pound Butter at Room Temperature
¼ Pound Parmesan Cheese, Grated
¼ Cup Heavy Cream, Warmed
Freshly Ground Pepper to Taste

Place a 6-quart or larger pot with 4 quarts of water over high heat. Add ¾ teaspoon salt. Bring to a boil. When boiling, add noodles, separating them with a long handle fork. Homemade noodles take ¼ of the time to cook than store-bought noodles.

Place the pan or bowl you will mix the pasta in over the pot. When the pasta is cooked, drain approximately 98% of the water.

Place noodles in the preheated pan or bowl along with the butter. Stir gently until the butter is melted, adding ½ of the cheese and ½ of the cream. Continue to mix and add the remainder of the cheese. If more moisture is needed, add the rest of the cream.

Stir and serve, adding freshly ground pepper.

Serves: 4

LEMON-TARRAGON PHEASANT

"Of life's saddest words and deeds are those of what might have been … go fishing!"

Roger Cruwys resides in Bozeman, Montana where he is inspired by the surroundings of *The Last Best Place* and where he has found the ideal environment to pursue his wildlife sporting art.

An avid sportsman, ex-pilot, guide and self-taught award winning artist, Roger's wildlife, dog portraiture and angling art have found acceptance throughout the county. His works have been featured in major galleries, exhibitions including the Easton Waterfowl Festival, private collections and in many national sporting magazines and publications including *Fly Fisherman*, *Field & Stream* and *Gray's Sporting Journal*. His work also includes numerous state waterfowl and trout/salmon stamp prints.

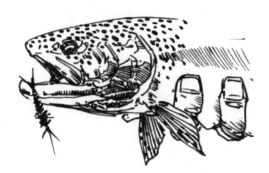

Years Fly Fishing
Over Forty

Favorite Rod
5 wt 9' Graphite

Rods Owned
Twelve

Favorite Flies
Dry – Elk Hair Caddis
Wet – Soft Hackle
Nymph – Flashback Pheasant
Tail and Baetis Nymph
Streamer – Woolly Bugger
Terrestrial – Beetle

Fly Invented
Nothing well known.

Favorite US River
Yellowstone (MT)

Home River
Genessee (NY)

Favorite Stream
Firehole (WY)

Home Stream
Gallatin (MT)

8 Skinless Boneless Pheasant,
Chicken or Partridge Breasts
2 Tablespoons Margarine or
Butter or Olive Oil, if Preferred
2 Cups Mushrooms, Sliced
2 Cloves Garlic, Diced
3 Tablespoons Dry Sherry
½ Teaspoon Dried, Crushed Tarragon
½ Teaspoon Lemon Pepper Seasoning
14 ½ Ounces Chicken Broth
1/3 Cup Flour, Cornstarch, if Desired
¼ Cup Sour Cream

In skillet melt margarine or butter on medium high heat. Add pheasant, chicken or partridge breasts, garlic, sherry, tarragon, and lemon pepper. Cook uncovered until meat is pink, 10 – 12 minutes.

Remove meat, add mushrooms and cook slightly. In screw top jar add chicken broth and flour. Shake until blended. Add mixture to skillet. Cook and stir until thickened. Stir in sour cream and return meat. Heat thoroughly, but do not boil.

Serve over hot noodles, or rice.

Serves: 3

"Fishing is simply a great excuse to visit cool places."

Ralph Cutter is a writer, instructor, author of *Sierra Trout Guide* and a co-owner with his wife, Lisa, of the California School of Flyfishing.

While mapping caves in Borneo for *National Geographic Magazine*, Ralph caught three new species of fish 1,400 feet underground on flies. He says he hasn't topped that feat, but is trying hard.

Ralph's many fly creations include the E/C Caddis, Martis Midge, Perfect Ant, Cutter's Little Yellow Stone, Goblin, and Teichert Caddis.

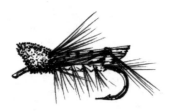

Years Fly Fishing
Thirty-five
Favorite Rod
5 wt 9' Graphite
Rods Owned
Over Twenty
Favorite Flies
Dry – E/C Caddis
Wet – Bird's Nest
Nymph – Bird's Nest
Streamer – Clouser Minnow
Terrestrial – Gartside Hopper

Flies Invented
See Comments
Favorite US River
They're all my favorites.
Home River
Truckee (CA)
Favorite Stream
It's a secret!
Home Stream
Little Truckee (CA)

6 Pack Sierra Nevada Pale Ale
1 Box Vegetable Thins
1 Pillow Pack Gallo Light Salami
1 ½ Pounds Pepper Jack Cheese
1 Fuji Apple
1 Variety Pack Pepperidge
Farms Cookies
1 Bottle Sierra Nevada Cilantro &
Garlic Chileno Peppers

Open all packages and spill contents onto tailgate of pickup, boat seat or granite boulder. Twist off beer cap and graze through the food in no particular order.

"Your odds of catching a truly big fish are inversely proportional to how much you actually deserve it."

Larry Dahlberg and his wife, Marilyn, live in Taylors Falls, Minnesota. Larry is a media host for *The Hunt for Big Fish* on ESPN. He has been elected to the *Freshwater Fishing Hall of Fame* and is a recipient of the *Henshaw Award*.

In addition to his many fly pattern inventions, including the Dahlberg Diver, Flashabou and the Balancer, Larry invented the blank-through off set bait casting handle.

Larry started out as a fishing guide at the age of eleven. Later he became video producer at *Infisherman* magazine.

By his own estimate, Dahlberg has caught more than 50 line class world records. Because he lets his fish go and they cannot be officially weighed, Dahlberg's name won't be found in the record books.

The globetrotting Dahlbergs fish worldwide, including Africa and Venezuela.

Years Fly Fishing
Forty-five

Favorite Rod
10 wt 9' Graphite

Rods Owned
Two Hundred

Favorite Flies
Dry – Dahlberg Diver
Wet – Blue Charm
Nymph – Deep Wiggler
Streamer – Matuka
Terrestrial – Wife, Marilyn

Fly Invented
See Comments

Favorite River
Zambezi for tigerfish.

Favorite US River
Snake (ID)

Home River
St. Croix (MN/WI)

Favorite Stream
The Jet Stream

Home Stream
Kinni (WI)

3 – 4 Pound Free Range Chicken
3 Tablespoons Sweet Curry
2 Tablespoons Ground Pepper
4 Tablespoons Fresh Ground Coriander
1 Tablespoon Salt
Fresh Garlic
Ginger Root
1 Cup Dark Beer
1 Cup Lemon Juice

Rinse chicken. Crush all spices together; curry, ground pepper, coriander and salt. Coat chicken inside and out with these spices. Place the coated chicken on a vertical roaster. Place roaster in a pan with 1-cup dark beer and 1 cup lemon juice. Tuck chopped garlic and ginger root under skin on breast of chicken. Protect chicken with 4" x 4" aluminum foil and place in a 450-degree oven for 1-½ hours. Reduce heat to 375 degrees if chicken looks too brown. Chicken is done when wing breaks off easily when lifted.

Serves: 4 depending on size of chicken

CORBETT DAVIS JR.

MANGO SNAPPER

"What I enjoy most about the sport of fly fishing is meeting new people and fishing with family and friends. Every trip is an adventure. Catching fish is a bonus."

Corbett Davis is a salt water fly fisher who resides in Gulf Breeze, Florida and operates a retail jewelry business in Pensacola. His greatest pleasure comes from fishing with great folks like Lefty Kreh, Nick Curcione, John Cole, Jeffrey Cardenas, his father and his son. He has caught a 25-pound permit on his fly rod.

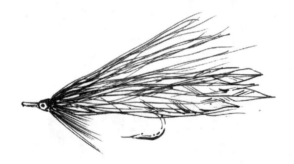

Years Fly Fishing
Sixteen in Saltwater

Favorite Rod
8 wt 9' 8" Graphite

Rods Owned
Twelve

Favorite Flies
Clouser Minnows and Deceivers

Fly Invented
Crab Mudgeon

Favorite US River
Kanetok (AK)

Home Waters
Gulf of Mexico and Pensacola Bay (FL)

4 Large Snapper Filets
2 Fresh Ripe Mangoes
1 Cup Mango Syrup,
or 2 Cups of Canned Mangoes and Juice
Garlic Powder
Salt and Pepper
Lime Juice
Flour
2/3 Cup Olive Oil
1/3 Cup Butter

Squeeze lime juice over filets. Salt and pepper to taste. Sprinkle with garlic. Dredge filets in flour. In large skillet add olive oil and butter. Fry filets on medium-high heat until nice and brown. Remove filets from pan. Repeat until all fish is fried. Reduce heat to low. Return all filets to skillet with oil and butter. Add mangoes with juice. Cover and let simmer for 5 minutes.

JACK DENNIS

"I fish once a year in honor of my grandfather, spending time in the spots we fished together, using his favorite flies. My grandfather taught me to fly fish so that I could live my life full of honesty, love of the outdoors, mystery and discovery. Everything in life is there to experience, truth, death, life and hope—eternal hope that life will always get better and just maybe we'll catch a bigger fish."

Jack Dennis is the founder of Wyoming Galleries and the Jack Dennis Outdoor Shops. His clients include everyone from U.S. presidents to movie stars. He introduced fly fishing to actors Tom Selleck, Don Johnson, Harrison Ford, Richard Pryor, Woody Harrelson and sports figures Arnold Palmer, Don Meredith, and Dr. J.

Jack's books, *Western Trout Fly Tying Manual, Volumes I and II*, have sold over 300,000 copies, making it one of the best known fly fishing books in the world. He has produced 15 fly fishing videotapes, winning several video of the year awards.

Jack lives with his wife, Sandra, in Jackson, Wyoming. He lectures worldwide over 100 days a year. His fly inventions include the Royal Humpy, Amy's Stonefly and the Kiwi Muddler.

Years Fly Fishing
Forty-seven

Favorite Rod
3 wt 8' 8" Graphite

Rods Owned
Eighteen

Favorite Flies
Dry – Adams Wulff
Wet – Soft Hackle Caddis
Nymph – Improved Pheasant Tail
Streamer – Kiwi Muddler
Terrestrial – Parachute Hopper

Flies Invented
See Comments

Favorite US River
Somewhere in Wyoming.

Home Stream
Snake (WY)

Favorite Stream
In the Alps of New Zealand.

Home Stream
A spring creek one-fourth mile from home.

GRILLED THAI SALMON

2 - 4 Pounds of Fresh Salmon Fillets
Olive Oil Based Mari Coconut Cream
Chili Sauce (Tamarind) – Olive Oil
Thai Spices
Sesame Fire Oil
Sweet Pepper and Pickle Relish
Lemon and Soy Sauce
Brown Sugar
Molasses and Honey

Marinade salmon with olive oil, lemon and soy sauce for 4 – 6 hours. Prepare hot coals, or hot gas grill. Cook fish fast but do not over cook. Prepare sauce by combining ¼ cup olive oil, 1 can coconut cream, ¼ cup Thai chili, Thai spices, 1 tablespoon sesame fire oil, ½ cup sweet pepper and pickle relish, 3 tablespoons honey, ½ cup brown sugar, teaspoon lemon, and 1 tablespoon molasses. Combine ingredients over medium heat to near boil and set aside. Lay salmon on grill, skin side down. Grill for 1 – 2 minutes. Separate burnt skin from fillet with spatula. Flip to other side. Baste heavily with Thai sauce on side not being grilled. Cook 2 minutes and flip again. Add more sauce to the cooked side that was just flipped. Cover grill, cook 1 more minute, move to a dish, add remaining sauce, and enjoy.

"If you want convention, comfort, and safety, stay home. If you want your life to be a joyous romp, get outside."

Jerry Dennis is a writer who lives in Traverse City, Michigan. He has written seven books of essays and stories about fishing and nature—multiple editions, and translations into Japanese, Chinese, German and Portuguese. Jerry also writes for *Sports Afield, Smithsonian, American Way, Gray's Sporting Journal* and *The New York Times*.

Books written by Jerry include *The River Home: An Angler's Explorations*; *A Place on the Water: An Angler's Reflections on the Home*; *Canoeing Michigan Rivers*; *It's Raining Frogs and Fishes: Four Seasons of Natural Phenomena and Oddities of the Sky*; *The Bird in the Waterfall: A Natural History of Oceans, Rivers, and Lakes*; and *From a Wooden Canoe: Reflections on Canoeing, Camping, and Classic Equipment*.

Another of Jerry's quotes about fly fishing comes from *The River Home* concerning the pursuit of trout: *"It's a restorative that cleanses us when we've become muddied and makes us healthy when we've become sickened. It's a brace against pessimism."*

Years Fly Fishing
Over Thirty
Favorite Rod
6 wt 9' Graphite
Rods Owned
Four
Favorite Flies
Dry – Parachute Hendrickson # 14 (during the hatch)
Wet – Soft Hackle Hare's Ear
Nymph – B.H. Stonefly
Streamer – Black Bow Bugger
Terrestrial - Hopper

Fly Invented
None, yet
Favorite US River
Manistee (MI)
Home River
Boardman (MI)
Favorite Stream
Burke Creek (MI)
Home Stream
Cedar Creek (MI)

2 One-Pound Skinned Salmon or Trout Filets
Fresh Tomato
Onion
Garlic
Oregano
Lemon
Salt and Pepper or Mrs. Dash

On a sheet of aluminum foil, arrange a bed of thinly sliced tomatoes, lemons and onions. Lay fillets on bed and cover with another layer of tomatoes, onions and sliced lemons. Season to taste with garlic, oregano, salt and pepper, or liberal doses of Mrs. Dash. Fold foil over and crimp edge. Place on covered grill for 15 minutes, turning once.

Serve when fish flakes easily with a fork. Serve with boiled red potatoes and a bottle of dry chilled white wine.

Serves: 2

"Stand on the table and shout hosannas!" – Jerry

"Whenever everything goes wrong, the fishing gets better."

Lenox Dick is a fly fishing writer and resides in Vancouver, Washington. He has been writing the *Interesting Fish Facts* column of *Salmon Trout Steelhead* magazine since August 1993.

Lenox's book, *Art and Science of Fly Fishing*, is in its third edition. He wrote the book, *Experience the World of Shad Fishing*, and co-authored *Walleye Fishing Simplified*.

In 1997, Lenox received the *Sheridan Anderson, Curtis Creek Manifesto Award* presented for contributions mightily to all aspects of fly fishing from Frank Amato Publications and the *Vern S. "Pete" Hidy Award* from the Fly Fishing Club of Oregon for significant contributions to angling literature.

Lenox writes regularly for publications such as *Hunting and Fishing News, Flyfishing, The Creel of the Fly Fishing Club of Oregon, Western Fly Fishing* and the New York Anglers Club's *Angler's Club Bulletin*.

Years Fly Fishing
Seventy
Favorite Rod
7 wt 9' Graphite
Rods Owned
Five
Favorite Flies
Dry – Adams
Wet – Soft Hackles
Nymph – Princess (Prince with Green Flashback Body)
Streamer – Blood Sucking Leach
Terrestrial – Not Provided
Fly Invented
Princess Nymph
Favorite US River
Deschutes (OR)
Home River
Not Provided
Favorite Stream
McKenzie (OR)
Home Stream
Not Provided

Shad

Broil boned shad in oven with lemon and butter.

RED BEANS & RICE

"I've only been trout fishing once and it was two weeks ago (May 1998) on the Deschutes where I caught my first ever rainbow after twenty years of warmwater fly fishing."

Captain Kirk Dietrich is a draftsman, part-time redfishing guide and a fly tyer residing in Arabi, Louisiana. He has had several articles published by Abenaki Publishers in *Fly Tyer* magazine. Orvis features several of his flies in their 1999 line-up.

Captain Dietrich came up with his Rattle Rouser when his friend, Tom Jindra, told him about Jon Cave's rattling flies and asked Kirk to come up with some patterns specific to fishing the central and western Gulf of Mexico.

Years Fly Fishing
Twenty-one

Favorite Rod
7 wt 9' Sage RPL+

Rods Owned
Eight

Favorite Flies
*Dry – Popping Bugs
Wet – Squirrelly
Nymph – G.R. Hare's
Ear and Girdle Bug
Streamer – Seaducer, Woolly
Bugger and Spoon Fly
Terrestrial – Sponge Spider*

Flies Invented
Squirrelly and Rattle Rouser

Favorite US River
Not Provided

Home River
*South East Louisiana
Marsh Estuary*

Favorite Stream
Not Provided

Home Stream
Not Provided

*2 Pounds Smoked Sausage
2 Pounds Kidney Beans
Large Onion – 2 Cloves Garlic
2 Green Bell Peppers – Handful of Parsley
3" Sprig of Rosemary (Optional) – 10 Bay Leaves
Separately Cooked Rice for Beans
Salt and Pepper to Taste*

Rinse and clean beans. Dump them in a large pot half-filled with water. Let the beans soak while performing other tasks.

Slice sausage into disks, thickness as desired, sauté in a frying pan and drain on paper towels.

Chop onions, bell peppers and garlic, by hand or food processor, and put in the pot. Add sausage, bay leaves, parsley, rosemary, salt, pepper and whatever else you desire. Cook over medium to low fire for 3 hours. You may want to crank up the heat for the first 20 minutes and then lower fire to simmer. After 3 hours, remove the pot from the heat and dump several trays of ice on top to help cool the mixture if saving for later freezing. This also makes the broth creamier.

Cook rice and serve beans over rice. Add bread, butter and 12 or so dashes of hot sauce, if desired.

Serves: 12 – 15

"The South isn't just a place for trout angling's unfortunates to while away unproductive hours between trips elsewhere anymore."

John Doty lives in Anderson, Tennessee where he is only 10 minutes away from the Clinch River tailwater and an hour from the Smokies. He is the Publisher of *TroutSouth* that in 1996 took first place honors in the prestigious Southeastern Outdoor Press Association competition.

TroutSouth, founded in 1995, is the first and only publication devoted solely to trout fishing in nine southern states, covering destinations, fly patterns, techniques, research, politics and personalities.

John launched the *Southern Trout Catalog*, the only one-stop source of books, tapes, maps and hatch charts relevant to the southern trout scene.

John is also an award-winning freelance writer/photographer and past President of the Southeastern Outdoor Press Association.

John says he was fortunate enough to marry an avid trout fisherwoman.

Years Fly Fishing
Sixteen

Favorite Fly Rod
5 wt 9' Graphite

Rods Owned
Four

Favorite Flies
The one that works on a particular water at a particular time.

Fly Invented
None

Favorite US River
Clinch (TN)

Home River
Clinch (TN)

Favorite Stream
Tellico (TN)

Home Stream
Tellico (TN)

© 2000 - Russell A. Hopper

1 Cup Quick-Cooking Oats
1 ¼ Cups Boiling Water
1 Cup Brown Sugar and 1 Cup White Sugar
½ Cup Shortening – 2 Eggs
1 1/3 Cups Flour
½ Teaspoon Cinnamon
1 Teaspoon Baking Soda
½ Teaspoon Salt
Small Box Raisins

Pour water over oats and let stand 20 minutes. Cream together brown sugar, white sugar and shortening. Add whole eggs, one at a time. Beat well after each addition. Blend/mix flour, raisins, cinnamon, baking soda and salt. Add flour and oat-mixture alternately to cream mixture, ending with flour. Bake 35 – 40 minutes at 350 degrees in a greased 8" x 16" pan or two 8" x 8" pans.

While cake is baking, make a topping by creaming together:

6 Tablespoons Butter – ¾ Cup Brown Sugar
¼ Cup Evaporated Milk – 1 Tablespoon Vanilla
1 Cup Chopped Nuts – 1 Cup Coconut

Mix well. Spread over cake after cake is baked. Put under broiler to heat. Cut in squares and serve.

Thomas W. Earnhardt

Extra Garlic Lemon Pesto*

"From trout streams to the Gulf Stream is a very short cast. No fish is off limits to a person with a fly rod."

Tom Earnhardt describes himself as an angler, writer, photographer, fly tyer, law professor, and attorney. He resides in Raleigh, North Carolina, but is a worldwide traveler and helped start fly fishing clubs in the Soviet Union.

Tom is the author of *Fly Fishing the Tidewaters*. He helped make false albacore catchable and exciting for southeastern anglers. His Alba Clouser fly, an ultra hair variation of the famed Clouser Minnow, is ideal for catching false albacore, bonito, and Spanish mackerel.

A fly fishing schizophrenic, Tom says he is often torn between his love of trout streams and salt water. His favorite salt water rod is an 8 weight 9' graphite.

Tom is a Contributing Editor to *Fly Fishing in Salt Water* and Southeastern Editor of *Fly Fisherman* magazine.

*"This recipe is protected by numerous patents, copyrights, and relatives from Sicily." – Thomas W. Earnhardt, Esquire

Years Fly Fishing
Forty-six
Favorite Trout Rod
4 wt 9' Graphite
Rods Owned
A Secret from My Wife
Favorite Flies
Dry – Blue Winged Olive
Wet – Coachman
Nymph – Hare's Ear
Streamer – Deceivers and Clouser Minnows
Terrestrial – Brown Fur Ant
Fly Invented
See Comments
Favorite US River
Bighorn (MT)
Home River
Roanoke (NC)
Favorite Stream
Gulf Stream-I love salt water.
Home Stream
Smith River (VA)

20 Fresh Sweet Basil Leaves
½ Cup Pine Nuts
8 Garlic Cloves, About 1 ¼ Bulbs
4 – 6 Small Sun Dried Tomatoes
½ Cup Olive Oil
1 Medium to Large Lemon
¼ Cup Grated Parmesan Cheese

Chop the garlic cloves in a food processor. Consistency should be between that of fine slaw and course paste.

Slice sun dried tomatoes into very thing strips. Do not put the tomatoes in a food processor.

Heat oil at very low heat in a small saucepan. Add mixture of basil, pine nuts and garlic. Add tomato strips. Simmer on very low heat for about 10 minutes while stirring frequently with wooden spoon. Do not let mixture brown or stick to the pan. At the 10-minute mark add juice of whole lemon, with some pulp, and grated Parmesan. Continue to stir for 1 – 2 minutes. Remove from heat. Sauce can be thinned with ¼ - 1/3 cup of water.

Serve over thin spaghetti for rave reviews. Enjoy!

Serves: 2 – 3 as main course or 5 – 6 as side dish

JEFF EDVALDS

"Never met a fish I didn't want to catch on a fly."

Jeff Edvalds is an award winning outdoor photographer and graphic artist whose work has appeared in or on the covers of *Gray's Sporting Journal, Field & Stream, Fly Fish America, Fly Fisherman Japan, Kodak Videotrips, American Angler, Warmwater Flyfishing, Saltwater Flyfishing, Fly Tyer, Fly Rod & Reel, Fly Fishing, Fly Fisherman, The Flyfisher, Fly Tackle Dealer, Salmon Trout Steelheader* and *Western Outdoors* among others. In addition to editorial, Jeff shoots assignment and stock (both above and underwater) for client presentations, brochures and catalogs, as well as calendars and books.

Jeff says he's always been somewhat unconventional; having learned to fly tie before learning to fly fish, or having multiple magazine covers before having any inside photo sales. His limited edition art work and flies are in rotation at William Cushner's Flyfishing Museum in Florence, Oregon.

When he's not floating in Alaska, flying through South America, underwater in the Yucatan or poling in the Bahamas, Jeff resides in Tacoma, Washington.

Years Fly Fishing
Twenty-one

Favorite Rod
4 wt 8' 6" Graphite

Rods Owned
Sixteen

Favorite Flies
Dry – Hairwing Caddis #14
Wet – March Brown
Soft Hackle
Nymph – Prince # 14
Streamer – Muddler
Minnow or Sculpin
Terrestrial – Red Ant

Flies Invented
E. T. Pupa, Woolly Bou and the F. L. Nymph

Favorite US River
Big Hole (MT)

Home River
Yakima (WA)

Favorite Stream
Silver Creek (ID)

Home Stream
Rocky Ford (WA)

CHICKEN-BROCCOLI CASSEROLE

6 Chicken Breasts, Cooked and Drained
3 Packages Frozen Broccoli, Cooked and Drained
Parmesan Cheese

Sauce
2 Cans Cream of Chicken Soup
1 Cup Mayonnaise
1 Tablespoon Lemon Juice
1 Teaspoon Curry

Place chicken and broccoli in a casserole dish. Chicken may be split into smaller pieces. Pour sauce over the chicken and broccoli. Top with Parmesan cheese and bake uncovered at 350 degrees for 1 hour.
Serve over rice.

Serves: 3 "wading tired" fly fishers or 4 – 6 regular people

"I have about come to the conclusion that about the most thing wrong with old age is that it's so damn inconvenient."

Charles Elliott has been associated with *Outdoor Life* magazine since January 1951 as either its Editor or a Contributing Writer. He is ninety-three years young, answers all correspondence, types on a real typewriter, and lives in Covington, Georgia.

Witnessing *Outdoor Life* through half it history, Charlie, as he calls himself, has been associated with many of fly fishing's legends. Legends such as Joe Brooks, Lee Wulff, Ray Bergman, J. A. McGuire, and others. His most recent book is entitled *Outdoor Life: 100 Years in Pictures*. More can be read about Charlie's life in the book *Outdoor Life: The Autobiography of Charlie Elliott* which he says depicts all his sins and transgressions.

All of Charlie's library, fishing and hunting and other outdoor gear, along with some 7,000 acres, have been turned over to the Charlie Elliott Wildlife Center in Georgia to be used as a class room for the young and middle school students of the State. He says his rod collection must number well over 100, and there are almost that many reels, with hundreds of lures, many still new in the original packaging.

Years Fly Fishing
Until I was not able to get out and break my 'toongass' on the slick rocks.

Favorite Rod
*5 or 6 Ounce 7' to 7' 8"
Leonard Bamboo*

Favorite Flies
*Dry – Black Gnat
Nymph – Tellico
Streamer – Parmachenee Belle
Salmon – Jock Scott*

Favorite Rivers and Streams
South Fork of the Yellowstone above Cody, Wyoming and the Bliss Creek that flows into it.

Home Waters
The trout creeks and rivers of the southern Appalachians, with Tellico, Jacks and Connasauga high on the list.

*Fresh Steam Side Channel Catfish Fillets,
Skinned and Dressed
3-Legged Cast-iron Pot or
Heavy Metal Pan 10" – 12" Deep
Paper Towels to Drain Fish and Hush Puppies
Sunflower Seed or Peanut Cooking Oil
Cornmeal
Onions
Large Potatoes, Cut for French Fries
Seasonings of Choice
Fermented or Distilled Spirits*

Make hush puppy mix by stirring cornmeal, water, chopped onion and seasonings and roll into 1" to 2" balls. Soak catfish fillets in a weak solution of salt water. Roll fillets in dry cornmeal.

Build a fire around the cast-iron pot. Fill ¾-full of cooking oil. Keep a small but hot fire under the pot until you can spit into the oil and it spits back.

Drop mealed fish in hot oil. When fillets float to the surface, lift out and drain on layers of paper towels. Keep oil hot and cook French fries and hush puppies the same way, cooking the hush puppies to a crusty brown.

Sip fermented or distilled spirits sparingly as the meal is being prepared.

RAY ELLIS

BEAUFORT CREAM OF CRAB SOUP

"The chase is the thing." – Silvio Calabi

Ray Ellis is an artist residing in Edgartown, Massachusetts. There have been ten books of his paintings, three with text by Walter Cronkite, including *Coastal Images of America* and *Martha's Vineyard.*

Ray was chosen as the artist for the 1998 White House Christmas card that depicts the newly redecorated State Dining Room with table set for a holiday dinner.

At first, Ellis didn't take the White House call seriously. *"I thought it was my brother's practical joke,"* the artist said.

Once convinced, he visited 1600 Pennsylvania Avenue and saw the room, which was still being redecorated. He painted the card to match expectations.

Ray says he started fly fishing and worm fishing in 1929, but has spent more time painting since 1969.

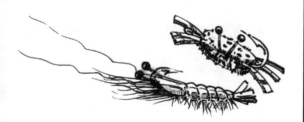

Years Fly Fishing
Forty
Favorite Rod
Graphite
Rods Owned
One
Favorite Flies
Not Provided
Fly Invented
None, yet
Favorite US River
Judith (MT)
Favorite Stream
Paradise Creek in the Poconos (NY)
Home Waters
Ponds on Martha's Vineyard (MA)

1 Pound Fresh Crab Meat
1 Onion, Chopped Fine
1 Tablespoon Butter
1 Cup Chicken Broth
1 Quart Half-&-Half
1 Tablespoon Chopped Parsley
½ Teaspoon Celery Salt
½ Teaspoon Mace
1/8 Teaspoon Pepper
½ Teaspoon Salt
Dash Cayenne
2 Tablespoons Flour
¼ Cup Dry Sherry

Sauté onion in butter. Add chicken broth and Half-&-Half. Stir well. Add seasonings and crab meat. Mix and simmer for 15 minutes. Do not boil. Make a paste of the flour and a little water and stir into the soup. Just before serving, add sherry. Remove from heat and serve immediately.

DAVE ENGERBRETSON

"Give 'em what they want, where they want it, and acting like they expect it to act."

Dave Engerbretson is a writer, photographer, fly fishing instructor, equipment designer, consultant to fly fishing companies, TV host and now a Contributing Editor for *Fly Fisherman* magazine. He has been a guide and commercial fly tyer, builds his own bamboo fly rods and currently serves on the Casting Instructor Certification Board of Governors for the Federation of Fly Fishers. Dave received the FFF's *Don Harger Lifetime Membership Award* in 1985.

Dave lives in Moscow, Idaho. He wrote the book *Tight Lines, Bright Water: Travels with a Fly Fisherman*.

Years Fly Fishing
Thirty-nine

Favorite Rod
*4 wt 7' or 6 wt 7 ½'
Self-built Bamboo*

Rods Owned
I have no idea.

Favorite Flies
*Dry – Dave's Hopper
Wet – Western Green Weenie
Nymph – My Damsel*
Streamer – Chickatuka*
Terrestrial – My Beetle*
Steelhead Fly – Purple Peril**

Flies Invented
All the above (*) plus the Bacon Ant and Spinner.

Favorite US River
Henry's Fork (ID)

Home River
Clearwater (ID)

Favorite Stream
Kinnikinnick, reserved for those who already know.

Home Stream
St. Joe (ID)

GRILLED SALMON ALA DAVE

Fresh Pacific King or Sockeye Salmon Filets

*Barbecue Sauce
Lemon Juice
Honey
Dijon Mustard
Margarine or Butter
Shallots, Freshly Chopped
Fresh Tarragon
Fresh Basil - Lemon Pepper
Toasted Almonds, Freshly Chopped*

Don't measure anything. Taste the sauce as you prepare it, and adjust the quantities to suit your own taste.

In a small saucepan, combine a cup of lemon juice, a tablespoon of Dijon mustard and a good dose of honey while heating the mixture over medium heat. Stir until the ingredients are melted and combined. Adjust the taste to your likes.

Turn the heat to low, add a palm full of basil and tarragon, a medium shallot, finely chopped, a dollop of margarine or butter, and sprinkle in a little lemon pepper. Simmer on low until ready to grill the salmon. Stir occasionally. Adjust the taste to your likes.

Continued on next page …

In a pie pan, toast some almond slivers in a little butter or margarine in a 300-degree oven for just a few minutes. When toasted and cooled, chop them finely in a grinder or food processor.

Place skin side of salmon filets down over charcoal in a wire fish basket. Coat the wire basket with cooking oil or spray. If using salmon steaks, coat both sides of the wire basket with oil. To enhance the smoky flavor of the meat, sprinkle water soaked hardwood chips over the coals while cooking.

While cooking, baste the flesh side of the salmon frequently with the sauce. Cook the meat until the surface turns a golden brown. When done, the skin will appear to be burned black and will stick to the basket. Check it with a fork. The meat should be opaque, moist, and flaky. It should not be dry and overly done. Slip a spatula between the skin and the meat to produce a perfect skinless filet for the plate.

Cook the salmon for approximately 10 minutes per side per inch of thickness. However, Dave turns the salmon frequently, and each time brushes it with the sauce to get plenty of herbs on the meat.

To serve, place on heated plates, give it one last baste with the sauce, and sprinkle with chopped almonds. Serve with Pinot Gris or your favorite dry white wine. Enjoy!

ED ENGLE

BOILED SHRIMP

"Rising trout do it for me."

Ed Engle is a fly fishing writer and guide residing in Manitou Springs, Colorado. He says his greatest achievement is that he can still tie a #22 midge imitation to a 6X tippet.

Ed is the author of *Fly Fishing the Tailwaters* and *Seasonal, A Life Outside*, a collection of essays about outdoors. He writes regular fly fishing columns for *Angler's Journal*, *Fly Tyer*, and *Warmwater Fly Fishing*. He has contributed to *Fly Fisherman*, *Gray's Sporting Journal*, *Fly Rod & Reel*, *American Angler* and *Saltwater Fly Fishing*. He is the current Southwestern Field Editor for *Fly Fisherman* magazine.

Ed is a devotee of split cane fly rods and trying to catch trout on very small flies. Ed says, *"My idea of the very best fishing is a cane rod and an out of the way small stream in the middle of nowhere in the Rockies. Trout rising on a beaver pond drive me to ecstasy."*

Actually, any rising trout drive Ed to ecstasy. He says, *"I just like seeing them come up, but that doesn't mean I'm not desperately searching my fly boxes for an imitation when they're doing it. It's plain, simple electricity and I will never get enough of it."*

Years Fly Fishing
Twenty-five

Favorite Rod
5 wt 8' 6" Split Cane Bamboo

Rods Owned
Twenty

Favorite Flies
Dry – Parachute Adams
Wet – Partridge and Green
Nymph – Pheasant Tail
Streamer – Zonker
Terrestrial – Schroeder Hopper

Fly Invented
None, yet

Favorite US River
Frying Pan (CO)

Home River
South Platte (CO)

Favorite Stream
St. Vrain Creek (CO)

Home Stream
Rough and Tumbling Creek (CO)

1 Gallon Water
1 Lemon, Sliced Thin
1 Onion, Sliced
¼ Cup Cayenne Pepper
3 Pounds Shrimp, With Peelings
1 Clove Garlic, Peeled
1 Cup Salt

Bring water, lemons, onion, garlic and cayenne pepper to a boil in a large pot. Simmer for 5 to 10 minutes.

Add shrimp. Bring to a boil and then boil shrimp for 3 minutes only.

Remove from heat and add 1 cup of cold water (to stop the boiling process) and salt to pot of shrimp. Let stand for 5 minutes and drain.

Serves: 4 – 6

"A close Louisiana friend, who knows about things like this, recommends smoking a cigarette while the shrimp are being eaten." – Ed

"We know more about fly fishing than ever before, all the know-how necessary; but I am still wondering, will there be a place for our grandchildren to fish?"

Chico Fernandez is well known for his first video, *The Art of Fly Casting*. His third video is entitled *The Art of Advanced Fly Casting*. These videos are based on Chico being a world-class caster and fisherman with over 40 years experience on fresh water and salt.

Chico lives in Miami, Florida where he photographs, writes, instructs and serves as a tackle consultant. He is also famous for his innovative fly tying. The Bonefish Special and the Bend-Back are two of his creations.

A staff writer for *Florida Sportsman*, Chico has many fly fishing world records to his credit including a 42-pound 5-ounce redfish on a fly rod and he was the first to land a white marlin on a fly rod.

Chico started fly fishing at the age of 13, went on to become an accountant and later budget director for Burger King Corporation. He says he started to hate it all and in 1975 gave it all up to become an outdoor writer and photographer. He says he has never looked back.

Years Fly Fishing
Over Forty

Favorite Rod
5 wt 8' 8" Graphite

Rods Owned
Too Many

Favorite Flies
Dry – Elk Hair Caddis
Wet – Coachman
Nymph – None
Streamer – My Own
Terrestrial – Dave's Hopper

Flies Invented
See Comments

Favorite US River
Not Provided

Home River
Not Provided

Favorite Stream
Not Provided

Home Stream
Not Provided

Fish Fillets
Salt – Garlic Powder
Day Old Cuban or French Bread
Eggs, Scrambled
Lemon or Key Lime

Fillet small, firm fishes (snapper, flounder, snook, grouper) and dry thoroughly. Season the fillets with a lot of lemon, salt and garlic powder. Let it set to absorb.

Take hard, day old bread and scrape into powder. Lay the fillets on the powdered bread. Then lay the fillets on the scrambled eggs. Lay again on the bread powder.

The old method, still in use in many areas, is to deep-fry the fillets by dipping them on a metal rack. But they can also be fried in a cast iron skillet. Use oil that is not too hot, or it will not cook through.

If deep-frying, the fillets will float to the surface when done. If in a skillet, by the time the fillets are browned they should be done.

Do not over cook. It is better to pull the fillets out too soon and have to cook some more, than overcooking.

"Buen provecho, amigos!" – Chico

ROB FIGHTMASTER

"In rod building and fly tying, I'm always doing something I think is innovative, but has probably been done by 100 other people."

Rob Fightmaster is a fly fishing guide and employee of The Sporting Tradition, an Orvis Endorsed shop located in Lexington, Kentucky where Rob resides. He also ties flies commercially, enjoys restoring old bamboo rods, and teaches fly fishing and fly tying classes at The Sporting Tradition and at the Lexington Community College. Rob is currently working on a book of maps of Kentucky streams.

Rob is a past President of the Bluegrass Chapter of Trout Unlimited and a current Board Member.

Year Fly Fishing
Eleven

Favorite Rod
5 wt 8' 6" Bamboo

Rods Owned
Thirteen

Favorite Flies
Dry – Parachute Adams
Wet – Soft Hackle Hare's Ear
Nymph – Pheasant Tail
Streamer – Mallard Minnow
Terrestrial – Rofi's
Hoppin' Sandy

Fly Invented
Rofi's Double Bead
Hellgrammite and others.

Favorite US River
Changes every year, but I like the Clinch in May. (TN)

Home River
Cumberland (KY)

Favorite Stream
Hazel Creek in the Smokies (NC)

Home Stream
Stoner Creek (KY)

NICOLE'S B.A. BAKED BEANS

1 Jar B & M Baked Beans
1 Can Kidney Beans
1 Can Butter Beans
1 Medium Onion, Chopped
½ Pound Cooked Bacon
¾ Cup Brown Sugar
¾ Cup Ketchup
1 Tablespoon Mustard
½ Cup Barbecue Sauce
½ Pound Cooked Ground Beef

Fry bacon and brown the beef. Slice bacon into bite size pieces. Combine all ingredients and place in a 13" x 9" casserole dish. Bake covered at 325 degrees for 40 minutes.

Serves: 6 – 8

"In an era of conservation, catch & release proves to be the only choice for the future of fish and fishermen alike."

Jon Fisher is the owner of New York's Urban Angler, Ltd. He has fly fished five continents and caught fish in over a dozen countries, developing techniques for catching game fish and non-game fish is areas where a fly rod has never been seen or used before.

Of special interest to Jon, is fishing in exotic locations where locals laugh at the thought of catching fish on a fly. Jon's motto is, *"If it can be caught on conventional tackle, it can be caught on a fly. The only problem arises when it is necessary to fish deeper than thirty feet. Beyond a depth of thirty feet, a fly is not a very efficient way of catching fish."*

Years Fly Fishing
Twenty-three
Favorite Rod
8 wt 9' Graphite IV
Rods Owned
Over Twenty-five
Favorite Flies
Dry – Griffith Gnat
Wet – Royal Coachman
Nymph – B.H. Pheasant Tail
Streamer – Black Ghost
Terrestrial – Foam Ant
Fly Invented
Super Fly
Favorite US River
Big Hole (MT)
Home River
Esopus (NY)
Favorite Stream
Bushkill (NY)
Home Stream
Bushkill (NY)

Whatever is Available

"I don't and can't cook, therefore, I rely on those around me, kind enough to include me. After a long day of fishing I find that anything put in front of me tastes twice as good as any meal after a day of real work. Just make sure there is plenty of salt, pepper and Tabasco on the table." – Jon

"Flyfishing is a lifetime of frustration interrupted by hours of sheer ecstasy."

Paul Fling is retired. He is a part-time guide and the author of four books and many magazine articles on fly tying and fly fishing. He resides in Howard, Colorado.

Paul has co-authored four books with Don Puterbaugh. *The Basic Manual of Fly-Tying* has become a classic in fly tying literature and is now in its second revised edition, having sold over 70,000 copies. Their other books include *Expert Fly-Tying, The Fly-Fisherman's Primer* (one of *The New York Review of Books* 'best forty thousand books in print'), and *Flyfishing Tips, Techniques, and Strategies from the Experts*.

Years Fly Fishing
Thirty-six

Favorite Rod
5 wt 9' Graphite

Rods Owned
Eleven

Favorite Flies
Dry – Foam Body Caddis
Wet – Caddis Emerger
Nymph – B.H. Pheasant Tail
Streamer – Muddler Minnow
Terrestrial – Hopper

Fly Invented
Pheasant Tail Prince Nymph

Favorite US River
Arkansas (CO)

Home River
Arkansas (CO)

Favorite Stream
Middle Fork of
South Platte (CO)

Home Stream
Middle Fork of
South Platte (CO)

2 Pounds Stewing Beef
2 Large Onions – 2 Stalks Celery
2 Cans Tomatoes – 4 Large Potatoes, Diced
1 Cup White Wine, 2 Cups if Fishing is Poor
Anything Else Lying Around Getting Old
2 Teaspoons Salt – 1 Teaspoon Pepper
¼ Cup Butter
2 Cloves Garlic
1 Tube Prepared Biscuits

Dig a hole twice the diameter of your Dutch oven and three times as deep. Line the hole with rocks and build a hot fire for two hours while preparing the ingredients. Brown the beef in the Dutch oven in the butter and diced garlic. Chop the vegetables, but not too fine, and add to the pot. Add the wine and bring to a soft boil. Cover and let simmer until the fire has burned down.

When the fire is out in the hole, lower the Dutch oven to the rocks on the bottom. Fill the hole with dirt, making sure the lid is tight on the Dutch oven. Go fishing for at least 4 hours. Uncover the oven, remove the lid and layer the top of the stew with the tube biscuits. Replace the lid and wait 30 minutes.

Lift the oven out of the hole and prepare to fight off the crowd that assembles.

CHRISTINE FONG

CATFISH & BLACK BEAN SAUCE*

"I like to photograph flowers, butterflies, insects and birds."

Christine Fong is a professional photographer, a collector of arrowheads, and spends most of her time producing *The Inside Anger*, a bimonthly newsletter reporting on and evaluating fishing destinations in western North America from Alaska to Mexico. *The Inside Angler* was first produced in 1992.

Christine's photographs have been published in all the leading outdoor periodicals including *Outdoor Life, Field & Stream, Sports Afield, Gray's Sporting Journal, Fly Fisherman, Fishing World, Fly Fishing,* and others. She has traveled extensively throughout the world with her fly fishing husband and partner, Michael Fong. They reside in San Francisco, California.

Christine caught her first bonefish on a fly in 1980.

Years Fly Fishing
Thirty-one
Favorite Rod
5 wt 9' Graphite
Rods Owned
Ten
Favorite Flies
Dry – Hendrickson or Sparkle Dun
Wet – Soft Hackle
Nymph – Pheasant Tail
Streamer – Black Leech
Terrestrial – Beetle or Ant
Fly Invented
None, yet
Favorite US River
Missouri (CO)
Home River
Fall (CA)
Favorite Stream
Henry's Fork of the Snake (ID)
Home Stream
Hat Creek (CA)

(*Steamed Catfish & Black Bean Sauce)

1 ½ Pounds Catfish Filets
2 Green Onions, Chopped
¼ Cup Salted Black Beans
1 Tablespoon Oil
2 Cloves Garlic
2 Quarter-sized Pieces of Fresh Ginger

Rinse black beans. Put garlic in a press. Grate ginger in a mortar. Make a paste of black beans, oil, garlic, and ginger. Cover catfish filets with black bean sauce. Steam for about 20 minutes or until meat flakes with a fork.

In last 5 minutes of cooking, add chopped green onions.

Serves: 4

"I fish constantly and enjoy it all."

Michael Fong is a first-generation Chinese-American. He resides with his wife, Christine, in San Francisco, California.

Michael is a former Editor of the Federation of Fly Fishers' *The FlyFisher* magazine and is currently a Contributing Editor to *Fly Fisherman* magazine. He and his wife have published *The Inside Angler*, a flyfishing newsletter, since 1992.

An outdoor writer and photographer whose works have been published in every national outdoor magazine that reports on fishing, Michael has fished extensively throughout North America, Central America, South America, New Zealand, the Bahamas and in Europe.

Organizations which he has supported include Trout Unlimited, United Anglers of California, California Trout, and the Nature Conservancy. The Umpqua Feather Merchants and Fenwick sponsor Michael's speaking engagements across the country.

Years Fly Fishing
Forty-nine

Favorite Rod
4 wt 9' Graphite

Rods Owned
Thirty-five

Favorite Flies
Dry – Many
Wet – Not Provided
Nymph – Many
Streamer – Many
Terrestrial – Many

Favorite US Waters
In the last five years, I have fished over 125 lakes and streams, mostly in the West.

Sashimi
Avocado
Lettuce Mix
Wasabi
Tortillas

This is a two-decker sandwich. Deep-fry three small tortillas. Mash avocados into a guacamole. Each layer of the sandwich consists of a bed of lettuce mix, guacamole, and sashimi with wasabi to taste.

NICK C. FORRESTER

"If you can't catch 'em, shoot 'em."

Nick Forrester and his wife, Francine, are the owners of Forrester's Frontier Travels based in Fort Smith, Montana. The resort is a collection of eight log buildings built in 1996 by Nick, Francine and their guides. Forrester's is an outfitting company offering guided fishing and hunting trips to both the BighornValley and Rocky Mountain Front.

Nick is a former wildlife biologist whose area of expertise, upland game birds, is not far afield from his current profession as an outfitter and guide. Francine is a chef trained in Manhattan. Her meals could remove the sting left by the worst day ever had in the field. Together, they go to extremes to please their guests.

Nick's favorite gun is a 12 Gauge Rugar, improved and modified. His favorite birds are sharptail, grouse, and huns. His favorite dogs are labs and shorthairs.

The above quote goes along with Nick's cast and blast trips. *"If the fish aren't biting, then we hunt duck and geese. And it goes the other way too,"* says Nick.

Years Fly Fishing
Ten
Favorite Rod
5 wt 9' Orvis Graphite
Rods Owned
Ten Orvis Rods
Favorite Flies
Dry – Midge
Wet – G.R. Hare's Ear
Nymph – Sow Bug or Scud
Streamer – C.H. Woolly Bugger
Terrestrial – Dave's Hopper
Fly Invented
None, yet
Favorite US River
Bighorn (MT)
Home River
Bighorn (MT)
Favorite Stream
Tongue (WY)
Home Stream
Tongue (WY)

GAME BIRDS & CHOKECHERRY*

*(*Game Birds & Chokecherry Sauce)*

Game Bird or Other Poultry Demi-glaze
Chokecherry Syrup
Black Cherry Juice
Raspberry Vinegar

Chokecherries are indigenous in most of Montana and Wyoming. The game birds will peck at the berries making this sauce the perfect accompaniment. Other berries such as cherries or other wild varieties would be best.

Demi-glaze is the reduction of any meat or poultry stock. After preparing and cooking your stock for at least 6 hours, strain through fine cheesecloth or other kitchen cloth, which you have placed in a strainer. Once you have strained the stock, reduce at low fire by ½ to ¾ths. Reserve.

Remove the game bird breasts carefully from the breastbone by following the contour of the bone with a very sharp boning knife. Reserve the bones in your freezer for later use. Under a trickle of running water, look carefully at the meat clearing away any feathers, gently scraping away blood clots and removing any remaining buckshot.

Continued on next page ...

If you are preparing this meal for others, be very picky here. Those not involved in your hunt might not find any of the above very appetizing. Lay breasts out on a sheet tray and remove moisture.

Prepare a seasoning mix by combining the following:

1 Teaspoon Salt
¼ Teaspoon White Pepper
1/8 Teaspoon Cayenne Pepper
½ Teaspoon Thyme

Any of the above amounts can be adjusted to taste. Sprinkle seasoning mix on bird and reserve.

Prepare a sauté pan by heating with clarified butter. It is important here to use clarified butter. If you cheat, you will have bits of burned butterfat in your sauce. Being careful not to get the butter too hot, add the meat and sauté until browned. This will only take a couple of minutes. Turn the breast and repeat. Do not cook through.

The breast should be pink under the fillet. Remove from the pan and return to the sheet tray. Place in a 350 degree oven for about 6 minutes, about the time it will take you to finish the sauce.

Continued …

Heat the reserved demi-glaze, pour off any fat remaining in the sauté pan and deglaze with at least one or more cups of demi-glaze. Stir, scraping up any bits of meat and let reduce slightly. Restrain demi through a cheese clothe back into a pan. To the demi, add ¼ cup of berry syrup, a bit of cherry juice and a couple of drops of high quality vinegar, preferably raspberry, and check the taste. Here you can add a drop of smoke essence, or a bit more fresh thyme. You may want to thicken with a bit of cornstarch. Serve over reserved breasts.

From their brochure … *"It's my last evening at Summit Station. The facing wall of Marias Pass goes pink in the setting sun. Through the dining room window, the guests, Francine and I watch a sow grizzly snuffle corn off the distant railroad tracks. 'It's something they do a lot,' Francine explains, 'especially in spring.' A train blasts its horn. The grizzly stands, sniffs the air, and rumbles into the woods. I take a sip of wine, and call out to Francine. 'I am satisfied in the extreme.'*

"She smiles a crooked little smile, and heads back to the kitchen, rosemary and garlic lingering in the air around me."

"The object of fly fishing is not to catch fish, but to catch a fish on a fly."

David Foster is the General Manager, Editor-in-Chief and first essayist for *Gray's Sporting Journal*. He became editor of *Gray's* in 1991 and lives with his wife, Sherry and nine-year-old daughter Alexandra in Augusta, Georgia. Under Dave, *Gray's* has taken a strong turn toward fly fishing and upland bird hunting as its primary editorial themes, both pursuits he unabashedly claims as his personal favorites. He hunts and fishes with his German wirehaired pointer, Savannah, and has to admit she prefers stalking the ponds and streams for fish more than she enjoys hunting birds.

Dave most enjoys his Southeastern trout streams, especially fishing for the little brookies that are denizens of small rills in very high places. When not fishing for trout, he enjoys "hunting" for 2-pound bluegill in farm ponds around Augusta.

*Note: You can add ½ cup of wine to the beans, in lieu of some of the water, at the beginning of cooking. Smoked or andouille sausage may be used instead of ham seasoning meat if you wish. In that case, brown sausage separately and drain well. Add it to the pot at the same time you put in the beans.

Years Fly Fishing
Sixteen

Favorite Rod
5 wt 9' Graphite

Rods Owned
Ten

Favorite Flies
Dry – Adams
Wet – Not Provided
Nymph – B.H. Hare's Ear
Streamer – Woolly Bugger
Terrestrial – Dave's Hopper

Fly Invented
None, yet

Favorite US River
Provo (UT)

Home River
Savannah (GA)

Favorite Stream
Soque (GA)

Home Stream
Noontootla Creek (GA)

© 2000 - Russell A. Hopper

1 Pound Dried Red Kidney Beans
1 Large Onion, Finely Chopped
5 Cloves Garlic, Peeled and Smashed
1 Bay Leaf
½ Teaspoon Red Pepper Flakes
½ Teaspoon Black Pepper
1 Tablespoon Salt
1 Ham Hock or ¼ Pound of Ham Seasoning Meat

Soak beans in water overnight. In a large heavy pot, brown the meat in about a tablespoon of oil for about 10 minutes. Add onion, garlic, and cook until onion is translucent, 5 – 7 minutes, over low heat. Add drained beans and remaining seasonings to pot. Add enough water to cover about 1 inch. Bring to a boil, with top off, stirring occasionally. Reduce heat to simmer and cover. Cook about 2 hours or until the beans are tender, stirring occasionally. You may need to add more water, depending on how much juice you like. Adjust seasoning as needed.

Serve over hot long grain (not Minute) rice, accompanied by a green salad, French bread and a glass of your favorite wine.

Serves: 6 adults generously

RON FOSTER

"Attention to detail is what separates the men from the boys."

Ron Foster is President of Hodgman, Inc. of Montgomery, Illinois. When asked about his accomplishments, Ron said he and his company created convertible waders and convertible wading jackets and that he owns more waders than any other individual in the world.

Years Fly Fishing
Twenty-six

Favorite Rod
5 wt 9' Graphite

Rods Owned
Twenty-five

Favorite Flies
Dry – Double Parachute Humpy
Wet – Woolly Bugger
Nymph – Hare's Ear
Streamer – Light Spruce
Terrestrial – Hopper

Fly Invented
Double Parachute Humpy

Favorite US River
Yellowstone (MT)

Home River
Fox (IL)

Favorite Stream
Tributaries to the Nowood (WY)

Home Stream
Bruce (IL)

CHILLED OLIVE SNACK

Ice Cubes
Dry Vermouth
Gin
Olive

Place 8 medium-sized clear ice cubes in a shaker. Add ¾ of a capful of dry vermouth. Add 3 to 4 ounces of gin (3 for small glass, 4 for large glass). Shake vigorously 8 to 10 times (8 times for 3 ounces of gin, 10 times for 4 ounces of gin). Immediately pour strained contents into a chilled stemmed martini glass. Add olive on a pick. Consume carefully ½ of liquid. Then eat ½ of chilled olive. Consume balance of liquid then finish olive snack.

Repeat process (exactly) as needed.

Serves: 1

"That day together on the river was like a thousand other pages from the book of any angler's memories. There was the clasp and pull of cold, hurrying water on our legs, the hours of rymthmic casting." – Sparse Grey Hackle

Craig Fraser is the restaurant manager of Arkansas' famed Gaston's White River Resort.

Years Fly Fishing
Not Provided

Favorite Rod
Not Provided

Rods Owned
Not Provided

Favorite Flies
Dry – Not Provided
Wet – Not Provided
Nymph – Not Provided
Streamer – Not Provided
Terrestrial – Not Provided

Favorite US River
White Water (AR)

Home River
White Water (AR)

Favorite Stream
Not Provided

Home Stream
Not Provided

6 Trout Fillets
4 Tablespoons Butter or Margarine
½ Cup Chablis Wine
3 Tablespoons Green Onion, with Tops, Chopped
12 Ounces Whipping Cream
6 Egg Yolks, Beaten
1 Teaspoon Seasoned Salt
1 Cup Cooked Crab Meat

In a heavy saucepan, simmer onions in butter for 3 minutes. Add wine and whipping cream, and simmer 10 minutes. Bring to a boil. Remove from heat. Add egg yolks, seasoning, and mix well. Add crabmeat and mix again. In a separate baking pan, place trout fillets skin side down. Brush meat with butter. Bake in oven at 400 degrees, approximately 10 – 15 minutes or until meat is flaky. Remove fillets and cover with supreme sauce. Return all to oven for 1 to 2 minutes. Remove and serve.

LUKE FRAZIER

GARLIC-BASIL SALMON

"First thirty minutes of the day and the last thirty minutes of the day."

Luke Frazier's home base is in Logan, Utah where he earns a living as a wildlife and sporting artist. Luke's innovative fly fishing paintings have appeared in *The Reader's Digest*, *Field & Stream*, *Gray's Sporting Journal* and *Alaska* magazines.

Years Fly Fishing
Twenty-one

Favorite Rod
5 wt 9' Graphite

Rods Owned
Sixteen

Favorite Flies
Dry – Elk Hair Caddis
Wet – Hare's Ear or
Soft Hackle Pheasant Tail
Nymph – Hare's Ear
Streamer – Yellow
Saddle Hackle
Terrestrial – Chernobyl Ant

Flies Invented
Yellow Elk Hair Caddis
Green Elk Hair Caddis

Favorite US River
South Fork of Snake (WY)

Home River
Logan/Blacksmith Fork (UT)

Favorite Stream
Blacksmith Fork (UT)

Home Stream
Blacksmith Fork (UT)

1 Salmon
1 - 2 Yellow Onions
1 Garlic
Basil to Taste
1 Green Pepper
1 Red Pepper
Salt and Pepper
Italian Salad Dressing
Foil

Place 2 large salmon fillets in a double layer of aluminum foil. Cover in sliced onions, garlic, basil and peppers. Add 10-ounce bottle of Italian dressing. Salt and pepper to taste. Seal with more aluminum foil. Put on a bed of coals for 20 – 25 minutes.
Delicious!

Serves: 4

"Alaskan bush cooking/fishing, it's the best way to cook them when you're camping light." – Luke

"I fish with rods found on river bottoms, with flies plucked from river brush."

Pete Fromm resides with his wife and sons in Great Falls, Montana. He is a Contributing Editor of *Gray's Sporting Journal*. His books include *Dry Rain; The Tall Uncut: Lives Amid the Landscapes of the American West; King of the Mountain: Sporting Stories; Indian Creek Chronicles: A Winter Alone in the Wilderness; Blood Knot;* and *Night Swimming*.

Pete says his claim to fame is that he fishes with a rod found on the bottom of the Snake River while he was a river ranger.

Besides winning the first *Traver Award*, Pete is the winner of *Pacific Northwest Booksellers Book Award* for 1994 and 1998.

Years Fly Fishing
Sixteen
Favorite Rod
Whatever I'm using.
Rods Owned
Three
Favorite Flies
Whatever works.
Fly Invented
Me?
Favorite US River
Confidential
Home River
Missouri (MT)
Favorite Stream
Confidential
Home Stream
Confidential

© 2000 - Russell A. Hopper

Brookies

Pull some brookies from a beaver pond. Build a small fire. Roast trout quickly, without any spices or additives. Devour.

Serves: Whoever's there

JAY "FISHY" FULLUM

"Fly tying and fly fishing is supposed to be fun."

Jay "Fishy" Fullum is a retired outdoor columnist for the *Albany Times Union* and the *Troy Record* newspapers, now working as a freelance writer, magazine columnist, photographer, illustrator and lecturer whose Creative Tying column is featured in each issue of *Fly Tyer* magazine.

Fishy is known for his beautiful, original flies, lucid written instructions, and eye-catching step-by-step artwork. He lives in Ravena, New York.

When he's not at the computer, playing with his watercolors and brushes, or the camera, he says he's usually on the water.

Jay's goal is to promote fly tying and fly fishing as an activity that is done because it is fun.

Years Fly Fishing
Forty Plus

Favorite Rod
2 wt 7' 9" Graphite

Rods Owned
Over Fifty

Favorite Flies
Dry – What's on the water.
Wet – Hare's Ear
Nymph – Fishy's Bead
Chain Nymphs
Streamer – Black Muddler
Terrestrial – Fishy's
Foam Hopper

Flies Invented
Dozens

Favorite US River
Mohawk (NY)

Home River
Hudson (NY)

Favorite Stream
Ruby (MT)

Home Stream
Hannacroix (NY)

NATIVE SPRING TROUT

2 Native 10" – 12" Spring Trout
Fresh Lemon Grass
White Pepper
Butter
Stir-fried Vegetables
White Rice
Fine Wine

Finely cut fresh lemon grass and white pepper are added to butter and the (whole) trout are pan fried until they flake.

Serve with stir-fried vegetables and white rice. A fine wine is also recommended.

Serves: 1 – 2 trout per person, depending on size

"Sorry, but I kill a couple for the pan each season." – Jay

BEN FURMINSKY

"You can have a great day fly fishing without catching any fish."

Ben Furimsky is known as the creator of the Bugskin-based Shine Tail, a generic salt water minnow pattern.

In his early twenties and a ski instructor, Ben is a professional fly tyer and guide. He is on the pro staff of Gudebrod and Eagle Claw and demonstrates his talents at numerous shows.

Ben resides in Crested Butte, Colorado and is the innovator of numerous fly patterns, in particular the Bugskin patterns. Bugskin is a light leather, which can provide realistic silhouettes, yet remains durable. Ben has caught over six bluefish on one fly, but not at the same time.

Ben's favorite obsession is striper fishing.

Years Fly Fishing
Twenty-one

Favorite Rod
8 wt 9' Graphite

Rods Owned
Six

Favorite Flies
Dry – Sulfur
Wet – Peacock
Nymph – B.H. Stonefly
Streamer – Woolly Bugger
Terrestrial – Deer Hair Ant

Fly Invented
Bugskin Shrimp

Favorite US River
Bighorn (MT)

Home River
Gunnison (CO)

Favorite Stream
White Deer (PA)

Home Stream
Slate (CO)

SALMON & ROASTED RED PEPPER

1 Pound Salmon Filets
1 Red Bell Pepper
1 Dried Whole Red Chili Pepper
Herb Seasoned Polenta
Tomato Basil

Roast one red bell pepper and skin. Place in a blender or processor with one dried red chili pepper (no stems) and chop fine. Fry a bed of polenta seasoned to taste. Ben uses tomato basil.

Bake two salmon filets, approximately ½ pound each, at 350 degrees until cooked.

Place salmon on bed of polenta and top with roasted pepper sauce.

Serve with vegetable and salad.

Serves: 2

DAN GAPEN SR.

DAN GAPEN'S SHORE LUNCH FISH

"Focus the call of … the Raven … the Sandhill Crane … the Loon … the Wolf … they are Wilderness."

Dan Gapen is a writer, tackle manufacturer and television host from Becker, Minnesota who started fishing with his father, Don Gapen, as a child. He has fond memories of pools where between four and six-pound brook trout were taken with his father.

Dan's father invented the Muddler Minnow in the late 1930s when he managed a lodge on the Nipigon River. The fly imitates the sculpin, a bottom feeder-dweller that has no swim bladder and is more like a lizard than a fish. Gapen developed the fly for the big Nipigon Brook Trout in Ontario.

The fly was popularized by Dan Bailey; a New Yorker transplanted to Montanta, with several variations, particularly the Marabou Muddler, which Bailey described as the top producer for big Montana trout.

Dan says he is very fortunate to have a gal who works for him by the name of Bobber Anne.

Years Fly Fishing
Not Provided

Favorite Rod
8 wt 8' Graphite

Rods Owned
Not Provided

Favorite Flies
Dry – Grizzel Wulff
Wet – Weighted Muddler #10
Nymph – Weighted
Muddler Minnow #14
Streamer – Muddler Minnow
Terrestrial – Weighted
Hare's Ear

Flies Invented
Capsize Streamer,
The Thief, and
Danny's Fancy

Favorite US River
Upper Mississippi (MN)

Home River
Mississippi (MN)

Favorite Stream
The Clouguet (MN)

Home Stream
The Rum (MN)

8 Deboned Fish Fillets
1 Can Baked Beans
1 Small Can Chopped Mushrooms
4 Frozen Potato Patties
1 Large Onion, Chopped
2 Cups Solid Crisco
Salt and Pepper to Taste
1 Brown Bag
1 Cup Flour

Place two 3-foot green logs 10-inches apart and begin a hot wood fire between them. Place fillets, flour, salt and pepper in a brown sack and shake until the fillets are fully covered. Place in a pan of hot Crisco, skin side down to prevent curling. Place potato patties in another pan with 2 spoons of Crisco. Cook 5 minutes, then add half the mushrooms and onions. Cook another 3 minutes. In a pot, place the beans and the rest of the onions and mushrooms. Salt and pepper to taste.

If all things begin on time, the meal should take about 20 minutes to cook.

"Fly flishing, unlike women, is something you can get better at as you get older."

Hugh Gardner is originally from Texas. He earned a Ph.D. and moved to Colorado in 1969, but didn't become a real fly fisherman until the mid-1980s, in need of some new horizons at age 40. *"Flyfishing became my spiritual salvation after a failed attempt at marriage,"* he says, *"and along with wilderness backpacking remains my favorite escape from the so-called real world."*

Occupationally, he has been a college professor, a political consultant, a national magazine writer, and an air transportation expert. He joined Trout Unlimited in the 1980s to fight Two Forks Dam and was honored for his work with the *Save the South Platte* award in 1990. He currently serves as Contributing Editor for *The Angling Report.*

In 1996, he wrote and produced a television documentary called *Incredible Journey of the Greenback Cutthroats,* a PBS show about restoration of Colorado's native trout. The program won nine awards at the 1997 International Wildlife Film Festival and was nominated for a television *Emmy* in 1998. His basement studio, Borderline Productions, is working on another TV documentary about ancient Indian cultures.

Years Fly Fishing
Sixteen
Favorite Rod
4 wt 8' 6" Hexagraph
Rods Owned
Ten
Favorite Flies
Dry – Stimulator
Wet – Swimming Caddis
Nymph – Prince
Streamer – Abel Anchovy
Terrestrial – Hopper
Fly Invented
None, yet
Favorite US River
Big Blackfoot (MT)
Home River
South Platte (CO)
Favorite Stream
Loon Creek (ID)
Home Stream
Bear Creek (CO)

© 2000 - Russell A. Hopper

Fresh Caught Fish
(Trout, Perch, Chubs)
Sharpened Willow Shoots
Salt and Pepper to Taste
Citrus Juice
Soy or Hot Sauce to Taste

Take a pack of Vietnamese Cub Scouts fly fishing. Catch nothing. Take scouts to local river with spinning rods and live bait. Catch a lot of little fish. Bring sack of little fish back to the family picnic, cutting willow sticks along the way. Sharpen sticks and insert through pelvic vent the length of the fish. Hold the fish over a campfire for 2 – 3 minutes until the skin is burned. Split, discard gut tube. Eat other delicious innards raw. Salt or dip the fish in a sauce of citrus juice, soy or hot sauce. Eat fish like corn on the cob, head to tail.

Serves: Family of 12 plus six scouts

Hugh's grant-supported Native Trout Education Project created new curricula for the public schools. In 1999, the project distributed free the Greenback video, weekly readers, teachers guides and native trout bookmarks to all K-12 schools in Colorado.

RUSTY GATES

AU SABLE WHITE CHILI

"One can become so involved in protecting a river, they forget to go fish."

Rusty Gates operates the famed Gates Au Sable Lodge where he serves as the high priest. *Fly Rod & Reel* magazine named Rusty *Angler of the Year* in 1995 for his stream conservation commitments.

Years Fly Fishing
Thirty-three

Favorite Rod
4 wt 8' Graphite

Rods Owned
Too Many

Favorite Flies
Dry – Parachute Anything
Wet – Wet Skunk
Nymph – What's that?
Streamer – Bunny Style Sculpin
Terrestrial – Dry
Skunk S.R.B

Fly Invented
S.R.B.

Favorite US River
Au Sable (MI)

Home River
Au Sable (MI)

Favorite Stream
Au Sable (MI)

Home Stream
Au Sable (MI)

1 – 1 ½ Pounds Cooked Chicken Breasts
2 Cups Finely Chopped Onion
2 Tablespoons Minced Garlic
1 Tablespoon Oil
1 Can (4 Ounces) Green Chilies
2 Cans (14 Ounces Each) Chicken Broth
3 Cans (16 Ounces Each) Northern Beans
2 Tablespoons Cumin
2 Level Tablespoons Oregano
¼ Tablespoon Cayenne Pepper

Sauté 2 cups finely chopped onion and 2 tablespoons minced garlic in 1-tablespoon oil until clear. Stir in 1-4 ounce can green chilies, 2-14 ounce cans chicken broth, 3-16 ounce cans northern beans, 1 – 1 ½ pounds cooked chicken breasts, 2 heaping tablespoons cumin, 2 level teaspoons oregano, and ¼ teaspoon cayenne pepper. Heat until boiling
Serve with cornbread.

Serves: 4 hungry people

PHIL GENOVA

"By offering the gift of fly fishing to a youngster, you are beginning a process that is sure to create a competent, educated, and dedicated steward of our resources." – from *First Cast—Teaching Kids to Fly-Fish*

Phil Genova is nationally known for his work as the founder and director of the Fly Fisher Apprentice Program. He has created a guidebook for use in schools, *First Cast, Teaching Kids to Fly-Fish*, that shares techniques for motivating and teaching kids to fly fish.

Phil resides with his wife, Judy, and their two sons in Spencer, New York. He is the Program Manager of Education and Communication at the Cortland Line Company, a former instructor in fresh water and salt water fly fishing education at Cornell University, a writer and a frequent lecturer.

Phil received the Paul G. *Mackenzie Award for Service* for five consecutive years and in 1995 was the recipient of the North East Council Federation of Fly Fishers' *President's Award for Excellence.*

Phil relaxes with a few pale ales and some venison sausage while cooling down from cooking his sauna roast duck. Phil says, *"It almost makes me look forward to winter."*

Years Fly Fishing
Thirty-five

Favorite Rod
7 wt 9' Graphite

Rods Owned
Eighteen

Favorite Flies
Dry – All the Wulffs
Wet – Royal Coachman,
Polar Bear Wing
Nymph – Hare's Ear
Streamer – Chartreuse and
White Clouser Minnow
Terrestrial – Not Provided

Fly Invented
Orange Weaner Salmon Fly

Favorite US River
Susquehanna (PA)

Home River
Susquehanna (PA)

Favorite Stream
Fall Creek (NY)

Home Stream
Fall Creek (NY)

SAUNA ROAST DUCK

3 – 5 Pound Duck
Two Peeled Apples
Dried Apricots – Raisins – Walnuts
Orange Juice and Other Fruits
Honey to Taste

Stuff duck with peeled apples to absorb flavors during cooking. Discard apples when done. Place duck in Dutch oven or other heavy cooking pot. Elevate duck on a rack to keep it off the fat. Poke several holes in the skin to allow the fat to escape.

Place covered pot and duck on corner of sauna stove before lighting. As stove heats up, so will the duck. It will cook, along with you, in the sauna.

While sauna is heating up, prepare sauce by chopping dried fruit and combing it with orange juice and honey to make a glaze for the duck.

As duck cooks, poke occasionally with a fork to let fat out. Poke a knife in several places toward end of cooking. If it goes in and out with no resistance, the duck is done.

Baste duck with sauce ½ hour before you and the duck are done. Serve remaining sauce at table.

"The marvelous aromas of the roasting duck will add to the pleasure of the sauna experience." – Phil

JERRY GIBBS

"Time is short; if you can get out, go fish."

Jerry Gibbs is a writer and photographer living in Newport Center, Vermont. He says his greatest accomplishment is in surviving 25 years in the publishing business.

Jerry is the Fishing Editor for *Outdoor Life* magazine and has written several books including *Outdoor Tip; Bass Myths; Advanced Tactics for Bass & Trout;* and *Steel Barbs, Wildwaters.*

He is an inductee of the *Freshwater Fishing Hall of Fame* and has fished across the United States, Canada, Europe, the Caribbean, Central and South America, Russia, New Zealand and Australia.

Years Fly Fishing
Over Fifty
Favorite Rod
5 wt – 9 wt
Depending on Quarry
9' Graphite
Rods Owned
Many, but never enough.
Favorite Flies
Dry – Adams
Wet – B.H. Woolly Bugger
Nymph – G.R. Hare's Ear
Streamer – Groceries, a Striper Fly
Terrestrial – Hopper
Fly Invented
Gibbs Smelt
Favorite US River
Alagnak (AK)
Home River
Clyde (VT)
Favorite Stream
Big Moore's Run (PA)
Home Stream
No-Name Creek (VT)

WOODCOCK & SAUCE*

(*Woodcock with Cranberry-Cassis Sauce)

<u>*Sauce for Breasts*</u>
3 Ounces Crème de Cassis Liqueur
3 Ounces Maple Syrup
2 Ounces Butter
½ Cup Orange Juice
1 Tablespoon Pommery or Dijon Mustard
1 Cup Fresh Cranberries
1 Ounce Gin

<u>*Woodcock Legs*</u>
Woodcock – Butter – Olive Oil – Chopped Garlic

Combine all sauce ingredients and simmer until berries soften. Add gin and heat through.

Remove woodcock breasts and halve them. Remove woodcock legs. Cook breasts in above sauce for a few minutes until they are a medium pink. Don't overcook. Sauté the white legs in butter, olive oil and chopped garlic. Serve legs as a side dish. If you want to be fancier, slice breasts and cook the slices in the sauce.

Serve with salad and green vegetable. Sliced kiwi fruit is a nice side dish.

Serves: 1 ½ – 2 woodcock per person

COOPER A. GILKES

"The only foolish question is the one that's never asked."

Cooper Gilkes is a guide and tackle shop owner living in Edgartown, Massachusetts. He is the co-organizer of Martha's Vineyard Striped Bass Catch and Release Fly Fishing Tournament, a Committee Member of Martha's Vineyard Bass and Bluefish Derby, and, since 1973, has been the Chairman of the Martha's Vineyard Youth Trout Tourney.

Years Fly Fishing
Forty-one

Favorite Rod
9 wt 9' Graphite

Rods Owned
Six

Favorite Flies
Dry – Light Hendrickson
Wet – Black Woolly Bugger
Nymph – Not Provided
Streamer – Mickey Finn
Terrestrial – Black Ant

Fly Invented
Saltwater Shrimp Fly

Favorite US River
Little Sandy (PA)

Home Waters
Estuaries surrounding Martha's Vineyard (MA).

VINEYARD QUAHOG CHOWDER

1 Quart Quahogs, Black Part Removed and Put Through Food Grinder
1 Pint Onions, Thinly Sliced
1 Quart Potatoes, Diced
1 Quart Half-&-Half, Heated
Pepper or Tabasco Sauce to Taste
6 Slices of Salt Pork, Diced

Fry out diced salt pork until it is light brown in color. Remove diced pork from kettle and drain on paper towels. Add sliced onions and fry until light yellow. Add potatoes, quahogs and pepper. Cover with quahog liquor, and if not enough, add water. Cook until the potatoes are done. Add heated Half-&-Half and bring to nearly boiling point. When a bubble appears, remove from the heat.

"For fish chowder, use steamed haddock, sea bass, cod or tautog which has been cooked until the meat falls from the bones. Then add the fish to the chowder base in place of the quahogs." – Coop

"A piece of pie is considered one-fourth of the pie."

Ken (Mr. Kastmaster) Glenn recently retired from the engineering department of a large multi-national company. As a result of his retirement, you could expect to find Ken on the waters, the golf course, or the couch, reading a book a week. However, in the interest of allowing his wife to retire earlier, Ken has give up his leisurely schedule and is now back in the work force. In addition to working, golfing, fishing and reading, Ken finds time to run.

Mr. Kastmaster is one of the six founders and four-term Treasurer of the Sons of the Cumberland, a Bowling Green, Kentucky non-profit fly fishing fellowship that practices catch and release fly fishing. Ken is accredited with the fellowship's Safety First slogan and designed a Cumberland River Hypothermia Fanny Pack.

Ken loves apple pie and his definition of a slice equals one-fourth of the pie.

Years Fly Fishing
Five Seasons
Favorite Rod
5 wt 9' Graphite
Rods Owned
Three
Favorite Flies
Dry – Adams
Wet – Hair Jig
Nymph – C.H. Woolly Bugger
Streamer – Hair Jig
Terrestrial – Japanese Beetle
Fly Invented
Kastmaster Streamer
Favorite US River
Cumberland (KY)
Home River
Cumberland (KY)
Favorite Stream
Trammel Fork (KY)
Home Stream
Trammel Fork (KY)

PASTRY FOR 9" TWO-CRUST PIE

2 Cups All-purpose Flour
2 Teaspoons Salt
2/3 Cup Plus 2 Tablespoons Shortening
4 – 5 Tablespoons Cold Water

Measure flour and salt into bowl. Cut in shortening thoroughly. Sprinkle in water, 1 tablespoon at a time, mixing until all flour is moistened and dough almost cleans side of bowl. Add 1 to 2 more teaspoons water if needed.

Gather dough, divide in half and shape into 2 balls. Flatten each ball into a round on lightly floured surface. Roll 2 inches longer than inverted pie pan. Fold into quarters. Unfold and ease into pan. Roll second round and cut slits to allow steam to escape.

Filling provided on next page …

APPLE PIE FILLING

¾ Cup Sugar
¼ Cup All-purpose Flour
1 ¼ Teaspoons Cinnamon
Dash Salt
6 Cups Thinly Sliced Pared Granny Smith Apples
2 Tablespoons Butter or Margarine

Heat oven to 425 degrees. Prepare pastry. Stir together sugar, flour, cinnamon and salt. Mix with apples. Turn into pastry-lined pie pan and dot with butter. Cover with slide top crust, seal and flute. Cover edge of crust with 2 to 3-inch strip of aluminum foil to prevent excessive browning. Remove foil last 15 minutes of baking.

Bake 40 to 50 minutes or until crust is brown and juice begins to bubble through slits in the crust.

D. L. GODDARD

"Today's kids are tomorrow's fly fishers."

D. L. Goddard is a fly tyer, teacher, outdoor writer, photographer and retired Miami Beach Police Captain who now resides in Easton, Maryland.

D. L. is a fly designer for Umpqua Feather Merchants and the Manager of Timonium Fly Fishing Shows. He is a regularly featured lecturer at many fly fishing shows across the country, instructing anglers in both fly fishing and fly tying.

Some of D. L.'s most famous fly patterns include the Mylar Minnow, the Glass Minnow, and the Stealth Fly.

Years Fly Fishing
Thirty-six

Favorite Rod
9 wt 9' Graphite

Rods Owned
Over Fifty

Favorite Flies
Dry – Not Provided
Wet – Not Provided
Nymph – Not Provided
Streamer – D. L.'s Stealth Fly
Terrestrial – Not Provided

Flies Invented
See Comments

Favorite US Bay
Barnegat Bay (MD)

Home Bay
Chesapeake (MD)

BAKED BLUEFISH

Fresh Bluefish
Mayonnaise
Old Bay Seasoning

Scale and fillet fresh bluefish. Preheat oven to 400 degrees. Place fillets in baking dish. Cover with mayonnaise and sprinkle on Old Bay Seasoning. Bake 10 minutes to the inch of thickness. Remove from oven and serve.

Serves: 2 – 10

ROBERT GORMAN

"No self in self—no self in things." – Lao Tzu

Robert Gorman resides in Brattleboro, Vermont with his wife, Judith, and his two achievements, Sasha and Melissa Gorman. He is a rod maker who was an apprentice to Sam Carlson and the founder and Master Craftsman of Green River Rodmakers. Being true to the quote provided, Robert doesn't own any fly rods.

Years Fly Fishing
Twenty-six

Favorite Rod
5 wt 7' 6" Bamboo

Rods Owned
None

Favorite Flies
Dry – Ted's Caddis
Wet – Ted's Caddis Nymph
Nymph – Ted's Caddis
Streamer – YUK!
Terrestrial – YUK!

Favorite US River
Deschutes (OR)

Home River
Deerfield (MA)

Favorite Stream
Green (VT)

Home Stream
Green (VT)

SPICY TOMATILLO SAUCE

1 Pound Tomatillos, Washed and Husks Removed
½ Medium Jalapeno, Ribs and Seed Removed, Coarsely Chopped
1 Poblano Pepper, Seeded, and Coarsely Chopped
1 Medium Green Pepper, Seeded, and Coarsely Chopped
4 Tablespoons Cilantro
1 Lime (Optional)
Vegetable Broth (Optional)

Bring a large pot of water to boil. Put in the tomatillos and return to boil. Remove with a slotted spoon when each tomatillo can be pierced with a fork, and drain under cold water. Place the tomatillos in the bowl of a food processor, add the remaining ingredients, and pulse until the tomatillos liquefy and the peppers are in tiny dice. Taste and add optional lime if the tomatillos are less acid/too sweet. If the mix seems too thick, thin with vegetable broth.

This sauce turns chicken, tortillas and sour cream into Pollo Verde.

Makes: 2 cups

JOSPEH V. GROBAREK

"Catch and release is not just a practice. It is a way of life, for the fish."

Joe Grobarek is the founder of the Fly of the Month Fishing Club, Inc. He resides in Lake Zurich, Illinois.

Joe once caught a 36-pound 7-ounce permit on a 12-pound class tippet, which, if killed, would have broken the 12, 16, and 20-pound International Game Fish Association records on a fly. However, Joe landed, measured, weighed and released the fish.

Years Fly Fishing
Thirty-six

Favorite Rod
9 wt 9' Winston XDLT

Rods Owned
Thirty-eight

Favorite Flies
Dry – Goddard Caddis
Wet – Polar Shrimp
Nymph – B.H. Zug Bug
Streamer – Spruce
Terrestrial – Dave's Hopper

Flies Invented
Werkin Merkin, El Pescador,
and the Bend Back Crab

Favorite US River
Green (UT)

Home River
None

Favorite Stream
Ontongon (MI)

Home Stream
Ontonagon (MI)

ROUND STEAK*

(*Round Steak in Mushroom Sauce)

2 Pounds Elk or Deer Round Steak
1 Can (16 Ounces) Mushrooms or
Fresh Mushrooms
1 Green Pepper, Cubed Small
1 Onion, Cubed Small
6 Cloves Garlic, Crushed
6 Cups Chicken Stock
½ Cup Olive Oil
Butter – Flour
Salt and Pepper to Taste

Flour round steak. Salt and pepper to taste. Brown on high heat until both sides are golden brown. Remove meat. Add olive oil, green pepper and onion and sauté until tender. Add chicken stock, crushed garlic and meat back to pan. Cover and simmer for 30 minutes. After 30 minutes, uncover and add mushrooms. Cover and simmer for an additional 15 – 20 minutes.

Remove meat. Thicken sauce with a mixture of ½ soft butter and ½ flour. Add meat back to the sauce.

Serve over medium pasta shells.

Serves: 4 – 6

"Work hard, fish harder."

Terry Gunn and his wife, Wendy, own Lees Ferry Anglers Fly Shop in Marble Canyon, Arizona. They also own Baja Anglers. Terry is a photographer, a noted fly casting instructor and an 18-year fly fishing guide. In his guiding, Terry says, *"I have met some of the finest people on this planet."*

Years Fly Fishing
Thirty-six
Favorite Rod
6 wt 9' Graphite
Rods Owned
Over Fifty
Favorite Flies
Dry – Royal Wulff
Wet – Soft Hackles
Nymph – Pheasant Tail
Streamer – Beadle's
Martin Fly
Terrestrial – Dave's Hopper
Flies Invented
The Alaskan Series
Favorite US River
Colorado at Lees Ferry (AZ)
Home River
Colorado at Lees Ferry (AZ)
Favorite Stream
Taylor (AZ)
Home Stream
Taylor (AZ)

Prime Cut Thick Steak
Lawry's Seasoning Salt

This method of cooking does not work well with steaks less than 1 inch thick.

Use a flattop grill or pan. The trick to cooking a quality steak is to cook it on a flat surface. The flat surface allows consistent searing of the steak and seals in the juices and flavor.

First, pat the steak with your favorite seasoning salt (Lawry's works well). Heat the pan to the hottest possible point. Sear the steak on both sides. Then reduce the heat by 20 percent.

The secret to cooking a good steak is to turn the steak frequently. Turn the steak every minute or more frequently. Frequent turning drives the juices to the middle of the steak. The goal is to keep the outside of the steak dry with no juices pushed through the steak.

It is important to remember that a steak cooked in this manner will appear more done than it is. Determine the level of doneness by pressing on the steak.

Follow this recipe and you will have the best steak that you have ever eaten.

Serves: 1

WENDY HANVOLD-GUNN

"One of the greatest things about this sport is that it's a never ending learning process."

Wendy Hanvold-Gunn is the co-owner and manager of Lees Ferry Anglers Fly Shop in Marble Canyon, Arizona. She is a noted fly casting instructor and fly fishing guide.

Wendy holds the International Game Fish Association's world record for a 136-pound striped marlin and wahoo caught on a fly rod. The record was established before there was a distinction between male and female world records.

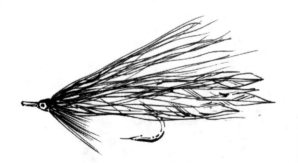

Years Fly Fishing
Thirteen
Favorite Rod
7 wt 9' Graphite
Rods Owned
Twenty-five
Favorite Flies
Dry – Unbelievable
Wet – Deer Hair Scud
Nymph – B.H. Midge
Streamer – Not Provided
Terrestrial – Not Provided
Fly Invented
None, yet
Favorite US River
Colorado at Lees Ferry (AZ)
Home River
Colorado at Lees Ferry (AZ)
Favorite Stream
Not Provided
Home Stream
Not Provided

TATER TOT CASSEROLE

2 Pounds Ground Beef
2 Cans French Cut Green Beans
2 Cans Cream of Mushroom Soup
Frozen Tater Tots

Brown ground beef and drain fat. Mix everything except tater tots. Put in a cake pan and cover with tater tots. Bake in a preheated 375-degree oven for 30 – 45 minutes.

Serves: 4 – 6

DAVID C. HALL

"The beauty of fly fishing is not measured in angling success, but in the environment in which it is practiced. Everyplace I fly fish is beautiful!"

David Hall of Glide, Oregon is the Manager of Quality Control for Umpqua Feather Merchants, an artist and a fly fishing guide. As Umpqua's person in charge of flies, Dave oversees the production of over 500,000 dozen (6,000,000) flies on an annual basis.

Dave has illustrated numerous angling books for Stackpole Publishing. He was the featured artist for the *Fly Fishing Experience* calendar. His works have been featured in *Fly Rod & Reel, Fly Fisherman, Fly Fishing in Salt Waters, Wild Steelhead, Atlantic Salmon, Gray's Sporting Journal*, and *Outdoor Life* magazines.

Hall created two steelhead fly patterns, the Hammer Down Caddis and the Flash Black Nymph.

Dave provided the pen and ink drawings used in this book, *Angler Profiles*.

Years Fly Fishing
Thirty-two

Favorite Rod
8 wt 10' Graphite

Rods Owned
Ten

Favorite Flies
Dry – Adams
Wet – Lead Wing Coachman
Nymph – Barr's P.M.D.
and B.W.O. Emerger
Streamer – Black
Rabbit Leech
Terrestrial – Schroeder's
Parachute Hopper

Flies Invented
See Comments

Favorite US River
North Umpqua (OR)

Home River
North Umpqua (OR)

Favorite Stream
Williamson River (OR)

Home Stream
North Umpqua (OR)

BARBEQUED ELK RIBS

1 Side Elk Ribs
¼ Cup Soy Sauce
¼ Cup Worcestershire Sauce
Juice of 1 Lemon
1 Onion, Chopped
½ Can Coke®
¼ Cup Oil
¼ Cup Wine Vinegar
1 Tablespoons Salt
1 Tablespoon Pepper
1 Tablespoon Ginger, Grated
3 Cloves Garlic

Mix all ingredients in a bowl. Place ribs in a roasting pan and pour mixture over ribs. Marinate 5 hours, basting every hour. Bake in oven at 350 degrees for 45 minutes, basting every 15 minutes.

Place on a barbecue grill for 15 minutes per side, basting every 10 minutes.

Serves: 6

"A fish doesn't know enough to be all that particular about flies, except maybe for fresh water trout sometimes. If it looks like a bug or a baitfish and it moves right, they'll eat it."

On May 8, 1998, Carl Hanson forwarded his information for inclusion in this book, *Angler Profiles*. He didn't include his favorite food recipe, just a recipe for living. Carl died in June of 1998 at the age of 84.

Carl Hanson was a well-known Florida fly tyer. He once said, *"Fishing is not my hobby—teaching is my hobby."* With that attitude, Carl held free tying and casting clinics every Tuesday night at his St. Petersburg home since 1950. He estimated that he had taught over 50,000 people how to tie flies and cast them.

Known as the original tier of the Glass Minnow, Carl liked to fish with a five-foot 2-weight split bamboo rod made by Jon Clarke, and a tippet tied from his wife's hip-length hair.

Years Fly Fishing
Seventy-five

Favorite Rod
2 wt 5' Bamboo

Rods Owned
Six

Favorite Flies
Dry – Home Made
Wet – Home Made
Nymph – Home Made
Streamer – Glass Minnow
Terrestrial – Ant

Fly Invented
See Comments

Home Waters
Salt Waters
of Bunces Pass (FL)

"Hurt as few people as you can. Help anybody. Enjoy life. Love people." – Carl

PHILIP HANYOK

"Big fish in small streams are an addiction."

Philip Hanyok has been the Managing Editor of *Fly Fisherman* magazine for the last thirteen years. He also writes *The Gearing Up Department* of that magazine and freelance articles for *Fly Fishing Retailer* magazine and other publications. He lives in Harrisburg, Pennsylvania.

Philip's recipe is of his own creation.

Years Fly Fishing
Twenty-one

Favorite Rod
6 wt 9' Graphite

Rods Owned
Twelve

Favorite Flies
Dry – Compra Dun
Wet – Woolly Bugger
Nymph – B.H. Hare's Ear
Streamer – Muddler Minnow
Terrestrial – Spider

Fly Invented
"No name" patterns of
my own modification.

Favorite US River
Pine Creek (PA)

Home River
Susquehanna (PA)

Favorite Stream
Falling Spring (PA)

Home Stream
Letort (PA)

CATFISH IN MUSHROOM CREAM*

(*Catfish in Mushroom Cream Sauce)

2 Large Catfish Fillets of ½ Pound Each
2 Tablespoons Butter, Plus Another Tablespoon
2 Tablespoons Shallots, Finely Chopped
3 Large Mushrooms Per Fillet, Sliced Paper Thin
½ Cup Half-&-Half or Cream
Parsley, Freshly Chopped

Rinse fish fillets under cold water and pat dry with a paper towel. Over medium heat, melt 2 tablespoons of butter in a non-stick pan. Fry the fish fillets in the butter uncovered, flipping the fillets when they are cooked half way through.

In a separate pan, melt 1 tablespoon of butter over medium heat and sauté the finely chopped shallots until they begin to turn transparent. Add thinly sliced mushrooms and sauté until nearly all liquid has evaporated. Reduce heat and add Half-&-Half to make enough sauce (about ¼ cup per fillet). As the sauce thickens over low heat, add chopped parsley to taste. Remove saucepan from heat. Place one fish fillet on each plate. Discard cooking butter. Spoon mushrooms and cream sauce on top of the fish. Serve with cooked orzo or rice and your choice of steamed vegetables.

Serves: 2

"Between fishing and bird hunting and making pictures of these wonderful vices, there are not enough days in the year."

Eldridge Hardie is a sporting artist who lives in Denver, Colorado. Eldridge was recently named as the Atlantic Salmon Federation's *Artist of the Year*. He has also been the Trout Unlimited's *Artist of the Year*. His work appears regularly in *Gray's Sporting Journal, Fly Fishing in Saltwaters, Sporting Classics, Pointing Dog Journal*, and several other magazines. Eight of the publications have included profiles.

Eldridge has illustrated many books, most recently Jose Ortega Y. Gasset's classic *Meditations on Hunting* and Paul Schullery's *Royal Coachman: The Lore and Legends of Fly-Fishing*. He painted covers for two Roderick Haig-Brown books.

The artist's works have been featured in invitational shows and exhibits throughout the U.S. and Canada.

Eldridge's best fish was a 20-pound hen sea-run brown that he caught in Rio Grande River in Tierra del Fuego, Argentina.

Years Fly Fishing
Forty-nine
Favorite Rod
5 wt 7' 5" Bamboo
Rods Owned
Eight
Favorite Flies
Dry – Adams
Wet – Rio Grande King
Nymph – G.R. Hare's Ear
Streamer – Hornberg
Terrestrial – Black Ant
Fly Invented
I don't tie.
Favorite US River
Bighorn (MT)
Home River
South Platte (CO)
Favorite Stream
Laramie (WY)
Home Stream
Bear Creek (CO)

Lean Breast Fillets

If using goose breast fillet, slice the fillet as you would with a bagel. Thinner pieces grill better than full thickness.

Do absolutely nothing in the way of seasonings, basting or marinating. Cook the fillets exactly as you would a steak on a barbecue grill. If you do not like rare to medium-rare steaks, forget it. You are not qualified to enjoy this dish.

Serve with wild rice, a tossed salad, French sourdough bread, and a good red wine.

Serves: Pair of fillets from mallard serves 1, from goose, 2 persons

"This is my campaign to educate all I can about what a delicacy wildfowl can be and how simple!" – Eldridge

"Please use flies with single barbless hooks and release most of the trout you catch!"

George Harvey is a legendary fly fishing innovator who retired from Penn State University in 1972, but has continued to teach throughout the U. S. and at State College every year since 1972. He resides in State College, Pennsylvania and is the recipient of *Fly Fisherman* magazine and the *Virtual Flyshop's* first *Lifetime Fly Tier Achievement Award*. The award was based on Harvey's starting the first full-credit college course in fly fishing at a major university, Penn State University. Since 1937, George has taught more than 45,000 students to fly fish and tie flies. His first non-credit class taught was in 1934.

In the 1960s, George helped the Metz Hatchery develop quality genetic hackles. His book, *George Harvey's Techniques of Trout Fishing and Fly Tying* has taught the sport to thousands. His night-fishing and Trico-fishing techniques were innovations when they were first introduced.

George Harvey: Memories, Patterns and Tactics is the Dean of American Fly Fishing's latest book.

Years Fly Fishing
Eighty-three
Favorite Rod
5 wt 8' 6" Graphite
Rods Owned
Fifteen
Favorite Flies
Dry – Harvey's Spruce Creek
Wet – Harvey's #1 Black
Nymph – Harvey's Peacock
Streamer – Harvey's Spruce Creek Streamer
Terrestrial – Elk Hair Ant
Flies Invented
Spruce Creek and the others listed above.
Favorite US River
Henry's Fork (ID)
Home River
Not Provided
Favorite Stream
Spruce Creek (PA)
Home Stream
Spruce Creek (PA)

Trout Fillets
1 Egg
Cup Flour
Vegetable Oil
Cracker Meal

Mix 1 egg to every cup full of flour. Add water until just a thin film stays on the finger. Use deep frying pan with 1 ½ inches of vegetable oil. Heat to boiling. Dip fillets in cracker meal. Cook the trout in boiling oil for about 3 minutes. Turn over every 1 ½ minutes.

"Serves as many as you have fillets for. I just had a fish fry for 21 people!" – George

George is 87 years young and hasn't missed a 1st day of fishing season since he was 6 years old. He caught his first trout at the age of 6—a six-inch brook trout that hooked itself. Geroge tied his first fly when he was 10 years old.

Harvey says his greatest enjoyment comes from teaching others to tie flies, cast, and catch and release trout.

TOM HAWTHORNE

"Be careful what you wish for, because someday you might get what you wished for."

Tom Hawthorne, a former helicopter certified mechanic, was introduced to fly fishing by his friend Ted Angle. Tom opened his Ozark Angler in 1998, starting with a modest inventory and just afternoon hours of operation. After just 4 months, he gave up the helicopter business to devote all his energies to the fly shop. Later that next year, Tom went west to guide for Bud Lilly's Trout Shop in West Yellowstone, Montana. The guide business grew so rapidly that he had to quit going to Montana. Today, after 10 years, his shop has grown to a 2-shop operation, employing 12 employees, with shops located in Little Rock and Heber Springs, Arkansas.

Tom's Heber Springs shop is located near the Little Red River in Arkansas, home of the current world record brown trout at 40-pounds 4-ounces.

Tom and his wife, Jennifer, live in Little Rock, Arkansas.

Years Fly Fishing
Twenty-one

Favorite Rod
Orvis Model 99 Bamboo

Rods Owned
A Few

Favorite Flies
Dry – Trude
Wet – Partridge and Peacock
Nymph – Pheasant Tail
Streamer – Llama
Terrestrial – Hopper

Fly Invented
Soft Hackle Brassie

Favorite US River
Madison below Quake Lake (MT)

Home River
Little Red (AR)

Favorite Stream
Firehole (WY)

Home Stream
Not Provided

PENNE PASTA*

(*Penne Pasta with Parsley & Artichoke)

Penne Pasta
Garlic
Artichoke Hearts
Fresh Parsley
Olive Oil
1 Cup Fresh Grated Parmesan Cheese
Fresh Cracked Pepper

Slice garlic very thin and sauté in olive oil. Cut up artichoke hearts and add to the oil and garlic. Also, add ¼ cup of water. Cook at high heat until water absorbed.

In separate pan, cook pasta. Drain and save ¼ cup of water for later. Add pasta to artichokes, along with ¼ cup of the saved water. Cook over high heat for 4 – 6 minutes or until hot.

In a large pasta bowl, sprinkle fresh parsley and 1 cup of fresh grated Parmesan cheese.

Toss gently and serve with fresh cracked pepper.

Serves: 4

CHRISTOPHER HELM

PFANENKUCHEN*

"If you need a quality tool and don't buy it, you've already paid for it." – Borrowed from an unknown person

Chris Helm is a recognized expert on fly tying with deer, elk and other animal hairs and has produced three videos on the subject. He operates his Whitetail Fly Tying Supply Company from Toledo, Ohio.

Chris also distributes the Comb Holder, and makes and markets the *Brassie Hair Packer*®, but did not invent the packer. His many videos are included in the *Hooked on Fly Tying* series.

When asked what flies he invented, Chris replied, *"None. There are already more flies than I have time to tie."*

Because there are really no streams in Chris' area that contain any worthwhile fish, he mostly lake fishes. His travels take him to places where he can fish for smallmouth bass and salt water species such as bonefish, permit and tarpon.

Years Fly Fishing
Over Thirty

Favorite Rod
9 wt 9' Graphite

Rods Owned
Ten

Favorite Flies
Dry – Humpy
Wet – Gray Hackle Peacock
Nymph – B.H. Pheasant Tail
Streamer – Spruce Fly
Terrestrial – Bullet
Head Hopper

Fly Invented
See Comments

Favorite US River
Lamar (MT)

Home River
Maumee (OH)

Favorite Stream
Hell Roaring in
Yellowstone Park (MT)

Home Stream
See Comments

(*Mother's German Pancake Recipe)

2 Cups Flour
1 Heaping Teaspoon Salt
2 Heaping Teaspoons Sugar
4 Eggs
2 Cups Milk
Fruit, if Desired

Mix flour, salt and sugar. Salt may be omitted and sugar may be reduced. Add flour with eggs and stir. Add 2/3-cup milk gradually. Add fruit, if desired. Continue adding 1 1/3 more cups of milk. Stir well.

Heat skillet or pan. Add a little Crisco before pouring batter. These pancakes are fairly thin.

Serves – 4

"These are the best pancakes I've ever eaten."
— Chris

BOB HENLEY

"In fly tying, fly fishing, and life in general, exhibit patience."

Bob Henley is the creator of Bob Henley's Tie-A-Fly Instructional Kits. He lives in Sacramento, California.

Beginning fly tiers often spend a lot of time gathering the right materials to tie the flies they want. To eliminate the frustration of looking for materials and to save tier's time, Bob has put together a series of 12 fly-tying kits that provides all the materials needed to tie a dozen flies of a particular pattern. His kits include tying thread, various sizes of hoods, and materials for tails, bodies, hackles, and other fly parts.

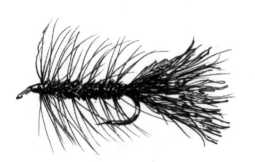

Years Fly Fishing
Fifty

Favorite Rod
3 wt 6' 6" Graphite

Rods Owned
Six

Favorite Flies
Dry – Humpy
Wet – Gray Hackle Peacock
Nymph – G.R. Hare's Ear
Streamer – Black
Woolly Bugger
Terrestrial – Black
Winged Ant

Fly Invented
Tie-A-Fly Concept

Favorite US River
Deschutes (OR)

Home River
American (CA)

Favorite Stream
Yellow Creek (CA)

Home Stream
Not Provided

POACHED TROUT*

(*Poached Trout in Sherry Wine)

2 Medium-sized Cleaned Trout
½ Teaspoon Dry Mustard
4 Tablespoons Butter or Oil
2 Tablespoons Soy Sauce
2 Teaspoons Honey
½ Cup Sherry Wine (California, of course!)
2 Cups Water
2 Tablespoons Flour

Combine 2 tablespoons butter or oil and the mustard in a large heavy skillet until well blended, using medium-high heat. Add the soy sauce, honey, wine and water. Stir well and heat to boiling. Simmer for 5 minutes. Add fish, cover, and continue cooking until flesh flakes easily.

Remove fish and cover to keep warm. Blend flour with remaining 2 tablespoons soft butter and add to sauce. Cook, stirring constantly until sauce is thickened.

Pour sauce over trout and serve. You may fillet the trout just before adding sauce.

Delicious with mashed potatoes topped with the same sauce!

Serves: 2

ANTHONY HIPPS

SPICY CROCK POT RED BEANS

"As a fly fisherman, I become a player in nature's symphony, with the fly rod and line as the instrument."

Anthony Hipps is an environmental research chemist. He lives in Lexington, North Carolina. Anthony developed the Hipps Hellgrammite which he says is a dynamite smallmouth bass fly.

Anthony is also a fly tying and fly casting instructor and former President of the Nat Greene Fly Fishers of Greensboro, North Carolina.

Years Fly Fishing
Seventeen

Favorite Rod
6 wt 8' Graphite

Rods Owned
Eleven

Favorite Flies
Dry – Elk Hair Caddis
Wet – Black Gnat
Nymph – B.H. Pheasant Tail
Streamer – Woolly Bugger
Terrestrial – Dave's Hopper

Fly Invented
Hipp's Hellgrammite
Smallmouth Fly

Favorite US River
Little (TN)

Home River
Yad Kin (NC)

Favorite Stream
Indian Creek (MT)

Home Stream
Abbotts Creek (NC)

¾ Bag Dry Red Kidney Beans
2 Tablespoons Honey
1 Tablespoon Salt
2 Teaspoons Cayenne Pepper
1 Teaspoon Louisiana Hot
Sauce or Tabasco Equivalent
¾ Pound Smoked Summer Sausage
1 Whole Chopped Onion
2 Chopped Jalapeno Peppers
Water to Cover
1 Cup Uncooked Minute Rice, Cooked Separately

Add beans to crockpot. Add honey and mix into beans thoroughly. Add remaining ingredients, except for rice, to the crockpot. Cover with 3 – 4 inches water (beans expand). Cook on low setting for 6 – 8 hours until beans are fully cooked. Ingredients and amounts can be varied to taste.

Cook 1 cup Minute Rice separately according to the directions on the box and boiling in water.

Best served over cooked rice with fresh, hot cornbread.

Serves: 3 – 6 hungry fisherpersons

"I'm glad to have seen fly fishing evolve from a minor sport in the 1950s to a much loved major sport in the 90s."

Henry Hoffman is the hackle raiser who from 1965 to 1995 produced super grade dry fly hackle, soft hackle and Chickabou™ under the name Hoffman's Hackle Farm. He resides in Warrenton, Oregon.

The fly tying innovator has created many fly patterns from rooster body feathers including Chickabou™, Knee Hackle, and Soft Hackle Flank Feathers.

In 1995, Henry developed a series of chickabou chironomid nymph patterns for lake fishing. On a purple nymph pattern, he caught a 26 ½" Lahontan cutthroat trout. Five days later he caught a 31" cutthroat, but no one was there at 7:45 in the morning to get a picture before the trout was released.

Years Fly Fishing
Forty-three

Favorite Rod
5 wt 9' Graphite

Rods Owned
Eight

Favorite Flies
Dry – Tan Deer Hair Caddis
Wet – Knee Hackle Special
Nymph – Chickabou Damsel
Streamer – Chickabou Sculpin
Terrestrial – Hopper

Flies Invented
Chickabou Crayfish and Others

Favorite US River
Deschutes (OR)

Home River
Necanicum (OR)

Favorite Stream
South Fork Boise (ID)

Home Stream
Big Creek (OR)

© 2000 - Russell A. Hopper

1 ½ Pounds Ground Beef
½ Medium Onion, Chopped
1 Can Cream of Chicken Soup
Grated Cheese
2 Pound Package Frozen Tater Tots
1 Can (4 Ounces) Sliced Mushrooms
1 Can Cream of Celery Soup

Press hamburger in bottom of 9" x 13" baking dish. Spread onion and mushrooms over hamburger.

Place frozen tater tots on top of onions and mushrooms. Mix celery and chicken soup, undiluted, in separate bowl and spread mixture over tater tots like frosting. Cover casserole with grated cheese.

Bake at 375 degrees for 15 minutes, reduce heat to 350 degrees and bake an additional 50 – 60 minutes.

Serves: 6

BRUCE HOLT

"Releasing a fish for future generations to enjoy is an emotional experience ... it's even more so when you know how good they taste!"

Bruce Holt is Director of Public Relations for G. Loomis, Inc. He is an avid angler, photographer and outdoorsman born in Oregon and raised in Idaho, where he first fly fished on the Middle Fork of the Weiser and Little Salmon rivers over 40 years ago.

Bruce has authored over a hundred articles on fishing around the world. In 1966, he set two IGFA world records in the six-pound fly tippet category, one for Chinook salmon and one for pink salmon.

Holt enjoys fly fishing for steelhead on Oregon's Deschutes River and catching big bluegill from area farm ponds, when he's not chasing smallmouth bass. His fishing buddies call him *Catfish* because he grew up on the Snake River and spent literally hundreds of hours on the water to just catch anything and the catfish were and are still one of his favorite non-fly fish.

Holt resides with future bride, Jean, in Kalama, Washington, near the Columbia River where he enjoys fishing for bass, sturgeon, salmon and steelhead, as well as hunting deer and elk in the nearby hills with both rifle and bow.

Years Fly Fishing
Over Thirty

Favorite Rod
7 wt 9' 6" Graphite

Rods Owned
Twelve

Favorite Flies
Dry – Coachman Bucktail
Wet – Teeny Nymph
Nymph – B.H. Prince
Streamer – Lefty's Deceiver
Terrestrial – Tied-down Caddis

Fly Invented
None, yet

Favorite US River
Deschutes (OR)

Home River
Kalama (WA)

Favorite Stream
Crooked River (OR)

Home Stream
Middle Fork Weiser (ID)

HALIBUT STEW

2 – 3 Pounds Cubed Halibut or Similar White-meat Fish with Firm Flesh
1 Large Onion, Chopped
6 – 8 Large Potatoes, Peeled and Chunked
4 – 6 Large Carrots, Sliced
2 – 4 Large Tomatoes, Chunked
12 – 20 Fresh Crawdad Tails, Cleaned
3 – 4 Bay Leaves
2 – 3 Tablespoons Seasoning Salt
1 Package (16 Ounces) Cajun Fish Boil Mix
1 Tablespoon Salt
1 Jar (32 Ounces) Salsa, Mild or Hot
1 Cup Rum

Soak fish and crawdad tails in strong salt water solution overnight. Rinse with cold water and have ready to put in stock.

Boil peeled potatoes in large pot with lots of water until semi-soft. Remove and cut into 2" chunks, keeping the water hot for stock. Slice carrots, chunk tomatoes and add to the "potato" water with the potato chunks. Add salt, seasoning salt, Cajun fish boil mix, bay leaves and chopped onion, bringing the entire mixture to a boil.

Continued on next page ...

Add fish and crawdad tails to broth, blending in the fish boil mix and rum. Allow entire mixture to boil for 20 minutes. Simmer for an additional 1-hour, adding any additional spices, as you like. Just remember the fish boil mix is spicy so you may wish to check the ingredients.

Serve in a bowl over hot rice.

"Tastes even better on day two, and can be frozen." – Bruce

GEORGE HOMMELL

"You don't need tarter sauce."

George Hommell was born in the Catskill Mountains in New York and fly fished for brook and rainbow trout when he was ten years old. After his first hitch in the military, he moved to Islamorada, Florida in the Florida Keys. After his second tour of duty in 1952, he became a fishing guide specializing in fly fishing for tarpon, bonefish and other sport fish.

Hommell has guided such luminaries as George Bush, Jack Nicklaus, Ted Williams and the angling legend, Joe Brooks. Ernest Hemmingway also once rescued him from a cargo boat delivery to Cuba.

George opened the World Wide Sportsman in 1967, and he and his silent partner, Billy Pate, sold it to Johnny Morris of Bass Pro Shops in 1995. He presently is the General Manager of the new World Wide Sportsman in Islamorada.

Many credit Hommell with founding the salt water fly fishing ethic highlighted in this *Angler Profile*.

Florida's pioneer flats guide, George Hommell, was featured in the May/June 1999 issue of *Fly Fishing in Salt Waters*.

GEORGE HOMMELL'S SALT WATER FLY FISHING ETHIC

"Respect other people's right to fish, know the layout, release your catch, and contribute to the future with your time, thoughts and money."

HOMMELL'S FISH FILET*

(*Hommell's 21ST Century Fish Filet)

Yellowtail Snapper or Other Fresh Fish
Butter
Salt, Pepper and Garlic Salt
Cracker Crumbs
Eggs

Take a fresh filet of fish, preferably a yellowtail snapper. Make sure there are no bones. Slip in melted butter after putting salt, pepper and garlic salt on both sides. Put in a rack and cook over charcoals for 5 minutes. Then mix up a batter of cracker crumbs, eggs and melted butter. Slip the fish back on the charcoals and cook for 20 minutes.

FIRE SIDE STEW

"There's casting, fishing, catching, and releasing, but I get a great deal of satisfaction from the sport by shopping and buying."

Russ (Flyrodruss) Hopper has only been fly fishing for six seasons, yet it consumes his waking moments, dreams and wallet. Russ is a certified public accountant and a certified alcohol and drug counselor. He resides in Bowling Green, Kentucky and is the author of this book, *Angler Profiles: A Collection of Some Legendary Anglers' Favorite Flies, Foods, Rods & Waters.*

Russ is the current President and one of the six founders of the Sons of the Cumberland, a Kentucky non-profit fly fishing fellowship that practices catch and release fly fishing. He holds membership in the Federation of Fly Fishers, the American Museum of Fly Fishing, the Catskills Fly Fishing Center and Museum, the Middle Tennessee Fly Fishers, Trout Unlimited, and the International Game Fish Association.

Russ enjoys seeing his two children, Kim and Warren, his wife's children, Getta and Angela, and fly fishing with his wife, Susan. He is in the process of writing a book entitled *Pet Peeves & Angling Etiquette.*

Years Fly Fishing
Six Seasons

Favorite Rod
5 wt 8' 6" Graphite

Rods Owned
Five

Favorite Flies
Dry – Royal Wulff
Wet – G.R. Hare's Ear
Nymph – B.H. Soft
Hackle Pheasant Tail
Streamer – C.H. Olive
Woolly Bugger
Terrestrial – Crayfish

Fly Invented
None, yet

Favorite US River
Pere Marquette (MI)

Home River
Cumberland (KY)

Favorite Stream
Trammel Fork (KY)

Home Stream
Trammel Fork (KY)

1 ½ Pounds Cubed Stewing Beef
1 Can (1 Pound, 13 Ounces) Whole Baby Carrots
1/3 Cup Buttery Flavored Oil
1 Can (8 Ounces) Tomato Sauce with Onions
Salt and Pepper
½ Teaspoon Thyme
¼ Cup Flour
1 Can (8 Ounces) Green Beans
1 Can (8 Ounces) Whole Baby Potatoes

Coat beef with flour, salt and pepper. Brown in oil at medium temperature and drain fat. Drain and reserve liquid from potatoes, carrots, and beans. Add water to make 2 cups. Add meat. Stir in tomato sauce and add thyme. Cover and simmer 1 ¾ hours. Add vegetables and simmer 15 minutes longer.

SUSAN HOPPER

"I fly fish so I can be with my husband."

Susan Hopper lives in Bowling Green, Kentucky where she is the Office Manager for a large regional furniture store, Betty & Tom's Country Charm. She has two children, Georgetta and Angela.

Susan's husband is Russ Hopper, the author of this book. She and Russ travel throughout the Southeast looking for exotic waters containing trout.

Years Fly Fishing
Four Seasons

Favorite Rod
5 wt 9' Graphite

Rods Owned
One

Favorite Flies
Dry – Royal Wulff
Wet – Hare's Ear
Nymph – B.H. Zug Bug
Streamer – Woolly Bugger
Terrestrial – Hopper

Flies Invented
None, yet

Favorite US River
Hiawassee (TN)

Home River
Cumberland (KY)

Favorite Stream
Trammel Fork (KY)

Home Stream
Trammel Fork (KY)

HOPPIN' JOHN SOUP

¼ Pound Pork Sausage, Preferably Hot
½ Cup Onions, Chopped
2 Carrots, Peeled and Diced
3 ½ Cups Chicken Stock
3 – 4 Cups Water
½ Teaspoon Salt or to Taste
½ Cup Uncooked Brown Rice
1 Package (8 Ounces) Frozen Black-eyed Peas
1 Package (8 Ounces) Frozen
Turnip Greens, Defrosted
½ Teaspoon Red Pepper Flakes

Brown sausage in a large pot or Dutch oven over medium-high heat. Pour sausage into colander to drain off fat. Wipe out pot and return sausage to pot.

Add onion and carrots. Cook for 5 minutes, stirring often, until the onions are soft. Add chicken stock and water. Bring to a boil and add salt and rice.

Lower heat to simmer. After 20 minutes, add black-eyed peas and greens. Cook 20 minutes longer until the rice and vegetables are tender. Add red pepper flakes and adjust seasoning to taste.

Serves: 6 – 8

"Don't ask what you will do to a fishing day; ask instead what beauty and surprise an angling day might hold for you."

Dave Hughes is one of the most published authors in the history of fly fishing, and one of the most popular speakers at sportsmen's shows, banquets, and fly fishing club meetings.

Dave co-authored the classic *Western Hatches* with Rick Hafele. The Portland, Oregon resident wrote the script for *Anatomy of a Trout Stream*. He authored *American Fly Tying Manual, Dry Fly Fishing, Nymph Fishing, Reading Trout Water, Strategies for Stillwater, Wet Flies,* and *Trout Flies.*

He is an Essayist for *Flyfishing* magazine, *Bug Basics* Columnist for *Fly Tying*, and *Fly Fishing Success* Editor for *Fly Rod & Reel*.

Awards given to Dave include the *Pete Hidy Memorial Award for Literary Achievement*, which was bestowed by the Fly Fishers Club of Oregon and the *Lew Jewett Memorial Life Membership* by the Federation of Fly Fishers.

The founding President of Oregon Trout fly fishes a hundred or so days each year.

Years Fly Fishing
Forty-three

Favorite Rod
4 wt 9' Graphite

Rods Owned
About 20

Favorite Flies
Dry – Beetle Bug
Wet – Hare's Ear
Nymph – Olive Bead Head
Streamer – Olive
Woolly Bugger
Terrestrial – Parachute Hopper

Flies Invented
All-Fur Wets

Favorite US River
Deschutes (OR)

Home River
Deschutes (OR)

Favorite Stream
Nameless

Home Stream
Nameless

© 2000 - Russell A. Hopper

Whole Chicken
2 Quarts Water
Potatoes, Quartered
Carrots, Chunked
Celery, Sliced
Onion, Diced
1 Tablespoon Chicken Bouillon
1 Tablespoon Spike

This recipe may be made with half of a chicken, 1 quart of water, ½ chicken bouillon and ½ tablespoon spike. Vegetables should be added to personal taste. Remove most of the fat from American chickens before boiling.

In a large pot with lid, add water, chicken, onion, celery, bouillon and spike. Start at a boil, reduce heat, and simmer for 1 hour. Add potatoes, carrots and simmer until soft.

"Casuela de Ave is a Chilean recipe that I first discovered when I was down there and had a cold. A compassionate cook at a lodge made it for me. There was a chicken missing in the yard flock, and feathers in the stew. It tasted great and cured the cold." – Dave

JOE HUMPHREYS

ALLENBERRY SWEET ROLLS

"Starting out, we're all equal before the trout."

Joe Humphreys taught fly fishing at Penn State University for twenty years, thus earning the name, The Professor. Joe, who resides in Boiling Springs, Pennsylvania, has fished for over 60 years in the United States and Canada.

In addition to his recent video productions, *A Casting Approach to Dry Fly Tactics in the Brush* and *A Casting Approach to Nymphing Tactics*, Joe has written two books, *Joe Humphreys' Trout Tactics* and *On The Stream with Joe Humphreys*.

Joe was an apprentice to George Harvey and the holder of *Pennsylvania's State Trout Record* (August 1977) of 15-pounds 5-ounces (34"). He also instructed former President Jimmy Carter in nymph fishing, former Secretary of Defense, Richard Cheney, and basketball coaching legend, Bobby Knight.

Honors bestowed on Joe include *Order of the Hat* by the Harrisburg Flyfishers Club and the *Wally Thompson Award* given by the Centre County Pennsylvania Conservation District.

Humphreys hosted the first national fly fishing series on U.S. television; *Fly Fishing Journal* and has represented the U.S. in the 1989, 1990 and 1992 World Fly Fishing Championships.

Years Fly Fishing
Over Sixty

Favorite Rod
6 wt 9' or 7' 6" Graphite

Rods Owned
Maybe Forty

Favorite Flies
Dry – Tailless Humpy
Wet – Royal Coachman
Nymph – Harvey Stonefly
Streamer – Red Fin Mylar
Terrestrial – Black
Deer Hair Ant

Fly Invented
Nymph patterns sold by Umpqua Feather Merchants.

Favorite US River
Madison (MT)

Home River
Juniata (PA)

Favorite Stream
Spring Creek (PA)

Home Stream
Spring Creek (PA)

2.5 Ounces Active Dry Yeast
10 Quarts of Warm Water
50 Pounds Pillsbury Sweet Roll Mix
Butter
Sugar
Cinnamon

Syrup
32 Cups Brown Sugar
8 Cups Granulated Sugar
8 Cups Water
6 Pounds Butter

Dissolve 2.5 ounces Active Dry Yeast in 10 quarts of warm water. Mix in 50 pounds of Pillsbury Sweet Roll Mix. Mix in a large mixer with a dough hook.

Divide dough into 5 portions and let rise to double in size. Work with each portion separately. Divide into six portions. Roll out into rectangle. Butter and sprinkle with sugar and cinnamon. Roll up Jelly Roll Style and cut off buns.

Arrange buns in pans of syrup. Let rise and bake at 350 degrees. Flip onto sheet tray.

To make the syrup, heat the syrup mixture to syrup stage. You will need 2 ½ times the amount above or 3 times for 50 pounds.

RICHARD IZMIRIAN

POTATO CHIPS & BEER

"Hey—what are you using?"

Richard Izmirian is Vice President of Communications for the Federation of Fly Fishers. According to Susan Williams, a foraging angler herself, Richard is one of those indefatigable fishing/fishing issues people. When not dealing with his terminal tackle or the issues of the day, he is questing for the perfect home brew. His current brew is Hexagenia Hefeweizen.

Richard is the founder of the Home Brew Flyfishers Club. The club provides various concoctions for consumption and auction at local fly fishing fundraising events.

He is active in resource management projects at the local, state and national level. Richard has been president, chair, committee member, participant, instructor, director, or vice president of numerous organizations.

In 1988, Richard was selected as the Golden West Women Fly Fishers' *Playmate of the Year.* He lives in San Carlos, California.

Years Fly Fishing
Twenty-five

Favorite Fly Rod
I love all my children.

Rods Owned
Closet Full

Favorite Flies
Whatever caught the last fish.

Fly Invented
Reinvented Many

Favorite US River
Anything Wild

Home Water
Pacific Ocean

Favorite Stream
Anything Wild

Home Stream
Cordilleras Creek (CA)

© 2000 - Russell A. Hopper

This is a favorite of the Big Dumb Guys Fly Fishing Club. After a long day on the river, there is nothing like ripping open a bag of chips and popping the cap on a bottle of home brew. The whiskey and cigars are for much later.

1 Bag Potato Chips
(Try Trader Joe's Hawaiian Style)
22 Ounce Bottle Home-Brew Beer or Ale
2 Glasses
Bottle Opener

It is important to open the bag of chips with gusto and style. Tearing with the teeth always makes a good presentation. Opening the beer, however, requires a degree of reverence seldom expected. Listen to the beer (stop crunching the potato chips for a moment). Pour carefully into the brace of glasses. If you pour out some sediment, however, don't worry—it is full of vitamins.

For a fat-free alternative, try substituting pretzels for potato chips.

"Give a toast to the day, the fish and their world, and friendship astream. Enjoy." – Richard

JIMMY JACOBS

"Much like a juvenile rainbow trout, I tend to travel up stream until I run out of water."

Jimmy Jacobs is the author of *Trout Fishing in North Georgia, Trout Streams of Southern Appalachia, Bass Fishing in Georgia* and *Tailwater Trout in the South*.

Jimmy is the Editor of *Georgia Sportsman* magazine and resides in Marietta, Georgia.

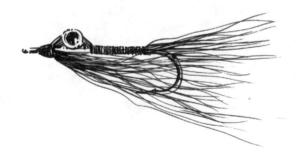

Years Fly Fishing
Thirty-six

Favorite Rod
2 wt 6' 6" Graphite

Rods Owned
Three

Favorite Flies
Dry – Royal Wulff
Wet – Not Provided
Nymph – B.H. Prince
Streamer – Chartreuse and
White Clouser Minnow
Terrestrial – Not Provided

Fly Invented
None, yet

Favorite US River
Conasauga (GA)

Home River
Chattahoochee (GA)

Favorite Stream
West Fork Montgomery Creek (GA)

Home Stream
Not Provided

COHUTTA MOUNTAIN CRAWDAD*

*(*Cohutta Mountain Crawdad Creole)*

1 Cup Shelled Crawfish Tails, Fresh
from a Mountain Creek
¼ Cup Margarine
½ Cup Flour
1 Small Can Mushrooms
1 Medium Chopped Vidalia Onion
2 Cups Water
¼ Teaspoon Thyme
2 Bay Leaves
¼ Teaspoon Cayenne Pepper

Sauté onion and mushrooms in margarine several minutes. Add flour, then stir in water slowly, stirring continuously. Add crawfish, or boiled fish, if crawdads are scarce, and seasonings. Cook five more minutes. Remove bay leaves. Salt and pepper to taste.

Serve over rice or biscuits.

Serves: 2 – 4 depending on level of hunger

DANN JACOBUS

"Somewhere in the mind of every angler is a mythical fish." – John Gierach

Dann Jacobus is a sporting and wildlife artist living in Warwick, New York.

Years Fly Fishing
Thirty-three

Favorite Rod
Graphite or Bamboo

Rods Owned
Fifteen

Favorite Flies
Dry – Red Quill
Wet – Isonychia Bivisible
Nymph – G.R. Hare's Ear
Streamer – Woolly Bugger
Terrestrial – Griffith's Gnat

Fly Invented
None, yet

Favorite US River
Neversink (NY)

Home River
Wawayonda Creek (NY)

Favorite Stream
Musionetcong (NJ)

Home Stream
Wawayonda Creek (NY)

CALAMARI IN MARINARA SAUCE

2 Pounds Cleaned Squid
3 Tablespoons Olive Oil
Garlic
Celery
Onion
3 Cans (8 Ounces Each) Tomato Sauce
Basil
Oregano
Salt and Pepper

Finely chop garlic, onion, celery, basil and oregano. Add to the saucepan containing 3 tablespoons olive oil. Sauté until transparent. Add 3 8-ounce cans tomato sauce and simmer about 20 minutes. Add cleaned squid after the bodies have been cut into rings about 1/8" in width. Add tentacles.

Cook for about 45 minutes. Add salt and pepper to taste.

Serve alone or over thin pasta.

Serves: 4

TOM JINDRA

"There are no secrets in fly fishing, only people who love their sport."

Tom Jindra is a journalist and President of the Federation of Fly Fishers. He lives in New Orleans and says he had the pleasure of fly fishing the Louisiana Coast when it was still a fly fishing frontier.

Tom's wife, Debra, volunteers at all the fly fishing conclaves. She also serves as Outreach Chairperson on the national as well as the southeastern level. When asked about her fly fishing, she said, *"I am not a fly fishing woman. I do this because this is what my husband loves. I've come to love the people and what the sport of fly fishing means, preserving and conserving. Friends forever in Fly Fishing!"*

Although not included here, Debra has a great recipe for *Chicken Andouille Gumbo*.

Years Fly Fishing
Thirty-one
Favorite Rod
7 wt 9' Graphite
Rods Owned
Six
Favorite Flies
Dry – Popping Bug
Wet – Not Provided
Nymph – Not Provided
Streamer – Clouser Minnow
Terrestrial – Not Provided
Fly Invented
None, yet
Favorite US River
Mississippi (LA)
Home River
Mississippi (LA)
Favorite Stream
Louisiana Marshes
Home Stream
Louisiana Marshes

SHRIMP DILLICIOUS

1 ½ Pounds Fresh Shrimp, Cleaned
Butter
1 Tablespoon Garlic Puree
¼ Cup White Wine
2 Teaspoons Cajun Magic or Other
Cajun Seasoning Blend
2 Teaspoons Dillweed
Fresh Black Pepper
2 Tablespoons Fresh Parsley
4 Ounces Heavy Cream
Freshly Grated Parmesan

Sauté shrimp in butter and garlic until pink and remove from the pan. Deglaze pan with wine.

Add the rest of the ingredients to the sauté pan. Heat through and reduce to half. Do not allow this to boil excessively, light bubbles just to simmer.

Add shrimp and heat for another two minutes stirring occasionally.

When the sauce is complete, pour it over freshly cooked fettuccine and sprinkle with Parmesan cheese. Rice is also good.

Serve it with a simple salad, crusty Italian bread, and a bottle of Chardonnay wine.

Serves: 2

TOM JOHNSON

"This is a lousy time to receive a request for an Angler Profile. We're in the middle of spring steelhead."

Tom Johnson is a fishing guide, professional fly fisherman and owner of the famed Johnson's Lodge in Baldwin, Michigan. His fly shop is one of the largest Orvis Endorsed outfitters. He also sells fly fishing boats.

Tom's team tied for first place in the World Fly Fishing Championship's Professional Division held in Jackson Hole, Wyoming in 1997. He came in third in the Individual Professional Division. Tom holds the International Game Fish Association's World Record for a mutton snapper on a fly. He has released a 15-pound 8-ounce bonefish, but had no certified scale. So Tom is still trying for an IGFA bonefish record.

Flies invented by Tom include the P. M. Wiggler, Johnson's Tarpon Crab, and The Big Johnson Bunny Shrimp for bonefish.

When Tom worked in Alaska as a guide on the Alagnak, he had to prepare shore lunches each day for clients. Every day was a salmon or char lunch so the preparations had to be different as Tom had the same clients for six days.

Years Fly Fishing
Twenty-seven

Favorite Rod
5 wt 10' Graphite

Rods Owned
Over One Hundred

Favorite Flies
Dry – Rubber Legged Mattress Thrasher
Wet – Woolly Spey Fly
Nymph – P.M. Blond Wiggler
Streamer – Johnson's Bunny Crab for Tarpon
Terrestrial – Ant or Dave's Hopper

Flies Invented
See Comments

Favorite US River
Pere Marquette (MI)

Home River
Pere Marquette (MI)

Favorite Stream
Moraine (AK)

Home Stream
The Baldwin (MI)

MUSTARD SALMON GLAZE

Salmon
Mustard
Mayonnaise
Sugar
Ritz Cracker Crumbs
Red or Sweet Onion Sliced into Half Rings

Prepare mustard glaze by using 1 part Sun Valley, Chrissy's or Dijon mustard and 2 parts mayonnaise. German-style or grain mustards do not work. Use French's yellow only as a last resort. Add sugar.

Grill salmon, skin side down. If there is no skin, use aluminum foil against the grill. With the flesh side up, brush or wipe on mustard glaze and grill 2 minutes. Dust with cracker crumbs then lay ½ onion rings on top of the body like scales (cute?). Cook an additional five minutes or until flesh is just done. Do not overcook as salmon gets real dry.

"The world of striped bass cannot be singled out as the realm of any one individual or group of individuals."

Nick Karas of Orient Point, New York is a journalist and ichthyologist. He has been an outdoors columnist for *New York Newsday* for the last 25 years and in time has written over 3,500 columns.

Nick served on the staff of *True*, as Assistant Outdoors Editor, then *Argosy* as Outdoors Editor. While with *Argosy*, he was also its Editorial Director for 20 annual outdoors-oriented publications.

His book—he has a dozen to his credit—*Brook Trout* was released in 1997 and is now in its third printing. *The Striped Bass* is in its second edition. He also puts out an annual *Guide to Saltwater Fishing* which serves salt water anglers who fish in New York Bight waters.

It's not unusual to see Nick and his wife, Shirley, walking down the bluff near their home and cast to feeding stripers and blues.

Years Fly Fishing
Fifty-six

Favorite Rod
5 wt 8' 6" Graphite

Rods Owned
Twenty-five

Favorite Flies
Dry – Royal Coachman
Wet – Paramechenee Belle
Nymph – G.R. Hare's Ear
Streamer – Mickey Finn
Terrestrial – Hopper

Fly Invented
Bass Wulff

Favorite US River
Connetquot (NY)

Home River
Nissequague (NY)

Favorite Stream
Sutton (Ontario)

Home Stream
Nissequague (NY)

1 Cup Boiled Flanked Bass, Free from Skin and Bone
3 Tablespoons Minced Olives
Mayonnaise
1 Cup Finely Minced Celery
1 Head Lettuce
Salt
Paprika
Lemon Juice

Mix the fish, celery, olives and mayonnaise together. Season with salt and lemon juice. Line a salad bowl with leaves of lettuce. Place the salad in the center and dust with paprika.

"Always do your best and never accept anything less."

Karry Karavolos is the President and Chief Executive Officer of Powell & Company. Powell has been manufacturing fly rods since 1910. The plant is located in Rancho Cordova, California.

Karry is the first woman CEO of a fly fishing company and the first Chief Financial Officer of the newly formed (1998) International Women Fly Fishers. She received her undergraduate degree from the University of San Francisco and her MBA from the University of Chicago.

In addition to the two fly rods owned by Karry, she has access to Powell's SSL Series, a moderately fast action fly rod perfect for fishing on still clear streams, the LGA, a fast action fly rod, and the ASX Series, a new ultra fast axcellerator action rod.

Years Fly Fishing
Three Seasons

Favorite Rod
5 wt 9' Graphite

Rods Owned
Two

Favorite Flies
Dry – Stimulator
Wet – Soft Hackle Partridge
Nymph – Pheasant Tail
Streamer – Thunder Creek
Terrestrial – Hopper

Fly Invented
None, yet

Favorite US River
Bitterroot (MT)

Home River
Lower Sacramento (CA)

Favorite Stream
Not Provided

Home Stream
Yellow Creek (CA)

© 2000 - Russell A. Hopper

---

30 Large Pasta Shells
2 Tablespoons Butter
1 Cup Zucchini, Quartered and Sliced
½ Cup Fresh Mushrooms, Sliced
½ Cup Green Onions, Sliced
4 Ounces Fresh Spinach, Washed,
Drained and Chopped
1 ½ Cups Low-fat Cottage Cheese, Drained
1 Cup Cooked Sliced Carrots
1 Cup Cooked Broccoli Florets
¼ Cup Grated Romano Cheese
½ Teaspoon Salt
½ Teaspoon Italian Seasoning
¼ Teaspoon Ground Pepper
1 Cup Pizza Sauce or Tomato Sauce

Cook pasta shells according to package directions. Drain, rinse and place in cold water. Set aside. Meanwhile in a large skillet over medium heat, melt butter. Sauté zucchini, mushrooms and onion in hot butter for 3 minutes. Stir in spinach and cook 1 minute longer. Remove from heat. Stir in cottage cheese, carrots, broccoli, Romano cheese, salt and seasoning. Set aside. Drain pasta shells.

Continued on next page . . .

Preheat oven to 350 degrees. Fill each shell with about 3 tablespoons vegetable cheese mixture. Spread a small amount of pizza sauce in the bottom of a 1 ½ quart rectangular baking dish. Place filled shells in baking dish. Spoon remaining pizza sauce over shells. Bake, uncovered, for 20 - 25 minutes or until hot.

Serve immediately.

"Of the many fly fishing methods, dry fly fishing is the easiest. One does not need to be an expert to hook fish on the dry fly, especially if a good hatch is in progress and fish are not too discriminating."

Randall Kaufmann is one of the leading experts on flies, fly fishing, and fly tying. His innovative and unique tying techniques have helped set the standard for commercial tying operations.

Randall's books include *American Nymph Fly Tying Manual, Tying Dry Flies, Fly Patterns of Umpqua Feather Merchants, Lake Fishing With A Fly* and *Bonefishing With A Fly*.

He is the co-owner of Kaufmann's Streamborn, Inc., a fly fishing mail order house with stores in Portland, Oregon, Seattle and Bellevue, Washington and Kaufmann's Fly Fishing Expeditions, Inc., a world wide travel service.

Excluding company owned rods, Randall owns Scott, Winston and Sage rods mostly in the 4 and 5 piece models for ease in travel.

Randall lives in Portland, Oregon.

Years Fly Fishing
Thirty-five

Favorite Rod
5 wt 9' Graphite

Rods Owned
See Comments

Favorite Flies
Dry – Stimulator
Wet – Timberline Emerger
Nymph – Kaufmann Gold Bead Rubber Leg Stone
Streamer – Kiwi Muddler, B.H. Rabbit Leach, Rubber Leg Woolly Bugger
Terrestrial – Cicada or Beetle

Fly Invented
Kaufmann Stone

Favorite US River
Anywhere in the West

Home River
Deschutes (OR)

Favorite Streams
High Sierras (CA) and New Zealand Wilderness Waters

Randall's favorite food recipe comes from *THYME and the RIVER* by Sharon Van Loan and Pat Lee.

Prepare and bake the crust. Set aside to cool.

CHOCOLATE NUT CRUST

4 Ounces Semisweet Chocolate, Finely Ground
1/3 Cup Finely Ground Walnuts
2 Cups Finely Ground Vanilla Wafers
6 Tablespoons Butter, Melted

Combine the chocolate, nuts, and ground wafers. Stir in the melted butter until well combined. Press onto the sides and bottom of a lightly buttered 10" tart pan. Chill 10 minutes. Bake in a preheated 375-degree oven about 10 minutes. Remove and set on a rack to cool.

Filling provided on next page . . .

CHOCOLATE MOUSSE FILLING

MOUSSE FILLING – CONTINUED

1 10" Tart Pan With Removable Bottom
1 Recipe Chocolate Nut Crust (See Prior Page)
1 Tablespoon Cold Coffee
1 Teaspoon Instant Coffee Powder
1 Teaspoon Vanilla Extract
1 Teaspoon Brandy, Rum or Nut Liqueur
3 Egg Yolks, Room Temperature
3 Ounces Unsweetened Chocolate
3 Ounces Semisweet Chocolate
12 Tablespoons Sugar
6 Tablespoons Water
3 Egg Whites, Room Temperature
Pinch of Cream of Tarter
1/3 Cup Whipping Cream

Prepare and bake the crust. Set aside to cool. Combine the coffee, instant coffee, vanilla, brandy and egg yolks. Set aside.

Chunk up the chocolate and place in the bowl of a food processor. Process until finely ground.

Combine 6 tablespoons sugar and the water in a small saucepan and heat on high, without stirring, until the sugar has dissolved and the mixture starts to boil. Turn on the food processor and very carefully pour the hot sugar syrup through the feed tube. Process until combined.

Scrape down the sides of the work bowl and let set 2 minutes to cool a bit. Then add the coffee-egg yolk mixture and process until smooth. Transfer to a mixing bowl.

Beat the egg whites and cream of tarter until foamy. Gradually add the remaining 6 tablespoons sugar and continue to beat until stiff, shiny peaks form. Stir ¼ of the whites into the chocolate-egg yolk mixture to lighten it. Gently fold in the remaining whites.

Whip the cream until soft peaks form and gently fold into the chocolate. Pour into the prepared crust and chill 4 - 5 hours or overnight.

Serves: 10

"If you're not having fun, it's time to do something else."

Kim Keeley of Victor, Idaho is a fly fishing guide and lead casting instructor for Reel Women Outfitters. She is also a member of the Powell & Company Factory Team and does casting demonstrations at trade shows across the U. S. Her streamer, the TeQueely, offered in the Orvis catalog, was rated a top new fly in 1998 by *Sports Afield* magazine.

When not working, Kim spends her time pursuing fish all over the world.

Years Fly Fishing
Twenty-one
Favorite Rod
7 wt 9' Graphite
Rods Owned
Twelve
Favorite Flies
Dry – Chernobyl Ant
Wet – Gone Right
Nymph – Soft Hackle
Pheasant Tail
Streamer – TeQueely
Terrestrial – Ant
Fly Invented
TeQueely
Favorite US River
Snake (WY)
Home River
Teton (ID)
Favorite Stream
French Creek (WY)
Home Stream
Fox Creek (ID)

Canned Black Beans
Garlic
Onion
Green Pepper
Cumin
Chili Pepper
Cayenne
Salsa
Cheddar Cheese
Sour Cream
Brown Rice
Tortillas
Twizzlers Red Licorice

Sauté garlic, onions and peppers. Add beans, spiced with cumin, chili pepper and cayenne. Wrap beans, rice and cheese in tortilla. Bake at 350 degrees for 20 minutes. Garnish with salsa and sour cream. Eat. Then eat Twizzlers for dessert or as an appetizer if you can't wait for the burritos to cook.

"Fly fishing guides don't have much time to cook, so here's a recipe for when you're on the fly!"
– Kim

"Sharing a pool, swapping a fly, making a new friend—that makes a fishing trip complete."

Dave Klausmeyer is a writer, editor and maker of split-bamboo rods who says his greatest achievement as a fly fisherman was the day he caught a trout on a fly he tied while using a split-bamboo rod he made with his own hands.

Dave lives in Steuben, Maine and is writing a fly tying book about traditional New England streamers. He is the Senior Editor for *American Angler, Fly Tyer* and *Salt Water Fly Fishing* magazines.

A buddy of Dave's once won a moose permit and Dave went along for the adventure. They spent the week prior to the hunt camping, hunting grouse, and calling moose. Located on an area containing several big bulls, Dave's friend shot a 935-pounder on the second day of the moose hunt. He and his friend dined on Moose Steak Tarragon that evening. Dave's friend was well prepared, bringing all the ingredients for the meal along for the hunt. Rather than using an oven, Dave's friend wrapped the steaks in foil and set them next to the fire. *"What a memorable trip,"* says Dave as he reminisces.

Years Fly Fishing
Over Thirty

Favorite Rod
4 wt 8' Bamboo

Rods Owned
Too Many to Count

Favorite Flies
Dry – Wulffs, Elk Hairs and Hendricksons
Wet – Royal Coachman
Nymph – Big Green Drakes
Streamer – Gray Ghost
Terrestrial – Dave's Hopper

Fly Invented
None, yet

Favorite US River
West Branch of the Penobscot (ME)

Home River
Narraguagus (ME)

Favorite Stream
Gravel Lake Stream (ME)

Home Stream
Not Provided

© 2000 - Russell A. Hopper

2 Pounds Moose Steak
2 Tablespoons Bacon Drippings
2 Medium Onions, Peeled and Sliced
½ Cup Flour
1/8 Teaspoon Each of Marjoram, Thyme
and Sweet Basil
1 Teaspoon of Salt
¼ Teaspoon Pepper
1 Can (8 Ounces) Mushrooms
1 Cup Beef Bouillon
½ Cup Tarragon or Red Wine Vinegar

In a heavy skillet, sauté the onions in the bacon drippings until lightly browned. Remove the onions to a separate dish.

Combine the flour, herbs, salt and pepper. Dip the meat into the mixture. Brown the meat in the skillet and drippings. When browned, sprinkle remaining herb flour over the meat. Add undrained mushrooms, onions, bouillon and vinegar.

Cover tightly and bake in a preheated 300-degree oven until tender, 2 or more hours.

Serves: 4 – 6

MALCOLM KNOPP

"An ounce of thought while fly fishing will catch pounds more trout."

Malcolm Knopp is an oil field chemist and an author. He is the co-author of the book *Mayflies: An Angler's Study of Trout Water Ephemeroptera*.

Malcolm's passion has always been fishing. As a young boy, and growing up in London's East End, he fished local ponds for perch, carp and other course fish. He remembers well a tolerant mother that allowed him to prepare stink baits and other formulations for carp in the kitchen sink. It was not until he was nineteen that he tried his hand at fly fishing and was instantly fascinated by the concept of imitating insects with wet and dry flies.

On emigrating to Western Canada in his mid-twenties to seek a job in the oilfields, Malcolm found the wealth of the Rocky Mountain streams and rivers to be full of trout willing to rise to the dry fly and insect life in more abundance and variety than ever imagined. His fishing partners have said that he now spends more time turning over stones and chasing airborne bugs than putting line to water. But they all agree on one thing—his passion has always been fishing.

Today, Malcolm lives with his wife, Sally, and daughter, Kathleen, in Alberta, Canada.

Years Fly Fishing
Thirty-three

Favorite Rod
5 wt 9' 6" Graphite

Rods Owned
Seven

Favorite Flies
Dry – Callibaetis Spinner on Lakes and PMD Cripple for Rivers Wet – PMD Soft Hackle Nymph – Tarcher Green Drake Streamer – A Very Big Woolly Bugger Terrestrial – Black Ant

Fly Invented
None, yet

Favorite US River
Clark Fork (MT)

Home River
Crows Nest (Alberta)

Favorite Stream
River Darenth (England)

Home Stream
Stauffer Creek (Alberta)

STEAMED MUSSELS IN A CROCK

50 Mussels
3 Finely Chopped Shallots
1 Tablespoon Butter
¼ Pint White Wine
¼ Pint Chicken Stock
4 Slices of Leek
1 Carrot, Sliced – 1 Bay Leaf
4 Sprigs Parsley – Lemon Juice
Salt and Freshly Ground Pepper
¼ Pint Double Cream (Optional)

Clean and beard mussels and place in a heavy cast iron saucepan. Add shallots, butter, white wine, chicken stock, leek, carrot, bay leaf and parsley. Cover and boil for 5 minutes or until the mussels are open. Remove from heat.

Season to desired taste with salt, pepper and lemon juice. Add cream, if desired. Bring to a boil again and serve.

This dish may be eaten as cooked or seasoned with a splash of malt vinegar to individual mussels. The dish also serves as an excellent appetizer when served with crusty French bread topped with mounds of butter (dipped into the broth) and followed by sips of a favorite white wine.

Serves: 4

VENISON/BEEF BARBECUE

"When is the last time you did something for the first time?"

Ed Koch is a retired author, guide, instructor, speaker and pioneer small-fly tying innovator. He resides in York Springs, Pennsylvania.

Ed is the author of *Fishing the Midge* and *Terrestrial Fishing*. He co-authored *Basic Fly Tying* with Norm Shires, *Terrestrials* with Harrison Steeves and is a Contributing Author to Art Flick's *Master Fly Tying Guide, Fishing Moments of Truth.*

A fly fisher since the age of six, Ed's first fly rod was a 9-foot, two-piece Heddon costing $3 in the 1940s when his father only made about $15 a week.

Ed has held the Pennsylvania State Record for a brown trout caught on a dry fly at 9-pounds. The Letort trout was caught in 1962. He is a past President of the Brotherhood of the Junglecock and the 1987 recipient of the *Order of the Hat.*

Years Fly Fishing
Fifty-four
Favorite Rod
2 wt 7' 9" Graphite
5' One Piece T/T Bamboo
Rods Owned
Fourteen
Favorite Flies
Dry – Trico
Shenk's No Name Midge
Wet – Not Provided
Nymph – Frank Sawyer's
Pheasant Tail
Streamer – Shenk's Sculpin
Terrestrial – Letort Cricket
Flies Invented
Tan and Olive Shrimp
Favorite US River
Juanita (PA)
Home River
Juanita (PA)
Favorite Stream
Spring Creek (PA)
Home Stream
Yellow Breeches (PA)

© 2000 - Russell A. Hopper

2 Pounds Venison Burger
1 Pound Hamburger
4 ½ Tablespoons Worcestershire Sauce
1 Bottle Chili Sauce
3 Small Onions, Minced
6 Tablespoons Brown Sugar
3 Tablespoons Vinegar
3 Tablespoons Dried Mustard

Brown meat. Add onions and cook until onions are glazed. Add remaining ingredients and simmer about 45 minutes.

Serves: About 6 sandwiches

"Great at camp or just after a long day's fishing." – Ed

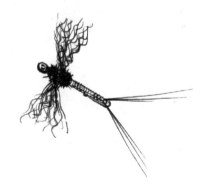

"Common sense ain't all that common."

Lefty Kreh is a legend in the sport of fly fishing. An outdoor writer for more than 40 years he has written for most every major outdoor magazine and currently holds positions with six outdoor magazines. He is Editor-at-Large for *Fly Fishing in Salt Water* and *Fly Fisherman*.

Lefty has fished all fifty states and is the inventor of the famed Lefty's Deceiver fly, which was reproduced and named on a US postage stamp. The Deceiver has been fished worldwide.

Lefty's recent awards include the American Sportfishing Association's *Lifetime Achievement Award* in 1997 and *Fly Rod & Reel* magazine's *Angler of the Year* for 1998.

Some of Lefty's books include *Fly Fishing with Lefty Kreh, Salt Water Fly Fishing, L. L. Bean Guide To Outdoor Photography, Salt Water Fly Patterns,* and *Lefty's Little Library,* a series of individual books, each devoted to a particular area of fly fishing. His newest book is entitled *Presenting the Fly*.

One of Lefty's proudest accomplishments comes from the fact that he has been married to his wife, Evelyn, for more than 50 years. They reside in Hunt Valley, Maryland.

Years Fly Fishing
Fifty

Favorite Rod
8 wt 8' 6" Sage Graphite

Rods Owned
Over One Hundred

Favorite Flies
Dry – Parachute Adams
Wet – Woolly Bugger
Nymph – Hare's Ear
Streamer – Clouser Minnow
Terrestrial – Ant

Fly Invented
Lefty's Deceiver

Favorite US River
Susquehanna (PA)

Home River
Potomac (MD)

Favorite Stream
Hunter (New Zealand)

Home Stream
Gunpowder Falls (MD)

© 2000 - Russell A. Hopper

---

2 Large Cans of Sauerkraut
8 Pork Chops, 1" Thick

Pour sauerkraut in a baking dish. Add about 3 cups of water. Lay pork chops on top of the sauerkraut.

Cook at 350-degrees until pork chops are done.

Serves: 8

Standing only 5 feet, 7 inches tall and weighting 190 pounds, he is known for the length and accuracy of his casting. He can throw a fly line without a rod, using only his hands.

Not only is Lefty a class fisherman, he is a class gentlemen who has given countless hours to helping new fly fishers get started in the sport. He has also contributed greatly to helping people like Bob Clouser, Kathy Beck and others by encouraging them to make their cast into the fly fishing world go just a little further to achieve excellence.

Lefty is a member of the *Fly Fishing Hall of Fame* and is equally famous as a photographer.

FANNY B. KRIEGER

BOUILLABAISSE

"I love the places and the moods where fly fishing takes place."

Fanny Krieger resides in San Francisco, California where in 1983 she co-started the Golden West Women Fly Fishers Club. In 1996, Fanny conceived and chaired the first International Festival of Women Fly Fishers, which brought women from across the globe to connect through a shared interest.

Fanny has been introduced into the *Fly Fishing Hall of Fame*. A tireless traveler who was introduced to fly fishing by her husband, Mel, over forty years ago, Fanny is an advisor to the Damsel Fly catalog, a source for women's outdoor clothing and gear.

Years Fly Fishing
Forty

Favorite Rod
5 wt 9' Graphite

Rods Owned
Three

Favorite Flies
Dry – Humpy
Wet – Not Provided
Nymph – Pheasant Tail
Streamer – Not Provided
Terrestrial – Not Provided

Fly Invented
None, yet

Favorite River
Small Creek in Northern California

Home River
California (CA)

Favorite Stream
Not Provided

Home Stream
Not Provided

1 Stalk Celery, Chopped
1 Medium Onion, Chopped
1 Clove Garlic, Finely Chopped
1 Stalk Leeks, Diced
½ Teaspoon Thyme
½ Bay Leaf
4 Tablespoons Olive Oil
2 Cups Crushed Tomatoes
1 Cup Bottled Clam Juice
1 Cup Dry White Wine
¼ Cup Fennel, Chopped
Pinch of Saffron
2 Tablespoons Parsley, Chopped
1 Small Lobster Cut into Pieces
12 Mussels, Scrubbed and Cleaned
12 Raw Shrimps
12 Scallops
1 Pound Red Snapper or Cod, Cut in Pieces

Sauté celery, onion, garlic, leeks, thyme and bay leaf in olive oil for 5 minutes.

Add tomatoes, clam juice, wine, fennel, saffron and parsley. Simmer 15 minutes.

Add seafood. Cook 15 minutes.

Serves: 6

MEL KRIEGER

CHARCOAL TROUT OVER SAGE

"Fly fishing is man's chance to get back to basics. To sweat. To get lost. To get chased by a bear."

Mel Krieger likes to blame his wife, Fanny, for all his indulgences. When asked to provide his favorite food recipe, he said, *"I expose myself!!! My good wife, Fanny, loves to eat a fresh caught trout—and we've adapted the sage-trout cookery that's been a winner. Honestly, it's rarely used on wild trout as I am a catch and release fanatic!"*

Mel is a world class instructor, having coached Steve Rajeff, the current world fly casting champion and heaver of 300-foot casts. He has also taught many others how to cast through his book, *The Essence of Flycasting*, and his videos, *The Essence of Flycasting Volumes I and II* and *Beginnings*.

The owner of the Mel Krieger School of Fly Fishing & Fly Casting has been recognized for over three decades as the top fly fishing instructor in America. He resides in San Francisco, California.

"Fishing lets the child in me come out." – Mel

Years Fly Fishing
Thirty-five

Favorite Rod
Not Provided

Rods Owned
Not Provided

Favorite Flies
Dry – Not Provided
Wet – Not Provided
Nymph – Not Provided
Streamer – Not Provided
Terrestrial – Not Provided

Fly Invented
The Bunny

Favorite US River
Not Provided

Home River
Not Provided

Favorite Stream
Not Provided

Home Stream
Not Provided

Trout or Other Fish
Sage

Prepare a bed of charcoals as usual. When the coals are ready, place a small supply of freshly picked sage directly over the coals. Let it burn a while. Then place a branch or two of sage over the grill and lay the trout, or any other fish, on it. Turn once. Do not overcook.

The same can be done with chicken or pork.

"The rich get richer!"

Doug Kulick is a maker of multi-piece bamboo fly rods under the name of Kane Klassics. Doug resides in Hayward, California.

Years Fly Fishing
Thirty-six

Favorite Rod
5 wt 9' Graphite
4 wt 3 Piece 7' Bamboo

Rods Owned
Over One Hundred

Favorite Flies
Dry – Muddler Steelhead,
Skated
Wet – Muddler Steelhead,
Covesse Cine
Nymph – B.H. Pheasant Tail
Streamer – Mickey Finn
Terrestrial – Ant

Fly Invented
Skatted Muddler

Favorite US River
McCloud (CA)

Home River
Trinity (CA)

Favorite Stream
Coffee Creek (CA)

Home Stream
Calavarous (CA)

© 2000 - Russell A. Hopper

Any Type Steak

Take any type of steak, barbecue and serve.

"Buy to match the hatch." – Doug

RICK KUSTICH

"Some of life's greatest rewards are reserved for the patient and persistent."

Rick Kustich is based in Grand Island, New York. He is an author, instructor, fly shop owner and the husband of Ann who provided the Rib Tickling Barbecue Ribs recipe.

Rick has authored three books: *Salmon River, New York River Journal; Fly Fishing The Great Lakes Tributarie;* and *Fly Fishing for Great Lakes Steelhead.* He has written numerous magazine articles about fly fishing.

Rick fly fishes approximately 100 times a year and holds an International Game Fish Association Catch & Release Tippet Class Record.

Years Fly Fishing
Twenty-seven
Favorite Rod
7 wt 10' Graphite
Rods Owned
Twenty-five
Favorite Flies
Dry – Thorax Parachute
Wet – Bunny Spey
Nymph – Pheasant Tail
Streamer – Hen Sculpin
Terrestrial – Hopper
Fly Invented
Catnip
Favorite US River
Missouri (MT)
Home River
Niagara (NY)
Favorite Stream
Wiscoy Creek (NY)
Home Stream
Oatka Creek (NY)

RIB TICKLING BARBECUE RIBS

4 Pounds Spareribs, Cut into Pieces
1 Cup Water – 1 Cup Catsup
1 Tablespoon Butter
1 Cup Onions, Finely Chopped
2 Tablespoons Worcestershire Sauce
¼ Teaspoon Salt
¼ Teaspoon Liquid Hot Pepper Seasoning
½ Cup Vinegar
3 Tablespoons Molasses
½ Teaspoon Ground Ginger
¼ Teaspoon Thyme
2 Teaspoons Dry Mustard
1 Teaspoon Paprika

Place ribs in single layer in 2 large baking pans. Pour ½ cup water in each pan. Bake covered in a 350-degree oven for 1 hour. In a large frying pan over medium heat, melt butter and add onions. Cook until soft. Add remaining ingredients, blend well and bring to a boil. Reduce heat and simmer uncovered for 10 minutes.

Remove ribs from the oven. Pour off water and fat. Put the ribs in one pan and add sauce. Return to the oven and bake uncovered for 1 more hour or until the meat is tender. Baste occasionally.

Serves: 4

AL KYTE

SOUR CREAM COFFEECAKE*

"The best fly fisherman is any angler who has worked actively to protect and maintain the trout water that remains."

Al Kyte and his wife, Barbara, reside in Moraga, California. Al is a Professor at the University of California where he has served for over 30 years. He has also taught fly fishing through the University of California Extension, the old Fenwick Fly Fishing Schools and his own fly fishing schools.

Al has been a guide on California's Upper Sacramento River, is the author of *Fly Fishing— Simple to Sophisticated* and several note worthy articles, a member of the Federation of Fly Fishers' Board of Governors for the Certification of Fly Casting Instructors, and serves as the only West Coast fishing advisor to Orvis. He has been a consultant for Orvis fly rod designs since 1993.

The recipe is provided by his wife, Barbara, from a cookbook she co-authored with Katherine Greenberg, *Muffins, Nut Bread and More*, published by Nitty Gritty Cookbooks of San Leandro, California.

Years Fly Fishing
Fifty-three
Favorite Rod
4 wt 9' Graphite
Rods Owned
Over Forty
Favorite Flies
Dry – Horner Deer Hair
Wet – Fay's Peacock Bomber
Nymph – C. K. Perlid Stonefly
Streamer – Kyte's Coho Candy
Terrestrial – Small Beetle
Flies Invented
C. K. Perlid and Coho Candy
Favorite US River
Nushagak (AK)
Home River
Upper Sacramento (CA)
Favorite Stream
Silver Creek (ID)
Home Stream
Butte Creek (CA)

*(*Spiced Sour Cream Coffeecake)*

1 ½ Cups All-purpose Flour
½ Cup Brown Sugar, Firmly Packed
1/3 Cup Granulated Sugar
1 Teaspoon Cinnamon
½ Teaspoon Nutmeg
½ Teaspoon Ground Ginger
½ Cup Vegetable Oil
2 Teaspoons Baking Powder
½ Teaspoon Baking Soda
½ Teaspoon Salt
1 Egg - ½ Cup Sour Cream

Preheat oven to 350-degrees. Stir together flour, sugars and spices. Blend in oil. Set aside ½ cup of this mixture. To the remainder, add baking powder, baking soda, salt, egg and sour cream. Mix well and spread into a greased, floured 8" x 8" x 2" baking pan. Sprinkle reserved mixture over batter. Bake for 30 minutes, or until cake tests done.

Serves: 9

"This recipe is a favorite of Barbara's and mine and is perfect to freeze and have on hand for unexpected guests." – Al

GARY LaFONTAINE

CHILE RELLANOS

"I didn't want to just fish—I wanted to write about fly fishing … and I wanted to seriously study fish … I've been fortunate enough to spend my life doing both of these things."

Gary LaFontaine of Deer Lodge, Montana is a writer, lecturer and publisher. He is the author of 1981's *Fly Fishing Book of the Year, Caddisflies,* 1990's *Fly Fishing Book of the Year, The Dry Fly: New Angles,* and 1993's *Fly Fishing Book of the Year, Trout Flies: Proven Patterns.* Gary's newest book is *Fly Fishing the Mountain Lakes.*

In addition to being President of Greycliff Publishing, which publishes instructive books and videotapes, Gary is a clinical psychologist.

When asked to provide the information included here, Gary replied, *"I travel and speak all winter. I fish all summer. This latest request hit me on the one week I had nothing to do."*

Gary was named *Fly Rod & Reel's Angler of the Year* in 1996. He is a prolific designer of flies, including the Emergent Sparkle Pupa and the Natural Drift Stonefly Nymph.

"Food + Cover + Resting Areas = Trout Heaven." – Gary

Years Fly Fishing
Forty-seven

Favorite Rod
3 wt 8' 9" Graphite

Rods Owned
Twenty-eight

Favorite Flies
Dry – Double Wing
Wet – Diving Caddis
Nymph – B.H. Twist
Streamer – Stub
Wing Bucktail
Terrestrial – Flex-Hopper

Flies Invented
See Comments

Favorite US River
Big Hole (MT)

Home River
Clark Fork of the Columbia (MT)

Favorite Stream
North Fork of the Blackfoot (MT)

Home Stream
Cottonwood Creek (MT)

---

2 (4 Ounce) Cans of Whole Green Chiles
2 ½ Pound Slab of Cheddar Cheese
1 Egg, Beaten
½ Cup Milk
Flour
Salt
Garlic Salt

Stuff chiles with cheese and set aside. Mix egg, milk, flour, salt, and garlic salt into a thick batter. Dip chiles in batter and fry in hot oil until golden brown.

"If at first you don't succeed, then try again: then quit. There's no use being a damned fool about it."

H. Lea Lawrence is a freelance writer who lives in Franklin, Tennessee. He has taken fish on the fly in waters all across North America, as well as in Europe and Africa.

Throughout his lengthy career, Lawrence has been published in more than 50 outdoor, travel, and general interest magazines, and is the author of six books: *Prowling Papa's Waters: A Hemingway Odyssey; The Fly Fisherman's Guide to the Great Smokey Mountains National Park; The Archer's and Bowhunter's Bible; The Small Game and Varmint Hunter's Bible; The Outdoor Photographer's Bible;* and *Natural Wonders of Tennessee, A Guide to Parks, Preserves & Wild Places.*

Years Fly Fishing
Fifty
Favorite Rod
4 wt 7' 6" Graphite
Rods Owned
Eight
Favorite Flies
Dry – Adams
Wet – Gray Hackle Yellow
Nymph – Tellico
Streamer – Woolly Bugger
Terrestrial – Black Ant
Fly Invented
None, yet
Favorite US River
Clarks Fork of the
Yellowstone (MT)
Home River
Hiawassee (TN)
Favorite Stream
Hazel Creek (NC)
Home Stream
Hazel Creek (NC)

Quail
Italian Dressing
Onion Gravy

Marinate whole quail overnight in Italian dressing. Drain quail, then brown in deep fat for no more than 5 minutes. Drain browned birds. Place in a light onion gravy. Then tightly cover a baking dish with foil. Bake at 375 degrees for 1 hour.

Serves: 2 quail per person

"Do not use wine or exotic seasonings, only salt and pepper. Wine makes the quail tough." – Lea

ART LEE

"Jealousy is like taking poison and waiting for the other guy to die."

Art Lee of Roscoe, New York has been described as the most instantly recognizable face in American fly fishing. He is the Editor-at-Large for *Fly Fisherman, Wild Steelhead & Salmon* and *The Atlantic Salmon Journal*.

A three-time winner of the *Orvis Writing Awards for Excellence in the Fields of Outdoor and Conservation Journalism,* Art has written hundreds of articles for national sporting publications.

When asked about his achievements, Art replied, *"That I would say is for others to judge. I have always done my best to give my best."*

Art's 1999 fly fishing books include *The Lore of Fly Fishing* and *On Blue Water,* the latter written in recognition of the Ernest Hemingway Centennial. Other books include *On Tying and Fishing the Riffling Hitch* and *Fishing Dry Flies for Trout on Rivers and Streams.*

Note – "Down went McGintry to the bottom of the sea." – "The line, if not the fly, is irresistible." – Art

Years Fly Fishing
Fifty

Favorite Rod
4 wt 9' Graphite

Rods Owned
Too Many

Favorite Flies
Dry – The Usual
*Wet – The McGintry**
Nymph – Bebe's Boar Hair
Streamer – Black Ghost
Terrestrial – McMurray Ant

Fly Invented
The Stardust

Favorite US River
Beaverkill (NY)

Home River
Beaverkill (NY)

Favorite Stream
Beaverkill (NY)

Home Stream
Beaverkill (NY)

GRAVLAX IN VIKING SAUCE

See Dick Pobst's and Paul Shultz's Recipes for Gravlax

<u>*Art Lee's Viking Sauce*</u>

1 ½ Cup Kraft Mayonnaise Salad Dressing
1 Tablespoons Gulden's Mustard
1 Tablespoon Honey
1 Tablespoon Dill Weed
3 – 4 Shakes Gravy Master for Coloring
Salt and Fresh Pepper to Taste

Mix all ingredients well. Serve thin slices of Gravlax on toast points with sauce in separate bowl for topping.

Gravlax is pressed salmon cured with salt, sugar and dill.

MATT LIBBY

"Fishing for everyone is fishing for no one."

Matt Libby is the owner of the famed Libby Camps in Ashland, Maine. He is the fourth generation of the Libby family to run the camps; the only set up of its kind in the East. His camps are set up with a flyout lodge with 10 outpost cabins and 40 streams and ponds.

Matt says his wife, Ellen, is an outstanding cook and has published a cookbook of her own.

Years Fly Fishing
Thirty-six

Favorite Rod
4 wt 9' Graphite

Rods Owned
Twelve

Favorite Flies
Dry – Goddard Caddis
Wet – Zug Bug
Nymph – Woolly Worm
Streamer – Gray Ghost
Terrestrial – Stimulator

Fly Invented
Riverkeep Special

Favorite US River
Allagash (ME)

Home River
Aroostook (ME)

Favorite Stream
Mooseleuk (ME)

Home Stream
Millinocket (ME)

BANOC BREAD

1 Cup Flour
½ Teaspoons Baking Powder
2 Tablespoons Sugar
Dash of Salt
1/3 Cup Water
Butter

Once streamside, mix all ingredients except butter, adding water slowly. Make 7 patties and cook in a frying pan over low heat in bubbling butter.

"Great to pack for emergency bread. Blackfly or mosquitoes optional as garnish." – Matt

JOHN LINDEN

"I'll bet those big holdover trout are just a little further downstream."

John Linden is a licensed psychologist and is employed by a large medical hospital in Bowling Green, Kentucky where he resides with his wife, Rhonda, and their two children, Callie and Sadie.

The Doctor says he was the 1997 recipient of *The Ole Sycamore Award* for the most flies lost in the same tree on his home stream, Trammel Fork.

John is one of the six founders and President Elect of the Sons of the Cumberland, a Kentucky non-profit fly fishing fellowship that practices catch and release fly fishing.

When not fly fishing, John prepares for 10K racing events.

Years Fly Fishing
Three Seasons

Favorite Rod
5 wt 8' 6" Graphite

Rods Owned
Two

Favorite Flies
Dry – Adams
Wet – Not Provided
Nymph – B.H. Prince
Streamer – C.H. Woolly Bugger
Terrestrial – Todd's
Japanese Beetle

Fly Invented
John's Treeless Rainbow Teaser (Larval Stage)

Favorite US River
Au Sable (MI)

Home River
Cumberland (KY)

Favorite Stream
A Secret

Home Stream
Trammel Fork (KY)

MOM'S RAW CHILI SAUCE

1 Peck Tomatoes, Plus a Few
2 Ribs Celery
12 Medium Onions
1 Quart White Vinegar
3 Red Hot Peppers
2 Green Peppers
1 Teaspoon Black Pepper
1 Teaspoon Ground Cloves
1 Teaspoon Cinnamon
1 Teaspoon Ginger
8 Cups Sugar
1 Cup Salt
8 Pint Jars

Skin tomatoes. Coarsely grind tomatoes, celery and onions. Add 1 cup of salt. Let stand overnight in refrigerator. Next day drain very dry to get the salty water out. Use colander, then sieve if necessary. In separate pan combine other ingredients and boil 5 minutes. Mix with tomatoes. Fill and seal in sterilized jars.

This is an excellent sweet, spicy relish for meat loaf, hamburgers and other meats.

Makes: 8 pints

TIM LINEHAN

"At the end of a long, hard day's fishing, I sleep well."

Tim Linehan lives with his wife and dogs in Yaak, Montana.

Originally from New Hampshire, Tim graduated from the University of New Hampshire in 1984 with a Bachelor of Arts degree/creative writing minor. He's been fly fishing and tying for many years and has been guiding on the Kootenai River since moving to Montana ten years ago.

In 1994, Tim started Linhan Outfitting Company, a fly fishing and upland bird hunting guide service based in the greater Kootenai River area. Linehan Outfitting Company employs six guides throughout the season. In 1995 Tim was selected as the *Montana Guide of the Year*.

Tim writes an outdoor column for the *Western News* newspaper entitled, *A Guide's Point of View*. His articles have appeared in *Fly Fisherman*, *The Retriever Journal*, *The Angler's Journal*, and *The Independent Record* newspaper. Tim is currently the host of Trout Unlimited Television, a Barrett Productions/ESPN2 television show.

For many years, Tim has been making presentation/slide shows for Trout Unlimited chapters, fly shops and trade shows.

Years Fly Fishing
Sixteen
Favorite Rod
4 wt 9' Graphite
Rods Owned
Eight
Favorite Flies
Dry – Sparkle Dun
Wet – Grouse and Green
Nymph – B.H. Prince
Streamer – Zonker
Terrestrial – Joe's Hopper
Fly Invented
None, yet
Favorite US River
Kootenai (MT)
Home River
Kootenai (MT)
Favorite Stream
Yaak (MT)
Home Stream
Yaak (MT)

JOANNE'S GROUSE CHOWDER*

(*Grouse, Wild Rice, Leek & Morel Chowder)

2 Ruffed Grouse or Other Wild Bird
2 Tablespoons Olive Oil – Salt and Pepper
¼ Pound Diced Bacon
2 Leeks, Thinly Sliced
2 Carrots – 2 Celery Ribs, Finely Chopped
6 Cups Chicken Stock
1 Can (14 Ounces) Tomatoes
1 Cup Red Wine – 2 Bay Leaves
1 Teaspoon Each of Rosemary and Fennel Seeds
1 Tablespoon Balsamic Vinegar
1 Tablespoon Butter – Fresh Parsley
½ Cup Wild Rice – ¼ Pound Morels

Remove the grouse breasts from the bone, rub with olive oil, season with salt and pepper, and set aside. Cut the remaining grouse into pieces.

In a stockpot, cook the bacon over medium heat until crisp. Remove bacon and drain on paper towels. Add grouse pieces to pot and cook until lightly browned on all sides. Remove grouse pieces to a plate. Reduce heat to low and add leeks to the pot. Cook until soft, 3 – 4 minutes. Add carrots and celery and cook 3 minutes longer.

Continued on next page . . .

Add chicken stock, tomatoes, wine, bay leaves, rosemary, and fennel. Return grouse pieces and bring to a boil over high heat. Reduce to low and simmer for 45 minutes. Add wild rice and continue to simmer until tender, about 30 minutes.

Melt 1-tablespoon butter over medium heat. Sauté mushrooms until tender, approximately 5 minutes. Remove grouse pieces from stock and pull off meat; discard skin and bones. Return meat to stock. Add balsamic vinegar. Grill or broil reserved grouse breasts to medium rare, about 3 minutes per side. Let sit for 1 – 2 minutes, then slice.

Ladle chowder into bowls. Add sliced breasts to top. Sprinkle bacon and mushrooms over breasts. Top off with fresh minced parsley.

"Why stick a hook into a fish if you don't intend to eat it?"

A. D. Livingston is a professional writer who lives in Wewahitchka, Florida where he cooks, philosophizes, and tinkers with tackle. A. D. has written over 20 books and many magazine articles. He is a Contributing Editor to *Gray's Sporting Journal*, where his *A. D. Livingston Recipe* is featured in each issue.

Some of A. D.'s books include *Cast-Iron Cooking: From Johnnycakes to Blackened Redfish; Venison Cookbook; Poker Strategy and Winning Play; Sausage, Cold Smoking & Salt Curing Meat; Fish, & Game; Luremaking: The Art and Science of Spinnerbaits, Buzzbaits, Jigs, and Other Leadheads;* and *Bass on the Fly.*

A. D.'s Bass on the Fly was dedicated to Dr. Helen N. Livingston, who seems to have forgiven him for losing her 8-pound largemouth at the net some years ago.

Years Fly Fishing
Forty-one
Favorite Rod
8 wt 8' 6" Fiberglass
Rods Owned
Twelve
Favorite Flies
Dry – Not Provided
Wet – Black Gnat
Nymph – Not Provided
Streamer – Unnamed
Terrestrial – Cricket
Fly Invented
Several, but unnamed.
Favorite US River
Chipola (FL)
Home River
Chipola (FL)
Favorite Stream
Judy Creek (AL)
Home Stream
Cypress Creek (FL)

Fish Fillets
Peanut Oil
Stone-ground White Cornmeal
Salt.

Use bass fillets or small trout. Large trout have a muddy taste. Yellow corn meal won't do. Heat peanut oil to 375 degrees in a cast-iron pot. Sprinkle the fish nicely with salt and cornmeal. Fry a few pieces at a time until nicely browned. Do not overcook. Drain fillets on a brown paper bag.

Serve hot with fried cornbread, tomato salad, and French fries or grits.

GARY LOOMIS

"Keep your line tight, but not too tight."

Gary Loomis, founder of G. Loomis, Inc., resides in the Woodland, Washington area.

A native of the northwest, Gary graduated from high school in 1960, served four years in the Navy as a machinist, and spent the next ten years working for a machine shop, manufacturing specialized equipment for lumber mills. However, his passion was to design a better fishing rod, so in 1974, Gary went to work for Lamiglas, where he ran their blank production facility for five years. It was during his initial years at Lamiglas that he pioneered graphite-fishing technology and has since gained a reputation as a leader in the carbon-fiber fishing rod industry.

In 1982, Gary started G.Loomis, Inc., designing and building all of his own production equipment from the ground up.

Having spent literally hundreds of hours fishing local rivers over the past few years, Gary saw a need to put something back into the sport, and has been instrumental in organizing FISH FIRST, a non-profit organization to help restore salmon and steelhead runs in the Lewis River. Their mission statement: *More and better fish in the Lewis River with no politics.*

Years Fly Fishing
Over Thirty
Favorite Rod
7 wt 9' GLX Graphite
Rods Owned
Many
Favorite Flies
Dry – Muddler Minnow
Wet – Woolly Bugger
Nymph – Bead Head
Streamer – Blue Spruce
Terrestrial – Joe's Hopper

Fly Invented
None, yet
Favorite US River
North Fork of the
Lewis (WA)
Home River
North Fork of the
Lewis (WA)
Favorite Stream
Black River (WA)
Home Stream
Cedar Creek (WA)

HALIBUT STROGANOFF

9" x 13" x 2" Baking Dish
Halibut Cut into ½" Steaks
1 Large Onion, Diced
2 Cups Grated Medium Cheddar Cheese
2 Cans Mushrooms, Sliced
2 Cans Cream of Mushroom Soup
1 Can Cream of Chicken Soup
1 Cup Best Foods Mayonnaise or Sour Cream
¼ Teaspoon Curry Powder
Johnny's Seafood Seasoning
Black Pepper
Parsley
Butter or Margarine
Egg Noodles

Place fish in the baking dish. Season liberally with Johnny's Seafood Seasoning and black pepper to taste. Cover the fish with all the diced onion, mushroom and cheese. In a mixing bowl, combine the soups, mayonnaise, curry powder and parsley. Mix well. Dot the fish with butter and pour the soup mixture over the fish. Bake at 350 degrees for approximately 1 hour or until fish flakes.

Serve with your favorite cooked egg noodles.

Serves: 6

IVAN L. MAHONEY

"Fly fishing is not a contest, have fun!"

Ivan Mahoney lives in Essex, Connecticut. He is the author of the book, *Trout Flies & Flowers*. His fishing partner, Veva Crozer, illustrated the book.

Ivan's book is based on the belief that flowers bloom, and insects hatch in a trout stream in the same specific order year after year. With his system, you only need to stop, smell, and most importantly, see the flowers for a moment. Select the fly that matches the natural plant and then enjoy the fishing.

Donna Warner, Editor-in-Chief of *Metropolitan Home* magazine, gave the Sautéed Trout recipe to Ivan. It was inspired many years ago by the chef at Restaurant Leslie in New York.

Years Fly Fishing
Thirty

Favorite Rod
*4 wt 7' Bamboo
by Ron Kuse*

Rods Owned
Fifteen

Favorite Flies
*Dry – Blue Wing Olive # 20
Wet – Kattermann
Nymph – Stenonema
Streamer – Muddler Minnow
Terrestrial – Ant*

Fly Invented
None, yet

Favorite US River
Farmington (CT)

Home River
Connecticut (CT)

Favorite Stream
Beaverkill (NY)

Home Stream
Mianus (CT)

SAUTÉED TROUT WITH BACON

*8 Slices Bacon
Freshly Ground Pepper
4 Cleaned Trout with Head and Tail Left On
(About ¾ to 1 Pound Each)
2 Shallots, Peeled and Sliced
4 Bay Leaves, Fresh if Possible
2 Cups Good, Dry Red Wine*

Fry the bacon slices in a large, heavy skillet. When brown, remove and drain on paper towels. Crumble into ½" pieces and set aside. Pour out and discard all but about 2 tablespoons of the bacon fat.

Pat trout dry with paper towels and pepper to taste. Turn the heat under the skillet to medium high and add the trout. Cook about 5 minutes a side, (the classic fish cooking rule is 10 minutes for every inch of thickness) or until crispy and brown.

Remove trout to warm dinner plates. Add shallots and bay leaves and sauté quickly over medium heat until shallots are transparent. Add red wine, stir to scrape up all the delicious brown bits, and simmer to reduce by half. Pour the sauce over the fish, add crumbled bacon and serve immediately.

Serve with dry red wine.

TRACIE MALER

"To enjoy fishing in the future, we must begin protecting our waters today. Please do your part by supporting the Federation of Fly Fishers."

Tracie Maler is the first woman member of the Federation of Fly Fishers to serve on the national Executive Committee as Vice President of Fund Raising. She resides in Memphis, Tennessee with her husband, Roger.

Tracie's first fish was caught with a rig that her dad made to keep her occupied and consisted of a tree branch, fishing line and a safety pin. She caught a fish and to land the fish she ran to the top of a rocky embankment dragging the fish behind her. *"So much for catch and release!"* says Tracie.

Her husband, Roger, introduced Tracie to fly fishing after they met in 1987. Their weekends are spent fly fishing out the back door of their cabin on the White River in Mountain Home, Arkansas. Vacations are spent stalking the flats for bonefish or traveling out west to trout fish.

In 1996, Tracie was twice voted *Women of the Year,* once by the FFF Southern Council, and again by the Mid-South Fly Fishers.

Tracie is Vice President of Maler Construction. She started fly fishing in 1987.

Years Fly Fishing
Twelve

Favorite Rod
5 wt 9' Graphite

Rods Owned
Four

Favorite Flies
Dry – Caddis
Wet – Red Fox
Squirrel Nymph
Nymph – Red Fox Squirrel
Streamer – Black
Woolly Bugger
Terrestrial – Not Provided

Fly Invented
None, yet

Favorite US River
San Juan (NM)

Home River
White (AR)

Favorite Stream
Crooked Creek (AR)
Gulf Stream (Bonefish)

Home Stream
Crooked Creek (AR)

HASH BROWN CASSEROLE

2 Pound Bag Frozen Diced Hash Browns
1 Can Cream of Chicken Soup
2 Cups Shredded Cheddar Cheese
8 Ounces Sour Cream
½ Cup Onion
½ Stick Melted Butter
Crushed Potato Chips or Corn Flakes

Mix all ingredients together, except for the potato chips or corn flakes. Place in a greased baking pan. Top with potato chips or corn flakes and bake at 350 degrees for 1 hour.

"I love this recipe not only for its flavor, but also its simplicity. When guests come fishing, I'll serve this with dinner and heat the leftovers for a perfect breakfast side dish." – Tracie

"My golden retriever Skipper says it best—the purpose of life is to have fun."

Al Marlowe resides in Evergreen, Colorado. He is a freelance writer, author of *Fly Fishing the Colorado River: An Angler's Guide* and *A Hiking and Camping Guide to the Flat Tops Wilderness*, a photographer and a guide.

Al contributed to the 1999 edition of *Field & Stream's Angling Encyclopedia*, writing the section on Colorado fishing. This is the book that updates A. J. McClane's edition of 1965.

In the past few years, Al has discovered the fun of warm water fly fishing. He says, *"Crappie and bluegill are great sport on a light rod."* He is still looking for a chance to hook a redfish on a fly in the flats off the Texas Gulf Coast.

In addition to streams, Al enjoys fishing high lakes in Colorado, particularly in the Flat Tops Wilderness area. He says it offers the angler lots of fishing in out of the way places.

Al says brook trout are plentiful in Colorado and are best eaten as soon as possible after catching.

Years Fly Fishing
Thirty-six

Favorite Rod
5 wt 8' 6" Graphite

Rods Owned
Six

Favorite Flies
Dry – Humpy with Peacock Herl Underbody
Wet – Clouser Minnow
Nymph – Halfback
Streamer – Woolly Bugger
Terrestrial – Hopper

Fly Invented
None, yet

Favorite US River
Roaring Fork (CO)

Home River
Colorado (CO)

Favorite Stream
Headwaters of the Colorado (CO)

Home Stream
Bear Creek (CO)

8 Brook Trout 6" – 10"
½ Cup Complete Pancake Mix
(Use only Complete Pancake Mix with Dried Milk and Egg)
½ Cup Yellow Cornmeal
Pepper and Salt
Powdered Cayenne
Oregano, Onion Powder, Paprika
Canola Oil

Prepare the fry mix at home and store in a sealed plastic bag. Heat a 10" – 12" iron skillet with canola oil on a stove or campfire. Use enough oil to cover the bottom of the skillet. It should be hot but not so hot as to burn the oil.

While the skillet is heating, put cleaned, but not necessarily skinned, brook trout in a plastic bag. It's best if they are slightly wet so the mix adheres. Add fry mix, close and shake until the fish are well covered.

Cook the fish, turning once, until they are crispy, a golden brown. When the oil is at the right temperature, it will cook without saturating the fish excessively.

Serve with fresh corn on the cob, lightly seasoned and buttered. Then wrapped in foil, and cooked until hot on the coals.

PAUL MARRINER

FRESH SMOKED TROUT

"Atlantic salmon fishing is as much about the whole experience as it is about merely catching fish."

Paul Marriner has angled for Atlantic and Pacific salmon, trout, bass, and other fresh and salt water species in a dozen countries around the world. He is a seven-time member of the Canadian team participating in the World and Commonwealth Fly Fishing Championships and was the Captain of the Canadian team between 1994 and 1996. Paul organized the Commonwealth Fly Fishing Championships in 1993 at Nimpo Lake, British Columbia. He has also made numerous appearances as a lecturer on fly fishing and fly tying.

A member of the Outdoor Writer's Associations of Canada and America, he is the North American Columnist for the Australian magazine *FlyLife*, a Columnist with *Fly Fish America, The Fishing News,* and *The Canadian Fly Fisher*, and a Regional Editor for *Outdoor Canada Magazine* and *Fly Fisherman's Virtual Fly Shop*. Paul has had several hundred articles published. He authored *Atlantic Salmon – A Fly Fishing Primer* that was an Outdoor Writer's award winning book in 1994.

Years Fly Fishing
Thirty-three
Favorite Rod
8 wt 10' Graphite
Rods Owned
Twenty
Favorite Flies
Dry – Klinkhamer Special (Trout) Bomber (Salmon)
Wet – Partridge and Orange (Trout) Miramichi Cosseboom (Salmon)
Nymph – Sawyer's Pheasant Tail
Streamer – Muddler Minnow (Trout) Marabou Muddler (Salmon)
Terrestrial – Black Foam Beetle
Flies Invented
Foam Post Emerger and DB Caddis
Favorite River
Miramichi (Labrador)
Home River
LaHave (Canada)

2 Wild 10" Brook Trout
Apple and Mesquite Chips

Take 2 wild brook trout caught within the past ½ hour, where resource permits.

Hot smoke in a backpackable Swedish Smoker with apple and mesquite chips.

Paul has also written *The Ausable River Journal* and *The Miramichi River Journal*. His latest book, *Modern Atlantic Salmon Flies*, appeared in March of 1999. In 1991 Paul won the *Gregory Clark Award* for outstanding contributions to the art of fly fishing.

According to Paul, his favorite stream is the Cornwallis and his home stream is the Mushamush. Both streams are located in Nova Scotia. Paul resides in Mahone Bay, Canada.

BOB MARRIOTT

"Fly fishing is a fraternity of friends you have yet to meet."

Bob Marriott is the owner of the famed Bob Marriott's Fly Fishing Store based in Fullerton, California. The store provides the largest mail order catalogue in the fly fishing industry and represents what is the world's largest fly fishing only store.

While increasing the size of the store, Bob does find time to sneak away to do some exploratory trips to Southern Venezuela, New Guinea and Siberia. On a Siberia trip he once hooked and landed a 52-inch Taimen. He has fished throughout the U. S., South America, New Zealand, and has been to Christmas Island several times.

Bob continues to commit himself to the improvement of the store and in recent years brought a travel center in house. He or one of his staff visit the locations he represents before sending an individual or group.

Years Fly Fishing
Over Thirty

Favorite Rod
5 wt 9' Graphite

Rods Owned
Twelve

Favorite Flies
Dry – Royal Humpy
Wet – Woolly Bugger
Nymph – G.R. Hare's Ear
Streamer – Lefty's Deceiver
Terrestrial – Black Ant
Bonefish – Tan/White Clouser

Fly Invented
None, yet

Favorite US River
Big Wood (ID)

Home River
Rio Colorado (Costa Rica)

Favorite Bonefish Flat
Christmas Island

Favorite Species
Bonefish

© 2000 - Russell A. Hopper

TURTLE CAKE

1 Box German Chocolate Cake Mix
(Super Moist is OK)
1 Package (14 Ounces) Kraft Caramels
½ Cup Butter, Not Margarine
½ Cup Evaporated Milk
1 Cup Chocolate Chips
1 Cup Coarsely Chopped Pecans

Mix cake according to package directions. Pour ½ of the batter into a greased and floured 9" x 13" pan. Bake at 350 degrees for 10 – 12 minutes.

Meanwhile, melt caramels together in the microwave or double boiler. Add butter and milk, stirring well.

Pour mixture over baked cake. Then sprinkle with chocolate chips and pecans. Pour remaining batter over all, spreading the batter out to the edges. Bake for an additional 20 – 30 minutes at 350 degrees.

Cook cake thoroughly before serving.

CRAIG MARTIN

"When fishing mountain streams, forget about matching the hatch, match the water with a high-floating, high-visibility fly."

Craig Martin is a full-time househusband and a part-time freelance writer. He says his greatest accomplishment is in adapting to total role reversal to create a positive environment for family life that allows plenty of time for hiking, backpacking, and fly fishing.

After growing up in the suburbs of Philadelphia, he fell in love with the West on his first trip beyond the Mississippi in 1975. He has lived in the West since 1980, exploring the mountains and deserts on foot, mountain bike, cross-country skis, or with a fly rod in hand.

Craig's books include the award winning *Fly Fishing in Northern New Mexico; Fly Fishing Southern Colorado: An Angler's Guide; 75 Hikes in New Mexico* and others. He penned *Fly Fishing Southern Colorado* with Tom Knopick and John Flick.

Martin lives in Los Alamos, New Mexico, with his wife, June, and children, Jessica and Alex, with whom he shares his outdoor adventures.

~ 150 ~

Years Fly Fishing
Fifteen

Favorite Rod
5 wt 8' 6" Graphite

Rods Owned
Three

Favorite Flies
Dry – Parachute Brown Wulff
Wet – Partridge and Gray Soft Hackle
Nymph – B.H.G.R.
Hare's Ear
Streamer – Little Brown Trout
Terrestrial – Dave's Hopper

Fly Invented
Rubber-legged Hopper

Favorite US River
Rio Grande (NM)

Home River
Rio Grande (NM)

Favorite Stream
Piedra River (CO)

Home Stream
East Fork of the Jemez (NM)

RIO GRANDE PIZZA

Crust Ingredients
1 ½ Teaspoons Active Dry Yeast
3 Cups Bread Flour
Pinch of Sugar and a Pinch of Salt
3 Tablespoons Olive Oil
2 Teaspoons Dried Mexican Oregano
1 1/8 Cups Warm Water

Topping Ingredients
1 Tablespoon Olive Oil
1 Tablespoon Chilpotle Peppers, Canned in Oil
2 Tablespoons Barbecue Sauce
1 Small Red Onion, Thinly Sliced
2 Chicken Breasts, Grilled and Shredded
3 Ounces Monterey Jack Cheese, Grated
3 Ounces Mozzarella Cheese, Grated
1/8 Ounce Chopped Fresh Cilantro

Place the ingredients for the crust in the order listed in a bread machine. Run the machine through the first kneading cycle. Then place the dough in an oiled bowl and allow to rise for 1 hour.

While the dough is rising, grill the chicken breasts until cooked through, about 6 minutes on a side. Combine Chilpotle peppers and barbecue sauce.

Continued on next page . . .

Preheat the oven to 500 degrees. Work the dough into a 15" pizza pan. Brush olive oil on the dough. Then smear the combined Chilpotle and barbecue sauce on top. Arrange the onion and chicken evenly on the crust. Sprinkle the cheese in layers on top of the chicken.

Bake in the upper third of the oven for 8 – 10 minutes or until the crust is golden brown. Remove the pizza from the oven and garnish with cilantro.

Serve with a Zinfandel or an India Pale Ale.

"All our creations are imperfect and float upon mixed currents. And we become solemn when we encounter smooth water, drifting rings, and a well-wrought fly. Perhaps it (fly-tying) allows the tyer to be a god in his own galaxy of gnats, to clamp a small world in the jaws of a vise." – Fly-Tying Methods

Darrel Martin is a Contributing Editor for *Fly Rod & Reel* magazine, writer and retired teacher living in Tacoma, Washington.

Darrel is the originator of the Dubbing Whirl, a small top-like dubbing twister, the Furler for furled leaders, and other tying items.

Books written by Darrel include *Fly-Tying Method* and *Micropatterns: Tying and Fishing the Small Fly*.

Favorite Rod – *"Depends on the quarry; from 3 to 12, mostly 4 to 6 weight graphites. For research, I have even used gut and horsehair lines."*

Rods Owned – *"Never quite enough is there?"*

Favorite Flies – *"I love all flies."*

Favorite Us Rivers – *"The upper Missouri, the lower Madison, the middle Yellowstone."*

Home River – *"The Yakima (WA)."*

Years Fly Fishing
Over Thirty-five

Favorite Flies
Dry – Changes daily.
Wet – Changes monthly.
Nymph – Changes weekly.
Streamer – Depends on location and quarry.
Terrestrial – Hawthorns, Hoppers and Spiders

Flies Invented
A few micropatterns and terrestrials.

Favorite Rivers
The Upper Zambezi (Zambia, Africa) and the Aqua Boa (Amazon, Brazil)

Favorite Streams
Test and Itchen (UK), Unec (Slovenia), Rocky Ford (WA), Nirihuao (Patagonia, Southern Chile) and Ohre (Czech Republic)

(*ČEVAPČIČI, Pronounced Che-bop-che-chee, A Traditional Yugoslavian, Field-dish for Sportsman)

Equal Parts Ground Beef and Ground Pork (For Moist Čevapčiči, Half of Pork Should be Pork Fat) Salt and Pepper Garlic

Combine ground meats thoroughly. Add salt, pepper and crushed garlic to meat. Mix ingredients and meats thoroughly. Make palm-size balls, about an inch-and-a-half in diameter each.

Place čevapčiči balls on open grill over a hot fire and cook thoroughly. During cooking, most fat will drip off into the fire.

Serve with bread such as fresh rye and drink. With a small, portable grate, cevapcici is easily prepared and cooked in the field.

Serves: Depends on your appetite

"Dober tek (bon appetit)." – Darrel

CRAIG MATHEWS

"Let's give something back to Yellowstone Park and its fishery."

Craig Mathews and his wife, Jackie, live in West Yellowstone, Montana. They are the owners of Blue Ribbon Flies which was founded in 1980.

Craig is also a writer and has written several books on fly fishing, including *Western Fly Fishing Strategies, Fly Patterns of the Yellowstone, Fishing Yellowstone Hatches* and *Yellowstone Fly Fishing Guide*. *Fly Patterns of the Yellowstone* was co-authored by John Juracek (1987) and *Yellowstone Fly Fishing Guide* was co-authored with Clayton Molinero (1997).

Craig's efforts to give something back to Yellowstone Park is reflected in his donation of a portion of the sales of *Yellowstone Fly Fishing* to the Yellowstone Park Foundation. In 1997, Craig and Jackie were awarded the *Yellowstone Park Protection Award* for their efforts.

The former Police Chief of Yellowstone, Montana is a regular contributor and member of the Angler's Club of New York and its bulletin.

Craig has a photograph of the time Nick Lyons hooked his wife on a back cast and she took off running.

~ 153 ~

Years Fly Fishing
Over Forty

Favorite Rod
4 wt 9' Graphite

Rods Owned
Over Twenty

Favorite Flies
Dry – Sparkle Dun – X Caddis
Wet – Partridge and Primrose Soft Hackle
Nymph – Mature Nature Stonefly
Streamer – Fly Fur Rainbow
Terrestrial – Foam Beetle

Flies Invented
Sparkle Dun, X Caddis and Others

Favorite US River
Madison (MT)

Home River
Madison (MT)

Favorite Stream
Firehole, Yellowstone National Park (WY)

CREAMY GROUSE PEQUIN PASTA*

*(*Creamy Blue Grouse Pequin Pasta)*

2 Grouse Breasts, Skin Removed, Boned & Diced
3 Tablespoons Clarified Butter
½ Pound Mushrooms, Sliced
1 Small Jar Pimientos, Chopped
1 Small Can Sliced Black Olives
2 Heaping Tablespoon Minced Garlic
1 Tablespoon Pequin (Crushed Red Pepper)
1/3 Cup Marsala
1 Cup Heavy Cream
1 Pound Linguini
Freshly Grated Parmesan Cheese
Green Onions, Chopped to Top

In an extra large skillet, heat the butter to medium high. Add the grouse and sauté for 2 – 3 minutes. Chicken, pheasant or wild turkey may be substituted for the grouse. Add the mushrooms, pimientos, olives, garlic and pequin. Sauté for 1 – 2 minutes until the mushrooms are tender. Add the Marsala and deglaze the pan. Cook the sauce for 1 minute. Add heavy cream. Stir well and continue cooking for 2 minutes until the sauce thickens.

Serve over linguine. Sprinkle on the Parmesan and green onions.

RICK L. MATTHEWS

"There is nothing better than taking kids fishing and watching the excitement they experience. They are the future keepers of our rivers and streams."

Rick Matthews says his greatest achievement in the fly fishing world was when he caught a 12-pound rainbow on a size 16 nymph he tied. *"No really, it's the truth!"* Rick says.

When not serving as a pharmacist for a large retail store, or fishing places like the Florida Keys or Belize, Rick spends quality time with his son, Sam, and his daughter, Morgan. He was fortunate enough to see his son and daughter when they caught their first fish at age four.

Rick resides in Bowling Green, Kentucky and is one of the six founders of the Sons of the Cumberland, a Kentucky non-profit fly fishing fellowship that practices catch and release fly fishing.

Years Fly Fishing
Ten

Favorite Rod
6 wt 9' Graphite

Rods Owned
Ten

Favorite Flies
Dry – B.W.O. Thorax
Wet – Giant Black Stone
Nymph – B.H. Hare's Ear
Streamer – Olive Yuk Bug
Terrestrial – Dave's Hopper

Fly Invented
None, yet

Favorite US River
Cumberland (KY)

Home River
Cumberland (KY)

Favorite Stream
A Secret

Home Stream
Another Secret

FROG MORE STEW

2 Pounds Shrimp
1 Pound Russet Potatoes
6 – 8 Small Ears of Corn
Old Bay Crab Seasoning
Kielbasa Sausage, Sliced into 7 -½" Pieces

Bring large kettle of water to boil. Add 2 – 3 tablespoons Old Bay Crab Seasoning. Add small russet potatoes with skin on them. Cook potatoes and Kielbasa 20 minutes or until done. Add corn on the cob and cook 5 – 6 minutes. Add shrimp and cook until shrimp shells turn pink. Remove shrimp as they float to the top. After all shrimp is cooked, pour off the water and dump the potatoes and corn on spread out newspapers.

Serves: 4

"It's somewhat messy, but a great dish!" – Rick

"I saw a man today with no smile, so I gave him one."

Todd Matthews resides in Bowling Green, Kentucky where he is employed as the Manager in an engineering department for a large multi-national corporation. He is the founder and owner of Last Cast Anglers, Inc. and serves as a fly fishing guide.

Todd is one of the six founders of the Sons of the Cumberland, a Kentucky non-profit fly fishing fellowship that practices catch and release fly fishing. He is past President of the fellowship, having served two terms. He won the *Cumberland River's First Annual One-Fly Event* in 1997.

Todd is active in the men's movement and travels around the country participating in men's workshops. However, he spends most of his off-the-water time with friends building his cabin, using bare hands and salvaged materials.

Todd attributes his interest in the waters to his grandfather who took him fishing at the tender age of six.

Todd's second favorite quote is, *"Get the net!"*

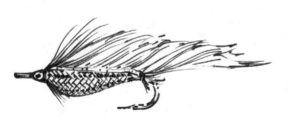

Years Fly Fishing
Seven Seasons

Favorite Rod
5 wt 9' Graphite

Rods Owned
Three

Favorite Flies
Dry – Dark Hendrickson
Wet – Blue Winged Olive
Nymph – Stonefly
Streamer – Woolly Bugger
Terrestrial – Japanese Beetle

Fly Invented
Little Leila

Favorite US River
Cumberland (KY)

Home River
Cumberland (KY)

Favorite Stream
Renox Creek (KY)

Home Stream
Whetstone (KY)

© 2000 - Russell A. Hopper

1 Boneless Chicken Breast
5 Small Potatoes
1 Ear Corn
1 Handful of Mushrooms
1 Handful of Baby Carrots
1 Yellow Onion, Cut into ¼ Slices
3 Cloves of Garlic, More if You Like
1 Can (16 Ounces) Stewed Tomatoes
¼ Cup Worcestershire Sauce
Salt and Pepper

Tear off approximately 2 feet of heavy-duty aluminum foil and place on flat surface. Slice chicken breast and place on foil. Add all vegetables. Fold all four ends of the foil to form a bowl. Add canned tomatoes, salt, pepper and Worcestershire Sauce. Wrap foil tightly at the top, and then roll up the ends.

Dinner can be placed in an open fire and will be ready in approximately 1 hour, or in an oven on 350 degrees for 1 hour.

Preparation is easier if done at home before going on a fishing trip.

Serves: 1

"It's not the destination that counts, it's the journey."

Gerry McDaniel is the developer of a unique map of Kentucky's premier trout fishery, *The Lower Cumberland River*. The map provides all the information needed for someone who has never been taken there before.

Gerry received quite a compliment when the Army Corps of Engineers ordered 4 of his books and said that it was the best reference material on the Cumberland River.

As a young boy with 2 brothers and a sister, Gerry was handed a fishing rod by his dad who wanted his son to keep busy and find something that he would enjoy. He began fishing in grade school and hasn't stopped since.

When not working as an upholsterer in Louisville, Kentucky, Gerry can be found guiding others on his beloved Cumberland River.

In 1999 Gerry caught a 42 ½-pound striper using his self-styled Mylar minnow. The Cumberland River (KY) catch earned him the fresh water 12-pound tippet line class fly rod world record for landlocked striped bass.

Gerry has provided his secret, but never before published Kentucky famous lasagna recipe.

Years Fly Fishing
Forty-one
Favorite Rod
8 wt 9' Graphite
Rods Owned
Twelve
Favorite Flies
Dry – Coachman Trude
Wet – White Woolly Bugger
Nymph – Stonefly
Streamer – White
Mylar Minnow
Terrestrial – Dave's Hopper
Fly Invented
Mac's X
Favorite US River
Yellowstone (MT)
Home River
Lower Cumberland (KY)
Favorite Stream
Soda Butte (MT)
Home Stream
Lower Cumberland (KY)

Hamburger
Italian Sausage
Minced Garlic
Onion, Freeze Dried
Tomato Paste
Water
Salt and Pepper
Pinch of Sugar
Tomatoes, Diced
Sage
Pasta Noodles
Ricotta and Mozzarella Cheese

Brown the hamburger, Italian sausage, garlic and onion in a skillet. Add the tomato paste and water. Add salt, pepper, sugar, diced tomatoes and a lot of sage. Simmer while cooking the pasta noodles.

Cook the pasta noodles until all the water is absorbed.

When the pasta is ready, layer the pasta, meat sauce and cheeses in a baking dish.

Top with a lot of Mozzarella and brown in the oven.

Serves: 6 – 8 or Gerry, if he's hungry

THOMAS McGUANE

"People are no damn good."

Tom McGuane is a writer who has been described as one of the finest American novelists of his generation and a national treasure. Tom resides in McLeod, Montana.

Fly fishing plays a supporting role in a number of his books, from *Ninety-Two in the Shade* set in 1960s Key West, to the contemporary Montana of *Nothing But Blue Skies*. His *Live Water* is a collection of fly fishing essays by the acclaimed novelist, screenwriter and fly fishing addict.

When asked about his greatest achievements, Tom says, *"I dress myself every morning. While no innovation, it is an achievement."*

Tom's photograph was featured on the September 1998 cover of *Fly Fisherman* magazine. The photograph captured Tom with a 25-pound sea-run brown trout caught on a Bomber dry fly in March 1998. It is the largest fish ever caught on a Bomber on the Rio Grande. Val Atkinson captured the moment on film.

"Angling is extremely time consuming. That's sort of the whole point." – Tom

Years Fly Fishing
Fifty-one

Favorite Rod
6 wt 9' Graphite

Rods Owned
Twenty

Favorite Flies
Dry – Adams
Wet – Grouse and Orange
Nymph – Prince
Streamer – Spruce Fly
Terrestrial – Joe's Hopper

Fly Invented
None, yet

Favorite US River
Yellowstone (MT)

Home River
Yellowstone (MT)

Favorite Stream
Rock Creek (MT)

Home Stream
Big Creek (MT)

MANGO TOMATILLO PESCADOR*

(*Mango Tomatillo Pescador Salsa)

1 Red Bell Pepper
1 Green Bell Pepper
1 Purple Onion
3 Mangoes
4 Tomatillos
1 Large Jalapeno
2 Tablespoons Cumin
½ Cup Pineapple Juice
½ Cup Cilantro
2 Cloves Garlic
3 Limes
¼ Cup Light Apple Vinegar

Slice 3 mangoes. Chop 1 purple onion, 4 tomatillos, 1 red bell pepper and 1 green bell pepper. Mash and chop 2 cloves of garlic. Slice 1 large Jalapeno finely. Add ½ cup pineapple juice. Add ¼ cup light apple vinegar. Squeeze 3 limes. Add 2 tablespoons cumin and ½ cup of cilantro. Stir well and refrigerate for 1-hour minimum.

"This salsa is great on chips, but is also terrific on fish!" – Tom

ANN McINTOSH

EYRE HALL CLAM CASSEROLE

"Whatever you do, do not park on or beside posted or private property."

Ann McIntosh is a freelance writer and fundraiser who resides in Monkton, Maryland. She is the inventor and author of *The Budget Angler* column in *Trout* magazine. Her book, *Mid-Atlantic Budget Angler*, is a guide to the best trout streams in Pennsylvania, New Jersey, Delaware, Maryland, Virginia, and West Virginia.

Years Fly Fishing
Twenty-one
Favorite Rod
5/6 wt 8' 6" Graphite
Rods Owned
Six
Favorite Flies
Dry – Patriot
Wet – Not Provided
Nymph – Green Weenie
Streamer – Not Provided
Terrestrial – Madame X

Fly Invented
None, yet
Favorite US River
South Fork of the Snake (ID)
Home River
Gunpowder (MD)
Favorite Stream
Spruce Creek (PA)
Home Stream
Western (MD)

© 2000 - Russell A. Hopper

5 Pounds Clams
Clam Juice, Bottled
Worcestershire Sauce
Butter
Pepper
Breadcrumbs

Open and grind clams until they are minced. Add 1 bottle of clam juice. Pepper to taste. Add 1 – 2 sticks of butter. Bake for about 1 hour. Add breadcrumbs to top after the clams have cooked down. Use Worcestershire Sauce as desired.

PATRICK F. MCMANUS

DEEP-FRIED TROUT

"The best time to fish is when it's raining and when it ain't." – R. Crabtree

Patrick McManus is a writer living in Spokane, Washington. He has written for newspapers and television stations. Pat is the current Editor-at-Large for *Outdoor Life* magazine and provides the *Last Laugh* column for the magazine where he often comments on his 45-plus year marriage to his wife, Darlene, referred to as Bun.

Pat has committed himself to writing for two hours each day. His first humor piece came back twice but was then picked up by *Field & Stream* magazine in 1968. Since then his works have appeared in *TV Guide, Sports Illustrated, Reader's Digest, The Saturday Evening Post* and other magazines.

Some of Pat's books include *Into the Twilight, Endlessly Grousing, How I Got This Way, They Shoot Canoes, Don't They?*, and *Never Sniff a Gift Fish*. He has had 13 books published.

Years Fly Fishing
Fifty-one

Favorite Rod
5 wt 9' Graphite

Rods Owned
Fifteen

Favorite Flies
Dry – Irresistible
Wet – B.H. Prince
Nymph – Bitch Creek
Streamer – Woolly Bugger
Terrestrial – Fur Ant

Fly Invented
None, yet

Favorite US River
Clark Fork (MT)

Home River
Clark Fork (MT)

Favorite Stream
Sand Creek (ID)

Home Stream
Sand Creek (ID)

12 Medium Trout
2 Eggs
4 Tablespoons Water
Cracker Crumbs, Finely Crushed
Flour Seasoned with Salt, Pepper and a
Touch of Onion and Garlic Powder
Vegetable Shortening or Salad Oil for Frying

Clean, scale and chill the trout. Leave whole unless they are over 9" in length. Otherwise, split lengthwise. Drain well. Beat the eggs with water. Roll the trout in the seasoned flour. Then dip in the egg/water mixture and roll in cracker crumbs.

Heat 3" of shortening or oil to 375 degrees and fry fish until they are golden brown and the flesh flakes easily.

Serves: 6

"This recipe was taken from 'Whatchagot Stew' by me and my sister, Patricia." – Pat

"I don't use light tippet, since the strikes are so fierce."

Ken Medling is a wrestling coach, biology teacher, outdoor writer, columnist, photographer and, along with Mark Williams, the co-owner of River Maps Company. His pictures and articles are published in various fly fishing magazines.

Ken lives in Amarillo, Texas and writes a monthly fly fishing column in *The Amarillo Globe News*. He is also the co-author of *Flyfishing Northeastern New Mexico*.

One of Ken's fly inventions, the Fred, is an Adams type fly with grizzly and brown hackle, gray muskrat body and golden pheasant tail.

Another favorite quote of Kenny's is, *"Hey, I finally got it right."*

Years Fly Fishing
Seventeen
Favorite Rod
5 wt 9' Graphite or 7' Diamondback on Small Streams
Rods Owned
Six
Favorite Flies
Dry – Stimulator
Wet – Not Provided
Nymph – Pheasant Tail
Streamer – Muddler Minnow
Terrestrial – Not Provided
Fly Invented
The Fred
Favorite US Rivers
Gallatin (MT) and Big Blue (CO)
Home River
Big Blue (CO)
Favorite Stream
Soldier Creek (CO)
Home Stream
Soldier Creek (CO)

2" Steak
Onions

Grill as many onions as you think that you can handle. Turn up the grill until it is roaring. Take your 2" steak, go outside and show it to the fire. Take it back in, put the steak on the bed of onions, and enjoy.

Serves: 1

"You can cook your steak to your own specifications, but I like mine to moo when I cut into it." – Ken

"Fly Fishing is a great outdoor sport for anyone at any age."

Maggie Merriman started the first women's fly fishing schools in the western U.S. in the 1970s. And in the early 80s designed and manufactured the first women's fly fishing vest. She was one of the first to have a product clothing and accessory line under her own label.

Maggie is based in West Yellowstone, Montana but is known throughout the world. She was invited as a special guest to the Chatsworth Angling Fair on the Duke of Devonshire's estate in Chatsworth, England where she represented the U. S. and female anglers at the Fair in 1998.

The recipient of many awards, Maggie received the Federation of Fly Fishers' 1995 *Woman of the Year Award*. She has also received the Federation's *President's Pin* and the *Lew Jewett Award*.

In addition to her fly fishing and instructors schools, Maggie gives slide shows, casting demonstrations and special seminars to clubs, conclaves and organizations. A member of the Outdoor Writers Association of America, Maggie has written numerous columns and articles in her career.

Years Fly Fishing
Fifty-three

Favorite Rod
4 wt 9' Graphite

Rods Owned
Too Many

Favorite Flies
Dry – Elk Hair Caddis
Wet – Soft Hackle
Nymph – Prince
Streamer – Woolly Bugger
Terrestrial – Hopper or Ant

Fly Invented
None, yet

Favorite US River
Yellowstone (MT)

Home River
Madison (MT)

Favorite Stream
Spring Creeks (MT)

Home Streams
Madison (MT), Firehole (WY)
and Henry's Fork (ID)

"I'm not a fancy cook ... so, I really don't have a great recipe. But, I love to visit the local Dairy Queen for a Hot Fudge Sunday ... particularly after a great day of fly fishing.

"Follow the signs to your closest Dairy Queen or Baskin-Robbins." – Maggie

"Anyone can make a living as a writer—just don't spend more than you make."

Deke Meyer has been a full time writer since 1982, with 11 books and numerous fly fishing articles published. His newest books (1999) are *Flyfishing Inflatables* and *Hot Bass Flies and Tactics*. Deke actually makes a living as a writer. He resides in Monmouth, Oregon.

Deke tied his first flies from a kit at the age of 13. His fly inventions include the Keel Sneaker, Gold Bead Rubber Legs, Keel Shrimp, Extended Body and Keel Flats Shrimp, Extended Body.

Favorite Rod – *"For graphite, it varies with the type of fish I'm trying to catch, how far I have to cast to catch them, and how big, heavy or wind-resistant the fly, and whether I'm traveling by plane. I also love to use well-tapered cane."*

Favorite Flies – *"Because I fish year-round and for a variety of fish under tremendously varying conditions, it boils down to the moment I pull that fly out of the fish's mouth—I love that particular fly at that particular moment. I would also add that presentation is most often more crucial than fly pattern."*

Years Fly Fishing
Thirty-five
Favorite Rod
See Comments
Rods Owned
Fifteen graphite and some cane.
Favorite Flies
See Comments
Flies Invented
See Comments
Favorite US River
Fly fishermen are an extremely fickle lot, and I'm no exception-if I'm on a river catching fish-that's my favorite, and I'm glad I don't have to fish just one.
Home River
Siletz (Or)
Favorite Stream
Brushy, un-navigable, fish-poor coastal streams, some with names, that offer minimal catching, but prime solitude.

© 2000 - Russell A. Hopper

HIGHWAY STEW

1 Can Pork n' Beans
Hamburger
Ketchup
Black Pepper

In a 10-inch well-seasoned, black, cast iron frying pan, fry hamburger until cooked. Pour off most of the grease. Add beans; stir until beans are heated. Add ketchup and pepper to taste, eat.

"As an apprentice writer, I often had more ambition than cash or cooking skills, so I made do with quick, cheap, easy and filling. I still don't care much about food, but find that it is a necessity. I get a lot more excited about bamboo rods or a good hatch.

"It isn't what you eat that counts—it's what the fish are eating, and can you present a fly that they want." – Deke

Home Stream – *"It keeps me forever humble to admit that the closest flowing water to me is Ash Creek, which supports little but a run of spawning bottlenose suckers in January. However, they are native. I've caught them on worms, but not flies."*

MIKE MICHALAK

VODKA SORBET

"Thank goodness people can't figure out the difference between what they want and need."

Mike Michalak is the owner of The Fly Shop based in Redding, California. He says he is proudest of being a good dad, husband and son. Then comes his business, which he built from scratch and bootstrapped with $1,250 into one of the largest businesses of its kind.

Mike says his business philosophy has been simple; *"Surround myself with talented people, good ideas and products, treat people well, and good things will happen."* He sends out over one-half million, hundred plus page four-color catalogs each year.

Mike's early mentor, Dan Blanton, helped him add distance to his casting.

Years Fly Fishing
Twenty-nine
Favorite Rod
5 wt 9' Graphite
Rods Owned
The Store
Favorite Flies
Dry – Elk Hair Caddis
Wet – 2 Wing
Nymph – A. P.
(Andre' Puyan)
Streamer – Clouser Minnow
Terrestrial – Whit Hopper
Fly Invented
Illamna Pinky
Favorite US River
Sacramento (CA)
Home River
Sacramento (CA)
Favorite Stream
El Gato (Chile)
Home Stream
Hat Creek (CA)

© 2000 - Russell A. Hopper

Lemon or Lime Sorbet
Absolut Citron Vodka

Put a generous scoop of lemon sorbet (frozen hard) in a margarita glass with a double shot of Absolut Citron Vodka. Marinate (also out of freezer). Garnish with lemon or lime slices.
Seconds are recommended.

"Anyone that know me knows I don't cook well, I eat well." – Mike

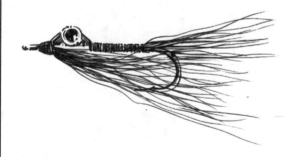

"Trout are too beautiful to kill. Please pinch barbs and release."

Jack Miller's nickname is One Weight Jack as he fishes with an Orvis one weight rod. Jack resides in Nashville, Tennessee. He is retired, but an active member of the Middle Tennessee Fly Fishers. Jack also supports Trout Unlimited.

Jack was born in Carlisle, Pennsylvania and walked to the famed LeTort to fish as a teenager in the late 1940s. He fishes about 70 days a year.

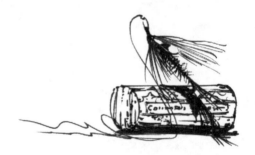

Years Fly Fishing
Fifty-two
Favorite Rod
1 wt 7' 6" Graphite
Rods Owned
Six
Favorite Flies
Dry – Pale Morning Dun
Wet – B.H. Pheasant Tail with Partridge Hackle in Silver
Nymph – Brown Bomber Soft Hackle
Streamer – Olive and Black Woolly Bugger with Eyes
Terrestrial – Hopper
Favorite US Rivers
Bighorn (MT) and San Juan (NM)
Home River
Caney Fork (TN)
Favorite Stream
Yellow Breeches (PA)
Home Stream
Mountain Creek (TN)

1 Pound Hamburger Meat
2 Cans Campbell's Vegetable Soup
Instant Rice

Fry hamburger as small meat balls until done. Mix in 2 cans of Campbell's Vegetable Soup until warm. Then add minute rice. Stir all ingredients together in a skillet until warm.

Serves: 6

ANNA MINICUCCI

BREAM ENSALADA

"If fly fishing is heaven, I've arrived."

A panelist at the first International Festival of Women Fly Fishers, Anna Minicucci lives in Providence, Rhode Island where she lectures, illustrates, cartoons, and writes on such diverse subjects as fishing, canoeing, shooting sports, theater, books, art, movies, outdoor photography, politics, and other subjects.

Anna has received numerous awards including the 1987 New England Outdoor Writers Association's *Sportsman of the Year Award*, the 1990 Rhode Island Hunting and Fishing Association's *Sportsperson of the Year Award*, and the 1998 Rhode Island Federated Sportsmen's Clubs, Inc.'s *Outdoor Sports Writer of the Year Award*.

She was the first Editor/Originator of *The Long Cast*, Trout Unlimited's Narragansett Chapter newsletter, is the first woman outdoor weekly Rhode Island Columnist and, in 1994, organized the Ladies of the Long Rod fly fishing group.

In 1996, Anna designed/created the original copyrighted art work entitled *Lady Fly Fisher Pine*.

Anna is a 1998 International Women Fly Fishers Board Member and the Editor for the IWFF Newsletter.

Years Fly Fishing
Twenty-three

Favorite Rod
*3 wt 8' 6" Graphite and 7' 6"
3 ½ Ounce Bamboo*

Rods Owned
Eighteen

Favorite Flies
*Dry – Comparadun
Wet – Professor
Nymph – Hare's Ear
Streamer – Matuku
Terrestrial – Jassids*

Fly Invented
David's Real Hair Nymph

Favorite US River
Yellow Breeches (PA)

Home River
Pawcatuck (RI)

Favorite Stream
Chickasheen Brook (RI)

Home Stream
Roaring Brook (RI)

*Several Poached Bream Filets
¼ Cup Extra Virgin Olive Oil
Cayenne Pepper to Taste
Cracked Pepper to Taste
Salt to Taste
Chopped Fresh Basil
½ Cup Diced Celery
¼ Teaspoon Lemon Juice
Chopped Black Olives
1 Clove Garlic, Crushed*

Poach filets. Flake when done and mix in other ingredients. Chill in refrigerator overnight, or for several hours.

Serve on a bed of lettuce of choice, or in combination with fresh spinach and watercress, with garlic bread.

Serves: 4

M. R. Montgomery

"Wild fish grow poorly in frying pans."

M. R. Montgomery, known to the various government record keepers as Maurice R. Montgomery Jr., and to all his acquaintances as Monty, describes himself as a newspaper man. He has been a journalist with *The Boston Globe* since 1971 and is the author of six books including *Way of the Trout* and *Many Rivers to Cross*. Monty resides in Lincoln, Massachusetts.

Monty was born in eastern Montana in 1938, raised partly in California, and now lives near Boston for reasons that he cannot quite explain. Over the past twenty-five years he has written on every subject except politics, a clean record he hopes to maintain until retirement. Other than fishing and a bit of gunning, he has no obsessive hobbies, although he has been know to plant the occasional tomato and a manageable number of antique rose varieties, these for the pleasure of his wife, Florence. He maintains small areas of both tallgrass and short-grass prairie in his yard that have attracted one moose, a coyote, and a few white-tailed deer. He has high if unrealistic hopes for a buffalo (*Bison bison*) someday.

Years Fly Fishing
Fifty

Favorite Rod
6 wt 9' Graphite

Rods Owned
Four

Favorite Flies
Dry – Bomber
Wet – Soft Hackles
Nymph – Breadcrust
or Prince
Streamer – Bitch Creek
Terrestrial – Dave's Hopper

Fly Invented
None, yet

Favorite US River
Madison-in-the-Park (MT)

Home River
Not Provided

Favorite Stream
Fish Creek (WY)

Home Stream
East Fork of the
Bitterroot (MT)

Fried Stocked Trout

Hapless, Very Fresh, Hatchery-fattened,
Domesticated Rainbow Trout, Less than 8 Hours
Out of the Stream
Butter
Salt
Black Pepper
1 Cup Flour

Shake 1-cup flour, 1 tablespoons each of salt and ground black pepper in six-pack brown paper bag. Gut trout. Cut out gills. Put thumb in trout's mouth, bend back head, break off head and pull skin off trout. Shake nude trout in flour. Fry very slowly with low heat in real butter.

Serves: 2 trout per manly appetite

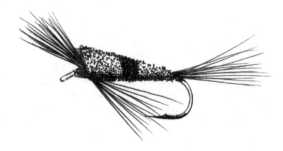

WINSTON MOORE

"Every fish landed should be released."

Winston Moore is a real estate developer residing out of Boise, Idaho. He is most famous in the fly fishing world for having caught over 138 Pacific sailfish on flies. He developed his famous Billfish Fly in the 1970s.

In addition to the 138 billfish, Winston has taken 6 marlin, over 6,000 bonefish, 95 permit, plus 230 tarpon, all on flies. He now fishes exclusviely for permit.

Winston once caught a 450-pound black marlin, which jumped more than 70 times before he finally brought it boat-side one-and-a-half hours later. When the marlin regained its strength, Moore fought it for another four hours before intentionally breaking the fish off.

In 1986, in Belize, Winston fought and brought to the boat a tarpon estimated by measurement formula at 212 pounds. He fought the fish for 6 hours and 10 minutes. It was hooked at 6:30 a.m. and brought to the boat at 12:40 p.m.

Years Fly Fishing
Over Sixty

Favorite Rod
10 wt 9' Graphite

Rods Owned
Thirty-one

Favorite Flies
Dry – Female Adams
Wet – Duck Tail Stayner
Nymph – Not Provided
Streamer – Integration
Terrestrial – Not Provided

Fly Invented
The Billfish Fly

Favorite US River
South Fork of the Boise (ID)

Home River
Don't claim one.

Favorite Stream
Cottonwood Creek (ID)

Home Stream
Won't tell.

COUNTRY HAM BALLS

2 Pounds Ground Country Ham, Cooked
1 Pound Breakfast Pork Sausage
2 Cups Breadcrumbs
3 Eggs

Sauce
2 Cups Brown Sugar
2 Cups Vinegar
1 Cup Water
2 Teaspoons Dry Mustard

Mix ingredients well and chill. Roll into bite-sized balls. Place in a shallow baking pan. Cover with sauce and bake in a 350-degree oven for 1 hour or until the balls are firm.

To make the sauce, mix ingredients in a small saucepan and bring to a boil. Use to cover baking ham balls.

Serves: Makes 4 – 5 dozen ham balls, depending on what size your roll them.

The author of this book, Russell A. Hopper, provides this recipe. *"I eat a lot, but don't cook."* – Winston

SKIP MORRIS

NOODLES WHATEVER

"Talent is no rarity—nearly everyone has it in several areas. I am lucky to have found something (fly fishing instruction) that works in harmony with my own particular talents."

Skip Morris is an author, speaker, instructor, professional fly tyer, and musician. He says that he has tried to advance closed-cell foam as a tying material and combine clear concise well-crafted prose and instruction with crisp, illustrative photography and art (and a dose of entertainment) in his books. Skips says a few folks even feel that he's succeeded.

The author of seven books and writer of four magazine columns lives in Port Ludlow, Washington. Some of his books include *Tying Foam Flies*, *The Art of Tying the Dry Fly*, *Concise Handbook of Fly Tying*, *The Custom Graphite Fly Rod*, *Fly Tying Made Clear and Simple*, and *The Art of Tying the Nymph*. He has also produced several videos including *The Art of Tying the Nymph*.

Skip tied his first fly at the age of 10 and was a professional fly tyer by the age of 13. Many of his flies are now in a collection at the William Cushner Fly Museum.

Skip plays jazz guitar one or two nights a week.

Years Fly Fishing
Thirty-six

Favorite Rod
6 wt 8' 8" Graphite

Rods Owned
Over Twenty-five

Favorite Flies
Dry – Morris Foam Stone
Wet – Not Provided
Nymph – Skip Nymph
Streamer – Clouser Minnow
Terrestrial – Ant Carol

Flies Invented
The Skip Nymph is my signature fly. Others include the Morrisfoam Stone, Skip's Dad, Skip's Furry Dragon, and Skip's Iced Chironomid.

Favorite Waters
I tried, but I just can't pick favorites.

© 2000 - Russell A. Hopper

Noodles of any Kind
Parmesan Cheese, Grated or Shredded
Ground Meat of any Kind
Butter or Margarine
Salt

As you are boiling the noodles, cook and crumble the ground meat. Drain the cooked noodles. Sprinkle them with the meat. Add a little butter and stir it all until the butter melts. Sprinkle Parmesan over the top. Add salt to taste.

"Any noodles—spaghetti, fettuccini, macaroni ... Any ground meat—lamb, beef, turkey ... Season the meat any way you wish. Vegetables on the side are a great compliment, or just cook them and mix them in. My wife, Carol, adds pepper to the finished dish. We eat this at least once a week, because we both really like it (and because I do most of the cooking)." – Skip

Serves: The hungry, but not fussy

"Don't catch a good fish. Catch an excellent fish."

Laurie Morrow is an outdoor writer and author of six books, including *The Woman Angler* and *Corey Ford Trout Tales*. She has been a contributor to magazines such as *Field & Stream, Petersen's Shotguns, Shooting Sportsman* and *The Gun Journal*, among others. She is Volvo's adventure travel journalist and writes a monthly magazine for the Volvo website. Mrs. Morrow is currently writing a five-book series on fishing and wingshooting destination travel for Orvis, called *The Orvis Sporting Travel Guides*. She resides in Freedom, New Hampshire.

Years Fly Fishing
Six

Favorite Rod
6 wt 8' 6" Orvis Power Matrix

Rods Owned
Not Provided

Favorite Flies
Dry – Black Gnat
Wet – G.R. Hare's Ear
Nymph – B.H. Olive Caddis
Larva
Streamer – Woolly Bugger
Salmon Fly – Cosseboom

Fly Invented
None, yet

Favorite River
Miramichi (Labrador)

Home River
Ossipee (NH)

Favorite Stream
Itchen (England)

Home Stream
Pine (NH)

© 2000 - Russell A. Hopper

The secret to fine cuisine—as any connoisseur of cooking will tell you—is the ingredients. The fresher the better, and that means fresh—picked, ripe-off-the-tree or just harvested from the farm. Frozen, canned, processed and additives—especially additives—are dirty words in the *Language of Food*. Why, commit any of these atrocities against food in France and you may very well run the risk of being guillotined. At the very least, you'd be run out of the country.

The same philosophy to freshness should always apply to fish. This is not to say that the instant you take a priest and perform last rites on a salmon that you should toss him into a sizzling frying pan. But quite frankly, you shouldn't really wait too long after that to prepare your catch for the table.

With this in mind, here's my best fish recipe. Ever.

FRESH TROUT

Rig a fly-rod and cast your favorite fly into a promising bunch of water. I prefer a Hawthorn on a No. 5 unless the fish aren't rising, in which case fishing the upstream nymph is the obvious way to go.

Continued on next page . . .

My water of choice is the River Itchen in England, one of the legendary chalk streams and also the water of choice of none other than Izaak Walton himself. The secret to this recipe is to be selective. Do not catch a good fish. Catch an excellent fish.

This fish you fish will, obviously, vary with the water you are fishing, however if you fish a chalk stream, then do not settle for anything less than a wild brown. A rainbow will not do, not from English chalk streams, because a rainbow in these waters is invariably a stocked fish. A stock brown is acceptable only if it is plump, say over 3-lbs. A wild brown over 2¼ pounds—why that's a fish fit for a king.

Once you hook a promising fish, play him well. Let him run, let him roll, but when he pouts and you eventually land him—assuming you are more clever than he and succeed in doing so—then be swift hearing his confession. After all, you are the victor over a warrior of the river.

There is much debate about whether to gut a fish by the side of the river or at home. I personally prefer the riverside ritual. I have no explanation for this, nor any reason that supports it. It's just what I do, and I'm sure that what you do is equally acceptable. Put the fish in a cooler until you get home. If your home is 3,000 miles away—as mine—then borrow a kitchen. I borrowed my friend's who lives in the New Forest, Hampshire. If you plead your case, chances are the hotel you are staying at will oblige.

Rinse the fish tenderly without rubbing it, inside and out. Prepare a hot bath of boiling water. It is important that you use a long, shallow fish pan with a tight cover. Use very little water—a couple of inches will do, as you're poaching the fish with steam. Too much water can make the flesh fall apart. Add a little salt and a few sprigs of fresh parsley. Gently place the entire fish into the pan and put the lid firmly on. Some people prefer to serve fish with the head on. I do not know whether or not this is your tradition, but I prefer to serve fish headless. We've already met under the best of circumstances, but from this point forward he is dinner.

Do not leave the stoveside, not for a second. Do not turn the fish, through you may need to nudge it with a spatula ever so gently to be sure it does not stick to the bottom of the pan. Remember, to maintain a rapid boil, you're poaching under high heat.

Continued on next page . . .

Keep the cover on for the first minute, lift it and be sure the fish is not sticking to the pan, replace the cover slightly askew for another two minutes and then after that, quite frequently, check the fish to make sure that it is not overcooking.

The flesh should be coral-pink in color. If it doesn't turn pink then silly you—caught a stocked rainbow, which is pellet-fed and has white flesh. The wild brown trout invariably feeds on crustaceans and shrimp, which account for its lovely color.

By capturing a native of the wild waters, you already have a pre-seasoned feast. Because the real secret, boys and girls, is this: The fish you caught and kept—the worthy one you culled from those you released—means you knew. You understood that the supreme flavor of a fish doesn't come from inundating it with oils and marinades and spices and herbs. The flavor has been developing over the entire life of the creature based on the delicious things that he himself has fed upon. It would be a sin to hide that natural flavor, and in the case of a superb fish like a wild brown, I guarantee there's nothing you could do to make it more superior than it, quite naturally, already is.

When the fish looks near done (the amount of time depends upon the weight of the fish), then gingerly test the middle portion of the fish with a fork and be certain the flesh is flaky and light.

Drain the water from the pan and with all the care you can muster, slide the fish onto a large, warmed platter, preferably Sevres (in a pinch, Crate & Barrel will do). Garnish it down the middle with fresh, thin lemon slices, and around the plate with parsley and, for color, sliced radishes. Serve with Hollandaise or a cream based horseradish sauce on the side. Fresh steamed asparagus and scalloped potatoes are an appropriate accompaniment in spring; yellow and green summer squash and rice are best for summer fare.

Present the brown trout to table with great pride and to the applause of your family and guests. One last tip—say a little grace. Nothing heavy or religious … just a word of thanks to the aquatic warrior who gave his life to nourish yours.

© 2000 - Russell A. Hopper

LORI-ANN MURPHY

LORI-ANN'S BEST APPLE PIE

"Catch and release offers an intimate relationship with nature without depleting the precious resource of wild fish."

Lori-Ann Murphy is one of the top women fly fishing guides in the country. She is an advisor for the Orvis Company and runs Reel Women® Fly Fishing Outfitters, based in Victor, Idaho. She runs six guides on the Snake River in Jackson Hole, Wyoming and the South Fork of the Snake River in Idaho.

She worked as the fly fishing consultant for Meryl Streep and Kevin Bacon in the movie, *The River Wild*. Her company has been featured on CNN's *Impact*, *The New York Times*, *Martha Stewart Living* and several prominent magazines.

Lori-Ann says her pie recipes have a lot of meaning in her fishing career. When she started guiding in Colorado, she baked the guides a pie in exchange for certain fishing spots she wanted for her clients. She used pies as a bribe in return for trade secrets and access to very wonderful fishing places.

Lori-Ann gives credit for her Easy Crust Recipe to Ruth McPhaden of Seattle, Washington and her Apple Pie Recipe to her friend, Chrissie Marshall, who Lori-Ann says, is the real pie queen.

Years Fly Fishing
A lifetime, but it has taken over my life the last 12 years.

Favorite Rod
1 Ounce 4 wt Orvis

Rods Owned
Too many to count.

Favorite Flies
Dry – Adams
Wet – Green Butt Skunk
Nymph – Tungsten
B.H. Pheasant Tail
Terrestrial – Schroeder's
Hopper

Fly Invented
None, yet

Favorite US River
I'm not telling.

Home River
See Comments

Favorite Stream
A spring creek in Wyoming.

Home Stream
Snow (ID)

2 Cups Unbleached White Flour
½ Teaspoon Salt
2/3 Cup Melted Butter
1/3 Cup Boiling Water

Mix melted butter and boiling water. Add to flour and salt. Toss lightly with a fork until the dough is formed. Divide in half and roll out the crust between 2 pieces of wax paper lightly floured.

12 Granny Smith Applies
Cinnamon – Nutmeg – Sugar – Flour – Butter
Half-&-Half

Peel the apples and cut into big bite size pieces. Place half of the apples into an unbaked pie shell. Assemble a small handful of flour, a healthy tablespoon of cinnamon and a half-cup of sugar and place over the apples.

Add the rest of the apple slices, and more flour, cinnamon and sugar. Dot with butter, about half a stick or ¼ cup. Pour ¼ cup Half-&-Half over the apples.

Cover with pie dough. Cut pie vents into the crust. Pour 1 – 2 tablespoons of Half-&-Half over the crust and sprinkle with sugar and nutmeg.

Bake at 350 degrees for 1 hour. Enjoy!

"There are as many reasons why and ways to fish as there are people who do it." – Russell Chatham

Nick Murphy is the President of Umpqua Feather Merchants, located in Glide, Oregon.

Years Fly Fishing
Twenty-seven

Favorite Rod
8 wt 10' Graphite

Rods Owned
Fifteen

Favorite Flies
Dry – Blue Wulff (Steelhead) and CDC Spent Caddis (Trout) Wets, Nymphs & Streamers – Ones with lots of feathers. Terrestrial – CDC Hopper

Fly Invented
Proprietary

Favorite US River
North Umpqua (OR)

Home River
North Umpqua (OR)

Favorite Stream
Rock Creek (MT)

Home Stream
Unnamed

Black Pudding
Irish Bacon
Eggs Up
Fried Tomatoes
Soda Bread
Fresh Butter
Marmalade
1 Pint Harp Lager

Fly to Shannon Airport, drive to Connemara Coast, order at any pub any time of day and wash down with a pint of Harp Lager.

Serves: 1

HARRY W. MURRAY

BROILED FLOUNDER & GINGER

"All fish feed on minnows and some large fish make them the main items on their diets."

Harry Murray resides in Edinburg, Virginia. He is a freelance writer of books and articles, the owner of Murray's Fly Shop, and according to some, he is the best all-round fly fisherman in the world. Harry's books include *Fly Fishing for Smallmouth Bass, Trout Fishing in the Shenandoah National Park* and *His Blessings Through Angling.*

In addition to running his fly shop, Harry is a pharmacist. He fishes for two species, trout and bass, and has provided his favorites in both areas.

Bass Rod — 7 wt 9' Graphite Murray/Scott
Trout Rod — 3 wt 6' 10" 3 Piece Murray/Scott
Bass Flies — Murray's Hellgrammite #4, 6, 8; Murray's Olive Strymph #6; Murray's Mad Tom #4, 6, 8; Murray's Shenandoah Blue Popper #6; Chuggar #8; and Slidder #6
Trout Flies — Mr. Rapidan Dry Fly #14, 16, 18; Murray's Black Strymph #10; Murray's Olive Strymph #10; Murray's Flying Beetle #14, 16; and Murray's Mr. Rapadan Bead Head Nymph #10, 12, 14

Years Fly Fishing
Forty

Favorite Rod
See Comments

Rods Owned
Forty

Favorite Flies
See Comments

Flies Invented
The Murray Series

Favorite US River
Trout – Rapidan (VA)
Bass – Shenandoah (VA)

Home River
Smith (VA)

Favorite Streams
Mossy Creek (VA)

Home Stream
Bass – Shenandoah River (VA)
Trout – Shenandoah National Park (VA)

2 Pounds Flounder
Salt and Pepper
Ginger
Butter or Margarine

Cut flounder into serving pieces. Sprinkle the pieces with salt, pepper, and ginger. Preheat the broiler about 20 minutes. Place the fish on the preheated broiler pan 2 inches below the flame (heat). Brush with butter or margarine, and dot generously. Broil 3 – 4 minutes on one side, and turn.

Brush with butter or margarine again and broil 4 minutes—or until light brown. Slip into a hot platter and serve with a sauce of your choosing.

Serves: 4 to 6

John Murray

"You should have been here yesterday."

John Murray is the owner of the Blue River Anglers of Schoharie, New York. According to John, one of his accomplishments is that he has developed some fly patterns that catch fish. He and his wife, Jeri, also offer some of the best patterns at prices that are amazing.

Years Fly Fishing
Sixteen

Favorite Rod
5 wt 8' Graphite

Rods Owned
Twelve

Favorite Flies
Dry – Elk Hair Caddis
Wet – Soft Hackle
Nymph – F.W. Stonefly
Streamer – Black Nose Dace
Terrestrial – Fur Ant

Flies Invented
Morning Glory, L.G. Smelt
and F.W. Stonefly

Favorite US River
Ausable (NY)

Home River
Mohawk (NY)

Favorite Stream
Catskill Creek (NY)

Home Stream
Schoharie Creek (NY)

Goulash

1 Pound Ground Beef
2 Cans Stewed Tomatoes
3 Cans Tomato Sauce
1 Pound Rigatoni
1 Onion
1 Tablespoon Garlic Powder
1 Tablespoon Italian Seasoning
1 Green Pepper
1 Red Pepper
2 Green Tomatoes
1 Tablespoon Black Pepper

Boil rigatoni until firm. Brown ground beef. Place firm rigatoni noodles and browned ground beef into a large pot. Add chopped/diced-sliced onion, sliced peppers and sliced green tomatoes. Stir in stewed tomatoes and sauce. Sprinkle in garlic powder, Italian seasoning and black pepper.

Cook over low to medium heat. Keep covered. Stir occasionally when it comes to a boil. Cook for about 1-½ hours.

Serves: 6

BOB NAUHEIM

"You can fool some fish all the time, and all fish some of the time, but you can't fool all the fish, all the time."

Bob Nauheim dwells in Santa Rosa, California. He has fished virtually worldwide. In fact, it was over 20 years ago that Bob was fishing with his Andros Island Bahamian bonefish guide, Charlie Smith, when the two of them collaborated at Charlie's Bonefish Haven to create the Crazy Charlie fly, a fly named after Smith. Bob is President of Fishing International.

Years Fly Fishing
Over Fifty

Favorite Rod
Graphite

Rods Owned
Twenty

Favorite Flies
Dry – Blue Winged Olive
Wet – Queen of the Waters
Nymph – Pheasant Tail
Streamer – Lefty's Deceiver
Terrestrial – Beetle

Fly Invented
Crazy Charlie

Favorite US River
Russian (CA)

Home River
Russian (CA)

Favorite Stream
Fall River (CA)

Home Stream
Gualala (CA)

TURKEY FRIED RICE

Turkey Breast
2 Cups Rice
Olive Oil
2 Slices Bacon
Chopped Onions
Handful of Peanuts
Soy Sauce
2 Teaspoons Sugar
½ Cup of Frozen Peas, Carrots
and String Beans
Spices

Boil 2 cups rice and let sit one day. Heat skillet and add olive oil. Cup up turkey breast and set aside. Fry rice. As browning, add 2 slices bacon and cook with rice. Then add turkey (precooked, if you like), chopped onions, and a handful of peanuts and stir-fry. Add soy sauce to taste. Then add 2 teaspoons sugar and ½ cup of frozen peas, carrots, and string beans. Mix, stir-fry and serve.

Serves: Several

"Structure forms the foundation of the fish's neighborhood, and from this foundation all else comes."

Bob Newman is the author of numerous books including *North American Fly-fishing* and *Flyfishing Structure*. In addition to being a writer, Bob says, *"I am an aquatic vagrant."* He is a Contributing Editor for *Fly Fishing in Salt Waters* magazine, the Rocky Mountain Regional Editor for *Fly Fish America* magazine and is retired from the United States Marine Corps.

The Longmont, Colorado resident edited the Sycamore Island Books anthology *Gray Ghosts and Lefty's Deceiver*. His much-anticipated study of salmonid prey, *The Troublesome Creek Chronicles: The Flyfisher's Guide to Trout and Salmon Prey* was released in 1999.

Years Fly Fishing
Thirty-two

Favorite Rod
5 wt 9' Graphite

Rods Owned
Over Twenty

Favorite Flies
Dry – Adams # 14
Wet – Parmachenee Belle
Nymph – G.R. Hare's Ear # 16
Streamer – Gray Ghost
Terrestrial – Dave's Hopper

Fly Invented
None, yet

Favorite US River
Throne on Prince of Wales Island (AK)

Home River
Big Thompson (CO)

Favorite Stream
Troublesome Creek (CO)

Home Stream
North St. Vrain (CO)

© 2000 - Russell A. Hopper

Moose Tenderloin
Monterey Jack Cheese
Red, Yellow, Orange and Green Peppers
Cayenne Pepper
Minced Garlic
Black Pepper
Swiss Chard
Acorn Squash
Burgundy Wine

Shoot one moose. Remove tenderloins. Over a campfire, place tenderloin, seasoned with cayenne pepper, black pepper and fresh minced garlic to taste, on a grill. Turn when light pink inside. Place sliced peppers on meat and cover with Monterey Jack cheese. After cheese melts, remove when you see fit.

Serve with a decent burgundy, Swiss chard and acorn squash.

Serves: One Marine or six sailors

SETH MICHAEL NORMAN

"Any damn fool can get complicated. It takes real genius to achieve simplicity." – Will Rogers (Maybe ...)

Seth Norman is a writer, fly fishing tackle manufacturer, Book Editor for *Fly Rod & Reel*, Associate Editor for *California Fly Fisher,* father to Sophie, Max, Cathy, Eric and Marc, and a regular contributor to magazines such as *Gray's Sporting Journal.*

A resident of Oakland, California, Seth is the author of *Meanderings of a Fly Fisherman* and *Flyfisher's Guide to Northern California.* He is the recipient of the *Harrah Award* for Public Interest Journalism, the *Golden Medallion for Journalism* and a *Pulitzer Prize* nominee.

Seth won the *Robert Traver Fly-Fishing Fiction Award* in August 1998 and the Federation of Fly Fishers' *Roderick Haig-Brown Award* for literary excellence which he says, *"Is an exceedingly kind effort made at least a decade early."*

Seth is a past President of the Grizzly Peak Fly Fishers.

Years Fly Fishing
Twenty-six
Favorite Rod
4 wt 9' Graphite
Rods Owned
Quiet a few.
Favorite Flies
Dry – Stimulator
Wet – Partridge & Green
Nymph – Brassie
Streamer – Alf
Terrestrial – Ant
(Size 8 to 17 Pattern)
Fly Invented
Seth's Fat Boy
(River Dragonfly Nymph)
Favorite US River
McCloud (CA)
Favorite Stream
Just ... can't ... remember ...
Home Stream
It's ... coming ... to ... me ...

DEATH DEFYING LIVERS*

(*Death Defying Chicken Livers)

8 Chicken Livers, or Game Bird "Equivalent"
8 Strips Bacon
Clove Garlic
8 Ounces Soy Sauce
Salt and Pepper
Paprika

Marinate livers in soy sauce for ½ hour. Crush garlic and insert small piece into center of liver. Add dash of pepper and a pinch of salt. Wrap bacon strip around liver, tightly. Sprinkle paprika liberally. Placed wrapped livers on broiler pan and broil until browned, approximately 8 minutes.

Serves: 4 people or Seth

BRIAN O'KEEFE

"Float & bloat! (An Alaskan line abroad where good fishing is surpassed by great food: King crab, spot prawns, halibut, salmon, etc.)"

Brian O'Keefe is a sales representative for Scott Rods, Scientific Angler, Frontier Flies and Ronny Waders. He is also a professional photographer specializing in fishing and athletic outdoor subjects. His photography work is featured in the slide show entitled *Trespassers Guide to Oregon.*

Brian resides in Bend, Oregon.

Years Fly Fishing
Thirty-six

Favorite Rod
4 wt 9' Graphite

Rods Owned
Forty

Favorite Flies
Dry – PMD Thorax
Wet – Steelhead
Caddis/Spey
Nymph – Damsel
Streamer – Alaska Fry
Terrestrial – Paloma R. (Chile)
Beetle

Fly Invented
Turd Bonefish Fly

Favorite US River
Beaverhead (MT)

Home River
Deschutes (OR)

Favorite Stream
American Creek (AK)

Home Stream
Malhuer (OR)

HATCHERY STEELHEAD

1 Hatchery Steelhead
Ginger Peach Jam

Fillet hatchery steelhead. Pull out little bones along lateral line with pliers. Cover meat with ginger peach jam. Barbecue skin side down.

Serves: 4 – 8

CHAD OLSEN

"Fly fishing is more than just the fish; it's about problem solving, the setting, camaraderie, passion, friendship, conservation, soul searching, romanticism, lifestyle and fun!"

Chad Olsen is a fly fishing guide, fly shop owner and journalist. He received the *Outstanding Volunteer Service Award* from the South Platte Chapter of Trout Unlimited in 1989. Chad is a supporter of Trout Unlimited, the Greater Yellowstone Coalition and the Beartooth Alliance.

The Bozeman, Montana resident owns the Greater Yellowstone Flyfishers, which includes a fly shop and guide service in Bozeman and one in Cooke City, Montana. Chad is also a published author and has appeared on several television shows.

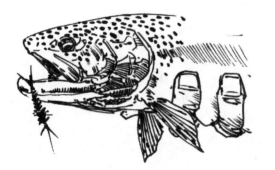

Years Fly Fishing
Fifteen

Favorite Rod
5 wt 8' 6" Graphite

Rods Owned
Ten

Favorite Flies
Dry – Stimulator
Wet – Halloween
Woolly Bugger
Nymph – B.H. Flashback
Hare's Ear
Streamer – Yellow Yummy
Terrestrial – Rubber
Leg Foam Beetle

Fly Invented
CDC Quill Caddis

Favorite US River
Yellowstone (MT & WY)

Home River
Gallatin (MT & WY)

Favorite Stream
Slough Creek (MT & WY)

Home Stream
Soda Butte Creek (MT & WY)

PHEASANT DIVAN

4 Pheasant Breasts, Cooked and Boned
1 Box Chopped Broccoli
2 Cans Chicken Soup
1/8 Cup Lemon Juice
Grated Cheddar Cheese
Breadcrumbs
½ Cup White Wine

Shred breasts and place in 9" x 11" pan. Add 1 box chopped broccoli. Mix 2 cans of chicken soup and 1/8 cup lemon juice. Pour over broccoli. Add a light layer of grated cheddar cheese and breadcrumbs. Refrigerate overnight. Add ½ cup white wine and bake at 350 degrees for 45 minutes.

Serves: 4 – 6

DAVID ONDAATJE

"Enjoy the ones that get away."

David Ondaatje is the President of R. L. Winston Rod Company. He has managed and owned the Company since 1991.

David continues to build Winston rods around quality, innovation and integrity. He was the co-designer of the popular 5-piece LT Trout Rod Series, the BL5 5-piece Rod Series, and the new Winston Perfect Reels.

Years Fly Fishing
Twenty-six

Favorite Rod
4 wt 8' 9" Graphite Winston

Rods Owned
Many

Favorite Flies
Dry – Parachute Adams
Wet – Popsicle
Nymph – Hare's Ear
Streamer – Not Provided
Terrestrial – Letort Hopper

Fly Invented
The Gnarly

Favorite US River
Big Hole (MT)

Home River
Beaverhead (MT)

BASMATI RICE

1 Cup Basmati Rice
1 ½ Cups Water
1 Teaspoon Vinegar
Salt
1 Teaspoon Light Vegetable Oil
Cooking Pot (3+ Cups)

Rinse 1-cup basmati rice repeatedly until the water is clear. Earlier rinsing will yield milky water. Put 1-cup basmati rice, 1 ½ cups water, 1 teaspoon of vinegar and 1 teaspoon vegetable oil in a pot. Mix and cover.

Bring to a boil, stirring gently. Simmer for up to 20 minutes or until the rice absorbs all water. Do not remove cover. Remove from heat. Let stand covered for 10 minutes. Add salt and other food.

Eat quickly!

Serves: 1 – 5

TOM OWEN

BAKED PASTA & VEGETABLES

"I was introduced to fly fishing at age eight and decades later no other endeavor has given as much satisfaction."

Tom Owen hails from Black Forest, Colorado where he enjoys success as an artist. While he says he has no personal innovations regarding fly fishing, he is an outstanding painter of trout and other game fish in a natural setting.

He is the winner of the *Gold Medallion* and the *Adirondacks Wilderness Award* from the National Exhibition of American Watercolors in Old Forge, New York, the *Juror's Choice* at the San Diego International Watermedia Exhibition, and the *Harriet Wexler Bartsch Memorial Award* by the National Watercolor Society in Los Angles, California.

Tom's works are represented by the Cogswell Galley, Vail and Colorado Springs, Colorado; El Centro Gallery, Santa Fe, New Mexico; the Sportsman Gallery, Atlanta, Georgia; and Warehouse Gallery at Camden Yards, Baltimore, Maryland.

Years Fly Fishing
Forty-one

Favorite Rod
5 wt 9' Graphite

Rods Owned
Six

Favorite Flies
Dry – Elk Hair Caddis
Wet – Golden Stone and Caddis Emerging
Nymph – RS2 and Hare's Ear
Streamer – Woolly Bugger
Terrestrial – Hopper

Fly Invented
None, yet

Favorite US River
Frying Pan (CO)

Home River
South Platte (CO)

Favorite Stream
Chalk Creek (CO)

Home Stream
Monument Creek (CO)

1 Each Red and Green Peppers Cut into Strips
Olive Oil
1 Eggplant ¾" Diced
2 Small Zucchini ½" Diced
1 Pound Mostocallis Pasta
1/3 Cup Chopped Parsley
Newman's Own Bombolina Pasta Sauce
½ Cup Shredded Mozzarella Cheese
½ Cup Mixed Mexican Cheeses, Monterey Jack, Cheddar Queso, and Asadero
½ Cup Freshly Grated Parmesan

Roast pepper strips on a large baking sheet with 3 tablespoons of olive oil for 35 minutes at 450 degrees. Place in a large bowl. Roast eggplant about 20 minutes with 3 tablespoons olive oil. Place in bowl. Roast zucchini about 25 minutes with 2 tablespoons of oil and toss into bowl with other vegetables. Salt and pepper to taste.

Cook pasta until al dente. Grease large baking dish (i.e. 10" round). Add ¼ cup parsley to pasta and toss. Stir in pasta sauce, mozzarella, Mexican cheeses and ½ the parmesan. Sprinkle remaining Parmesan and parsley over the pasta. Bake at 375 degrees for 35 – 40 minutes, until bubbling.

Serves: 8 – 10

MARGOT PAGE

"Little rivers run deep."

Margot Page is the author of *Little Rivers: Tales of a Woman Angler*. She worked in the publishing field for Nick Lyons during the1980s. Margot was the first woman Editor of the American Museum of Fly Fishing's quarterly magazine, *The American Fly Fisher*.

Margot was one of the first literary voices in the explosion of women into fly fishing during the last decade. She is on the board of Casting for Recovery, a national nonprofit program teaching fly fishing to breast cancer survivors. Margot also served on the Steering Committee of the 1997 International Festival of Women Fly Fishers, held in Baja, Mexico.

Sparse Grey Hackle was Margot's grandfather. She resides in East Arlington, Vermont with her daughter, Brooke.

Margot did not take up fly fishing until she was a grown woman.

"I am alone. Peace wraps me like an airy miracle. Slow and light." – Little Rivers

Years Fly Fishing
Fifteen

Favorite Rod
6 wt Graphite

Rods Owned
Can't count how many.

Favorite Flies
Dry – Hendrickson
Wet – Woolly Bugger
Nymph – Any Bead Head
Streamer – Woolly Bugger
Terrestrial – Hopper or Yellow Humpy

Flies Invented
None, yet

Favorite US River
Any Alaskan river.

Home River
Battenkill (VT)

Favorite Stream
Wild and woolly Cape Cod for salt water.

Home Stream
Mettowee (VT)

© 2000 - Russell A. Hopper

THE CROWD PLEASER*

(*Artichoke/Feta Fusilli)

3 Jars Marinated Artichokes
2 Garlic Cloves – 1 Pound Fusilli Pasta
½ Package Feta Cheese
½ Cup Fresh Parmesan Cheese
3 Tablespoons Fresh Italian Parsley
1 Teaspoon Each Salt and Pepper
½ Cup Dry White Wine
¼ Cup Calamata or Greek Olives

Cook fusilli until al dente and drain. In a large pot, dump the artichokes and oil from the jars. Use kitchen scissors to halve. Turn burner on low. Add chopped or crushed garlic cloves, parsley, salt and pepper. Let simmer for a few minutes. Add wine, crumbled feta cheese, parmesan and let marry. Then add cooked fusilli, olives and toss. Let heat through then serve with a green salad, hearty red wine, crusty bread, and blue-checked napkins. Candles too.

Serves: 4

"This is an easy, elegant meal that my twelve-year-old daughter requests weekly. You can even toss in some quartered sautéed zucchini for some extra green jazz. Yum." – Margot

DIANE B. PALLOT

"There is nothing artificial about the moment of inspiration."

Diane Pallot is a flight attendant, freelance writer and photographer living in Mims, Florida with husband Flip.

A multi-talented woman, Diane has been a production assistant for the television series, *Saltwater Angler*, a designer of women's swim suits and is active in conservation and animal protection groups. Her articles appear in fishing books, cat books, and calendars.

Diane has appeared frequently on the *Walker's Cay Chronicles* television series. She also participates in casting clinics for various charities for children and other organizations.

Diane's passions are fly fishing and felines. Having four cats, she is often seen casting a hookless fly to one or more of these feisty participants.

Years Fly Fishing
Sixteen

Favorite Rod
8 wt 8' 6" Graphite

Rods Owned
Seven

Favorite Flies
Dry – Royal Wulff #14
Wet – Woolly Bugger
Nymph – Hare's Ear
Streamer – Clouser Minnow
and the Kreh Half-n-Half
Terrestrial – Cats

Fly Invented
Mothra

Favorite US River
St. Johns (FL)

Home River
St. Johns (FL)

Favorite Stream
Buffalo (AR)

Home Stream
Not Provided

PARMESAN RED SNAPPER*

(*Parmesan Red Snapper ala Florida)

6 Red Snapper
6 Tablespoons Butter – Salt and Pepper
8 Tablespoons Shallots, Minced
7 Tomatoes, Peeled, Seeded and Chopped
3 Cups Each Dry White Wine and Heavy Cream
3 Tablespoons Parsley
Locatalli Romano, Reggiano or Any Fine
Freshly Grated, Bulk Parmesan Cheese

In a baking dish, make a single layer of the fillets. Dot fish with butter and season with salt and pepper. Sprinkle shallots and 6 chopped tomatoes over the fillets. Then add wine and bake at 350 degrees for 15 minutes. Remove fish from oven and turn to broil.

Drain off cooking liquid to a saucepan and over high heat, reduce the liquid to ½ cup. Lower heat and gradually add cream, stirring constantly. Heat sauce, but do not boil. Add parsley and more salt and pepper, if necessary. Pour sauce over the fillets and garnish with 1 remaining chopped tomato. Place under broiler until sauce is browned. Remove and sprinkle with Parmesan.

Serves: 4 – 6

FLIP PALLOT

"Best time to fish is when it's raining and when it ain't."

Flip Pallot started his career as a commercial banker before becoming a guide to anglers and hunters. These days, Flip is a consultant to manufacturers of outdoor clothing, fishing, and hunting tackle. He is a partner in the Hell's Bay Boatworks, makers of cutting edge fishing boats.

Flip is perhaps best known in the fly fishing community as the host of ESPN's award winning *Walker's Cay Chronicles* television program.

This winner of the very first Islamorada International Bonefish Fly Tournament has held many salt water world fly rod records and was nominated to the *3-M Scientific Anglers Hall of Fame* as well as *Who's Who in the Southeastern United States*.

Featured in many outdoor films, Flip has also written widely for outdoor publications and has written a book entitled *Memories, Mangroves & Magic*. He is a Contributing Editor for *Fly Fishing in Salt Water* magazine.

Based out of Mims, Florida, Flip is the guy who gets to spend time with Dianne Pallot.

Years Fly Fishing
Forty-one

Favorite Rod
8 wt 8' 6" Graphite

Rods Owned
Twenty

Favorite Flies
Dry – Royal Wulff
Wet – Clouser Minnow
Nymph – Stonefly
Streamer – Lefty's Deceiver
Terrestrial – Dave's Hopper

Fly Invented
Prince of Tides

Favorite US River
Buffalo (AR)

Home River
St. Johns (FL)

Favorite Stream
Not Provided

Home Stream
Not Provided

BACKSTRAP BONANZA

2 Venison Tenderloins
1 Bottle Crystal Hot Sauce
Garlic Salt

Slice backstraps into 2-inch medallions. Sprinkle with garlic salt on both sides. Fire grill with live oak, white or red oak, or mesquite. When the wood has burned to coal, place the seasoned medallions on the hot grill and add a dollop of Crystal Hot Sauce to each medallion. Braise outside. Serve rare.

"This dish also works well with domestic pork tenderloin served with apple sauce." – Flip

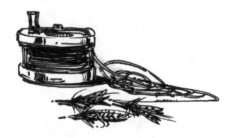

ERNIE PAQUETTE

"You can't catch 'em from the couch." – Ernie
"Anglers have kept up to 30 fish per man per day during the spawn, and now they wonder where their fish have gone!" – From the floor of the Tennessee Legislature

Ernie Paquette is the owner of South Harpeth Outfitters based in Kingston Springs, Tennessee. He is also a fly fishing guide, photographer, instructor, outdoor writer and restaurant owner.

He says he and his wife have created two handsome, kind and smart young fishermen.

Ernie is the 1996 winner of the *Friend of Fisheries Award* from the American Fisheries Society and the winner of the *Excellence in Craft Award* from the Tennessee Outdoor Writers Association.

His writings have been included in *Warmwater Fly Fishing* magazine.

Note to Recipe: The novice should make the sweet potato hash first. Ernie has cooked this meal so many times he can do both at the same time. It's one of his most requested shore lunches. Serve with vine ripened tomatoes and a buttery Chardonnay. Enjoy!

Years Fly Fishing
Sixteen
Favorite Rod
5 wt 9' Graphite
Rods Owned
Twenty
Favorite Flies
Dry – Sulphur Dun #14
Wet – Adams Soft Hackle
Nymph – Golden Stonefly
Streamer – Ernie's Cockle Bugger
Terrestrial – Dave's Black Hopper
Fly Invented
Ernie's Cockle Bugger
Favorite US River
White Water (AR)
Home River
Caney Fork (TN)
Favorite Stream
Abrahms Creek (Smokies)
Home Stream
South Harpeth (TN)

SALMON PESCADOR*

(*Salmon Pescador with Blackberry Sage Sauce & Sweet Potato Hash)

Farm Raised Salmon Filets, Boneless
Salt and Pepper
Fresh Garlic
Sage
Seedless Blackberry Preserves
3 – 4 Medium Onions, Diced
3 – 4 Precooked Sweet Potatoes, Nuked in a Microwave for 5 – 10 Minutes the Night Before and Refrigerated
Olive Oil

Heat ¼ cup of olive oil in a skillet. Generously season the salmon filets with salt and pepper. When the oil begins to smoke, carefully drop in the filets. Quickly brown each side and remove from the pan. Add 1 – 2 onions, 1 pinch of sage, 1 teaspoon garlic and sauté until tender. Add 4 heaping tablespoons blackberry preserves, melt and incorporate with the onions. Place salmon on a plate and top with blackberry sauce.

In another skillet, heat ¼ cup olive oil and 1 tablespoon minced garlic. Sauté 2 diced onions and add in chunks of pre-cooked sweet potatoes. Cook until brown. Salt and pepper to taste.

JON W. PARKER

MOM'S POTATO PANCAKES*

"Nothing great was ever achieved without enthusiasm." – Ralph Waldo Emerson

Jon Parker retired to Saratoga, Wyoming from Ballston Lake, New York where he operated a steel fabricating business and was actively engaged in making bamboo fly rods. He continues to make and market hand planed split bamboo rods under the Parker Rod name.

Years Fly Fishing
Fifty-six
Favorite Rod
6 wt 8' Parker Bamboo
Rods Owned
Twelve
Favorite Flies
Dry – Henryville Caddis
Wet – Cary Special
Nymph – Brassie
Streamer – Nine-Three
Terrestrial – Ant
Fly Invented
None, yet
Favorite US River
Missouri (MT)
Home River
North Platte (WY)
Favorite Stream
Hog Park Creek (WY)
Home Stream
French Creek (WY)

(*Mom's Favorite Potato Pancakes)

3 Cups Shredded/Grated Potatoes, Drained
2 Eggs Slightly Beaten
¼ Onion, Grated
3 Tablespoons Flour
1 ¼ Teaspoons Salt
¼ Teaspoon Pepper

Mix all ingredients together. Fry in 1/8" oil or Crisco at 350 degrees for 8 minutes or until desired doneness. Drain on brown paper or paper towels. The potatoes may be shredded/grated with a food processor.
Serve with applesauce and sour cream.

"This is great for a quick supper or served as a side dish." – Jon

R. M. "Pete" Parker

"Ain't life grand?"

Pete Parker lives in Indian Hills, Colorado, but fishes the Pacific coast of Baja, Mexico and around the world. His famed Pete's Slider helped him capture the world record for black skipjack on a fly, 13-pounds. Pete has an IGFA world record for a giant trevally on 12-pound tippet and a 54-pound Pacific bonito. He says he is only one of two people who have taken a wahoo on monofilament. Pete's weighed 51-pounds.

Pete earns a living in computer sales and through International Sportsmen's Expositions. He is also a contract fly tyer for Umpqua, ties flies for the Federation of Fly Fishers Museum and the FFF's National Conclaves.

His flies are regularly featured in books and magazines. In addition to Pete's Slider, he invented the Tuna Helper, Pete's Mackerel and other patterns.

When not fishing, Pete takes a spin around the dance floor. He is a champion ballroom dancer.

Years Fly Fishing
Fifty-six

Favorite Rod
5 wt 8' Bamboo

Rods Owned
Thirty-seven

Favorite Flies
Dry – Adams
Wet – Pete's 50/50
Nymph – G.R. Hare's Ear
Streamer – Pete's Slider
Terrestrial – Black Ant

Flies Invented
See Comments

Favorite US River
Green (UT)

Home River
South Platte (CO)

Favorite Stream
Middle Fork South Platte (CO)

Home Stream
Bear Creek (CO)

Pedros Ceviche

2 Pounds Whatever Fish Caught,
Filleted and Cubed ½"
12 Limes
2 Medium Tomatoes, Diced
12 Serrano Chilies, Diced
1 Medium Onion, Diced
1 Sprig Cilantro, Crumbled
2 Shot Glasses Olive Oil
2 Shot Glasses Red Wine
2 Shot Glasses Comemorativo Tequila
1 Tablespoon Coarse Black Pepper
1 Tablespoon Whole Seeds of Cumin

Combine ingredients in a glass or ceramic covered bowl. Let marinate for at least 2 hours, better overnight.

Serve on a leaf of Iceberg Lettuce.

Serves: 4 – 6 hearty eaters

BILLY PATE

"All in all considered, I believe that friendships are the greatest reward of fly fishing."

Billy Pate and his wife, Jodi, divide their time between Winter Haven and Islamorada, Florida where they both continue to chase International Game Fish Association Fly Rod Records.

One of the most celebrated fly fishing anglers of our time, Billy Pate has set more than 25 IGFA fly world records. These records include both the first black marlin and blue marlin ever caught on a fly.

Billy has won the Gold Cup Tarpon Fly Championship four times, the Hawley Tarpon Fly Tournament, the World Invitational Bonefish Fly Championship, and twice won the International Billfish Fly Championship. He has jumped more than 4,000 large tarpon and 1,000 billfish, and fly fished in more than 25 countries visiting Argentina 28 times and Costa Rica more than 30 times.

George Hommell and Billy Pate co-founded World Wide Sportsman, a tackle shop and fishing travel agency in Islamorada.

Over the years, Billy has been a frequent contributor to many outdoor fishing magazines.

Perhaps Billy's greatest recent catch was when he married his wife, Jodi.

Years Fly Fishing
Fifty-three

Favorite Rod
12 wt Original Fenwick Graphite (Tarpon).

Rods Owned
Not Provided

Favorite Flies
Tarpon Fly – Little Brown Streamer – Pate Pancora

Fly Invented
Pate Pink Sailfish Fly

Favorite US River
North Umpqua (OR)

Home River
St. Lucie (FL)

Home Stream
North Umpqua (OR)

Favorite Tarpon Waters
Homossassa (FL)

PECAN PIE

1 Cup (4 Ounces) Shelled Pecans
3 Eggs
3 Tablespoons All-purpose Flour
1 Cup Granulated Sugar
1 Cup Light Corn Syrup
3 Tablespoons Softened Butter
1 Tablespoon Vanilla
1 Unbaked 8" Pastry Shell

Preheat oven to 350 degrees.

Beat the eggs thoroughly in a deep bowl. The texture is better if the eggs are hand beaten. Mix the flour and sugar and add gradually to the mixture in the bowl. Add corn syrup gradually.

Add the pecans and the softened butter, beating to blend the butter thoroughly, about 300 strokes. Add the vanilla. Pour the mixture into an unbaked pastry shell.

Bake for about 1 hour. The pie should be brown on top, with the custard set, but still somewhat soft in the center.

Let the pie cool at room temperature—not in the refrigerator—at least 1 hour before cutting.

Serves: 6 – 8

JODI PATE

"My favorite fishing is big game fishing for bill-fish, all marlins, sailfish, and of course, tarpon."

Jodi Pate initiated the letter-writing campaign that persuaded the International Game Fish Association to allow women to have their own salt water fly rod world record category. She then went out to land a world record white marlin catch when she caught an 82-½ pound white marlin on a 20-pound tippet in Morocco. The battle lasted two hours and 45 minutes.

The wife of world class angler Billy Pate, who holds over 25 world records on a fly, Jodi fishes between 120 and 150 days a year. She now has eight records approved and six pending.

Jodi met her husband through the one and only personals ad he ever placed, in a Portland-area newspaper. Billy, who owns property in Southern Oregon, placed the ad at the instance of his Oregon based attorney. *"He was looking for someone who could go from blue jeans to a cocktail dress and must love the outdoors,"* Jodi says, happily.

Jodi is the first woman to catch four billfish species on a fly and has twice won the Women's Championship International Black Marlin Fly Classic in Australia.

Jodi is the first President of the newly formed International Women Fly Fishers. IWFF was formed on Halloween Weekend in 1998. Their goal is to have 1,000 members by the year 2000.

Years Fly Fishing
Ten
Favorite Rod
13 wt 9' Fisher Bluewater Graphite (Billfish)
12 wt Powell (Tarpon)
Rods Owned
Five
Favorite Flies
Black Marlin Fly – Slimey Mackerel
White Marlin and Pacific Sailfish Fly – One tied by Richard Whitner.
Dolphin Fly – Fat Albert by Kate Howe
Streamer – Pate's Pancora
Fly Invented
None, yet
Favorite US River
St. Lucie (FL)
Home River
Umpqua (OR)
Home Waters
Florida Keys in Islamorada

PEANUT BUTTER PIE

1 Cup Peanut Butter
½ Pound Cream Cheese, Softened
1 Cup Sugar
2 Tablespoons Melted Butter
1 Cup Whipped Cream
2 Teaspoons Vanilla
1 Graham Cracker Crust
Chocolate Frosting
Nuts

Mix together peanut butter, cream cheese, sugar and melted butter. Fold in whipped cream and vanilla. Put into prepared graham cracker crust and chill for 6 – 8 hours.

Top with any chocolate frosting that has been thinned out a bit so you can drizzle it back and forth on top of the pie. Finally, sprinkle with chopped nuts.

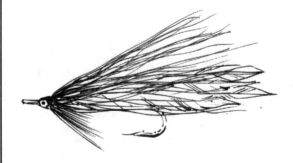

"I am still fishing all over the world."

Howard Patterson is a retired railroad electrical engineer who has fished in every state except Oregon and California, every province in Canada, Europe, Mexico, Central America and South America, including Brazil and Venezuela. He resides in Louisville, Kentucky.

Howard's fishing companions have included the legendary Lee Wulff, Lefty Kreh, Flip Pallot and Dave Whitlock. However, Howard prefers his annual trips with his long-time friends. When not making trips, he prefers a relaxing day on Lake Nolin fly fishing for bass from a boat.

During his many travels, Howard has caught some trophy fish. The Silver Salmon in Alaska is one of his most favorite fish to catch: his biggest was 27 pounds. He has also caught a King Salmon that topped the scales at 60 pounds. He also enjoys catching Peacock Bass in Brazil (12 pounds), and Bonefish and Tarpon in Venezuela.

In previous years, Howard has won awards as the top fly caster when entered in some major casting tournaments.

Howard once took his wife with him to Alaska where he fished for 60 days while she watched and did other things. Lucky man!

Years Fly Fishing
Sixty-five
Favorite Rod
9 wt 9' Graphite
Rods Owned
Sixty
Favorite Flies
Dry – Elk Hair Caddis
Wet – Woolly Bugger
Nymph – B.H. Hare's Ear
Streamer – White Shad Color
Terrestrial – Hopper
Fly Invented
Blue & Gray Damsel
Favorite US River
Green (UT)
Home River
Cumberland (KY)
Favorite Stream
Big Snow Bird (NC)
Home Stream
Rock Creek (KY)

Fresh Caught Fish
Ice Cubes
Buttermilk
Corn Oil
Breadcrumbs

Start with a live fish. Put fish on a stringer. Clip the gills on both sides. Return to water and allow all the blood to bleed out of the fish. Filet the fish. Cut out the small dark line in the center of the fillet. Cut out any brown meat or fat. Wash fish. Place in a container and cover with ice cubes. Leave overnight.

The next day, wash again and place in a bowl. Pour buttermilk over the fish, return to the refrigerator, and leave until you get ready to cook the fish.

Heat corn oil until hot (Howard means hot hot). Remove fish from buttermilk and dip in breadcrumbs. Then cook in hot oil until done.

LEIGH H. PERKINS

RUFFED GROUSE

"The only reason to fish is to enjoy oneself."

Leigh Perkins is the Chairman of Orvis, which he took from a small $500,000 annual business to an international business with sales exceeding $200 million a year. Leigh and his wife, Romi, reside in Manchester, Vermont. Romi is the author of *Game in Season: The Orvis Cookbook*.

Leigh invented the zinger for anglers clip, once caught a masheer in India on a dry fly and was the first to catch a permit on a fly at Boca Pailia, Yucaton. He also directed that the one-weight rod be built.

Serving on 16 different conservation boards, Leigh has served for ten years on the Board of Governors of The Nature Conservancy. He recently directed that $25,000 be given to the Kentucky Chapter for use on the Green River project and has pledged another $25,000.

Leigh has fished with many of the great fly fishing legends including Joe Brooks.

Leigh's two sons, Perk and Dave, now run Orvis, giving Leigh even more time to devote to his conservation interests, fishing and hunting.

Years Fly Fishing
Sixty-two
Favorite Rod
1 wt 7' 6" Graphite
Rods Owned
Unknown
Favorite Flies
Whatever it takes to catch fish that day.
Fly Invented
None, yet
Favorite US River
The one I am currently fishing.
Home River
Battenkill (VT)
Favorite Stream
Changes yearly.
Home Stream
Battenkill (VT)

© 2000 - Russell A. Hopper

Roast Grouse
Bacon

Place plucked ruffed grouse that has been hanging 4 days, in a shallow pan. Cover the breast with 3 strips of bacon for basting. Place in a 350-degree oven for 30 – 35 minutes until the internal temperature of the grouse is 140 degrees.

Serves: 1 bird per person

According to Paul Bruun, *"Leigh enjoys culinary pranks. He is widely known—perhaps notorious would be a better word—for his wild duck soup. His devoted friend, the late Vern Bressler, urged the master chef to at least pluck the feathers from the duck heads he sometimes substitutes when short of duck bones."*

C. BOYD PFEIFFER

MARINATED CHICKEN BREASTS

"If we wish to preserve our fishing and our environment, we must stabilize our population—nationally and world-wide. With the constantly increasing demands of more people—90 million more of which are added to the world's population each year—all conservation efforts are ultimately for naught. Conservation organizations should be using some of their funds to pay for vasectomies and condoms—and national and international world leaders must face this ultimate environmental problem now regardless of how difficult it is or how sensitive the subject."

Boyd Pfeiffer is a writer and photographer. His work has appeared in over 75 magazines. He has contributed columns to over 13 publications and provided script writing for segments for Orlando Wilson and Roland Martin. His book credits number over 15 and his writing and photography awards add up to over 50. Some of Boyd's books include *Modern Tackle Craft*, *Bug Making*, *Fly Fishing Basics*, and *Fly Fishing Salt Water Basics*.

Boyd says, *"My best and luckiest achievement was marrying my wife, Jackie, who died of cancer in 1997 after 34 years of marriage, and our three children, Debbie, Greg and Jeff."* Boyd resides in Phoenix, Maryland.

Years Fly Fishing
Fifty
Favorite Rod
8 wt 9' Graphite
Rods Owned
Four dozen fly rods.
Favorite Flies
Dry – Bivisible
Wet – Black Gnat
Nymph – Gray or Muskrat
Streamer – Lefty's Deceiver
Terrestrial – Black
McMurray Ant
Flies Invented
The Invincible and many others.
Favorite US River
Potomac (MD)
Home River
Potomac (MD)
Favorite Stream
Big Hunting Creek (MD)
Home Stream
Big Hunting Creek (MD)

Boneless and Skinless Chicken Breasts

<u>*Marinade Sauce Ingredients*</u>
Caesar Salad Dressing
Concentrated Lemon Juice
Worcestershire Sauce
Soy Sauce
Mustard
Ketchup
Orange Goo
Arby's Horseradish Sauce
Barbecue Sauce
Old Bay Seasonings
Paprika
Pepper

Mix roughly equal portions of the liquid marinade sauce ingredients. The orange goo is what you get with carry out Chinese restaurant egg rolls. Leaving out one or two items probably won't hurt anything.

Puncture chicken breasts repeatedly with a fork and marinade for several hours with the sauce.

Cook rapidly on hot heat (pan or grill) until cooked through.

Serves: 1 – 2 breasts per person, unless they are gluttons

FREDRICK PFISTER

"A knowledgeable reader is better than a 6X leader."

Fred Pfister is a guide and the owner of Lexington, Kentucky's The Sporting Tradition, a fly tackle shop, which he says he has owned and operated profitably for 13 years.

Years Fly Fishing
Thirty-one

Favorite Rod
5 wt 9' Graphite

Rods Owned
Six

Favorite Flies
Dry – Trude
Wet – Caddis Emerger
Nymph – B.H. Soft
Hackle Pheasant Tail
Streamer – Mallard Minnow
Terrestrial – Flying Ant

Fly Invented
Cigar Minnow

Favorite US River
Green (UT)

Home River
Lower Cumberland (KY)

Favorite Stream
Au Sable (MI)

Home Stream
Rock Creek (KY)

MARINATED VENISON CHOPS

Deer Chops
Caribbean Jerk Marinade

Marinate chops for 3 days. Slap on grill until done. Eat while drinking German Pilsner. Enjoy!

Serves: 2 chops per man, lots of beer

"Buy a Scott today."

Stephen Phinny is the President of the Scott Rod Company, based in Montrose, Colorado. Both he and his company are active supporters of river and fishery conservation in Colorado and throughout the United States, including providing funding for Trout Unlimited's whirling disease research projects.

Stephen brought Scott Fly Rods to Colorado and has grown the company from a small custom shop in Berkeley, California to one of the top rod manufacturers in the world.

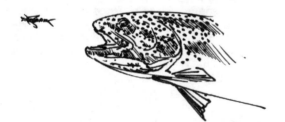

Years Fly Fishing
Thirteen

Favorite Rod
4 wt 8' 6" Scott Eclipse (SES 854)

Rods Owned
Forty Scotts

Favorite Flies
Dry – Parachute Adams
Wet – Blue Dun
Nymph – Pheasant Tail
Streamer – Dark Spruce
Home Stream Fly – Lime Trude
Terrestrial – White Winged Black Ant

Favorite US River
San Miguel (CO)

Home River
San Miguel (CO)

Favorite Stream
South Fork San Miguel (CO)

Home Stream
South Fork San Miguel (CO)

© 2000 - Russell A. Hopper

Nice New York Strip Steak
or
Filet Mignon
Charcoal
Barbecue Grill
Worcestershire Sauce

If you can figure out what the trout are eating, you can prepare a quality steak using the above ingredients.

TOM PICCOLO

"I never met a fish I didn't like."

Tom Piccolo is a fly fishing Manager of Bayou Specialties in New Orleans, Louisiana. Since 1994, he has been a celebrity fly tyer at the ISE Sportsmen's Show in San Mateo, California, and a guest fly tyer at the Federation of Fly Fishers' Southeastern Conclave.

Tom's fly designs include the Pic-A-Bugger, Tom's Wool Head Bunker, Pic's Poggie, Pic's Pink Mirro lure and others. His flies have appeared in many books including *Flies for Salt Water; Flies for Bass and Pan Fish; Secrets of the Saltwater Fly; Saltwater Flies: Over 700 of the Best; Inshore Fly Fishing;* and *Fly Fishing the Coast.*

Fly Fishing for Stripped Bass is the title of Tom's video.

Years Fly Fishing
Thirty-two

Favorite Rod
*T & T Horizon 908-4
8 wt 9' 4 Piece Graphite*

Rods Owned
Too Many

Favorite Flies
*Dry – Chuck's Caddis, Madam X or Gene's Gold Redfish Popper
Wet – Woolly Bugger
Nymph – Chartreuse/Red or Natural Shrimp with an Attitude – Pic's Woolly Crab
Streamer – Pic's Poggie
Terrestrial – Black Ant with Rubber Legs*

Flies Invented
See Comments

Favorite US River
Housatonic (CT)

Home River
*Housatonic
where I grew up.*

COURTBOUILLON ALA CREOLE

*6 Fine Slices Redfish (3 Pounds)
1 Tablespoon Shortening
2 Tablespoons Flour
12 Well Smashed Allspice
3 Sprigs Each of Thyme, Parsley, and Marjoram
3 Bay Leaves – Juice of 1 Lemon
1 Large Onion and 1 Clove Garlic
6 Large Tomatoes or 1 Pint Can
1 Glass Claret Wine – 1 Quart Water
Salt and Cayenne to Taste*

Wash and clean redfish and slice it into fine pieces. Make a Roux by putting 1 tablespoon of shortening in a deep pan or kettle. When hot, gradually add 2 tablespoons of flour, stirring constantly to prevent burning. Throw in 10 – 12 well-mashed allspice, 3 sprigs each of chopped thyme, parsley, bay leaf and sweet marjoram, 1 clove of garlic and 1 large onion, finely chopped. Add tomatoes. Pour in 1 glass of good claret, add 1 quart of water, and let it boil well. Then add salt and cayenne to taste. After boiling for 5 minutes, add fish, putting it in slice by slice. Add juice of a lemon, and let boil 10 minutes. Serve over rice, mashed potatoes or potato croquettes.

Serves: 6

DICK POBST

"The nature of both trout and trout-stream insects is that there are definite patterns of hatching; the trout discern those patterns and use them to feed selectively."

Dick Pobst is a fly fishing dealer, representative and writer. His shop is the Thornapple Orvis Shop in Grand Rapids, Michigan. He is the originator of the Keel Flies and Keel Hooks.

Dick's books include *Fish the Impossible Places*, *Trout Stream Insects* and *Caddisfly Handbook*. His videos include *Super Hatches* and *Trout Madness*.

Years Fly Fishing
Over Thirty

Favorite Rod
3 wt 8' 4" Graphite

Rods Owned
Not Provided

Favorite Flies
Dry – Whatever is hatching.
Wet – Not Provided
Nymph – Not Provided
Streamer – Not Provided
Terrestrial – Not Provided

Fly Invented
Keel Fly

Favorite US River
Muskegon (MI)

Home River
Muskegon (MI)

Favorite Stream
Elk Creek (CO)

Home Stream
Rogue (MI)

GRAVLAX*

(* Pressed Salmon Cured with Salt, Sugar and Dill)

1 Salmon or Steelhead Filet
2 Tablespoons Dill Weed
¼ Cup Salt
¼ Cup Sugar
White Pepper

Rub the spices into the fish. Put in a flat Pyrex cake pan. Put another Pyrex cake pan on top. Let stand in refrigerator for one day. Pour off the brine. Cover with plastic wrap and store in the refrigerator. Keeps about one week.

Slice thin, and serve with Mustard Sauce.

Mustard Sauce
¼ Cup Dijon Mustard
¼ Cup Salad Oil
1 Jigger White Wine
¼ Cup Brown Sugar
White Pepper
Fennel

Mix the ingredients and serve with Gravlax.

PRESS POWELL

BROILED WILD DUCK

"Fly fishing is a simple sport which consists of many simple techniques."

Press Powell is a fly fishing tackle manufacturer from Chico, California. His grand father, E. C. Powell, began making the famed Powell Rods in 1910. Press says the manufacturing of quality fly rods is in his blood. He has helped develop, manufacture and sale bamboo, graphite and fiberglass fly rods.

Years Fly Fishing
Forty-six

Favorite Rod
5-6 wt 9' 6" Powell Graphite

Rods Owned
Over Sixty

Favorite Flies
Dry – Adams
Wet – Rio Grande King
Bucktail Soft Hackle
Nymph – Pheasant Tail or
Bird's Nest
Streamer – Spruce Fly
Terrestrial – Hopper

Fly Invented
None, yet

Favorite US River
Pit (CA)

Home River
Sacramento (CA)

Favorite Stream
Big Sheep Creek (MT)

Home Stream
Chico Creek (CA)

1 Wild Mallard or Pintail Duck
Onions
Celery
Salt and Pepper
Seasoning Salt

Season 1 fat wild mallard or pintail duck and stuff with onion and celery.

Preheat oven to broil. Place duck in a pan on a small rack and broil for not more than 23 minutes. You do not have to turn the duck.

Serves: 1 – 2

STEVEN D. PRICE

"The inside of a trout stream is good for the inside of a man."

Steve resides in Manhattan where he earns a living as a writer and editor. He is the author of over 20 books including *The Ultimate Fishing Guide*. Steve is the co-author with Jimmy Houston of *Caught Me A Big 'Un ... and Then I Let Him Go!*

Steve's interest in fishing began as a boy when he spent many hours fishing the lakes and streams of Westchester County and the Catskills in upstate New York with his father. Since then, he has fished extensively, both in the U.S. and abroad.

Steve enjoys combining fly fishing with his other passion, horseback riding. In that regard, he has fished and ridden – *"trout and trot"* or *"hackle and hack,"* as he calls it – from the Rocky Mountains to Wales. In fact, hair from the manes and tails of favorite horses has found their way into homemade streamers.

Years Fly Fishing
Thirty
Favorite Rod
5 wt 9' Graphite
Rods Owned
Six
Favorite Flies
Dry – Royal Coachman
Wet – Royal Coachman Wet
Nymph – B.H.G.R.
Hare's Ear
Streamer – Mickey Finn
Terrestrial – Foam Ant
Fly Invented
None, yet
Favorite US River
White (CO)
Home River
Not Provided
Favorite Stream
Connetquot (NY)
Home Stream
Connetquot (NY)

CHICKEN PALE EVENING*

(*Steve Price's Chicken Pale Evening Well-Done)

1 Pound Boneless Chicken
Breasts, Cut into Cubes
Breadcrumbs or Flour for Dredging
4 Tablespoons Butter or Margarine
½ Pound Mushrooms, Cut into Small Pieces
1 Package (10 Ounces) Frozen Broccoli Spears
½ Cup White Wine or Lemon Juice

Dredge chicken breasts in breadcrumbs or flour. Set aside.

Melt 1 tablespoon butter or margarine, add the chicken and sauté over a medium flame for 5 – 6 minutes until brown. Turn the chicken over so that the other side of all the pieces is cooking. Add the mushrooms and broccoli, then cover the saucepan. After another 5 minutes, add the wine or lemon juice and cook for another 2 minutes or until tender. Don't let the chicken stick together.

Serve over pasta or rice.

Serves: 2 – 3

STEVE PROBASCO

"They're in there!"

Steve Probasco is an award winning, full-time outdoor writer and photographer living in Raymond, Washington. He is the Editor-in-Chief of *Northwest Fly Fishing* magazine.

Steve's articles and photographs appear regularly in magazines like *Fly Fisherman, Fly Fishing Salt Water, American Angler, Fly Tyer, Fly Fishing, Fly Tying, Salmon Trout Steelheader, Field & Stream* and others.

The author of nine fly fishing books and one video on fly tying is a seminar speaker/fly tier at the Federation of Fly Fishers International Fly Fishing Shows.

Steve's books include *The Art of Fly Tying: An Angler's Complete Handbook and Kit; River Journal Big Hole; Yakima River; Fishing Washington's Endless Season: A Year 'Round Fishing Guide; Fly Fishing Desert and High Arid Lakes;* and *Steelhead River Journal Hoh.*

The Probasco line of fly inventions includes the Night Leech, Sandshrimp and a whole pile of others.

Years Fly Fishing
Thirty-six

Favorite Rod
4 wt 9' Graphite

Rods Owned
Twenty-seven

Favorite Flies
Dry – Elk Hair Caddis
Wet – Gray Hackle Yellow
Nymph – G.R. Hare's Ear
Streamer – Spuddler Minnow
Terrestrial – Ant

Flies Invented
See Comments

Favorite US River
Big Hole (MT)

Home River
Hoh (WA)

Favorite Stream
South Fork Willapa (WA)

Home Stream
South Fork Willapa (WA)

PROBASCO'S FISH STEW

2 Pounds Whitefish of Choice, Chunked
4 Cups New Red or White Potatoes, Chunked
2 Cups Baby Carrots, Chunked
2 Cups Green Beans
2 Cups Pearl Onions
2 Cups Mushrooms, Cut in Half
2 Cans ((15 Ounces Each) Stewed Tomatoes
2 Cloves Garlic, Minced
Chives or Parsley for Garnish
1 Cube Butter, Sliced in Patties
Cajun Spice to Taste
Johnny's Seafood Seasoning to Taste

Steam vegetables until just tender. Potatoes will take longer than mushrooms and beans, so be careful. In a pot, layer butter, fish chunks and vegetables. Add garlic and spices. Pour the 2 cans of stewed tomatoes over all. Bring to a boil and then simmer for 10 minutes, just until the fish flakes. Garnish with fresh chives or parsley.

Serve with garlic bread. Yum!

"This is a fast and easy to make fish stew that anyone who likes fish will love. It can be made with all fresh ingredients, or canned vegetables may be substituted making this a snap to throw together in the field." – Steve

"Well, she says I keep repeating myself, but that's because she doesn't hear me the first time."

Datus Proper is a writer and Contributing Editor to *Field & Stream* magazine. Datus lives with his wife in Belgrade, Montana. When asked about his personal achievements, Datus replied, *"She still needs me, and she still feeds me, now I'm sixty-four."*

Datus' books include *Pheasants of the Mind: A Hunter's Search for a Mythic Bird* and *What the Trout Said.*

Favorite Rod – *"A 7' 9" bamboo by Charles Ritz with silk line to match. But fishing is more fun than fiddling with tackle, so I usually just take an 8-foot, 3-weight graphite that's set up in the garage."*

Favorite Dry Fly – *"The one on the water — which, on the stream closest to me, is likely to be a trico in any stage."*

Favorite Wet Fly – *"Hair-wing coachman, fished upstream a few inches below the surface. This is for brook trout, but others keep molesting it."*

Favorite Nymph – *"The one that is emerging when I'm there."*

Years Fly Fishing
Fifty-two
Favorite Rod
See Comments
Rods Owned
During my years in Ireland, I picked up all kinds of rods and reels made from 1840 on. Now I need to take an inventory and sell them. Nevermind yesterday; today is what counts.
Favorite Flies
See Comments
Fly Invented
See Comments
Favorite US River
Big Hole (MT), when it has water in it.
Favorite Stream
Humility Creek, out back of the house. I stride to it and slink back.

© 2000 - Russell A. Hopper

"I won't repeat it here because it took a whole chapter in my pheasant book. As to trout, the ones we eat are usually small brookies rolled in flour, pan-fried in peanut oil, and served with butter and fresh lemons. Trout Meuniere, in short." – Datus

Favorite Streamer – *"Don't use 'em much anymore. Bird season here opens September 1, when I might otherwise try a minnow imitation."*

Favorite Terrestrial – *"Beetle, maybe ant."*

Fly Invented – *"My great defect, as a fly-tyer, is that I cannot tie the same fly more than three times without making some change. This means that every fourth fly is an invention of sorts. But one that gets frequent use is the Perfect Dun, as described in my first book."*

"Innocence is a wild trout. But we humans, being complicated, have to pursue innocence in complex ways." – Datus

JAMES PROSEK

EASTON CONNECTICUT APPLE PIE

"Contrast makes virtue apparent."

James Prosek is an undergraduate student at Yale University, an author and artist. He resides in Easton, Connecticut.

James' works include *Trout: An Illustrated History*; *Joe and Me: An Education in Fishing and Friendship*; and his 1999 release, *The Complete Angler: A Connecticut Yankee Follows in the Footsteps of Walton.*

When James was fifteen, a ranger named Joe Haines caught him fishing without a permit. Instead of trying to flee, James surrendered. That single event started James on a life of fly fishing.

By the age of 20, James had photographed and sketched virtually every species and subspecies of trout in North America. All told, he has painted 71 true trout and char. It has been said that James Prosek qualifies to become the Audubon of the fishing world. He has also been compared to bird illustrator, Roger Tory Peterson.

James' website is www.troutsite.com.

Years Fly Fishing
Fifteen

Favorite Rod
5 wt 9' Graphite

Rods Owned
Twenty-five

Favorite Flies
Dry – Caddis Emerger with CDC
Wet – Soft Hackle
Nymph – B.H. Caddis Larvae
Streamer – Black Ghost
Terrestrial – Ant

Fly Invented
Popcorn Fly
(Emerger Pattern)

Favorite US River
Housatonic (CT)

Home River
Housatonic (CT)

Favorite Stream
Farm River (CT)

Home Stream
Mill River (CT)

6 - 8 Russet Apples from the North Slope of Slady's Orchard in Easton, Connecticut
¾ Cup Sugar
2 Tablespoons All-purpose Flour
2 Teaspoon Cinnamon
Dash Ground Nutmeg
Quick Pie Crust
2 Tablespoons Butter
Dash Salt

Combine sugar, flour, spices and a dash of salt. Mix with the apples. Line a 9" pie plate with pastry. Fill with apple mixture. Dot with butter. Adjust the top crust. Cut slits to let the steam escape. Seal. Sprinkle with sugar. Bake at 400 degrees for 50 minutes until done.

Serves: 4 – 8

JAMES PUCKETT

CHILI VERDE BURRITOS

"To learn to see, to learn to hear, you must do this —go into the wilderness alone." – Don Jose
"No snow flake falls in an inappropriate place." – Zen saying

Jamie Puckett is a building contractor based in Park City, Utah. He is an avid fly fisher who says he generously contributes to Trout Unlimited and supports Zero Limit fishing.

Jamie loves and enjoys skiing the beautiful Wasatch Mountains, biking through Moab, golfing and riding his Harley Davidson. He says he lives in gorgeous Park City, Utah with his wife and baby girl. *"I am a very very lucky man to be surrounded by such beauty,"* says Jamie.

Years Fly Fishing
Eleven

Favorite Rod
5 wt 9' Graphite

Rods Owned
Five

Favorite Flies
Dry – Parachute Adams
Wet – Barr Emerger PMD
Nymph – Pheasant Tail
Streamer – Woolly Bugger
Terrestrial – Cicada

Fly Invented
None, yet

Favorite US River
Beaverhead (MT)

Home River
Provo (UT)

Favorite Stream
A Secret

Home Stream
A Secret

1 Pound Pork Tenderloin,
Cut in 1" Pieces and Browned
2 Large Russet Potatoes, Washed and Diced
4 – 6 Carrots, Washed and Sliced
1 Large Onion, Chopped
1 Each – Green, Red and Yellow Pepper
6 – 8 Fresh Tomatillos, Sliced
1 Jalapeno, Chopped (Optional)
1 Can (4 Ounces) Green Chilies, Drained
2 Cans (22 Ounces Each) Green Verde Sauce
2 Tablespoons Salt – 2 Tablespoons Pepper
1 Teaspoons Red Pepper
2 Tablespoons Cilantro or 1/3 Cup Fresh Snipped

In a large pot, bring to boil potatoes and carrots. Cook uncovered until tender and most of the water has evaporated. Add onion, all peppers, tomatillos, jalapenos, green chilies and Verde sauce. Bring again to a boil.

Reduce heat and add all spices and browned pork. Simmer for 20 minutes or until thickened. For great vegetarian burritos, omit the pork.

Assemble burritos with warm tortillas and lots of cheese and tomatoes, smothered, if desired. Enjoy!

Serves: 8 – 10

PAUL QUINNETT

"I never met a fish I didn't like."

A man with two careers, Paul Quinnett is both a freelance writer and a clinical psychologist. Paul is an award-winning journalist with over 500 stories, essays and columns published in America's premier outdoor magazines. He has also written four books in psychology including his best-selling *Suicide: The Forever Decision.*

Paul is the Fishing Columnist for *Sporting Classics Magazine.* His mentor and best-selling humorist, Patrick F. McManus, in a serious moment, once wrote, *"Paul Quinnett is one of the finest essayists writing today."*

His best selling *Pavlov's Trout: The Incompleat Psychology of Everyday Fishing* was Paul's first attempt to bring his two great loves of his life together and has been predicted to become a fishing classic. Other books by Paul include *Fishing Lessons: Insights, Fun, and Philosophy from a Passionate Angler*, and *Darwin's Bass: The Evolutionary Psychology of Fishing Man.*

Despite Paul's teaching developmental psychology, none of his three children has turned out badly. He lives with his wife of three decades in Cheney, Washington.

Years Fly Fishing
Forty-seven

Favorite Rod
5 wt 8' 6" Graphite

Rods Owned
Fourteen

Favorite Flies
Dry – Adams
Wet – Buggers
Nymph – Scud
Streamer – One that catches browns.
Terrestrial – Joe's Hopper

Fly Invented
Paul's Pulverizing Pike Practitioner

Favorite US River
St. Joe (ID)

Home River
St. Joe (ID)

Favorite Stream
One without a crowd.

Home Stream
Crab Creek (WA)

© 2000 - Russell A. Hopper

TERIYAKI CRAPPIE

Skinless Filets from 4 Crappies
Top Grade Olive Oil
Quality Soy Sauce
Sake and Sugar
Fresh-squeezed Garlic
Salt and Pepper
Fresh-cut Asparagus
Flour
Short-grained Japanese Rice (Nikko Nikko)

Rinse rice three times, pouring off excess white water, and steam in rice maker for 20 – 30 minutes until done. Once rice is done, turn twice and allow to rest before dinner. Heat skillet searing hot. While warming up, stir equal parts of soy sauce and sugar in bowl and add ¼ cup of sake and 2 cloves of pestle-ground fresh garlic to sauce.

Salt and pepper filets to taste. Roll in flour and drop in heated olive oil for 1 minute each side. Remove filets and drain off excess oil. Add soy-sugar-garlic (teriyaki) sauce to pan and quickly add filets. Cook 1 minute, turn and cook 1 minute more. Remove from pan and serve with fresh-steamed asparagus, hot rice and a cool white wine (Washington State Johannesburg Resiling). After dinner, go Japanese with tangerine wedges, sweet rice cake or white ice cream custard.

PETER RAFLE

"Hip deep in clear, cold water, with fish rising, and bugs hatching, it's awfully hard to worry about anything but the next cast."

Peter Rafle is the current Director of Communications for Trout Unlimited. Prior to this, Peter edited TU's *Trout* magazine from 1992 to 1997. Peter is an outstanding spokesperson for American's leading trout and salmon conservation group. He resides in Springfield, Virginia.

A man of many talents, Peter is a graduate of Yale University where he was a member of the rowing crew and a member of a rock band. He also holds a brown belt in the Korean martial art of Tae Kwon Do.

Peter invented the Shad-Bugger fly which is tied on a #6 long shank hook with fluorescent chenille, marabou tail, and as much lead as a person can wrap on the hook. His advice when casting the fly is, *"Wear a helmet."*

Peter's recipe is a great way to stretch a small bag of birds.

~ 205 ~

Years Fly Fishing
Twenty-one

Favorite Rod
3 wt 8' 6" Graphite

Rods Owned
Seven

Favorite Flies
Dry – Stimulator #12
Wet – Peacock and Partridge
Soft Hackle
Nymph – B.H. Hare's Ear
Streamer – Mickey Finn
Terrestrial – Letort Cricket

Fly Invented
See Comments

Favorite US River
Upper Delaware (NY)

Home River
Potomac (VA)

Favorite Stream
Rose (VA)

Home Stream
Beaverkill (NY)

CURRIED QUAIL*

(*Curried Quail with Sausage & Couscous — Adapted from "Gourmet Magazine")

Breasts of Six Quail
¾ Pound Sausage, Browned if Preferred
1 Cup Peas
1 Cup Sliced Carrots
1 Tablespoon Curry Powder, More to Taste
1 Small Onion
2 Tablespoons Butter
1 Can Chicken Broth
½ Cup Water
1 ¾ Cup Couscous

Chop the onion fine, and sauté in 1 tablespoon of butter until softened. Add curry powder and cook 1 minute more, stirring. Add the broth, quail breasts, sausage, peas, carrots, and water to a saucepan. Bring to a boil. Lower heat and simmer 15 – 20 minutes or until the carrots are tender. Pour off 2 ¼ cups of liquid into another saucepan. Add the remaining 1 tablespoon of butter and couscous. Bring to a boil. Remove from heat and cover. Allow couscous to stand 5 minutes.

Serve quail and sausage over the couscous.

Serves: 4

"These brook trout will strike any fly you present, provided you don't get close enough to present it."—Blalock's Rapidan Paradox from *Fly Fishing through the Midlife Crisis*

Howell Raines is a journalist and the current Editorial Page Editor of *The New York Times*. In 1992, he won the *Pulitzer Prize* for *Grady's Gift*, a *New York Times Magazine* article about his friendship with Gradystein Williams Hutchinson, a black woman, in segregated Birmingham.

Howell is the author of *Whiskey Man, Fly Fishing through the Midlife Crisis* and *My Soul is Rested*, which is considered an essential work on the history of the civil rights movement.

Years Fly Fishing
Forty-six

Favorite Rod
4 wt 9' Graphite

Rods Owned
Ten

Favorite Flies
Dry – Royal Wulff
Wet – Hornberg
Nymph – Prince
Streamer – Clouser Minnow
Terrestrial – Letort Cricket or
Whitlock Hopper

Fly Invented
None, yet

Favorite US River
Rapidan (VA)

Home River
Not Provided

Favorite Stream
Not Provided

Home Stream
Not Provided

1 Copy of "Fly Fishing through the Midlife Crisis" – Turned to Page 133

"Fresh tomatoes of the kind not found in supermarkets, peeled and sliced.

"Fresh corn on the cob, preferably Silver Queen picked on the day it is cooked.

"Fresh, baby green onions with the tops trimmed and the outer skin peeled off or quartered Vidalia onions from Georgia or quartered Bermuda onions from Texas.

"Cornbread, made according to the recipe on the Indian Head cornmeal bag. (Do not use any recipe that calls for sugar. Corn bread with sugar is an abomination and demeans the death of any fish with which it is served.)

"Quartered lemons.

"Hellman's Tartar Sauce. (You can make your own. Frankly, I never figured I could top Hellman's, a noble product in my book.)

"Some of these items are seasonal, and if you substitute, do so with something like fresh spinach or collard greens or okra that is not going to compete with the fish. If you lay on too many side dishes, you lessen the impact of the fish, and the meal will leave you feeling both heavy and with your central craving unfilled." – Howell Raines

STEVE RAJEFF

OYSTERS WANDAFUL

"Fishing can be whatever you wish to make it. Angling is most rewarding to the boy or girl who puts the most into it." – Tom McNally

Steve Rajeff works as the Director of Research and Development for G. Loomis Rods. He lives in Battle Ground, Washington.

Steve is a 24 time North America and 13 time *World All Round Casting Champion*. His longest fly cast was 306 feet.

Steve grew up only five minutes away by bike from the Golden Gate Angling and Casting Club where he met Mel Krieger. Mel taught Steve how to cast better. At Mel's insistence, Steve entered his first tournament. He ended up in last place. In his next tournament two weeks later, Steve scored a 97. Mel cast a 95.

In 1986, Gary Loomis invited Steve, a lifelong, die-hard fisherman and expert rod designer since the 1970s, to try out his prototype IMX fly rod, a 9-foot, 6 weight. One month later, Steve joined G-Loomis.

Years Fly Fishing
Over Thirty

Favorite Rod
G. Loomis Graphite

Rods Owned
Over Two Hundred

Favorite Flies
Dry – Adult Stonefly
Wet – Exuma Shrimp
Nymph – Chartreuse Ricophelea (Green Rock Worm)
Streamer – Surf Candy
Terrestrial – Dave's Hopper

Fly Invented
Parachute Down Wing Midge

Favorite US River
Kulik (AK)

Home River
East Fork Lewis (WA)

Favorite Stream
Traful (Argentina)

Home Stream
Not Provided

Oysters on the Half Shell
Marinara Sauce with Garlic
Cooked Creamy Spinach, Chopped
Ground Parmesan Cheese

Take 1 dozen oysters on the half shell and place them on the barbecue grill. Put marinara sauce, then spinach, and then Parmesan cheese on top of the oysters.

Barbecue for 2 minutes to cook oysters and melt the cheese.

Serves: 4 as appetizers

"I fish because fishing humbles a man, and humility is a rare virtue."

Steve Raymond is a semi-retired editor. He is the author of seven fly fishing books, including _Kamloops, an Angler's Study of the Kamloops Trout; The Year of the Angler; The Year of the Trout; Backcasts, a History of the Washington Fly Fishing Club, 1939–1989; Steelhead Country; The Estuary Flyfisher_; and _Rivers of the Heart_.

Raymond's book, _The Year of the Angler_, was chosen by the American Booksellers Association for special presentation to the White House Library.

He has received the Federation of Fly Fishers' _Roderick Haig-Brown Award for Literary Excellence_ and his books have twice been honored with the _Governor's Award_ at the Washington State Festival of the Arts. He also received the _Letcher Lambuth Angling Craftsman Award_ from the Washington Fly Fishing Club.

A native of Bellingham, Washington, Raymond graduated from the University of Washington and served as a Navy officer before starting a 30-year career as a reporter, editor, and manager at _The Seattle Times_. He edited a _Times_ series that won the 1984 _Pulitzer Prize_ for feature writing.

Years Fly Fishing
Fifty-three

Favorite Rod
6 wt 6' 10" Graphite

Rods Owned
Over Thirty

Favorite Flies
Whichever one I happen to be using at the time.

Flies Invented
Golden Shrimp, Cutthroat Candy and Judge Boldt

Favorite Waters
North Fork Stillaguamish (WA)

© 2000 - Russell A. Hopper

"I don't eat fish; I consider it a form of cannibalism." – Steve

Raymond has served as President of the Washington Fly Fishing Club, Vice President of the Museum of American Fly Fishing, and Secretary of the Federation of Fly Fishers. He is a former Editor of the Federation's magazine, _The Flyfisher_, and currently is Consulting Editor for _Fly Fishing in Salt Waters_ magazine.

Raymond and his wife, Joan, make their home in Seattle, Washington.

GEORGE W. REIGER

"Loyalty is the first quality of a dog." – H. L. Mencken

"Ah! Another day in which to excel." – Price Mosher

George Reiger is the Conservation Editor for *Field & Stream* and *Salt Water Sportsman* magazines. He resides in Locustville, Virginia.

George is the author of sixteen books including *Profiles in Saltwater Angling, Fishing with McClane, The Undiscovered Zane Grey, Fishing Stories, The Silver King, The Striped Bass Chronicles* and *The Bonefish*. His writing awards include the *Excellence in Craft Award* from the Outdoor Writers Association of America, the *Writing Achievement Award* from CBS Publications, and he was a Pulitzer finalist for *Wanderer on My Native Shore*.

Reiger once worked for *Field & Stream* magazine and was a friend of the late A. J. McClane.

Years Fly Fishing
Forty-five

Favorite Rod
It all depends on what I'm fishing for.

Rods Owned
A couple dozen, including a few too many with broken tips.

Favorite Flies
Whatever works.

Fly Invented
None, yet

Favorite Water
The Atlantic

Home Waters
The 2 acre pond next to my house and the Chesapeake Bay.

© 2000 - Russell A. Hopper

CREPES BABA

2 Cups All-purpose Bleached Flour
1 Beaten Egg
¾ – 1 Cup Milk, Beaten in and Well Mixed

Heat iron skillet super-hot. Add tablespoon canola oil. Pour in batter. Flip when cooked on one side. Reduce heat to merely "very hot" after cooking first crepe.

Serve with bonafide maple syrup.

Serves: 2

"The ingredients above make 10 – 12 crepes— enough for one very hungry angler! Double the ingredients for 3 or 4 anglers." – George

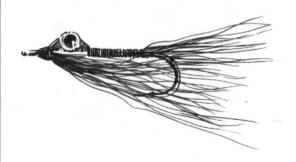

BOB RICHARDS

"No matter where you go in life, there you are."

Bob Richards is a thirty-year employee of Bowling Green, Kentucky's General Motor's Corvette Division. Bob fishes often with his friend, Russ Hopper. His wife, Betty, encourages him to fish in order to get him out of the house on weekends.

Prior to moving to Bowling Green, Kentucky, Bob fished the big rivers of the north for walleye, salmon, and other species of fish.

During Bob's first fly fishing outing, he broke the end of his rod tip trying to catch a sycamore tree. He was scheduled for a Vietnam Veteran trip to Washington, D.C. and was fearful that he wouldn't be home to receive his rod in time for his next fishing trip. Bob called L. L. Bean and explained his dilemma. They not only sent his rod to Washington; they even upgraded his rod at no additional cost.

Years Fly Fishing
Two Seasons

Favorite Rod
6 wt 9' Graphite

Rods Owned
Two

Favorite Flies
Dry – How can it be in the water and be dry?
Wet – Green Woolly Bugger
Nymph – The one that catches fish.
Streamer – Woolly Bugger
Terrestrial – Hopper

Fly Invented
None, yet

Favorite US River
Cumberland (KY)

Home River
Cumberland (KY)

Favorite Stream
Trammel Fork (KY)

Home Stream
Trammel Fork (KY)

© 2000 - Russell A. Hopper

MARTHA'S BEAN CASSEROLE

1 Can Pork and Beans, Drained
1 Can Kidney Beans, Drained
1 Package Frozen Lima Beans, Cooked and Drained
1 ½ Cups Celery, Chopped
1 ½ Cups Onions, Chopped
1 Cup Chopped Green Pepper
1 Teaspoon Dry Mustard
2 Cups Tomato Catsup
1 ½ Cups Brown Sugar
1 Teaspoon Garlic Juice or Salt

Mix all ingredients together and put in a large baking dish. Bake at 350 degrees for 45 minutes.

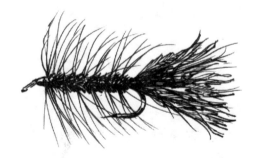

"My wife hooked, played, and landed me skillfully—and I am the lucky one!"

Bruce Richard's father started him fly fishing and is still a frequent companion. His mother, an avid outdoorswoman, allowed them as much fishing time as they wanted.

Bruce and his wife, Suzanne, met when she was a student in one of Bruce's fly fishing schools. She is his favorite fishing buddy. They live in Midland, Michigan.

The Scientific Anglers/3M employee is a Product Development Engineer and the designer of many popular modern fly line tapers. Bruce is the author of *Modern Fly Lines* that is included in the *Lefty's Little Library of Fly Fishing* series. He is a member of the Federation of Fly Fishers' Casting Certification Board of Governors and the AFFTA Board of Directors.

Years Fly Fishing
Thirty-five

Favorite Rod
5 wt 9' Graphite

Rods Owned
Don't Know

Favorite Flies
Dry – Deer Hair Caddis
Wet – Little Black
Caddis Pupa
Nymph – Hare's Ear
Streamer – Clouser Minnow
Terrestrial – Low
Water Hopper

Fly Invented
Flash Gordon

Favorite US River
Lamar (MT)

Home River
Au Sable (MI)

Favorite Stream
Cedar (MI)

Home Stream
Cedar (MI)

¼ Cup Olive Oil
Anchovy Paste, 2" from Tube
1 Teaspoon Dijon Mustard
Juice of 1 Lemon
1 Clove Garlic, Crushed
1 Teaspoon Worcestershire Sauce
6 Drops Tabasco Sauce
1 Teaspoon Tarragon Vinegar
1 Teaspoon Cracked Pepper
1 Raw Egg
¼ Cup Grated Parmesan Cheese
1 Cup Croutons
1 Head Romaine Lettuce

Mix all ingredients together well, except croutons and lettuce, in a large salad bowl. Add torn lettuce and toss. Add croutons and toss again. Serve. Top with additional Parmesan and cracked pepper if desired.

Serves: 4

CARL RICHARDS

GROUPER FINGERS

"The South is just a prettier place to fish and the water is almost always crystal clear."

Carl Richards is a dentist who lives in Rockford, Michigan. He has co-authored numerous volumes about trout and trout insects, including *Selective Trout, Emergers*, and *Fly Fishing Strategy*, all regarded as instructional classics. Carl co-authored these books with Doug Swisher. Carl's latest book, *Tailwaters of Southern Appalachia*, is co-authored with John Krause.

Selective Trout is one of the most influential and popular fly fishing books of the twentieth century.

Carl and Doug Swisher were introduced to the world by the legendary Joe Brooks who ran the story *New No-Hackle Dry Fly* in the August 1970 issue of *Outdoor Life* magazine. The team of Richards and Swisher developed their no-hackle dry fly on the Au Sable, after capturing insects from the river, placing them in aquariums for study and photographing them to compare with the naturals.

Carl now spends a considerable amount of his time on Tennessee's Clinch River and Kentucky's Cumberland River. He says this area is the next new Mecca of dry fly fishing.

Years Fly Fishing
Sixty
Favorite Rod
5 wt 9' Graphite
Rods Owned
Twenty
Favorite Flies
Dry – No-Hackle
Wet – Caddis Pupa
Nymph – Sulphur
Streamer – Chico Fly
Terrestrial – Ant
Flies Invented
No-Hackle and Para-Drake
Favorite US River
Clinch (TN)
Home River
Muskegon (MI)
Favorite Stream
South Holston (TN)
Home Stream
Au Sable (MI)

Grouper and Breadcrumbs

Directions – Deep fry.

CHUCK ROBINSON

"It's like this, and you know how that is."

Chuck Robinson is a Certified Fly Casting Instructor. He lives in Nashville, Tennessee and has recently served two terms as President and is a current Board Member of the Middle Tennessee Fly Fishers, an active member group of the Federation of Fly Fishers. Chuck's leadership, and a lot of other hard working fly fishers, built the Middle Tennessee Fly Fishers into the largest single group of the Federation. Hats off to Chuck!

Chuck has been noted to cast the fly line into the backing when demonstrating his casting abilities.

Once a year, Chuck takes his daughter back to his native Montana. Unfortunately, it seems his vehicle conveniently breaks down at nearly every stream.

Years Fly Fishing
Twenty-five

Favorite Rod
4 wt 7' 6" or 7' 8" Bamboo

Rods Owned
Over Twenty

Favorite Flies
Dry – Blue Wing Olive
Wet – Any Soft Hackle
Nymph – Red Fox Squirrel
Streamer – Sparse Bucktail
with Gold Body
Terrestrial – Hopper

Fly Invented
Just variations of
some favorites.

Favorite US River
Bighorn (MT)

Home River
Caney Fork (TN)

Favorite Stream
Elk (TN)

Home Stream
Caney Fork and Elk (TN)

VENISON MEDALLIONS

Venison
Milk
Tabasco
Flour
Olive Oil
Plastic Bag

Slice venison across grain ¼" thick and pound to tenderize. Put milk in shallow dish and add Tabasco until a hot pink. Put flour in plastic bag. Dip venison in milk and shake in flour. Fry quickly in olive oil. Do not over cook!

BOB RODGERS

"If I can see you, you're getting too close."

Captain Bob Rodgers is a Florida Keys fly fishing guide who stalks bonefish, permit and tarpon with a fly rod. He and his famed wife, Sandy, are regular contributors, as both writers and photographers, to numerous fly fishing magazines and operate from Tavernier, Florida.

Bob is a fly designer who designed the Peabody Fly for trout, the Depth Charge for bonefish, the Siuslaw Shrimp for steelhead and the Buchanan Special and Tarpon Crab for tarpon.

Known for his design capabilities, Bob is a fishing lodge consultant and has developed a flats boat for lodges in foreign destinations. He has made numerous television appearances, is a tackle consultant and a frequent lecturer who uses slide presentations.

Years Fly Fishing
Thirty-one

Favorite Rod
9 wt 9' Graphite

Rods Owned
Thirty-five

Favorite Flies
Dry – Adams
Wet – Peabody
Nymph – G.R. Hare's Ear
Streamer – Tarpon Crab
Terrestrial – Foam Ant

Flies Invented
See Comments

Favorite US River
North Umpqua (OR)

Home Waters
The Flats of the Keys (FL)

Favorite Stream
McKay Creek (OR)

Home Stream
Gulf Stream (FL)

POLLO RODRIQUEZ*

*(*Pollo Rodriguez with Green Chile Quesadillas)*

1 Chicken – Limes
Mojo Marinade or Italian Dressing
10 Flour Tortillas
Roasted, Peeled Green Chiles
(If Fresh, 5 Large – if Canned, 3 Cans)
¾ Pound Grated Mild Cheddar or
Mixed Cheddar – Monterey Jack Cheese
Salsa Picante – Fresh Cilantro

Cut chicken into 10 pieces and marinate in Mojo Marinade or Italian Dressing for 4 hours. Grill over medium flame, or coals, for approximately 35 – 45 minutes. Just before putting on the grill, however, squeeze lime juice over each piece of chicken.

While chicken cooks, heat tortillas one at a time in a dry skillet, folding in half after the first turn and filling with a large piece of chile and a handful of grated cheese.

Cook each side over medium heat until the cheese begins to melt and the tortillas have light brown spots.

Serve with picante sauce and sprigs of fresh cilantro.

Serves: 4

CRAIG ROGERS

SPAGHETTI WITH SCALLOPS*

"You can't catch fish in the same hole for too long."

Craig Rogers makes his home in Narberth, Pennsylvania and is a freelance artist specializing in fishing subjects. He says that the first time anyone tried one of his flies, his father, using the Brainteaser Shrimp, caught a bonefish with an estimated weight of over 15-pounds which would have qualified for the 12-pound tippet record at the time, had it not been released.

Craig is primary a salt water fisherman who started fly fishing at the age of seven. As a child his father would take him fishing near his house in Montana. He has since fished the Florida Keys, Costa Rica and Belize.

Years Fly Fishing
Fifteen, but not enough.
Favorite Rod
8 wt 9' Graphite
Rods Owned
Four
Favorite Fly
Rhody Flat Wing Deceiver
Fly Invented
Brainteaser Shrimp
Favorite Waters
Atlantic Ocean

*(*Spaghetti with Scallops & Sea Bass)*

2 Cubed Fillets of Chilean Seabass
1 Dozen Scallops
¼ Cup Moroccan Olives
3 Tablespoons Capers
2 ½ Cups Tomato Sauce, Homemade
or Store Bought
2 Teaspoons Garlic
4 Tablespoons Olive Oil
1 ½ Ounces Anisette
1 Box Spaghetti
Salt to Taste

Heat boiling water and cook spaghetti until al dente. At the same time, heat olive oil in a large sauté pan. Add garlic and stir until it begins to brown. Add seabass and scallops. Sauté for 1 minute over high heat. Add olives and capers. When fish is nearly cooked, deglaze pan with anisette. Add tomato sauce and salt to taste. Simmer until sauce is hot.

Serve over a bed of spaghetti.

Serves: 3 – 4

SIMPLE TOMATO SAUCE

"If you have the choice whether to be right or to be kind, be kind!"

Neal Rogers and his wife, Linda, are physicians and book publishers residing in Butte, Montana. He says his greatest accomplishment was in marrying Linda—the best fishing partner and photographer ever.

Neal and Linda's company, Earth & Great Weather Publishing Company, is the publisher of *Saltwater Fly Fishing Magic* and *Flip Pallot's Memories, Mangroves & Magic*. They are Contributing Photographers to *Fly Fishing in Salt Waters*. Their specialty is action and scenic photographic.

Linda, a retired pediatric physician, was introduced to fly fishing by her father when she was 10 years old and says she was one of the few women she knows who received a fly rod and reel as a high school graduation gift.

Neal is an ear, nose and throat doctor who started fly fishing at the age of seven.

Years Fly Fishing
Forty-six

Favorite Rod
8 wt 9' Graphite Loomis IMX or an Orvis Battenkill

Rods Owned
Twenty-seven

Favorite Flies
Dry – Adams
Wet – Gotcha
Nymph – Prince
Streamer – Borski Orange Butt Tarpon Fly
Terrestrial – Hopper

Fly Invented
Bone Crusher Crab

Favorite US River
Big Hole (MT)

Home River
Big Hole (MT)

Favorite Stream
Beaverhead (MT)

Home Stream
Beaverhead (MT)

2 Cans (14 Ounces Each) Whole Peeled Tomatoes
3 Tablespoons Olive Oil, Virgin
2 Teaspoons Dried Basil
2 Teaspoons Dried Oregano
5 Large Garlic Cloves, Crushed in a Press

Place tomatoes in a saucepan and crush by squeezing them each by hand. Add oil, basil, oregano and garlic.

Bring to a boil and then simmer for 25 minutes or more.

Serve over pasta. As a variation, fried ground beef may be added to the sauce. Also, top the pasta with mozzarella cheese, cover with the sauce and bake until the cheese is melted.

"Simple and great—can be made on camping trips or in the finest kitchen." – Linda

"Fly fishermen should stop taking themselves so seriously."

Tom Rosenbauer is the former Editor of *The Orvis News* and the current Catalog Manager for Orvis. He resides in Arlington, Vermont. Tom has penned several books including *Reading Trout Streams: An Orvis Guide; Prospecting for Trout: Flyfishing Secrets from a Streamside Observer;* and *Casting Illusions: The World of Fly-Fishing.*

Tom is a regular contributor to magazines such as *Fly Rod & Reel, Fly Fisherman, Field & Stream* and *Audubon.* He invented a magnetic net holder and is responsible for introducing the bead head nymphs to the United States.

When not in his office, Tom fishes the Battenkill at lunchtime.

Years Fly Fishing
Thirty-four
Favorite Rod
2 wt 7' 9" Graphite
Rods Owned
Varies since I am always testing new models.
Favorite Flies
Dry – Parachute Hare's Ear
Wet – 2/0 Chartreuse Lefty's Deceiver
Nymph – Pheasant Tail
Streamer – Black Ghost
Terrestrial – Quick Sight Beetle
Fly Invented
CDC Rabbit's Foot
Favorite US River
Delaware (NY)
Home River
Battenkill (VT)
Favorite Stream
Forget it!
Home Stream
No way!

© 2000 - Russell A. Hopper

4 Eight-inch Brook Trout
Salt and Pepper
Onions
2 Dozen Wild Chanterelles

Catch 4 eight-inch brook trout. Knock them on the head. Cut onion. Gather 2 dozen wild golden chanterelles mushrooms in late July—August no more than 5 feet from the edge of the brook. Throw onion, mushrooms, salt and pepper into a skillet left on the stream bank last year and place on a wood fire on a metal grate that you also left with the frying pan.

"If you kill more than 4 brook trout, substitute any species of amanita mushrooms for the chanterelles." – Tom

Note – Amanita mushrooms are poisonous.

JIM ROWINSKI

"Never be satisfied with what you did yesterday."

Jim Rowinski is the Product Manager for L. L. Bean Fly Fishing where he was instrumental in developing the Aqua Stealth Wading Shoes. The shoes are believed to be helpful in preventing the spread of whirling disease in trout, caused by a parasite that is believed to be transferred from one stream to another by waders and wading boots.

Jim lives in Yarmouth, Maine.

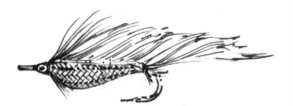

Years Fly Fishing
Thirty-one

Favorite Rod
5 wt 8' 6" Graphite

Rods Owned
Sixteen

Favorite Flies
Dry – Light Cahill #14
Wet – Quill Gordon
Nymph – Hare's Ear
Streamer – White Zonker
Terrestrial – Black Ant

Fly Invented
Katie Ann Streamer

Favorite US River
Gallatin (MT)

Home River
Bois Brule (WI)

Favorite Stream
Bois Brule (WI)

Home Stream
Bois Brule (WI)

MINNESOTA DUCK

4 Wild Ducks
2 Apples
Celery
2 Cans Consommé
1 Can Water
2 Cups Uncooked Wild Rice
4 Slices Bacon, Cooked and Crumbled

Sauce
1 Cup Butter
1 Cup Sherry
½ Cup Bourbon
Jar (5 Ounces) Currant Jelly
¾ Cup Worcestershire Sauce

Stuff each duck with ½ apple and a stalk of celery. Put ducks breast down in a pan and pour consommé and water into pan. Cover and bake at 350 degrees for 3 hours.

Pour sauce over ducks after turning them over in the pan. Bake for 20 minutes more, uncovered.

Serve sliced duck over wild rice with sauce and crumbled bacon.

To make sauce, slowly heat all ingredients until the jelly melts. The sauce may be thickened with cornstarch, if desired.

Serves: 6 – 8

DAVID RUIMVELD

"May all your dry flies float."

David Ruimveld is a wildlife and sporting artist who resides in Vicksburg, Michigan. Having two beautiful daughters, Kasey and Jenna, and staying married to his wife, Ginny, while being a self employed, self published, not so rich or famous, sporting artist which gives him the greatest excuse to research new paintings while hunting and fishing is David's greatest achievement.

Years Fly Fishing
Thirteen

Favorite Rod
4 wt 8' Graphite

Rods Owned
Ten

Favorite Flies
Dry – Caddis and Adams
Wet – Not Provided
Nymph – Prince
Streamer – Muddler Minnow
Terrestrial – Brown Cricket

Fly Invented
None, yet

Favorite US River
Missouri (MT)

Home River
Muskegon (MI)

Favorite Stream
Not Provided

Home Stream
Not Provided

FISH DOPE*

(*A Dutch Fish & Butter Sauce Dish)

1 Pound Icelandic Cod Cut in 1 ½ Inch Cubes
6 Medium Potatoes
¾ Cup Butter
2 Tablespoons Cornstarch
Parsley
Salt

Boil potatoes in ½ teaspoon salt. Drain the water, reserving 2 cups liquid for the sauce. Mash potatoes as usual.

Boil 3 cups of water with ¼ teaspoon salt. Place cod cubes in and bring back to a boil for 1-½ minutes. Drain fish.

Melt ¾ cup butter in the saved potato liquid. Thicken with 2 tablespoons cornstarch, softened with water to a gravy consistency.

Place mashed potatoes in a buttered 9" x 9" serving dish. Add drained fish to butter sauce. Pour fish and butter sauce over the potatoes. Garnish with parsley.

This dish may be made ahead of time and heated in the oven or in a microwave.

RICK RUOFF

"Let's get back to basics—keep fishing simple and fun."

Rick Ruoff is a veteran guide working out of the flats of the Florida Keys. He has been guiding for over 25 years and is based in Islamorada, Florida where he routinely catches and releases trophy-sized bonefish. He divides his time between homes in Islamorada and southwestern Montana.

Fly Rod & Reel magazine chose Rick as its first *Guide of the Year* in 1987. He is a member of the Orvis Saltwater Advisory Council.

Rick is an outdoor writer and a master fly tyer. His fly inventions include the Absolute Flea, Deep Flea, Backcountry Flea, Backcountry Popper and the Tarpon Lay-up Fly.

Years Fly Fishing
Thirty-seven

Favorite Rod
7 wt 9' Graphite

Rods Owned
Sixty

Favorite Flies
Dry – Backcountry Popper
Wet – Muddler Minnow
Nymph – Bonefish Absolute
Streamer – Tarpon Lay-up
Terrestrial – Crowe Beetle

Flies Invented
See Comments

Favorite Waters
Florida Keys

TAMARIND SORBET

1 ½ Pounds Tamarind Seeds, Shelled
1 ½ Gallon Water
2 ½ Cups Sugar

Boil all ingredients together until reduced by 1/3, about 30 minutes. Cool.

Strain pulp to remove seeds and stems. Place mixture in an ice cream maker for 10 – 12 minutes. Freeze for 2 hours before serving.

JIM RYALL

"He who pisseth into the wind shall find no comfort from the spray."

Jim Ryall designs and manufacturers fly reels. His company, J. Ryall Machine Works, is based in San Carlos, California.

Years Fly Fishing
Fifty-six

Favorite Rod
6 wt 8' 6" Graphite or Bamboo

Rods Owned
Twelve

Favorite Flies
Dry – Adams
Wet – Not Provided
Nymph – Prince
Streamer – Not Provided
Terrestrial – Not Provided

Fly Invented
None, yet

Favorite US River
Not Provided

Home River
San Francisco Bay (CA)

Favorite Stream
Highland Creek (CA)

Home Stream
Not Provided

PATTE MONTEREY

1 Can Sardines
1 Tablespoon Sweet Relish
2 Tablespoons Sour Cream
1 Teaspoon Mayonnaise
Small Jar Black Lumpfish Caviar

Mash sardines and add everything but caviar. Spread on cracker and top with dash of caviar.
For variation add pepper or Tabasco to taste.

Serves: 1 if you like sardines

WILL RYAN

"Buy low, sell high."

Will Ryan teaches writing at Hampshire College in Massachusetts. He says his greatest achievement is in fishing with the same family and friends every year; trying to catch the same species (bullheads, trout, salmon, bass, pike, stripers, and steelheads); and enjoying himself more every time he goes.

Will has contributed angling stories to most major sporting magazines. He has also written the exceptionally useful bass fishing book, *Smallmouth Strategies for the Fly Rod*.

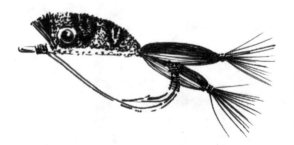

Years Fly Fishing
Thirty-five
Favorite Rod
6 wt 8' 6" Graphite
Rods Owned
Ten including spinning and bait casting.
Favorite Flies
*Dry – Elk Hair Caddis (Clipped Hackle)
Wet – Leisenring Spider
Nymph – Weighted Stonefly
Streamer – Thunder Creek Marabou, Tied in 9-3 Pattern
Terrestrial – Tap's Bass Bug*
Fly Invented
Sparkle Grub Smallmouth Bass Fly
Favorite US River
West Branch Penobscot (ME)
Home River
St. Lawrence (NY)
Favorite Stream
Bouquet (NY)
Home Stream
Lamoille (VT)

ROAST DUCK*

(*Mallard, Black Duck, Wood Duck, Scaup)

*One Plucked Duck
½ Cup Vermouth
½ Cup Applesauce
¼ Cup Tarragon
1 Apple Cut up
½ Pepper, Cut up
1 Onion, Cut up
Stuffing*

Stuff duck cavity with stuffing, onion, pepper, and apple. Pour mix of applesauce, vermouth, and tarragon over the duck. Roast in a shallow pan at 375 degrees for 30 – 45 minutes, depending on taste.

Serves: 2 per bird

BOB RYON

"As always, I'm a day late and a dollar short."

Bob Ryon is a banker, beginning fly tyer, and a member of the Board of Directors of the Middle Tennessee Fly Fishers, an active member group of the Federation of Fly Fishers. Bob serves on the Board of Directors as Outings Chairman. He lives in Franklin, Tennessee.

Years Fly Fishing
Nine

Favorite Rod
7 wt 8' 6" Graphite

Rods Owned
Two

Favorite Flies
Dry – Parachute Adams
Wet – March Brown
Nymph – Pheasant Tail
Streamer – Clouser Minnow
Terrestrial – Ant

Fly Invented
None, yet

Favorite US River
Clinch (TN)

Home River
Elk (TN)

Favorite Stream
Indian Creek (TN)

Home Stream
Big Swan Creek (TN)

HUNGRY JACK CASSEROLE

1 Pound Ground Beef
1 Teaspoon Salt
1 Can (16 Ounces) Pork 'n Beans
¾ Cup Barbeque Sauce
2 Tablespoons Brown Sugar
1 Tablespoon Instant Minced Onions
1 Cup Grated Cheese
1 Can Biscuits

Brown ground beef in cast iron skillet and drain. Add next five ingredients and heat until bubbly in skillet. Then pour into 2-quart casserole dish. Spread grated cheese and add biscuits. Bake at 375 degrees for 25 – 30 minutes.

The many varieties of barbeque sauce, cheeses and pork 'n beans give you a lot of options to create your own favorite variation.

JACK SAMSON

"Making the delivery is a lot easier when your rod and line are in harmony."

Jack Samson is a pioneer in salt water catch and release fishing. In 1980, he was the first to tag and release a marlin weighing more than 1,000 pounds. He was a co-winner of the First International Invitational Billfish Fly Tournament in 1989. And the first person to land both Atlantic and Pacific sailfish and all five species of marlin on a fly.

Jack is the former Editor-in-Chief of *Field & Stream* magazine and the author of 21 books on the outdoors, including *Salt Water Flyfishing, Permit on a Fly, Billfish on a Fly* and *Lee Wulff*, a biography of the legendary Lee Wulff.

The International Game Fish Association, of which Jack is a representative, gave him its annual *Conservation Award* for his March 1995 Saltwater column in *Fly Rod & Reel* magazine. Jack is a Contributing Editor for that magazine.

Jack resides in his native Santa Fe, New Mexico. It was from there that he went on to fly 52 combat missions in B-24 Liberators for General Claire Lee Chennault's Flying Tiger 14th Air Force in China. He covered the Korean War as a United Press correspondent and was later awarded a *Nieman Fellowship* to Harvard.

Years Fly Fishing
Sixty
Favorite Rod
8 wt 9' Graphite
Rods Owned
Twenty
Favorite Flies
Dry – Elk Hair Caddis
Wet – Woolly Bugger
Nymph – Chocolate Emerger
Streamer – Rio Grande
Terrestrial – Not Provided
Flies Invented
Jack's Fighting Crab and Green Mantis Shrimp
Favorite US River
Rio Grande (NM)
Home River
Rio Grande (NM)
Favorite Stream
San Juan (NM)
Home Stream
San Juan (NM)

BROILED DORADO (DOLPHINFISH)

Dorado Fillet
Garlic
Melted Butter
Fresh Lime Juice

Broil fresh Dorado fillet over charcoal. Layer with butter and garlic. Squirt with fresh lime juice.

"We all mellow with age, and I have to admit I now find solitude far more appealing than the size or pedigree of the fish." – Jack

JIM SCHOLLMEYER

ASPARAGIS ORIENTAL

"It use to be 'dry fly or die.' Now it is 'fish till I die.'"

Jim Schollmeyer is a photographer and writer. He makes his home in Salem, Oregon.

Jim has written *Hatch Guide for Western Streams; Hatch Guide for Lakes: Naturals and Their Imitations for Stillwater Trout Fishing;* and *The Hatch Guide for the Lower Deschutes River.* He co-authored *Fly Casting: Illustrated in Color* with Frank Amato. *Trout Flies of the West* and *The Fly Tyer's Benchside Reference to Techniques and Dressing Styles* was co-authored with Ted Leeson.

A Federation of Fly Fishers member for over 20 years, Jim is active in the Santiam Flycasters in Salem, Oregon and a founding member of Oregon Trout. He was the Federation's 1998 recipient of the *Arnold Gingrich Memorial Award.*

Years Fly Fishing
Twenty-nine

Favorite Rod
4 wt 8' 6" Graphite

Rods Owned
Fifteen

Favorite Flies
Dry – Deer Hair Caddis
Wet – Soft Hackles
Nymph – Pheasant Tail
Streamer – Bunny Leech
Terrestrial – Foam
Body Hopper

Fly Invented
Deer Hair Caddis

Favorite US River
Bighorn (MT)

Home River
Deschutes (OR)

Favorite Stream
North Fork of the Tung (WY)

Home Stream
Fall River (OR)

1 ½ *Pounds Asparagus*
3 *Teaspoons Butter*
1 *Teaspoon Chicken*
Stock or 1 Cube
1 *Teaspoon Salt*
1/8 *Teaspoon Celery Salt*
1/8 *Teaspoon Ginger*
1 *Teaspoon Soy Sauce*
White Pepper to Taste

Slice asparagus at extreme diagonal angle. Melt butter in skillet; add stock base and seasonings. Mix well, add asparagus and toss gently over high heat. Cover and cook for 2 minutes. Add soy sauce and serve.

Serves: 4

DOROTHY SCHRAMM

TTRJ BREAKFAST

"Kitchens are dangerous."

Dorothy Schramm is a rod builder and owner of Rodsmith™, an angling related arts business. She has customers in most U. S. states and several foreign countries. Her rods are known as tools of fine craftsmanship, and feature her multiple coat, minimal finish.

Dorothy, a Federation of Fly Fishers Certified Casting Instructor, teaches women's schools throughout the U. S. and estimates helping introduce fly fishing to over 700 women. If she is not over the top of her waders in volunteer work, you can find her haunting local rivers, listening for the heartbeats of steelhead.

Recognized for her tireless volunteer work for the Federation of Fly Fishers, Dorothy is the recipient of the *Lew Jewett Life Membership Award* and the 1998 *Woman of the Year Award*. She has also received the *Lefty Kreh Award* in 1997, sharing the honors with Ray Schmidt. Another award in 1998 was the Great Lakes Councils' FFF *Order of the River Keeper*.

Dorothy is a co-founder and current President of Flygirls, a women's fly fishing network. She is based in Pentwater, Michigan.

Years Fly Fishing
Twenty-one

Favorite Rod
7 wt 9' Graphite

Rods Owned
Thirty Something

Favorite Flies
Dry – 100% CDC Caddis
Wet – Any Soft Hackle
Nymph – Hare's Ear by D. Schwartz
Streamer – St. Paul Fly Tyer's Meat Fly
Terrestrial – Luca's Beetle

Fly Invented
100% CDC Caddis

Favorite US River
Mississippi (MN)

Home River
Pere Marquette (MI)

Favorite Stream
Drew Creek (WI)

Home Stream
Pentwater (MI)

Cereal
Milk

Pour the cereal into a bowl. Add milk. Eat with a spoon. It's O.K. to drink any extra milk from the bowl by tipping it to the mouth.

"At this time, I climb into the car, turn to my husband, Jim, and say, 'To the river, James.' (TTRJ)" – Dorothy

"This is as honest as a recipe you will get." – Dorothy

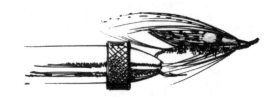

PEPPER VENISON STEAK STIR-FRY

"Always take time to go fishing with your kids."

Don Schroeder is a bamboo fly rod maker who lives in Janesville, Wisconsin. He says his greatest achievement is in being able to become a full time bamboo rod builder.

Years Fly Fishing
Thirty-one

Favorite Rod
5 wt 7' 9" Bamboo

Rods Owned
Ten

Favorite Flies
Dry – Adams
Wet – Black Ant
Nymph – Pheasant Tail
Streamer – Black
Woolly Bugger
Terrestrial – Black Ant

Fly Invented
None, Yet

Favorite US River
Yellowstone (MT)

Home River
Bois Brule (WI)

Favorite Stream
Soda Butte (MT)

Home Stream
Black Earth Creek (WI)

1 Pound Venison Steaks, Cubed
3 Cups Hot Cooked Rice
½ Cup Beef Broth
½ Cup Classic Stir-Fry Sauce
2 Teaspoons Cornstarch
1 Tablespoon Oil
2 Garlic Gloves, Minced
1 Green and 1 Red Bell Pepper,
Cut into ½" Pieces
1 Medium Onion, Cut into ½" Pieces

While rice is cooking, in a small bowl, combine broth, stir-fry sauce and cornstarch. Blend well and set aside.

Heat oil in a large skillet or wok over medium high heat until hot. Add venison and garlic. Cook and stir 3 – 5 minutes or until venison is browned. Remove from skillet. Cover to keep warm.

Reduce heat to medium. In the same skillet, combine bell peppers and onion. Cook and stir 5 – 7 minutes or until vegetables are crisp and tender.

Stir cornstarch mixture until smooth and add to skillet. Cook and stir 2 – 3 minutes or until sauce is thickened and bubbly. Stir in venison. Cook until thoroughly heated.

Serve over rice.

"I try to leave the stream a little better than I found it, whether it's picking up trash, old leader packs or old monofilament."

Ed Shenk is a retired planner and a legendary 30-year fishing instructor for the Allenberry School of Flyfishing. He is also an author and a professional fly tyer. Ed resides in Carlisle, Pennsylvania. In keeping with Ed's quote, he has planted many willows along the Letort, some of which are now 60 – 70 feet tall.

Flies invented by Ed include the Letort Cricket, Shenk Hopper, Shenk Sculpin, Shenk Minnow, Shenk Cress Bug and the Double Trico. His most recent book is entitled *Ed Shenk's Fly Rod Trouting*. He is working on his second book, *Ed Shenk—65 Years with a Fly Rod.*

Ed is the recipient of numerous conservation awards including *The Order of the Hat,* the first *Limestoner Award* and the Charles K. Fox *Rising Trout Award.*

Shenk has fished Patagonia, Argentina four times with world famous Bebe Anchorena who hosted Joe Brooks and the *American Sportsman* television series. Ed also fished numerous times with the late Joe Brooks. President Jimmy Carter also fished with Ed.

Years Fly Fishing
Sixty-five

Favorite Rod
Short Rods 5' – 6'

Rods Owned
Too numerous to mention.

Favorite Flies
Dry – Shenk Sulfur
Wet – Hare's Ear
Nymph – Cress Bug
Streamer – Shenk Sculpin
Terrestrial – Letort Cricket

Flies Invented
See Comments

Favorite US River
Madison (MT)

Home River
Yellow Breeches (PA)

Favorite Stream
Letort Spring Run (PA)

Home Stream
Letort Spring Run (PA)

"Nothing tastes better to me along the stream than grilled hamburger or hot dogs." – Ed

Ed Shenk's fellow fly fisher, Joe Humphreys, forwarded the Allenberry recipe for their famed rolls. Since it is such a huge recipe, maybe it can be shared between these two legendary anglers.

MARTY SHERMAN

"I have mastered the art of power napping."

Marty Sherman is a former magazine editor and is co-owner of River Graphics with his wife, Joyce. They specialize in catalog, book, newsletter and brochure production and design. The Shermans live in Portland, Oregon. He and his wife enjoy doing conservation work, especially spawning surveys for wild steelhead.

Marty, a fly fisher since the age of nine, says, *"My favorite fishing is for wild summer-run steelhead. I would rather catch these fish with a bamboo rod, old Hardy reel and a fly pattern older than I am."*

Years Fly Fishing
Over Forty

Favorite Rod
8 wt 9' Bamboo Made by Ed Hartzell

Rods Owned
Over Ten

Favorite Flies
Dry – Steelhead Bee
Wet – Tranquilizer
Nymph – McMillan Stone
Streamer – Muddler Minnow
Terrestrial – Moose Turd

Fly Invented
Stewart

Favorite US River
Kalama (WA)

Home River
Sandy (OR)

Favorite Stream
Drift Creek (OR)

Home Stream
Drift Creek (OR)

SMOKED SALMON OR STEELHEAD

3 – 5 Pounds Salmon or Steelhead Fillets
3 Cans Unsweetened Frozen
Apple Juice Concentrate
¼ Cup Salt
Garlic Powder to Taste
Soy Sauce to Taste – ¼ Cup Lemon Juice
Worcestershire Sauce to Taste

Mix apple juice concentrate, salt, garlic, soy sauce, lemon juice and Worcestershire Sauce. Pour over fish fillets placed in a glass or plastic container.

Let fillets soak in refrigerator for 3 days. After 3 days, remove fish from brine. Place fillets on a towel for 1 day in the refrigerator.

To smoke, place the fillets, skin side down, on a rack. Fill the chip pan with chips that have been soaked 20 – 50 minutes. Smoke for 10 – 16 hours, or until done, depending on the temperature outside.

Keep the chip pan filled. Use hickory chips or alder.

Serves: 1 – 6

"This recipe was given to me by Larry Palmer."
– Marty

JOHN SHEWEY

"I grew up fly fishing and to this day I pursue myriad species on many waters. Yet rising trout to dry flies and casting dry lines and classic flies for summer steelhead remain my most cherished angling pursuits: In the former I never tire of watching my fly disappear from the surface and in the latter I find my most intimate and unobtrusive involvement in the river and its surroundings. In both cases I am trying to bring the fish to the fly rather than pursuing the less reverent act of bringing the fly to the fish."

John Shewey is a writer, photographer and purveyor of Atlantic salmon tying materials. The Salem, Oregon resident created the Spawning Purple steelhead fly and several others. His favorite U.S. rivers include the Henry's Fork in Idaho for trout and the North Umpqua in Oregon for steelhead. His home rivers are Oregon's North Santiam for steelhead and the Deschutes for trout.

John is the author of nine fly angling books as well as numerous articles. Some of his books include *Fly Fishing Pacific Northwest Waters: Trout and Beyond II, Alpine Angler* and *Mastering Spring Creeks.*

Years Fly Fishing
Twenty-six

Favorite Rod
9 wt 9' 6" Graphite

Rods Owned
Twenty

Favorite Flies
Dry – Jughead and Parachute Adams
Wet – Soft Hackle Zug Bug
Nymph – Pheasant Tail
Streamer – Spawning Purple
Terrestrial – McMurray Fur Ant

Flies Invented
See Comments

Favorite US River
See Comments

Home River
See Comments.

Favorite Stream
Silver Creek (ID) and West Fork Stillwater (MT)

Home Stream
Middle Deschutes (OR)

CILANTRO STEELHEAD*

(*John Shewey's Cilantro Steelhead Barbecue)

Fresh Summer-run Steelhead of Hatchery Origin (Please don't kill the natives!)
2 Bunches Fresh Cilantro, Washed
2 Bunches Fresh Green Onions, Chopped
4 Limes, 2 Halved for Squeezing and 2 Sliced
Butter
Olive Oil
Black Pepper and Garlic Powder
Fresh Grated Romano or Parmesan Cheese

Catch steelhead on a well-tied fly and filet (skin off). Start barbecue. Cut 2 lengths of heavy-duty aluminum foil, longer than the filets. Grease the foil with olive oil and sprinkle with a little garlic powder, a little black pepper and fresh-squeezed lime juice. Lay each filet on a separate foil sheet and fold foil into a boat. Lightly dust each filet with black pepper and garlic powder; add several pats of butter to each filet and sprinkle each with lime juice. Place foil boats on barbecue (medium heat), close tops of foil boats and cook for a few minutes to melt the butter.

Continued on next page . . .

Open the boats and squeeze lime juice onto each filet, somewhat liberally; line each filet with lime slices, then add chopped green onion, but not too much. Close foil and cook for about 2 minutes. Re-open foil, and sprinkle each filet with grated Romano; then, over each filet, spread an entire bundle of fresh cilantro (washed); add a little more lime juice and re-seal the foil boats.

Finish cooking. Cook time is about 10 minutes per inch of thickness, so expect total cook time to be 12 – 15 minutes. Sample thickest section with a fork to make sure it is done but do not overcook.

Serve immediately with a fine Oregon Pinot Noir (e.g. Witness Tree, St. Innocent, Bethel Heights, Laurel Hood) or Gewurztraminer.

GRAVLAX

"I learned to fish prenatally from mother."

Paul Shultz is an attorney and current President of the Catskill Fly Fishing Center and Museum, that is located in Livingston Manor, New York.

When asked what his home stream was, Paul replied, *"The Little Beaverkill, which flows through the backyard and where my sons were baptized."*

Years Fly Fishing
Fifty-eight

Favorite Rod
4 wt 9' Graphite

Rods Owned
Over Fifty

Favorite Flies
Dry – Royal Wulff
Wet – G.R. Hare's Ear
Nymph – Bead Head
Streamer – Mickey Finn
Terrestrial – Joe's Hopper

Fly Invented
None, yet

Favorite US River
Bighorn (MT)

Home River
The Beaverkill (NY)

Favorite Stream
Willowemoc Creek (NY)

Home Stream
The Little Beaverkill (NY)

5 Pounds Fresh Atlantic Salmon Fillets
1 Cup Sugar
½ Cup Table Salt
Pinch White Pepper
Bunches of Fresh Dill

Catch the salmon (legally) with a Cullman's Special (personally tied by Lee Wulff) or purchase a fresh, farm-raised salmon.

Blend seasonings and spread on the fish. Cover generously with dill. Wrap the fillets separately and snugly with aluminum foil. Place in a baking dish and weigh with a brick. The weight is necessary to draw juices, creating the marinade.

Refrigerate for 3 days, turning over the packets every 12 hours, and replacing the brick.

Remove the foil, gently scrape off and discard the seasonings. Gently dry the fish. Place the fillets on a platter.

Serve with capers, chopped onion, lemon squeezes, and fresh dill on crackers or toast points.

CAM SIGLER

"The more time the fly is in the water and not in the air, the better your chances of catching a fish."

Cam Sigler owns an import/export-sourcing firm that designs flies and other outdoor products. His company is based in Vashon Island, Washington.

Cam's first love is fly fishing in salt water, something he does from Mexico, Costa Rica, Guatemala and other great locations. He invented the Big Game Tube Flies and Mini Tubes for fishing these waters.

Other inventions include flats booties, lace up waders and mariners gloves. Cam also has a book out, *Guide to Fly Fishing,* written for the beginning and intermediate level fly fisherman.

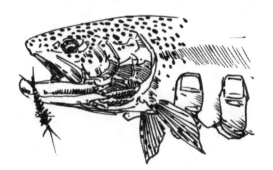

Years Fly Fishing
Forty-six

Favorite Rod
4 wt 9' Graphite

Rods Owned
Thirty-five

Favorite Flies
Dry – Trude Coachman
Wet – Woolly Bugger
Nymph – Hare's Ear
Streamer – Deceiver
Terrestrial – Black Ant

Flies Invented
See Comments

Favorite US River
Williamson (OR)

Home River
Yakima (WA)

Favorite Stream
Henry's Fork (ID)

Home Stream
Rocky Ford Creek (WA)

DUTCH OVEN FRIED CHICKEN

6 – 8 Pieces Chicken
1 Egg
1 Stick Butter
Salt and Pepper
1 Tablespoon Water
2 Cups Flour or Pancake Mix
1 Old Fashioned Cast Iron Dutch Oven for Outdoor Cooking (12 – 14 Inches with Legs)
10 – 12 Pieces Charcoal for the Bottom
12 Pieces Charcoal for the Top

Melt 1 stick of butter in the oven. Slice and wash the chicken. In a bowl, combine 1 egg and 1 tablespoon water per chicken, beating slightly. Place the chicken in the egg mixture to sit while the oven is heating.

Put 2 cups flour or pancake mix in a paper bag. Put in the chicken and shake to cover all pieces. Place the chicken in the Dutch oven, dark meat in the center, white meat on the outsides. Let brown for 1 – 2 minutes. Turn and brown on the other side. Cover and cook for 1 – 1 ½ hours until tender. Remove the chicken from the Dutch oven and generously season with salt and pepper. Drain on paper towels for a minute before serving.

Serves 3 – 4

HARRY LEE SLONE

"Unless I break a rod a year, I haven't really fished my best."

Harry Slone lives in Roanoke, Virginia. He is the author of the book *Virginia Trout Streams*, and recently produced a video entitled *Southeastern Trout Streams* that examines fly fishing for trout in the South.

Harry's book, originally published in 1990, is in its third printing (1999) and contains new information on private pay-for-fish streams, plus updates on public streams. A lifetime fly fisherman, Slone wrote the book after seeking the healing powers of trout waters and fly fishing after the loss of his wife in 1987.

Years Fly Fishing
Sixty-one

Favorite Rod
1 Ounce 7' 6" Graphite

Rods Owned
Ten

Favorite Flies
Dry – Adams #16
Wet – Prince Nymph #14
Nymph – B.H. Hare's Ear
Flashback #16
Streamer – Muddler
Minnow #12
Terrestrial – Fire Fly #14

Fly Invented
None, yet

Favorite US River
Jackson (VA)

Home River
Smith (VA)

Favorite Stream
Mossy Creek (VA)

Home Stream
Bullpasture (VA)

GRILLED TROUT

12 Quality 10" – 12" Farm-Raised Trout
Fresh Rosemary
Dill
Thyme
Basil
Bacon Slices
Lemon, Sliced
Wet Hickory Chips

Place trout in a 200-degree oven with a slice of bacon on each one. Cook until bacon is transparent, about 20 minutes. Meanwhile cover charcoal grill with foil. Cut a semi-circle from one end, punch holes in the remaining foil. Cover the foil with fresh herbs, then lemon slices.

Remove bacon slices from the trout, placing trout on the herbs and lemon bed. Add wet hickory chips to the whitened charcoal through the open end of the foil.

Cover the charcoal kettle and cook until the trout are done, about ½ hour, depending on heat of coals.

Serve with a chilled dry white wine.

Serves: 8

MARK SOSIN

"For the fly fisherman, the catch is incidental."

Mark Sosin is an award winning journalist, photographer and television producer. He is best known as the on-camera host of *Mark Sosin's Saltwater Journal* broadcast to all 50 states and several foreign countries on *TNN Outdoors*. More than 3,000 of his articles have been published in major magazines and he has written 26 books.

The Boca Raton, Florida resident is a leading educator, a Director of The Billfish Foundation and a former Trustee of the University of Florida's Whitney Laboratory.

Mark came up with the idea to keep salt water fly world records and wrote the original rules now maintained by the International Game Fish Association. He was also the first to dead drift a fly in a chum slick and publicize the results.

Mark is a past President of the Outdoor Writers Association of America and recipient of their *Excellence In Craft Award* and their *Ham Brown Award*. He is in the *International Fishing Hall of Fame* and *Freshwater Fishing Hall of Fame*.

Mark started fly fishing some 60 years ago. He fished with flies for trout, but says a worm and spinner combination was deadly.

~ 235 ~

Years Fly Fishing
Over Sixty

Favorite Rod
10 wt 9' Graphite

Rods Owned
Over One Hundred

Favorite Flies
Dry – Adams
Wet – Not Provided
Nymph – Bub's Best
Streamer – Muddler Minnow
Terrestrial – Not Provided

Fly Invented
Markee's Marshmallow

Favorite US River
I am a salt water fisherman.

Home River
Not Provided

Favorite Stream
Flat Brook (NJ)

Home Stream
South Branch (NJ)

BROILED YELLOWTAIL SNAPPER*

(*Tommy Greene's Recipe by Mark Sosin)

Yellowtail Snapper Fillets
Hellmann's Mayonnaise
Salt and Black Pepper
Cayenne Pepper
Celery Salt
Parsley Flakes
Shaved or Crushed Almonds, Walnuts or Pecans

Coat each fillet, on each side, with a coating of Hellmann's mayonnaise sufficiently thick so it is covered. Usually a sixteenth to an eighth-inch thick. Season each fillet with salt, cayenne pepper, black pepper, celery salt and parsley flakes. Begin with nominal seasoning and with experience gradually increase to suit your taste.

Place the fillets in a baking dish and sprinkle with a generous amount of nuts. Bake in a pre-heated oven at 400 degrees for 8 – 10 minutes, or until the fillets begin to flake when tested with a fork. Watch carefully the last couple of minutes, so you don't overcook. Finally, place the baking dish in the broiler for just a minute, until the mayonnaise is brown on top. Test the fillets for flakiness and remember that thin fillets cook quicker than thick ones. Takes about 3 minutes in a microwave.

GARY SOUCIE

MUSTARD SURPRISE CHICKEN

"When all is said and done, the principles of fish attracting and catching remain the same no matter how much the brand names and product lines change."

Gary Soucie was the Executive Editor for *Audubon* magazine for twelve years and was on the senior editorial staff of *National Geographic Magazine.* Formerly the Editor for *American Angler* magazine, he is presently Executive Editor for two medical magazines. He lives in Pearl River, New York, with his wife, Marina Brodskaya, whom he met on a salmon-fishing trip to Russia.

Gary is the author of several books including, *Traveling with Fly Rod and Reel, Hook, Line and Sinker* and *The Complete Angler's Guide to Terminal Tackle.* He is also the Editor of *Home Waters: A Fly Fishing Anthology.* Gary is presently writing a book on tying and fishing woolly worms and woolly buggers. Frank Amato Publications will publish *Woolly Wisdom.*

Some of Gary's accomplishments include being Chairman of the Coalition Against the SST, a Co-founder and Vice Chairman of the League of Conservation Voters, and Executive Director of Friends of the Earth. He also says he never met a fish he didn't like.

Years Fly Fishing
Seventeen

Favorite Rod
5 wt 8' 6" Graphite

Rods Owned
Fifteen

Favorite Flies
Dry – Royal Wulff
Wet – Miller Woolly Worm
Nymph – Small and Brown
Streamer – Muddler Minnow
(Salmon) and Lefty's
Deceiver (Salt Water)
Terrestrial – Letort Cricket and
Foam Ant

Fly Invented
None anyone has heard of.

Favorite US River
The next one I fish.

Favorite Home River
I keep changing my mind.

Favorite Stream
Sava-Bohinjka (Slovenia)

Home Stream
Too restless to settle on one, I guess.

© 2000 - Russell A. Hopper

1 Chicken, Cut into Serving Pieces
Salt and Pepper to Taste
Yellow Mustard*

Salt and pepper chicken. Dredge chicken in mustard, covering completely. Place chicken in a shallow, uncovered, greased baking pan or dish. Bake for 1 hour in a preheated 350-degree oven. The chicken will be coated in a thin, puffy crust that seals in all of the flavor and moisture. And the mustard taste will be very, very subtle.

* *"Use cheap, yellow, hot dog mustard—No Dijon, no honey mustard, no top-drawer stuff."* – Gary

DALE C. SPARTAS

ROAST GOOSE

"Nothing ventured, nothing gained. Also, think globally, act locally."

Dale Spartas is an outdoor photographer, specializing in fly fishing adventures. He lives in Bozeman, Montana with his wife, three children and three dogs.

More than 100 magazines have used Dale's work for their cover. He is a Contributing Editor for *Gray's Sporting Journal* who has featured over 49 of his essays.

Dale's works are included in four books: *Little Book of Fly Fishing, Just Labs, Just Goldens* and *101 Uses for a Lab.*

Born in Connecticut, Dale read about Montana in Joe Brook's columns and fantasized about living out west. In 1988, he and his family realized Dale's dream when they moved to Montana.

The Contributing Photographer of *Fly Fishing in Salt Water, Gray's Sporting Journal* and *Sports Afield Magazine* started fly fishing at the age of 10.

Years Fly Fishing
Thirty-eight

Favorite Rod
5 wt 9' Loomis Graphite
4 wt 7' 6" Winston Bamboo

Rods Owned
Twenty

Favorite Flies
Dry – Byron's Cut
Wing Caddis
Wet – Not Provided
Nymph – Flashback
Peasant Tail
Streamer – Whitlock's Sculpin
Terrestrial – The Lowly Ant

Fly Invented
None, yet

Favorite US River
Henry's Fork (ID)

Home River
Gallatin (MT)

Favorite Stream
Not Provided

Home Stream
Not Provided

1 Plucked Canadian, Specklebelly or Snow Goose
1 Lemon
Paul Newman's Italian Salad Dressing
Stove Top Dressing
Salt and Pepper
Vinegar
Butter
Apples and Grapes
Old Hickory Barbecue Sauce

Take the goose from the freezer and thaw. Once thawed, soak in cold water with salt and white vinegar for 2 – 3 hours. Pat dry inside and out. Salt and pepper the cavity. Make the stove top dressing. After the dressing is made, add the grapes and apple chunks to the dressing and stuff the goose. Rub lemon juice on the outside. Then do the same with the Newman's Dressing. Put the goose in the refrigerator for 2 – 24 hours.

Use a charcoal Webber Grill. Get the coals as hot as they can get, keeping the upper and lower flues all the way open. Put the goose in and cook at high for 10 minutes. Take the top off the Webber Grill and baste the goose with the barbecue sauce. Close the flues to ¼ opening and slow cook a large goose (10 – 12 pounds) for another 45 minutes, 35 minutes for a small goose.

SHANE STALCUP

"If you want to become a more successful fisherman, get armed with more knowledge."

Shane Stalcup is a fly tyer and materials manufacturer. He is one of the most innovative fly tyers in the world. His realistic, and effective, patterns come about from tying flies in front of a 40-gallon tank complete with aquatic insects.

After some 15 years of tying flies for shops around his Denver, Colorado area, he decided to launch his first catalog in 1993.

Famed fly tyer, A. K. Best declares Shane as a good teacher, explaining the why's and how's of his materials, discoveries and their use. This teaching style is reflected in Shane's videos, *Tying Bass Flies, Tying Mayflies Flies, Tying Lake Flies, Tying Caddis Flies, Tying Midges, Tying Emergers, Tying Streamers* and *Tying With CDC (Cul de Canard)*.

Shane's favorite friends are his two black labs, Maggie and Yogi. They reside in Denver, Colorado.

Years Fly Fishing
Twenty-six

Favorite Rod
5 wt 9' Graphite

Rods Owned
Eight

Favorite Flies
Dry – Emerging Dun
Wet – Bead Diving Caddis
Nymph – Gilled Nymph
Streamer – Hare Fry
Terrestrial – Flying Ant

Flies Invented
All of the Above

Favorite US River
Frying Pan (CO)

Home River
South Platte (CO)

Favorite Stream
Not Provided

Home Stream
Not Provided

CHICKEN & MASHED POTATOES*

*(*Fried Chicken, Mashed Potatoes and Gravy)*

Chicken
Flour
Salt and Pepper
Oil
Milk
Red Potatoes

Cut up the chicken and clean. Put the flour in a bag and shake the chicken in it. Put the chicken in a hot frying pan. Season with salt and pepper to taste. Cook for about 45 minutes to 1 hour. Take the chicken from the pan, but leave the droppings. Add some flour to the oil. Let it brown then add milk while stirring. Salt and pepper to taste.

To make the mashed potatoes, take one red potato per person and cook in the microwave or boil until done. Mash with added milk for desired thickness. Season to taste.

BOB STEARNS

GOOSE NUGGETS

"We need to take far better care of our natural resources."

Bob Stearns makes his home in Miami, Florida with his wife Shirley. He is currently a Contributing Editor and also the Boating and Saltwater Fishing Columnist for *Field & Stream* magazine, as well as the Electronics Editor for *Saltwater Sportsman*. Plus a regular contributor to *Saltwater Fly Fishing*, *Trailer Boats*, and others. He has also appeared many times in such publications as *Outdoor Life*, *Sports Afield*, *Boating*, *American Angler*, *Yachting*, and *Fishing World*.

Bob has a degree in Meteorology and spent six years as a weather officer in the Navy, plus another seven in environmental research with the University of Miami's School of Marine and Atmospheric Research. He started writing for outdoor magazines in 1969, made the transition to full time in this occupation in 1973, and has to date authored over 1,500 articles.

He is the author of *The Fisherman's Boating Book* and the revision author of *The Saltwater Fisherman's Bible*. He has also contributed chapters and photography to many other books.

Bob has fly fished since he was 18 years old.

Years Fly Fishing
Over Thirty

Favorite Rod
5/6 wt 9' Graphite

Rods Owned
Who's counting?

Favorite Flies
Dry – Muddler Minnow
Wet – My own designs.
Nymph – Not Provided
Streamer – My own designs.
Terrestrial – Not Provided

Flies Invented
Pinfish, Snapping Shrimp and Others

Favorite US River
Goodnews (AK)

Other Favorite Waters
The world's best fresh and salt-water fishing spots.

Goose Breasts
Milk
Orange Juice
1 – 2 Eggs
Seasoned Italian Breadcrumbs
Olive Oil

Cut goose breasts into bite-sized pieces. Soak in milk for 12 – 14 hours in refrigerator. Wash and soak in orange juice 4 – 5 hours. Drain orange juice and add 1 – 2 eggs. Dust with breadcrumbs. Cook in skillet 2 – 3 minutes per side, using a very thin layer of olive oil.

Serves: One medium-sized goose serves 2

JIM STEWART

"There are those that think they can. And those that think they can not. And both are right!"

Jim is a retired architect and currently counsels in the early retirement planning field. He resides in Tampa, Florida.

Jim's training helped him design a fly tying apron troll and develop the horizontal layering of colors in spun deer hair. He has created many fly patterns including the Dancing Frog, Lucky Wiggler, Chub Darter, Bend Back Dragon, Moth, and his most famous, Snook-A-Roo.

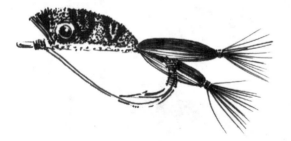

Years Fly Fishing
Forty-nine

Favorite Rod
9 wt 9' Graphite

Rods Owned
Six

Favorite Flies
Dry – Spun Deer Hair and Stewart's Snook-A-Roo
Wet – Stewart's Bug Eyed Brim Killer
Nymph – Not Provided
Streamer – Stewart's Fuzzy Wuzzy
Terrestrial – Not Provided

Fly Invented
See Comments

Favorite US Waters
Lake Kissimmee and Lake Cypress (FL)

"CRACKER" EGGS

Onions, Chopped
Green Pepper, Chopped
Olive Oil
Velveeta Mild Mexican Cheese
Milk
Eggs
Butter

The quantity of each ingredient depends upon the quantity of people. The recipe is based on 1 egg per person.

Take 1 thin slice of sweet onion, chopped. Add 1-¼" slice sweet green pepper, chopped. Sauté in a small amount of olive oil in the microwave for 1 minute 30 seconds. Save the bowl.

With a hand mixer, whip the egg and 1 tablespoon of milk. Add ¼" thick slice of Mexican cheese. Add peppers and onions. Drain the olive oil.

Melt 1 pad of butter in a hot skillet. Pour in the egg mix and scramble until cooked.

Serves: 1 egg per person

ED STORY

CHRISTMAS LADIES SUNDOWNER

"Fly fishing just for the fun of it."

Ed Story lives in St. Louis, Missouri where he is President of Feather-Craft Fly Fishing Outfitters. Ed says his claim to fame is hard labor. He likes to plug his company when possible and says he'll send a free catalog if readers call 1-800-659-1707.

Years Fly Fishing
Over Fifty
Favorite Rod
All Graphites and Bamboos
Rods Owned
Three Hundred
Favorite Flies
Dry – FC Crackleback #12
Wet – FC Crackleback #12
fished sub-surface.
Nymph – FC Pine Squirrel
Streamer – FC Pearl Shiner
Terrestrial – All
Fly Invented
Feather Craft Crackleback
Favorite US River
All with trout and smallmouth.
Home River
Current (MO)
Favorite Stream
Upper Roaring Fork (CO)
Home Stream
Meramec (MO)

1 Jigger Leroux Rock and Rye with Natural Fruit
Sprite® Soda
Lemon
Maraschino Cherry

Take 1 jigger Leroux Rock and Rye with Natural Fruit to a hi-ball glass. Add Sprite® soda to near top. Add lemon twist. Add maraschino cherry. Stir to create bubbles.

This is the first publishing of Ed's secret formula.

Serves: 2

"Only for the ladies at Christmas or New Years —never any other time of the year." – Ed

E. NEALE STREEKS

STUFFED PORK LOIN*

"The day always ends – from guiding in the wind … and then comes beer."

Neale Streeks calls himself a fishing guide, hack writer and stockroom boy who didn't die on a motorcycle, didn't make any money, and doesn't have skin cancer, yet. He resides in Great Falls, Montana.

Neale has written four books: *Drift Boat Strategies: Rowing and Fishing Skills for the Western Angler*; *Seasons of the Trout: Strategies for the Year-Round Western Angler*; *Drift Boat Fly Fishing: A River Guide's Sage Advice*; and *Small Fly Adventures in the West: A Guide to Angling for Larger Trout*.

After cooking Neale's Smith River Style Stuffed Pork Loin, he says, *"Sip wine, look at the scenery, and sigh – it's been a long day."*

Years Fly Fishing
Thirty
Favorite Rod
5 wt 8' 6" Graphite
Rods Owned
Eight
Favorite Flies
Dry – Parachute Adams
Wet – My Caddis Emerger
Nymph – B.H. Pheasant Tail and Montana Nymph
Streamer – Besides a Woolly Bugger? Egg Head Copper King
Terrestrial – Dave's Hopper
Flies Invented
Just the usual bastardizations.
Favorite US River
Missouri or Smith in the 80's.
Home River
Missouri (MT)
Favorite Stream
Hakataramea (New Zealand)
Home Stream
Missouri, a rather large stream!

(*Stuffed Pork Loin – Smith River Style)

Pork Loin, Pre-cut for Stuffing
Teriyaki Sauce
Onions
Green and Red Peppers
Granny Smith Apples
Apricot Jelly
Swiss Cheese
Celery

Marinate loin in Teriyaki Sauce for 1 hour. Sauté onions, celery, peppers and apples in oil until just done. Whatever else is in the cooler can substitute. Cool slightly.

Drain loin; stuff with Swiss cheese, sautéed vegetables and a touch of apricot jam. Close end of loin with toothpicks.

Wrap loin in foil and cook over charcoal for ½ hour, turning regularly. Uncover. Remove foil and cook over coals an additional 15 – 20 minutes, basting occasionally with marinade.

Cut 2" thick circles and serve with mashed potatoes, gravy, and glazed carrots.

Serves: 4 – 6

DOUG SWISHER

"The selectivity of trout has always been the most difficult and charming of the numerous problems that confront the fly-fisherman."

Doug Swisher is a true legendary fly fisher. His co-authored book, *Selective Trout*, is the all-time best-selling book in the fly fishing community. Along with Carl Richards, he also co-authored *Fly Fishing Strategy, Tying the Swisher/Richards Flies, Stoneflies* and *Emergers*.

Doug has written and performed in seven video-tapes, including *Advanced Fly Fishing Strategies, Tying the Hatch Simulators, Basic Fly Casting, Advanced Fly Casting, Tying the Attractors* and *Fly Fishing for Bass.*

A premier fly tyer, Doug has created over 60 fly patterns. Some of these patterns include the Madam X, No-Hackle, Velcro Streamer and Fluter. He also ran the first fresh water and salt water schools and started the kickboat revolution.

Doug resides in Naples, Florida.

~ 243 ~

Years Fly Fishing
Fifty-one

Favorite Rod
5 wt 9' Graphite

Rods Owned
Over Thirty

Favorite Flies
Dry – Speckle – X
Wet – Mono Caddis Pupa
Nymph – Prince
Streamer – Velcro Streamer
Terrestrial – Double Parachute Hopper

Flies Invented
See Comments

Favorite US River
Missouri (MT)

Home River
Bitterroot (MT)

Favorite Stream
Paloma (Chile)

Home Stream
Nez Perce (MT)

VEAL PICCATA

8 Veal Scaloppine, Pounded Thin
Flour for Dredging, Seasoned
with Salt and Pepper
3 Tablespoons Butter
3 Tablespoons Olive Oil
½ Cup Dry White Wine
2 Lemons, Juiced

Take veal pounded as thinly as possible and dip it into flour. Shake off excess. Heat butter and oil in a wide, heavy skillet over medium-high heat. When bubbling, lay in veal. Brown on first side, about 2 minutes. Turn; brown other side 1-minute. Do not crowd skillet; work in batches if skillet will not accommodate all scaloppine. Tip skillet and drain most of fat. Add wine. Let sizzle and cook down about 3 minutes while scraping up any bits of meat that may cling to the skillet. Add lemon juice. Place meat in overlapping fashion on warm platter. Pour thin sauce over.

Serve garnished with buttered carrots, oregano zucchini and fried eggplant sticks.

"Sorry, I don't cook." – Doug

LOU TABORY

"Locations devoid of food are generally devoid of game fish."

Lou Tabory is considered the dean of the Northeast saltwater fly fishing. He has been fly fishing in salt water for over 30 years and has authored two books: *Inshore Fly Fishing* and *Lou Tabory's Guide to Saltwater Baits and Their Imitations.*

Lou has been an outdoor writer for over 25 years and has written for almost every fishing magazine in the business, among them *Field & Stream, Saltwater Fly Fishing* and *Fly Fisherman.* He is a current Contributing Editor for *Fly Fishing in Salt Waters.*

A tireless lecturer, Lou has given more than 1,000 talks and demonstrations on marine fly fishing over the past 20 years.

Lou operated the first salt water fly fishing school in the Northeast, is a member of the Orvis Salt Water Advisory Team, and the Federation of Fly Fishers' Casting Instruction Certification Program.

One of Lou's most famous fly patterns is the Snake Fly.

Lou makes his home in Ridgefield, Connecticut.

Years Fly Fishing
Forty-one

Favorite Rod
10 wt 9' Graphite

Rods Owned
Many

Favorite Flies
Dry – 210 Foam Popper
Wet – Epoxy Sand Eel
Nymph – Shrimp Fly
Streamer – Slab Side
Terrestrial – Cinder Worm

Fly Invented
Snake Fly

Favorite US River
Rips between Fishers Island and Watch Hill (RI)

Home River
Mouth of the Housatonic (CT)

Favorite Stream
Gulf Stream

Home Stream
Burial Hill Creek (CT)

BAKED STUFFED SPINY LOBSTER

1 Whole Spiny Lobster
Shrimp Scallops or Artificial Seafood
Bread and Breadcrumbs
Portabello Mushrooms
Shitake Mushrooms
Oyster Mushrooms
Fresh Parsley
Lemon and Lime
Garlic and Olive Oil
Oregano
Onions
Butter

Split lobster and lay open in half. Sauté mushrooms and onions with garlic in oil, butter and parsley.

Cut bread in ½" cubes. Brown to make croutons. Mix croutons with mushroom mixture. Add oregano and choice of seafood. Stuff body cavity with mixture. Sprinkle stuffing with breadcrumbs. Squeeze juice of lemon and lime on top. Add some butter.

Cook slowly for 1 hour on grill or in oven. Finish by crisping surface under broiler.

Use a mixture of butter, olive oil and garlic on the side.

SAM TALARICO

"I honestly feel the people you meet during your life forges your character. I have met my best friends around the world fly fishing and doing my photography."

Sam Talarico is a photographer and a hardwood lumber dealer residing in Mohton, Pennsylvania. He has been making wine for over 30 years and has won several national awards for this activity.

Sam's passion for photography begin at Woodstock in 1969 and this love has taken him to exotic places all over the world

A very special part of Sam's life is Do/Wop. He sings lead with the Pretenders, a Do/Wop, oldies group that has been together for 38 years. The group has performed with such notables as the Platters, the Duprees and Patti Labell and the Bluebells.

Sam's photography has been published in books, magazines, calendars, and travel and sports equipment brochures including *Gray's Sporting Journal, The New York Times, Fly Fishing Salt Water, Fly Fisherman, The Orvis Company, Patagonia, L. L. Bean* and *Lefty's Little Library*, to name a few.

Sam is a Contributing Photographer to *Fly Fishing in Salt Water* magazine.

Years Fly Fishing
Thirty-six

Favorite Rod
8 wt 9' Graphite

Rods Owned
Twenty

Favorite Flies
*Dry – Royal Wulff
Wet – Woolly Bugger (Trout)
and Clouser Minnow
(Salt Water)
Nymph – G.R. Hare's Ear
Streamer – Zonker and
Lefty's Deceiver
Terrestrial – Disco Cricket*

Fly Invented
Who has time?

Favorite US River
I fish mostly salt water.

Home River
Susquehanna (PA)

Favorite Stream
Mossy Creek (VA)

Home Stream
Tulpehocken (PA)

HOT-CHENGTU CHICKEN

2 Whole Chicken Breasts

Marinade
*1 Tablespoon Cornstarch
1 ½ Tablespoons Rice Wine,
Dry Sherry or Any White Wine
1 ½ Tablespoons Soy Sauce
Other Ingredients
6 – 8 Green Onions
1 Cup Water Chestnuts, Sliced
1 – 2 Ripe Tomatoes
3 Tablespoons Fresh Ginger, or More
3 Tablespoons Chopped Garlic, or More
1 Tablespoon Hot Bean Paste (Chef Chow)
½ Cup Unsalted Peanuts or Cashews
Bamboo Shoots*

Seasonings
*2 Tablespoons Cornstarch
3 Tablespoons Dark Soy Sauce
2 Teaspoons Rice Vinegar
1 Teaspoon Sugar
½ – 1 Teaspoons Salt
2 Teaspoons Sesame Oil
1 Tablespoon Ground Szechwan Pepper Corns
1 – 2 Tablespoons Ketchup
1 Cup Peanut Oil*

Continued on next page . . .

TO PREPARE SAM'S CHICKEN

Bone the chicken breast and cut the meat into cubes. Mix the **Marinade**. Then mix with the chicken and marinate at least 10 minutes.

Cut the green onions into 1-inch lengths. Cut the water chestnuts into thin slices. Stem and half the tomatoes, and cut into wedges. Chop the ginger and garlic rather finely.

In a bowl, mix the **Seasonings**, first mixing the cornstarch with the soy sauce and vinegar, adding sugar, salt and finally mixing in the sesame oil, ground Szechwan pepper and ketchup.

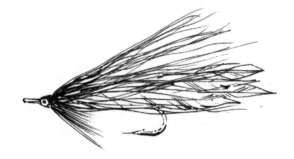

TO COOK SAM'S CHICKEN

Heat about 2/3 cup of cooking oil in a wok until very hot. Add the chicken cubes a few at a time as the chicken turns white. Remove and drain.

Heat 3 tablespoons of cooking oil in the wok and stir fry the bamboo shoots briefly. Drain and remove.

Heat 3 – 4 tablespoons of cooking oil in the wok until very hot. Add the hot bean paste, ginger, garlic and green onion. Stir fry until you notice a distinct spicy smell and the ginger and the garlic have absorbed the red color from the hot bean paste. Add the peanuts and stir for a moment. Then add the prefried chicken and the bamboo shoots and water chestnuts. Stir briefly until everything is well mixed and heated. Then give the **Seasonings** a stir and add along with the tomato wedges. Stir briefly and let the tomatoes heat through.

Check for salt or soy and remove to a serving dish. Serve hot over a bed of rice.

Serves: 4

DICK TALLEUR

"Two things are great fun on top. One of them is dry fly fishing. Keep it up!"

Dick Talleur is a noted fly fishing and fly tying author. He is a Columnist for *Fly Tyer* and *American Angler* magazines, the author of eight books, and countless magazine articles and photographs.

Dick speaks Russian as a second language and in 1993 managed a fishing camp on the Pana and Varzuga rivers in Russia. In 1996 and 1997, he managed a similar program on the Yokanga river.

Dick's fly fishing books include *Pretty And Practical Salmon Flies, Mastering The Art Of Fly Tying, The Fly-Tyer's Primer, Fly Fishing For Trout, The Versatile Fly Tyer, Talleur's Dry Fly Handbook, Modern Fly-tying Materials, Talleur's Basic Fly Tying* and *The L. L. Bean Fly Tying Handbook*. A completely new edition of *Mastering The Art of Fly Tying* is scheduled for publication early in the year 2000. Dick is also featured on 14 *Hooked on Fly Tying* videos.

Dick lives with his Russian wife, Vera, in Manchester, New Hampshire. His brother's wife, Denise, provided Dick with her original shrimp recipe.

Years Fly Fishing
Forty-three

Favorite Rod
5 wt 9' Graphite

Rods Owned
Thirty

Favorite Flies
Dry – Dorato Hare's Ear
Wet – Wild Turkey
Nymph – Pheasant Tail
Bead Thorax
Streamer – Marabou
Black Ghost
Terrestrial – Foam Beetle

Fly Invented
Perla Stonefly

Favorite US River
Main Delaware (NY)

Home River
None at this time.

Favorite Stream
DePuy's Spring Creek (MT)

Home Stream
None

DENISE'S SHRIMP

2 Pounds Raw Cleaned Shrimp
3 – 4 Cloves Fresh Garlic, Minced
3 Scallions, Minced
2 Tablespoons Olive Oil
Plus ¼ Cup Olive Oil
1 Bottle Clam Juice
Lemon Pepper Seasoning
2 Tablespoons Butter
1 Cup Finely Chopped Fresh Basil,
or ¼ Cup Dried Basil
1 Tablespoon Chives, Chopped
Romano Cheese, Preferably Fresh Ground
Vermicelli Pasta

In the 2 tablespoons of olive oil, sauté the garlic, scallions, and shrimp until the shrimp are just cooked through, but without too much heat.

Add ½ bottle of clam juice and a sprinkling of lemon pepper. Then add another ¼ cup of olive oil, the butter, basil and chives. Simmer until everything is hot.

Meanwhile, cook the pasta. When it's done, toss everything together with the Romano cheese, and serve.

Serves: 3 – 4

GARY P. TANNER

"I hope I never forget just how much fun popping for panfish can be—we all need to introduce kids to this great sport, and this can be a wonderful way to begin them."

Gary Tanner is the Executive Director of the American Museum of Fly Fishing, located in Manchester, Vermont.

Years Fly Fishing
Over Twenty

Favorite Rod
4 wt 9' Graphite

Rods Owned
Eight

Favorite Flies
Dry – Hendrickson
Wet – Not Provided
Nymph – G.R. Hare's Ear
Streamer – Woolly Bugger
Terrestrial – Letort Hopper

Fly Invented
None, yet

Favorite US River
Metawee (VT)

Home River
Battenkill (VT)

Favorite Stream
Not Provided

Home Stream
Not Provided

BREAM ITALIAN

Bluegill or Any Sunfish
Italian Breadcrumbs
Milk and Egg Batter
Lemon Wedges
Cocktail Sauce

Fillet bluegills. Dredge fillets first in an egg and milk batter, then coat with Italian style breadcrumbs. Deep fry quickly in the hottest oil possible. Drain. Serve with lemon wedges and cocktail sauce.

This recipe makes a wonderful appetizer—better than shrimp cocktail!

Serves: Depends on your fishing skills

WILLIAM G. TAPPLY

"Are we here to have fun, or to fish?" – Bill Rohrbacher, Bighorn Guide

William Tapply grew up hunting and fishing with his father, H. G. "Tap" Tapply. Bill is a writer, and teaches his trade at Emerson College and Clark University. He lives in Harvard, Massachusetts.

Bill writes the *Reading the Currents* column for *American Angler* magazine and is a Contributing Editor for *Field & Stream* magazine. He has written five fishing books and 16 mystery novels.

The most recent fishing book written by this author is *A Fly-Fishing Life*.

Years Fly Fishing
Fifty-one

Favorite Rod
4 wt 9' Graphite

Rods Owned
Twenty

Favorite Flies
Dry – Sparkle Dun
Wet – Soft Hackle
Nymph – Pheasant Tail
Streamer – Woolly Bugger
Terrestrial – Foam Beetle

Fly Invented
Mongrel Bugger

Favorite US River
Bighorn (MT)

Home River
Swift (MA)

Favorite Stream
DePuy's Spring Creek (MT)

Home Stream
A Secret

EDIBLE SEA DUCK

2 Dead Ducks, Such as Elder or Old Squaw
2 Cups Shitake Mushrooms
1 Cup Cheap Red Wine
¼ Pound Butter
Milk
Salt
Fresh Ground Pepper
Wild Rice
Fresh Asparagus
Expensive Red Wine
Fresh Greens

Breast out ducks and slice off the meat. Marinate in milk for 24 hours in the refrigerator.

Rinse the meat slices and marinate in the cheap wine for 12 hours.

Sauté the meat with the fresh mushrooms in butter. Sprinkle with salt and fresh ground pepper. Do not over cook, as this dish is best rare.

Serve over wild rice with fresh asparagus and expensive red wine and fresh greens.

Serves: 4

"Quit wishing … go fishin'."

Howard Taylor is the former long and suffering Secretary/Treasurer of the Middle Tennessee Fly Fishers, an active twenty year member group of the Federation of Fly Fishers. He was elected to serve as President of the group for 1999.

Howard has been a general contractor for the past twenty-three years. He and his wife of twenty-six years, Bernie, reside in Antioch, Tennessee.

For the past five years, Howard has led the fly fishing classes for the *Become an Outdoors Woman* program offered by the Tennessee Wildlife Resources Agency.

Howard conceived the idea of a knotless fly line/leader connection/strike indicator (all in one unit) that allows a solid connection without the use of the loop-to-loop method plus a highly visible strike indicator.

Howard loves to fish his home river at night, an activity NOT for the inexperienced, nor for the faint at heart. Asked how he could fish in total darkness, Howard responded, *"Fly fishing at night is like making love to a beautiful woman in a dark room. If you can't operate by feel, you have no business being there!"*

Years Fly Fishing
Twenty-one

Favorite Rod
2 wt 7' 6" Graphite

Rods Owned
Fifteen

Favorite Flies
Dry – Foam Humpy
Wet – Brown Bomber, Variant
Nymph – Damsel
Streamer – White Angel
Terrestrial – Foam Beetle

Flies Invented
White Angel and
Howard's Helluan

Favorite US River
Caney Fork (TN)

Home River
Caney Fork (TN)

Favorite Stream
Harpeth (TN)

Home Stream
Harpeth (TN)

© 2000 - Russell A. Hopper

Beef Steak, Pork Chop or Ground Chuck
Potatoes
Onions
Carrot
Mushrooms
Canned Corn
Cooking Oil
Flour
Salt and Pepper to Taste

The day before a planned trip, prepare your choice of meat. Cut into bite size pieces. Completely cook all other ingredients, seasoning as you prefer. Cool and wrap tightly in heavy-duty aluminum foil. If preparing several days prior to a trip, allow to cool and then freeze. Keep frozen until day of the trip.

Each packet can be warmed by boiling in water over campfire coals or, in a bind, the truck engine manifold. In dire straits this fully cooked meal could be eaten cold.

Prepare several at a time and freeze for future use. Another positive point of this packet is that no cooking utensils are required and there's no clean up—eat directly from the packet.

"The sport of fly fishing has no preferred gender. The fish could care less what sex the jerk is on the other end of the line."

Wanda Taylor is the co-owner of Taylor Fly Fishing Schools based in Calhoun, Tennessee. She is the first woman to be certified by the Federation of Fly Fishers as a Certified Master Fly Casting Instructor.

Wanda is also the first woman Orvis Endorsed guide in the Southeast and her husband, Captain Gary Taylor, was the 1993 – 94 *Orvis Guide of the Year*. He is a Certified Casting Instructor.

Taylor's favorite coast is Hilton Head Island, South Carolina where she likes to fish for redfish. Her favorite spot for false albacore is Nagshead, North Carolina.

Wanda is a graduate of the Orvis Guide School, the Joan Wulff School of Fly Fishing, as well as from Lefty Kreh's instructors course on *How to Teach Teachers to Teach*.

When not on the waters, Wanda can be found assisting with Trout Unlimited, Federation of Fly Fishers, TWRA's Beyond Becoming an Outdoor Women Program, and Casting for Recovery, a program designed for women recovering from breast cancer.

Years Fly Fishing
Sixteen

Favorite Rod
5 wt 9' Graphite (Trout)
9 wt 9' Graphite (Salt)

Rods Owned
Fifteen

Favorite Flies
Dry – Parachute Adams
Wet – LaFontaine Deep Diving Caddis
Nymph – B.H. Prince
Streamer – Mini Muddler/Red & White Lefty's Deceiver
Terrestrial – Beetle

Fly Invented
Taylor's Quigley

Favorite US River
Green (UT)

Home River
Hiwassee (TN)

Favorite Stream
DePuy's Spring Creek (MT)

Home Stream
Abram's Creek (TN)

1 Pound Fresh Shrimp
12 Medium Red Potatoes
6 Peaches and Cream Corn on the Cob
Smoked Beef Sausage
Olive Oil or Butter
3 Vidalia Onions
Old Bay Seasoning
8 Ounce Can of Beer
Crusty Sour Dough Bread

In a large deep pot, place the potatoes and cover slightly with water. Add 1 tablespoon Old Bay Seasoning and simmer.

In a skillet, brown the sliced sausage in 1 tablespoon of olive oil or butter. Add to the potatoes along with the corn and onions. Simmer until tender.

In a skillet, steam the shrimp in beer and Old Bay Seasoning to taste. Do not over cook. Shrimp will turn pink when finished.

Drain and serve with crusty sourdough bread.

Serves: 6

JIM TEENY

"You've got to get down deep to catch the fish."

Jim Teeny resides in steelhead country's Gresham, Oregon. He is the owner of Jim Teeny, Inc. and the holder of 10 International Game Fish Association Fly Rod World Records.

Jim's IGFA records for fish on the fly include sockeye salmon, chum salmon, pink salmon, sheefish, whitefish and northern pike, but he has released many other fish that would have been world's records had they been submitted for judging.

Jim hosted his own television series that ran for six years, is featured in several instructional videos and is the author of *The Teeny Technique for Steelhead & Salmon* that is included in the *Lefty's Little Library of Fly Fishing* series.

Known as the Submarine Man, Jim Teeny's 1988 video entitled *Catching More Steelhead* won the best *How to Video* for the nation and received *The Teddy Roosevelt Award*.

Jim's sinking fly line and nymph designs have proven to be popular worldwide. He has recently designed a new wading shoe that he says is the most comfortable wading shoe ever made. The shoe is easy to get in and out of and doesn't have laces.

Years Fly Fishing
Since Age Twelve

Favorite Rod
10 wt 9' Graphite

Rods Owned
Never Enough

Favorite Flies
Dry – What?
Wet – The Teeny Nymph
Nymph – The Teeny Nymph
Streamer – The Teeny
Flash Fly
Terrestrial – The Teeny Leech

Flies Invented
All the above.

Favorite US River
Kalama (WA)

Home River
Sandy (OR)

Favorite Stream
Sandy (OR)

Home Stream
Eagle Creek (OR)

BARBECUED SALMON FILLETS

Salmon Fillets
Salt and Pepper
Garlic Powder
Dill, Chopped
Tomatoes, Sliced
Onions, Sliced
Aluminum Foil
Teriyaki Sauce

Place fillets on aluminum foil, folding edges of the foil up slightly to hold in the moisture. Sprinkle fish with salt, pepper, garlic and dill. Top with tomatoes and onion slices.

Place the foil on a preheated barbecue grill. Medium to medium high heat works best. Cooking time depends on the thickness of the fish.

The fish is done when a spatula easily inserts into the fish at its thickest part.

Baste with teriyaki sauce while the fish is cooking. Cut the fish in the portion size you want. The skin will stay stuck to the foil.

TOM THEUS

"Any day on the water fly fishing is a great day."

Tom Theus is a show director, a lecturer on both salt water and fresh water fly fishing, a public speaker with Joan Whitlock's Speaker Bureau, and a conductor of fly casting schools. He helped develop the Federation of Fly Fishers' Casting Certification Program.

The outdoor writer, who resides in Boiling Springs, South Carolina, writes for the *Spartanburg Herald* newspaper and is a past President of Education for the Federation of Fly Fishers, past President of the Tampa Bay Fly Fishing Club and the Greenville, South Carolina Fly Fishing Club. Both clubs are active member groups of the Federation of Fly Fishers.

Years Fly Fishing
Twelve

Favorite Rod
5 wt 8' 6" Graphite

Rods Owned
Eight

Favorite Flies
Dry – Parachute Adams
Wet – March Brown
Nymph – Pheasant Tail
Streamer – Gray Ghost
Terrestrial – Dave's Hopper

Fly Invented
Tom's Jig for Salt Water

Favorite US River
Yellowstone (MT)

Home River
Davidson (NC)

Favorite Stream
Soda Butte (MT)

Home Stream
Looking Glass (NC)

TANGY GRILLED CHICKEN

6 Broiler/Fryer Chicken Quarters
½ Stick Butter
½ Cup Chopped Onions
½ Cup Red Vinegar
½ Cup Soy Sauce
1/3 Cup Orange Marmalade
½ Teaspoon Salt
½ Teaspoon Pepper
½ Teaspoon Paprika

Melt butter in a skillet, add onions and cook until done. Stir in vinegar, soy sauce and marmalade. Stir.

Season chicken with salt, pepper and paprika. Place chicken in a glass bowl. Pour marinade over chicken. Cover and refrigerate 3 hours.

Grill chicken. Turn and baste with remaining marinade every 10 to 15 minutes. Cook until a fork can be inserted in the chicken with ease, 45 – 60 minutes.

E. DONNALL THOMAS JR.

"Fly fishing should be fun. People who take it too seriously should be shot!"

Don Thomas practices medicine in Lewistown, Montana and says he has accomplished absolutely nothing. However, he has written several books including *To All Things a Season: Twelve Months Afield with Fly Rod; Dream Fish & Road Trips: Fly-Fishing Tales from Alaska, Montana, & Beyond; Fool Hen Blues: Retrievers and Shotguns and the American West*; and *Longbows of the Far North: an Archer's Adventure in Alaska & Siberia*.

Don also contributes articles to various sporting journals and is a Contributing Editor for *Gray's Sporting Journal*.

Years Fly Fishing
Forty-one

Favorite Rod
4 wt 7' 6" Graphite

Rods Owned
Ten

Favorite Flies
Dry – Egg Sucking Leech
Wet – Egg Sucking Leech
Nymph – Egg Sucking Leach
Streamer – Egg Sucking Leach
Terrestrial – Egg Sucking Leach

Fly Invented
Dirty Dog and
Halibut Special

Favorite US River
Yellowstone (MT)

Home River
Judith (MT)

Favorite Stream
A Secret

Home Stream
Another Secret

POLITICALLY CORRECT SEVICHE

1 Pound Halibut Fillet
2 Limes
½ Cup Fresh Cilantro
½ Cup Green Onions, Chopped
Dash Garlic Salt and Tabasco

Slice raw fish into thin strips. Cover the sliced fish with the juice of 2 limes. Let stand 1 hour. Drain lime juice. Add chopped cilantro and onions. Season with garlic salt and Tabasco.

Serve chilled with crackers.

"Since halibut are deep water fish of little general interest to fly anglers, no one will object to eating it even though this does not necessarily make sense." – Don

DOC THOMPSON

"There are only two things more natural than catching browns on a dry fly, and since we're not going to be rolling around in the dirt we might as well be catching browns on dries." – Doc's response to why people won't be using any nymphs or streamers on a particular guide trip.

"They rise like a fastball, and just when you expect another fastball, they throw you a change-up just to keep you thinking." – Doc's comments on how the native Rio Grande cutthroat rise to dry flies, and why so many anglers miss their rise.

Doc Thompson is a professional guide, freelance writer, author and owner of High Country Anglers in Cimarron, New Mexico. He is co-writing *Fly Fishing Northeastern New Mexico* with Mark D. Williams and Ken Medling. His article, essays and photographs have been published in *The Angling Report, Fly Fish American* and *Dallas Morning News.*

Doc created what he calls the choke-up hair brush roll cast.

Doc first created and served his Ponil Feast Pumpkin Cheesecake for the *First Somewhat Annual Thanksgiving Day Feast* held along the banks of the middle Ponil.

Years Fly Fishing
Since about eleven years old.

Favorite Rod
4 wt 8' Orvis Tight Loop
5 wt 8' 6" Hexagraph
4 wt 7' 9" Bamboo by Ken Cole, Rod Maker

Rods Owned
Finally down to four.

Favorite Flies
Dry – Parachute Adams with Black Hackle
Wet – Brown Partridge
Nymph – Pheasant Tail
Streamer – Do not use.
Terrestrial – Hopper

Fly Invented
GC Emerger

Favorite US River
Rio Grande (NM)

Home River
Cimarron (NM)

Favorite Stream
Streaked Creek (NM)

Home Stream
Rio Costilla (NM)

© 2000 - Russell A. Hopper

PUMPKIN CHEESECAKE*

(*Doc's Ponil Feast Pumpkin Cheesecake)

Crust
2 – 2 ½ Cups Graham Cracker Crumbs
1 ½ Sticks Melted Butter – 1 Handful Sugar

Filling
4 Boxes (8 Ounces Each) Cream Cheese
8 – 10 Ounces Pumpkin Pie Filling
7/8 Cup Sugar – 2 Eggs – 2 Dashes Nutmeg
2 Dashes Real Vanilla Extract
1 – 2 Dashes Real Almond Extract

Mix all crust ingredients in a bowl and press into a greased 9" – 10" spring pan. Cool in the refrigerator until needed. In a large bowl, blend softened (room temperature) cream cheese, sugar and eggs until smooth. Add vanilla, almond and nutmeg, and blend. Mix in pumpkin pie filling until well blended. Pour filling into the cooled crust, gently shaking until evenly spread. Bake in a preheated 450-degree oven for 8 – 10 minutes. Turn oven down to 200 – 225 degrees and bake for about 40 minutes. Check until almost done baking. Then cool in turned off oven with door cracked. When completely cooled, remove from the oven and place in refrigerator. Serve the next day.

Serves: 6 – 10

RICHARD TISCH

SHRIMP WITH RIGATONI

"The charm of fishing is that it is the pursuit of what is elusive, but attainable; a perpetual series of occasions for hope." – John Buchan

Richard Tisch is a lawyer residing in Pound Ridge, New York. He is the President of the Board of Trustees of the American Museum of Fly Fishing in Manchester, Vermont. Richard also serves as a Director of The Anglers' Club of New York and is a member of the Potatuck Club in Newton, Connecticut.

Years Fly Fishing
Thirty-seven

Favorite Rod
5 wt 8' 9" Graphite

Rods Owned
Ten

Favorite Flies
Dry – Adams, Catskill Tie, or a Ginger Bivisible
Emerger – Snowshoe Hare, Pink Thread
Wet – Green Highlander
Nymph – G.R. Hare's Ear
Streamer – Muddler Minnow
Terrestrial – Black Beetle

Fly Invented
None I will admit.

Favorite US River
Yellowstone (MT & WY)

Home River
Potatuck (CT)

Favorite Stream
Ausable (NY)

5 Tablespoons Olive Oil
2 – 3 Cups Tomatoes, Peeled and Cubed
½ Cup White Wine – Salt and Pepper
1 Teaspoon Finely Chopped Garlic – ¼ Cup Chopped Fresh Basil – 1 Teaspoon Oregano
1 ½ Pounds Medium Shrimp, Peeled, Deveined
1 Pound Rigatoni
½ Pound Feta Cheese

Heat 2 tablespoons olive oil in a skillet and add garlic. Cook briefly. Add tomatoes and cook for 1 minute. Add wine, salt, pepper, basil and oregano. Cook over medium heat.

Peel and devein the shrimp, leaving the tails on. Apply salt and pepper to the shrimp.

Heat 3 tablespoons of olive oil in a large skillet and add shrimp. Cook quickly for 1 minute, until the shrimp turns red. Sprinkle with red pepper flakes.

Preheat oven to 400 degrees. Spoon shrimp and juices into a baking dish. Sprinkle feta cheese over shrimp and spoon sauce over. Place baking dish in oven and bake for 10 minutes.

Cook rigatoni and drain. Serve hot rigatoni with shrimp mixture spooned over.

Serve: 4

TOM TRAVIS

"I am most interested in how many fish you can catch tomorrow, without me, than I am in how many you catch today with me!"

Tom Travis is a fly fishing guide and contract pattern designer for Orvis, who offers more than 20 of Tom's fly patterns. He guides out of Livingston, Montana. It is from Tom's guiding experiences that his quote is provided.

Tom has written articles for the *Flyfisher, Fly Fish America, American Angler, Fly Fishing Quarterly* and *Anglers Journal* magazines. He and Rod Walinchus co-authored *Fly Fishing the Yellowstone River: An Angler's Guide.*

Some of Tom's fly pattern creations include the Extended Body Gray Drake and the Travis Para Midge.

Tom is a regular attendee at the Federation of Fly Fishers Conclaves, providing workshops, programs and serving as speaker.

Years Fly Fishing
Forty-four

Favorite Rod
4 wt 8' 4" Graphite

Rods Owned
Eighty

Favorite Flies
Dry – Extended Body Gray Drake
Wet – Hare's Ear
Nymph – B.H. Pheasant Tail
Streamer – Lite Spruce and Western Feather Streamer
Terrestrial – Hopper

Flies Invented
See Comments

Favorite US River
Henry's Fork (ID)

Home River
Yellowstone (MT)

Favorite Stream
Firehole (WY)

Home Stream
DePuy's Spring Creek (MT)

MONTANA BAKED BEANS

1 Can VandeKamp Premium Baked Beans
3 Tablespoons Worcestershire Sauce
2 Tablespoons A-1 Bold & Spicy Steak Sauce
1 Cup Pace Thick & Chunky Salsa
¼ Cup Hunt's Smoky Hickory Barbeque Sauce

Mix ingredients together. Let set overnight. Serve hot or cold.

AL TROTH

"Fishing to rising trout is without a doubt the most fun. Unfortunately fish do not always cooperate."

Al Troth is a professional fly tyer, photographer, writer, fly designer, and retired guide and fly fishing outfitter. He was a schoolteacher back East. Since 1973 he and his wife reside in Dillon, Montana.

Al designed the Terrible Troth, but his best-known fly creation is the familiar Elk Hair Caddis. The Elk Hair Caddis is a generic fly, but can be used to imitate a stonefly by simply changing the size and color. Al also created a couple of dozen other fly patterns, including the Troth Olive Pheasant Tail and the MacHopper.

Before retiring from guiding in 1996, Al tied flies seven months of the year and then guided the other five. He caught his first trout at the age of 11. It was a 14" brown caught on a Fan Wing Royal Coachman.

Years Fly Fishing
Fifty-seven
Favorite Rod
5 wt 9' Graphite
Rods Owned
Ten
Favorite Flies
Dry – Elk Hair Caddis
Wet – Dark Cahill
Nymph – Olive Pheasant Tail
Streamer – Black Marabou
Muddler Minnow
Terrestrial – MacHopper
Flies Invented
See Comments
Favorite US River
Big Hole, Beaverhead and Madison (MT)
Home River
Beaverhead (MT)
Favorite Stream
Poindexter Slough (MT)
Home Stream
Poindexter Slough (MT)

BANANA NUT BREAD

½ Cup Butter
1 Cup Sugar
2 Eggs, Well Beaten
2 Ripe Bananas, Mashed
2 Cups Flour
1 Teaspoon Soda
Pinch Salt
¾ Cup Broken Pecans

Cream butter and sugar. Add eggs and bananas. Mix well. Stir in dry ingredients and nuts. Mix well. Bake in 2 well-greased loaf pans at 350 degrees for 50 – 60 minutes.

Serves best when in icebox. Then toast and butter.

The author of this book, Russell A. Hopper, provides this recipe, as Al says he has been diagnosed with Parkinson's Disease.

JOHN R. TROY

"If they're not hitting today, what makes you think they'll be hitting tomorrow?"

John Troy is a cartoonist living in Hardwick, New Jersey with his wife, Doris. He is the author of 10 books including: *Ben, Ben Again, Ben Unleashed, Ben at Large, The Authorized Ben Treasury, You Should Have Been Here Yesterday, Fly Fishing !#@%&*!*, and *The Great Outdoors #@%&*!* John teaches fly casting and cartooning in New Jersey.

Years Fly Fishing
Over Fifty

Favorite Rod
6 wt 8' 6" Fenwick, HMG Graphite

Rods Owned
Thirty

Favorite Flies
Dry – Black Gnat or Black Quill
Wet – Male Beaverkill
Nymph – Hare's Ear
Streamer – Dace #12
Terrestrial – Dry Muddler
Minnow as a Hopper

Fly Invented
Dace with Marabou Back

Favorite US River
Paulins Kill (NJ)

Home River
Paulins Kill (NJ)

Favorite Stream
Jacksonburg Creek (NJ)

Home Stream
Jacksonburg Creek (NJ)

CHILI DOG

Roll
Fine Onions
Mustard
Hot Dog
Chili

Take roll, fine onions, mustard, hot dog, and then chili—in that order. No chili con carne!
Eat from one end to the other.

GENE TRUMP

"Even ugly flies catch fish."

Gene Trump is a part-time outdoor cartoonist, humorist, writer and a full-time fly fishing fool. He resides with his wife, Virginia, in Corvallis, Oregon.

Gene's articles, humor stories and cartoons are frequently published in *Field & Stream, Fly Fisherman, Virtual Flyshop, Salmon-Trout-Steelheader, Flyfishing & Tying Journal,* and numerous other media. His cartoon book, *Fly Fishing Only,* is published by Abenaki Publishing.

Gene's many fly pattern innovations include the Spartan, Bubble Bug, Tied Down Brown, Bristle Brown, Royal Nymph, Dry Montana, YBP, Saint Nick and Snow Flake.

In responding to the Angler Profile request, Gene says, *"I have fly fished for twenty-four years and may get the hang of it yet."* He adds, *"My favorite rod is Graphite, but I would probably love bamboo if given the chance to afford one. My favorite nymph is my wife, Virginia, and as for terrestrials, hoppers are good, but extraterrestrials are a different story."*

Years Fly Fishing
Twenty-four

Favorite Rod
5 wt 9' 6" Graphite

Rods Owned
Twelve, but don't tell my wife.

Favorite Flies
Dry – Parachute
March Brown
Wet – John's Green
Soft Hackle
Nymph – B.H. Olive
Hare's Ear
Streamer – Spartan
Terrestrial – Joe's Hopper

Flies Invented
See Comments

Favorite US River
The Lamar (WY)

Home River
The Siletz (OR)

Favorite Stream
South Santiam (OR)

Home Stream
South Santiam (OR)

VIRGINIA'S SPARE RIBS

3 Pounds Boneless Country-Style Spare Ribs
2 Cups Catsup, More if Desired
1 Onion, Sliced into Rings
1 – 2 Teaspoons Minced Garlic
1/8 Cup Vinegar
½ Cup Water
2 Tablespoons Each of Soy Sauce,
Worcestershire Sauce and Brown Sugar
1 Small Can Crushed Pineapple
¼ Teaspoon Chili Powder or to Taste
Pepper, Celery Salt and Spices to Taste

Prepare sauce by combining all ingredients, except for the ribs. Bring to boil, then simmer for 15 minutes or until the sauce slightly thickens.

Trim most of the fat from the ribs. Brown on each side. Do in batches if necessary. Once the ribs are seared/browned, combine the sauce with the meat in a Dutch oven or roasting pan and cook at 350 degrees for 1 hour. Stir and bake for another hour, checking to make sure the sauce isn't drying out.

Remove the cover from the pan and bake for 20 – 30 minutes so the top of the meat browns. Use the broiler for the last 5 minutes or grill the meat for a crunchy, browned top.

LARRY TULLIS

"Regrettably, on most occasions fly fishing is no longer a sport of solitude."

Larry Tullis is the father of Madison Jeremiah Tullis. He is also the author of seven books, a photographer, guide, lecturer and fly shop expert. Larry is the past President of the Utah Valley Fly Rodders and helped in the design of modern kick boats.

Larry's premier appearance in book form was *Green River, UT*. He went on to hook up with Lefty Kreh and produced the third volume on trout in *Lefty's Little Library of Fly Fishing*. Other books include *Nymphs: Tying & Fishing; Henry's Fork, Volume 3*; and *Nymphing—Bottom to Top*.

Publisher John Randolph once said, *"Larry Tullis understands the instincts of trout and their survival behavior as well as any fly fisher who has dared to write about it."*

Larry resides in Salt Lake City, Utah.

"Gear does not make a fly fisherman." – Larry

Years Fly Fishing
Twenty-five

Favorite Rod
4 wt 9' Graphite

Rods Owned
Over Fifty

Favorite Flies
Dry – Double Ugly
Wet – Woolly Rabb-eye
Nymph – Spectrumized Fur Bug
Streamer – Tullis Wiggle Bug
Terrestrial – Cicada

Flies Invented
Wiggle Bug, Tube Damsel, Woolly Rabb-eye

Favorite US River
Henry's Fork (ID)

Home River
Green (UT)

Favorite River
Rio Nirchuao (Chile)

Home Stream
Provo (UT)

BEAR BAIT SPAGHETTI SAUCE

1 Pound Ground Beef
1 Cup Chopped Onion
2 Tablespoons Salad Oil
2 Cloves Garlic, Minced
2 (1 Pound Each) Cans Tomatoes (4 Cups)
2 (8 Ounces Each) Cans Tomato Sauce (2 Cups)
1 (3 Ounces) Can Mushrooms (2/3 Cups)
¼ Cup Chopped Parsley
1 ½ Teaspoons Oregano
1 Teaspoon Salt
½ Teaspoon Sugar
¼ Teaspoon Thyme
1 Bay Leaf
1 Cup Water

Brown onion in hot oil. Add beef and garlic, then brown. Drain grease and water.

Add final ingredients and simmer, uncovered, for 2 hours (½ hour and less water if you're hungry) until thick. Remove bay leaf.

Serve on normally prepared spaghetti pasta.

Serves: 4 – 6

"This sauce can also be used to make pasta pie or lasagna." – Larry

Daniel D. Turner

Hot Dog Chili Mac

"To fish, fine and far off, is the first and principal rule of Trout Angling." – Charles Cotton

Daniel Turner of Thornton, Colorado is a past Eastern Rocky Mountain President of the Federation of Fly Fishers. He says that he is currently retired.

Years Fly Fishing
Ten

Favorite Rod
5 wt 9' Graphite

Rods Owned
Four

Favorite Flies
Dry – Blue Winged Olive
Wet – Not Provided
Nymph – Mysis Shrimp
and Pheasant Tail
Streamer – Not Provided
Terrestrial – Ant

Fly Invented
None, yet

Favorite US River
Frying Pan (CO)
Yellowstone (MT)

Home Rivers
South Platte (CO)
and Blue River (CO)

Favorite Stream
Not Provided

Home Stream
Not Provided

1 Package (8 – 10) Franks
1 Can (15 Ounces) Chili with Beans
¼ Cup Heinz 57 or Pincante Sauce
Kraft Macaroni and Cheese

Fix macaroni and cheese as directed by the box. Slice hot franks into small slices. Add chili and Heinz 57. Mix everything together and heat thoroughly.

Serves: 4 – 6

"The system works! All anglers must put something back into the system if we are to have fishing in the future."

Peter Van Gytenbeek is the Publisher and Editor-in-Chief of *Fly Fishing in Salt Waters*. He was the first full time Executive Director of Trout Unlimited from 1969 – 74 and President of the Federation of Fly Fishers from 1983 – 84. Peter has served multiple terms on both organizations' Boards of Directors.

Long active in conservation causes, Peter conceived the alteration of the Flaming Gorge Dam in Utah, which insured the fishing we have there today.   He was President of the American Sportsman's Club and of R.O.M.C.O.E (Rocky Mountain Center on Environment), a unique regional organization which successfully mediated environmental conflicts and was conceived and supported jointly by business and environmental organizations.

Peter started fishing at age five and fly fishing at age seven. His school years were spent in Florida and the Northwest. He later moved to Colorado and expanded his fishing territory to the rest of the U. S., Canada, Mexico and the Bahamas. He resides in Seattle, Washington.

Years Fly Fishing
Fifty-six

Favorite Rod
8 wt 9' Graphite

Rods Owned
Over Twenty

Favorite Flies
Dry – Elk Hair Caddis
Wet – Woolly Bugger
Nymph – Stonefly
Streamer – Light Spruce
Terrestrial – Black Ant

Fly Invented
None, yet

Favorite US River
Rio Grand (CO)

Home River
Skagit (WA)

Favorite Stream
Middle Fork South Platte (CO)

Home Stream
Yakima (WA)

© 2000 - Russell A. Hopper

Chinook or Coho Salmon Filet
3 Parts Miracle Whip
1 Part Spicy Brown Mustard
2 Parts Brown Sugar
Dash of Soy Sauce

Broil salmon until approximately 5 minutes from being cooked to your satisfaction. Mix ingredients with a spoon until you have a thick sauce. Spread over filet and return to the oven. Repeat in 2 minutes. Remove as the sugar begins to burn, approximately 3 minutes.

Serve.

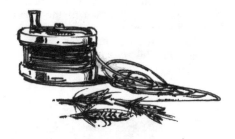

Mark Van Patten

Mark's Methane Madness

"Stop! Twelve o'clock! Big brown trout, forward cast!"

Mark Van Patten resides in Jefferson City, Missouri. He is a Stream Team Coordinator for the State of Missouri's Adopt A Stream Program and past President of the Southern Council of the Federation of Fly Fishers.

The Southern Council of the Federation of Fly Fishers named Mark *Conservationist of the Year* in 1990 and *Man of the Year* in 1991. In 1993, Mark's Stream Team was awarded the international *McKinnzee Cup* for stream conservation. He has received numerous other awards for his outstanding work.

Mark is a published author, has held various positions, including Chairman of the Board, with the Missouri Outdoor Communicators, a Missouri based outdoor writers group. He also received a *Life Membership Award* from the Missouri Outdoor Communicators in 1996.

Years Fly Fishing
Thirty-three

Favorite Rod
4 wt 8' Graphite

Rods Owned
Fourteen

Favorite Flies
Dry – Renegade
Wet – Partridge and Orange
Soft Hackle
Nymph – Prince
Streamer – Dark Olive
B.H. Woolly Bugger with
Peacock Body
Terrestrial – Mark's Hopper

Fly Invented
Mark's Hopper

Favorite US River
Madison (MT)

Home River
Gasconade (MO)

Favorite Stream
Roubidoux (MO)

Home Stream
Roubidoux (MO)

© 2000 - Russell A. Hopper

1 Pound Ground Beef
1 Pound Sirloin, Cubed
1 Cup Merlot Wine
3 Cloves Garlic, Chopped Fine
1 Cup Coffee
1 Teaspoon Thyme
2 Cans (8 Ounces Each) Red Beans
2 Habanero Peppers, Chopped Coarse
1 Medium Onion, Chopped Coarse
½ Cup Brown Sugar
3 Tablespoons Black Molasses
6 Bay Leaves
Salt and Pepper to Taste

Brown meat with garlic, thyme, onions, Habenero, salt, and pepper. Add Merlot, brown sugar, molasses, bay leaves, beans with juice in the cans, and coffee. Simmer until the chili cooks down to a thick base.

Serve with chopped raw onion and shredded cheese on top. This chili is hot! You might want to adjust the number of peppers to your taste. You can also add chili powder to taste. Tastes great in a Dutch oven over a campfire. Have plenty of cold beverages on hand before eating.

Serves: 6

"Troutfishing enthusiasts look upon the Beaverkill as America's stream."

Ed Van Put is a Principal Fish and Wildlife Technician for New York State Department of Environmental Conservation. He resides in Livingston Manor, New York.

Ed is the author of *The Beaverkill: The History of a River and Its People.*

Ed believes that presentation and accuracy are the two most important steps in successful trout fishing. He only fishes with a double tapered floating line and utilizes, compared to most fly fishers, very few patterns. His other favorite dry flies include a Pheasant Tail Midge #22, Elk Hair Caddis #14, and a Royal Wulff #14.

Years Fly Fishing
Forty-seven

Favorite Rod
8' Orvis Bamboo
8' One Piece Vince Cummings Glass

Rods Owned
Twenty-two

Favorite Flies
Dry – Adams
Wet – Royal Coachman
Nymph – Zug Bug
Streamer – Black Ghost
Terrestrial – Occasionally a Black Ant.

Fly Invented
Able Mable

Favorite US River
Delaware (NY)

Home River
Beaverkill (NY)

Favorite Stream
Any stream in the Catskills (NY).

Home Stream
Willowemoc Creek (NY)

© 2000 - Russell A. Hopper

Seafood!

JAMES D. VINCENT

JIM'S ORIENTAL BARBECUE FISH

"The fish you release is your gift to another angler and remember, it may have been someone's similar gift to you." – Lee Wulff

Jim Vincent, of Blackfoot, Idaho, specializes in the manufacture of fly lines through his company, Rio Products. He is also an excellent photographer.

Jim's claim to fame is the development of spey lines, leaders, tippet material and custom fly lines. He has also written for various outdoor magazines for over fifteen years and developed some pretty interesting techniques for catching steelhead on a dry fly.

Years Fly Fishing
Thirty-six

Favorite Rod
*5 wt 8' 6" Graphite
or Bamboo*

Rods Owned
Seventy-five

Favorite Flies
*Dry – Emerger
Wet – Soft Hackle
Nymph – Black A.P.
(Andre' Puyan)
Streamer – Marabou Leech
Terrestrial – Ant*

Flies Invented
Several

Favorite US River
Henry's Fork (ID)

Home River
Henry's Fork (ID)

Favorite Stream
Skeena (ID)

Home Stream
Clearwater (ID)

*2 Large Fillets
(Salmon, Steelhead or Large Trout)
½ Teaspoon Wasabi Mustard
¾ Cup Soy Sauce
¼ Cup Honey
1 Tablespoon Fresh Ginger, Chopped
¼ Cup White Wine*

Prepare a fire on the grill and let the coals burn until they are low and even heated.

Take ¾ cup of soy sauce and mix with ½ teaspoon of mustard, ¼ cup of honey, 1 tablespoon of chopped fresh ginger and ¼ cup of wine. Mix well and cover fillets with mixture. Put fillets on grill about 8" above fire coals. Be sure to leave the skin on! Cover with aluminum foil to just cover the flesh as the skin takes the heat. Cooking time is about 30 minutes for 5 to 6 pounds of meat. The idea is to slowly cook.

When done, cut pieces out of the skin with a spatula and serve directly.

"Nice to meet you; do you have any bass or trout on your irrigation pond?"

Rudy Von Strasser is the owner of Freestone Winery in Napa Valley. He's the one who tied together fine wine, nature and the art of fly fishing with his wine label designs. His 95 Sauvignon Blanc depicts a class fly painted by Eldridge Hardie.

Rudy says, *"California has no water. It's all shipped in from other states."* He says his fly invention is based on the collie-dog salmon streamer, but from Rudy's longhaired days.

Years Fly Fishing
Thirty-one
Favorite Rod
4 wt 9' Graphite
Rods Owned
Four
Favorite Flies
Dry – Humpy
Wet – Rusty Rat for Salmon
Nymph – B.H. Hare's Ear
Streamer – Muddler Minnow
Terrestrial – E. T.
Fly Invented
Rudy-dog
Favorite US River
Madison (MT)
Home River
Smith (CA)
Favorite Stream
Not Provided
Home Stream
Not Provided

Alder-Chip Smoke Bags
from Finland

Stick trout into an Alder-Chip Smoke Bag that Rudy's wife's relatives shipped in from Finland. Enclose 2 sugar cubes. Close. Place on fire until done.

Serves: 2 – 4 depending on fish size

"I love easy cooking." – Rudy

"Colossal ignorance, greed and out of control egos define modern fly fishing. Such degradation springs from ignoring the truth found in 500-years documented flyfishing wisdom. Flyfishers are unread, unlearned and ignorant thereby vulnerable to not only flyfishing failures but financial exploitation. Writers, editors, producers and sellers of product suffer an equal lack of wisdom; however, their afflictions are compounded by heaping helpings of arrogance and avarice. Please remember history proves there is very, very little honestly new to flyfishing; ignorance and arrogance damage fish, flyfishing, caring flyfishers, ethics, manners and morals."

John Waite lives in Spokane, Washington and is the author of *Serious Flyfishing with Survey Results*. He is the nation's leading supplier of legal polar bear hair, dubbing and flies. John says, *"With adequate research, it becomes evident that it is very difficult to invent any new fly pattern. They may be modified and possibly improved."*

John continues to fight for the good of flyfishing and common flyfishers, but says he finds that most people prefer to be fooled, believe myth and hyperbole.

Years Fly Fishing
Thirty-nine

Rods Owned
Who cares? I have too many and collect a few. Rods should be kept in their none-too-important perspective.

Favorite Flies
Dry – Hair Caddis
Wet – Wet Coachman
Nymph – Polar Bitch Creek
Streamer – Bi-Buck, Brown and White
Terrestrial – Hair Caddis

Fly Invented
See Comments

Favorite US River
North Umpqua (OR)

Home River
None I claim.

Favorite Stream
None, I like many.

Home Stream
Not Provided

© 2000 - Russell A. Hopper

Slice Cold Shoulder
Slice Sharp Tongue
Bread of Choice

Take above ingredients and make a sandwich.

The author of this book, Russell A. Hopper, provides this recipe and the recipe is no reflection on his own current mother-in-law.

"I am not a cook." – John

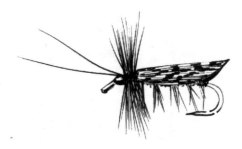

LANI WALLER

"The long way is the short way in the long run."

Lani Waller is the owner of Worldwide Anglers, an international fly fishing travel program promising trips of a lifetime. He is based out of Sausalito, California.

Lani is a current Field Editor for *Fly Fisherman* magazine, an Editor-at-Large for *Wild Steelhead & Salmon*, and a frequent contributor to other fly fishing magazines.

A fly fisher since 1956, Lani has watched a small, quiet sport grow into a major outdoor activity practiced by enthusiastic people from all walks of life and from all parts of the world.

Lani has fished many of the premier waters around the world, but long ago earned a reputation, as one of the Northwest's most knowledgeable steelhead anglers and guides. This knowledge has landed Lani in many videos such as *Fly Fishing for Pacific Steelhead, Advanced Fly Fishing for Pacific Steelhead* and *Fly Fishing for Trophy Steelhead.*

Years Fly Fishing
Forty-three

Favorite Rod
8 wt 9' 6" Graphite

Rods Owned
Thirty-six

Favorite Flies
Dry – Waller-Waker
Wet – Signal Light
Nymph – Muskrat
Streamer – Electric Leech
Terrestrial – Not Provided

Fly Invented
Waller-Waker

Favorite US River
Not Provided

Home River
Babine (BC)

Favorite Stream
Babine (BC)

Home Stream
Babine (BC)

© 2000 - Russell A. Hopper

OLD IRISH FUDGE PIE

¼ Pound Butter
2 Squares Unsweetened Chocolate
1 Cup Sugar
3 Eggs, Beaten
¼ Cup Flour
1 Pinch Salt
¼ Cup Chopped Pecans
1 Teaspoon Vanilla

Melt butter and chocolate over low heat. Add sugar, then beaten eggs and mix well. Stir in flour, salt and pecans. Beat well. Add vanilla and pour into a buttered pie pan. Bake at 350 degrees for about 25 minutes or until set. Top with whipped cream or ice cream.

The author of this book, Russell A. Hopper, provides this recipe, as Lani Waller didn't provide a favorite recipe.

JOE J. WARREN

"Attitude is everything, that one cast could be for the big one!"

Joe Warren is a bio science fisheries technician and the author of *Tying Glass Bead Flies*, the first and only comprehensive fly tying book using glass beads. He has performed in two fly tying videos: *Glass Bead Flies for Trout* and *Warm Water Glass Bead Flies*. He resides in Carson, Washington.

Joe has created 48 original fly patterns with glass beads.

Years Fly Fishing
Twenty-six

Favorite Rod
5 – 6 wt 8' 6" Fiberglass

Rods Owned
Over Twenty-five

Favorite Flies
Dry – Bead Butt, Elk Wing Caddis
Wet – Killer Caddis
Nymph – Pebble Bead Stonefly
Streamer – Woolly Bugger
Terrestrial – Joe's Drowning Ant

Flies Invented
See Comments

Favorite US River
North Platte (WY)

Home River
Klickitat (WA)

Favorite Stream
Armstrong Spring Creek (MT)

Home Stream
Big White Salmon (WA)

BEEF CURRY*

(*Beef Curry Over Steamed Rice & Fried Eggs)

1 Pound Chunk Meat
½ Onion, Diced
3 Tablespoons Curry Powder
Seasoning Salt and Pepper, To Taste
6 Cups Water
1 Large Carrot, Chopped
3 Potatoes, Chopped
¼ Cup Flour

Brown meat with seasoning salt and pepper. Then sauté onion. Add curry powder and stir thoroughly. Add water and bring up to a boil. Turn down heat to simmer for 1 hour. Add carrot and potatoes. Cook for 1 more hour. Then add flour and stir until thickened and flour is completely cooked.

Serve over steamed rice. Fried eggs overeasy are highly recommended on the rice before adding curry. Try soy sauce for added flavor.

Serves: 6

"Great cold weather meal!" – Joe

"There are very few new flies, just new names."

Charlie Waterman has been with *Gray's Sporting Journal* since its beginning and is a current Contributing Editor for *Gray's* and *Fly Fishing in Salt Water*. He lives in DeLand, Florida and spends a great deal of time fishing the brackish water of Florida's southwest coast. Both he and his wife, Debie, are avid fly fishers.

Charlie's *Hunting Upland Birds* was first published a quarter of a century ago. Other books include *Black Bass & the Fly Rod, Field Days*, and *Gun Dogs and Bird Guns*. *Mist on the River*, is about his remembrances of the legendary Dan Bailey. Charlie was awarded the Outdoor Writers Association *Excellence in Craft Award* in 1977.

Gray's Sporting Journal tells a story about Charlie's awakening to changing times. It seems Charlie was fishing a creek out West, when he hooked a pretty fair rainbow when an 11-year-old in chest waders came up behind him and netted the fish for him, after which the grade-schooler told Charlie his leader tippet was too heavy and his hook barb was not sufficiently bent down. After making some changes in Charlie's tackle, the boy said: *"Now try it again."* Sorry, Charlie!

Years Fly Fishing
Seventy Five

Favorite Rod
9 wt 9' Graphite

Rods Owned
Twenty-eight

Favorite Flies
Dry – Caddis Imitation
Wet – Silver Outcast
fished as a wet fly.
Nymph – Gray Midge Pupa
Streamer – Silver Outcast
Terrestrial – Dave's Hopper

Fly Invented
See Quote

Favorite US River
Smith (MT)

Home River
St. Johns (FL)

Favorite Stream
Nelson's Spring Creek (MT)

Home Stream
Not Provided

2 Pounds Shrimp
1 Pound Crabmeat
2 Medium Sized Onions
2 Cans (1 Pound Each) Tomatoes
6 Stalks Celery
¾ Cup Flour
2 Large Green Peppers
1 Pound Fresh Okra
Pinch Thyme
Bay Leaf
Salt and Pepper to Taste
1 Cup Warm Water
Minced Parsley
1 Can Tomato Juice
1 Hot Habanero Pepper, Chopped

Put 1 tablespoon shortening in a skillet and add chopped celery, onion, peppers and seasonings. Cook the vegetables until they are tender.

Brown the flour and 4 tablespoons butter in another skillet. When the vegetables are tender, add the browned flour, okra and tomatoes, stirring constantly. Add the tomato juice, shrimp and crabmeat. Cook over low heat for at least 1 hour. Do not cover while cooking.

Serves: 8

JIM WATT

"I have the best and easiest job in the world."

Like his wife, Jim Watt is also in the television business. He produces and co-hosts with Kelly, ESPN's *Fly Fishing Video Magazine* series. Jim says his greatest personal achievement is that he's lucky enough to make a living working with his best friend, Kelly, doing something they love. They spend more than 120 days a year fly fishing in a wide variety of places from Tierra del Fuego, Argentina to Alaska.

Their company, Bennett/Wyatt Entertainment, Inc., has produced over 160 videos on the subject of fly fishing since they started their fly fishing series in 1987. In addition to producing the fly fishing series, Jim and Kelly work as a video production crew for clients like ABC's *20/20, World News* and *Good Morning America* programs.

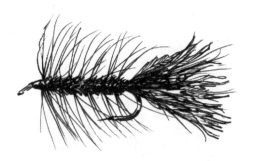

Years Fly Fishing
Forty-seven

Favorite Rod
4 wt 9' Graphite

Rods Owned
Too Many to List

Favorite Flies
Dry – Humpy
Wet – Woolly Bugger
Nymph – Bread Crust
Streamer – Kelly's Princessa
Terrestrial – Hollywood Cicada

Fly Invented
Pancora Martin

Favorite US River
Henry's Fork (ID)

Home River
Yakima (WA)

Favorite Stream
Quillen (Argentina)

Home Stream
Snoqualmie (WA)

STUFFED FREE RANGE CHICKEN

1 Free Range Chicken (4 Pounds)
3 Pounds Hot Italian Sausage
8 Cups Stuffing Mix or Breadcrumbs
4 Tablespoons Poultry Seasoning
2 Tablespoons Cracked Black Pepper,
Added to Breadcrumbs
1 Cup Raisins
1 Cup Walnuts, Chopped
1 Can (8 Ounces) Chicken Broth
2 Cups Onion, Chopped
2 Cups Celery, Chopped
1 Cake Butter

Brown sausage and add to the breadcrumbs.

Melt butter in the same pan and sauté the onion and celery.

Add poultry seasoning and pepper to the onion and celery, mixing well. Add the mixture to the breadcrumbs and toss. Add walnuts, raisins and toss. Add chicken broth and toss it again.

Stuff the chicken and roast in a 400 degree oven for 1 hour and 30 minutes.

Jim adds a bag of cranberries, boiled for about 10 minutes with a cup of brown sugar, 2 tablespoons allspice and a cup of water. He personally prefers a Pinot Noir as an accompanying wine.

KELLY WATT

ROCK SHRIMP CAPELLINI

"Filming fly fishing with your best buddy is a great way to make a living."

Kelly Watt lives in Issaquah, Washington with her husband and partner, Jim Watt. Their company, Bennett/Watt Entertainment, Inc., is in the television and video production business. Clients include ABC and ESPN in addition to their independent projects. They have produced over 160 home videos about fly fishing and have had a regular television program, *Fly Fishing Video Magazine*, on ESPN since the early 1990's. In producing all these videos and television shows, she feels very lucky that she gets to travel all over the world and fish some incredible water.

Before preparing Kelly's Rock Shrimp Capellini, she asks that you have everything else done in preparation for your meal before you start the shrimp. She says it goes very fast and doesn't lend itself well to hanging around on the stove very well.

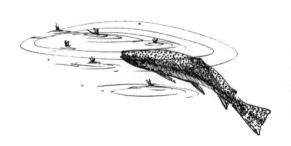

Years Fly Fishing
Fifteen
Favorite Rod
4 Piece 8 wt 10' Graphite
Rods Owned
Too Many
Favorite Flies
Dry – Parachute Adams
Wet – C.H. Woolly Bugger
Nymph – Prince
Streamer – Kelly's Princessa
Terrestrial – B & B Hopper
Fly Invented
Kelly's Seductress
Favorite US River
Colorado (CO)
Home River
Yakima (WA)
Favorite Stream
Riva Davia (Argentina)
Home Stream
Snoqualmie (WA)

1 Pound Bag Capellini Noodles
2 Pounds Fresh Rock Shrimp
4 Tablespoons Margarine
1 Tablespoon Fresh Garlic, Crushed
2 Pinches Red Pepper Flakes
Cracked Black Pepper to Taste
2 Tablespoons Lemon Juice

In a saucepan, cook capellini noodles until desired firmness. Do not drain until rock shrimp mixture is done, so noodles stay hot.

Once capellini is cooked, melt margarine over medium high heat in a sauté pan. Add garlic, red pepper flakes and black pepper. Stir and add rock shrimp to margarine mixture and stir constantly. Add lemon juice. Remove from heat once shrimp is heated through, shrimp is still translucent but has more of an orange color to it. Do not over cook or shrimp will be very tough.

Drain capellini and return to saucepan. Add rock shrimp mixture from sauté pan and toss together with capellini. Salt and pepper to taste.

Serve immediately. Good luck!

Serves: 8

CRAIG WEAVER

SALLY SUMMER'S CHEESECAKE

"Lust for gear is widespread among American men. We think that if we have the right equipment, we will acquire expertise and that expertise will bring happiness." – Howell Raines

Craig Weaver resides in Goodlettsville, Tennessee where he is in the orthotic and prosthetic business. He is a member of The Middle Tennessee Fly Fishers, an active member group of the Federation of Fly Fishers.

Craig and his wife, Sally, fish throughout the middle Tennessee area as well as in exotic places like Belize.

Sally is the cousin of Becky Hopper, sister-in-law of the author of this book, *Angler Profiles*.

Years Fly Fishing
Thirteen

Favorite Rod
7 wt 9' Graphite

Rods Owned
Five

Favorite Flies
Dry – Adams
Wet – Black Gnat
Nymph – B.H. Prince
Streamer – Woolly Bugger
Terrestrial – Ant

Fly Invented
None, yet

Favorite US River
San Juan (NM)

Home River
Caney Fork (TN)

Favorite Stream
Slickrock (TN)

Home Stream
Gasper (KY)

2 Cups Graham Cracker Crumbs
Sugar
½ Cup Melted Butter
16 Ounces Cream Cheese
2 Eggs
Vanilla
1 Cup Sour Cream

Mix 2 cups graham cracker crumbs, ½ cup sugar and ½ cup butter. Press into bottom and sides of a 9" spring baking pan.

Cream 16 ounces of cream cheese until softened and smooth. Blend in 2 eggs, 2/3 cups sugar and 1 teaspoon of vanilla. Pour into crust and bake at 375 degrees for 20 minutes. Remove from oven and let stand 15 minutes.

Combine 1 cup of sour cream, 2 tablespoons of sugar and 1 teaspoon of vanilla. Spread over top of cheesecake. Return to 425-degree oven for 10 minutes.

Cool overnight in refrigerator.

Serves: 10

KATHARINE WEBER

PRATIE OATEN*

"You do it for those moments of casting your thoughts beneath the surface of the water to see if you can conjure up a fish."

Katharine Weber is a writer, book critic and novelist who teaches fiction writing at Yale. She lives in Bethany, Connecticut, but spends summers in Ireland, where her two daughters enjoy fishing for mackerel from their dinghy.

Katharine's novels include *Objects in Mirror Are Closer Than They Appear* and *The Music Lesson*.

Landing a 13-pound salmon on a Brown Fairy, on the Toliqre River, with only one turn left in the knot, is one of Katharine's greatest achievements.

Years Fly Fishing
Twenty-one

Favorite Rod
Whatever

Rods Owned
Two

Favorite Flies
Dry – Parmacheene Belle
Wet – Brown Fairy
Nymph – Not Provided
Streamer – Not Provided
Terrestrial – Not Provided

Fly Invented
None, yet

Favorite Waters
Lots of angling in West Cork, Ireland, where I have a house near the Ilen River.

© 2000 - Russell A. Hopper

(*Irish Potato Pancakes)

6 Potatoes
1 Cup Oatmeal
2 Tablespoons Butter
Salt and Pepper to Taste
½ Cup White Flour
All Ingredients are Approximate and Variable

Boil 6 potatoes and mash them as if for lumpy mashed potatoes. Leave the skins on. Leftover mashed potatoes work fine, too.

Add 1 cup of oatmeal (Quaker Oats) straight from the container, not cooked. Add ½ cup flour, white or whole wheat. Mix together, but don't over mix. Salt and pepper to taste.

In a large skillet or sauté pan, melt 2 tablespoons butter. With clean hands, form patties of mixture and then fry in butter at medium heat for 8 – 10 minutes until browned on one side. Turn and brown on the other side.

Drain the pancakes on paper towels before serving. Make a lot. People love them.

Serves: 6ish – *"Six medium potatoes, as above, will serve 6 people, or 4 hungry people, or 2 very hungry people."* – Katharine

RAY J. WHITE

BLACK BEAN SOUP

"The recipe provided was the meal just after catching my first three trout on the night of a giant mayfly hatch in June 1946 at age 11, the first time I ever went trout fishing. I have been hooked on it ever since—and it led to a career."

Ray White, *Fly Fish America's* wild fish expert, lives in Edmonds, Washington. He began his career as an aquatic biologist for the Wisconsin Conservation Department, where he evaluated habitat management and developed gear and methods for inventorying stream fish populations. Now a retired professor of fisheries science, Ray serves as a fishery resource consultant, particularly on stream habitat restoration.

Ray has published many works on trout stream habitat and its management. He does most of his fishing in Montana and at his rustic, streamside cabin in central Wisconsin—the very same place where he caught his first trout and discovered black bean soup.

Years Fly Fishing
Forty-four

Favorite Rod
6 wt 8' 6" Graphite

Rods Owned
Eighteen

Favorite Flies
Dry – Adams
Wet – None in particular.
Nymph – Cinnamon
Streamer – Hornberg
Terrestrial – Pochmann
Hopper Trudes

Fly Invented
Blond Adams

Favorite US River
Madison (MT)

Home River
Mecan (WI)

Favorite Stream
A Secret

Home Stream
Mecan (WI)

1 Can Black Bean Soup Concentrate
1 Can Water

Open a can of black bean soup concentrate. Dump contents of can into saucepan. Add 1 can of water and stir. Heat to near boiling. Pour into soup dishes and eat.

DAVE WHITLOCK

SPINACH DIP

"If the water is already crowded, do not make matters worse by squeezing in, too."

Dave Whitlock lives in Mountain Home, Arkansas where he and his wife run their Dave & Emily Whitlock Fly Fishing Schools.

For ten years, Dave ran the L. L. Bean fly fishing schools. He also wrote the *L. L. Bean Flyfishing Handbook* and contributed *Fly Fishing for Trout* to Lefty Kreh's *Lefty's Little Library of Fly Fishing*.

Dave has illustrated many fly fishing books including President Jimmy Carter's *Outdoor Journal*.

A strong devotee to conservation efforts, Dave has contributed to The Federation of Fly Fishers' *Whitlock-Vibert Box Handbook*, a product of seven years research with the Whitlock-Vibert Box, an instream incubation and nursery system for trout, char and layed salmon eggs.

In 1981, Dave received the FFF's *Conservation Man of the Year Award,* as well as the Buz Buszek *Fly Tyer's Award*, the highest honor bestowed in the fly fishing world. In 1997, he was inducted into the *National Freshwater Hall of Fame*.

Dave is the Editor-at-Large for *Fly Fisherman* magazine.

Years Fly Fishing
Not Provided

Favorite Rod
Not Provided

Rods Owned
Not Provided

Favorite Flies
Dry – Adams and Royal Wulff
Wet – Dave's Damsel Nymph
Nymph – G.R. Hare's Ear
Streamer – Near Nuff Sculpin
Terrestrial – Dave's Hopper
and Near Nuff Crayfish

Flies Invented
Dave's Hopper, Near Nuffs
and Many Others

Favorite US River
White (AR)

Home River
White (AR)

Favorite Stream
Little Norfork (AR)

Home Stream
Not Provided

10 Ounces Frozen Spinach
(Thaw and Squeeze Out Later)
2 Packages (8 Ounces Each) Cream Cheese
2 Cups Cheddar Cheese, Grated
2 Tablespoons Covenders Greek Seasoning
1 Can Rotel, Drained

Mix all ingredients and cook at 350 degrees for 30 – 45 minutes.

EMILY WHITLOCK

"It shall be a rule for me to make as little noise as I can when I fish." – Izaak Walton

Emily Whitlock has been an avid outdoors woman most of her life, learning to fish when she was 7 years old. She has degrees in botany and biology and is a conservationist in the true sense, willing to work for preservation of the natural world.

Emily and her husband, Dave, combined their talents in 1991 and have lectured, instructed and fished together around the United States and abroad.

A natural teacher, Emily is also an accomplished photographer and assists Dave in all of his writing and video projects.

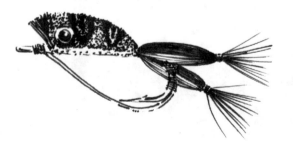

Years Fly Fishing
Not Provided

Favorite Rod
Not Provided

Rods Owned
Not Provided

Favorite Flies
Dry – Adams
Wet – Dave's Damsel Fly
Nymph – G.R. Hare's Ear
Streamer – Near Nuff Sculpin
Terrestrial – Dave Whitlock

Fly Invented
None, yet

Favorite US River
White (AR)

Home River
White (AR)

Favorite Stream
Little Norfork (AR)

Home Stream
Not Provided

SPINACH DIP

"See Dave's Spinach Dip." – Emily

RICHARD WHITNER

"Life is like fishing. Keep casting. You never know when you'll catch one, or two or more. But don't ignore the fishless days either. You can sometimes learn more on those days, than the days you caught a creel full. P. S. Practice Catch & Release."

Richard Whitner is the Manager of The Sporting Life Outfitters in New Orleans, Louisiana. He is in the process of creating a whole new series of flies using Flexo tubing.

Richard is also the creator of the famed The Pops, a fly named after all the dads who took their kids fishing, which is one of the Flexo tubing series flies.

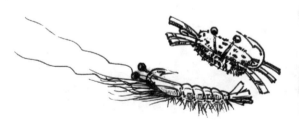

Years Fly Fishing
Twenty-nine

Favorite Rod
9 wt 9' Graphite

Rods Owned
Fifteen

Favorite Flies
Dry – The Pops
Wet – Show's Soft Shell Crab
Nymph - Kiraw
Streamer – Magna Herring
Terrestrial – Flexo
Arrowhead Squid
(All Salt Water Flies)

Flies Invented
Show's Soft Shell Crab,
Flexo Arrowhead Squid
and The Pops

Favorite US River
Hudson (NY)

Home River
Mississippi (LA)

Favorite Stream
Walkill (LA)

Home Stream
The Gulf (TX)

NEW YORK CHEESECAKE

Crust Ingredients
1 1/3 Graham Cracker Crumbs
¼ Cup Sugar
3 – 4 Pats Butter

Cheesecake Ingredients
4 Packages (8 Ounce Each) Cream Cheese
1 ¾ Cups Sugar
3 Tablespoons Flour
1 Teaspoon Vanilla
1 Teaspoon Lemon Juice
6 Eggs
¼ Cup Heavy Cream

Mix crust ingredients and layer in the bottom of a 10" cheesecake pan and dust on sides.

Mix cheesecake ingredients, except cream, and mix well until creamy. Add cream and mix well. Pour into the cheesecake pan.

Preheat oven to 450 degrees. Bake for 10 – 12 minutes. Turn the oven to 200 degrees and bake for 1 hour.

Open the oven door, leaving oven open just a crack, and leave cake in the oven for 15 minutes.

Turn the oven off. Leave the cake in the oven for 30 more minutes.

Cool in the refrigerator and serve.

GEORGE A. WIEGERS

"Trout Unlimited has made me more aware of the variety of interests and opinions that trout and salmon fishermen have."

George Wiegers describes his occupation as sportsman. The Vail, Colorado resident is also the retired Managing Director at Dillon Read in New York and current Chairman of Wiegers & Company. He has over 30 years in investment banking, financing corporate development for major industrial, media and communication concerns.

George is current Chairman of Trout Unlimited. Upon accepting the position of Chairman, George set an initial goal of increasing TU's membership some 5,000 members to 100,000 total membership by September 1989. That increase was achieved and Trout Unlimited continues to grow.

Years Fly Fishing
Twenty-six

Favorite Rod
3 wt 9' Graphite

Rods Owned
Six

Favorite Flies
Dry – Elk Hair Caddis or Royal Wulff
Wet – Scud
Nymph – G.R. Hare's Ear
Streamer – Muddler Minnow
Terrestrial – Ant

Fly Invented
None, yet

Favorite US River
Colorado (CO)

Home River
Colorado (CO)

Favorite Stream
Skylark Creek (CO)

Home Creek
Skylark Creek (CO)

© 2000 - Russell A. Hopper

SNAPPER HASH

1 Credit Card or Cash
1 or More Airline Tickets
1 Taxi with Driver

Go to New York City. Walk into the Zavenga Restaurant and order.

EDWARD F. "TED" WILLIAMS

BIG ISLAND POND PERCH FILLETS

"No hectic raging in our species' blood—not discounting thirst, hunger, substance addiction and sexual lust—is more compelling than the urge of one human being to change the written words of another." – Williams' First Maxim of Journalism

Ted Williams is a fish and wildlife writer who resides in Grafton, Massachusetts. He says his greatest achievement is in raising a family by freelance writing.

Ted served as *Gray's Sporting Journal's* Managing Editor and then Contributing Editor from 1976 until 1989. He has been writing on environmental issues, with special attention to fish and wildlife conservation, for 29 years. His conservation columns appear regularly in *Audubon* and *Fly Rod & Reel* magazines. He is a Conservation Editor for *Fly Rod & Reel* and Editor-at-Large for *Audubon*.

The Insightful Sportsman: Thoughts on Fish, Wildlife & What Ails the Earth is Ted's most recent book.

Ted is often confused with Ted Williams of baseball fame who also shares this Ted Williams' love for fishing.

Years Fly Fishing
Forty-two

Favorite Rod
4 wt 9' Graphite

Rods Owned
Twenty-five

Favorite Flies
Dry – Cahill
Wet – Muddle Minnow
Nymph – Woolly Bugger
Streamer – Gravel Gertie
Terrestrial – Black Ant

Fly Invented
The Ruggles

Favorite US River
Goodnews (AK)

Home River
Ware (MA)

Favorite Stream
Hyla Brook (MA)

Home Stream
Hyla Brook (MA)

8 – 12 Yellow Perch
Milk
Flour
Unsalted Butter
Ritz Crackers

Catch 8 – 12 yellow perch over nine inches long. Fillet them. Pop yellow worms from fillets with a sharp knife. Wash fillets. Soak fillets in milk for 45 minutes. Dust fillets with flour. Thinly spread unsalted butter and Ritz Cracker crumbs between the fillets. Insert fillets in a crock-pot. Cover with butter and Ritz Cracker crumbs.

Bake in hot crock-pot for 30 minutes.

MARK D. WILLIAMS

"I never met a trout I didn't like."

Mark Williams is a writer. He has authored *Freshwater Fly-Fishing: Tips from the Pros; Trout Fishing Map Book; Southwest: A Guide to the Classic Streams and Lakes; Trout Fishing Sourcebook; Knots for Fly Fishers; Backpacking Flyfisher;* and *Fly Fishing Southwestern Colorado.*

The author, who lives in Dallas, Texas with his wife, Amy, writes a monthly column for the *Amarillo Globe News.*

Years Fly Fishing
Sixteen

Favorite Rod
4 wt 8' Graphite

Rods Owned
Over Twenty

Favorite Flies
*Dry – Mathew's X-Caddis
And Stimulator
Wet – Mathew's X-Caddis
Nymph – B.H. Prince
Streamer – Light Spruce Fly
Terrestrial – Beetle*

Fly Invented
None, yet

Favorite US River
Yellowstone (MT)

Home River
Mountain Fork (OK)

Favorite Stream
Big Blue Creek (CO)

Home Stream
Henson Creek (CO)

© 2000 - Russell A. Hopper

ORANGE JELLO-O CAKE

*White or Yellow Cake Mix
¾ Cup Water
¾ Cup Wesson Oil
1 Package Orange or Lemon Jell-O
4 Eggs*

Beat all ingredients together at one time. Pour into a tube pan and bake at 375 degrees for 25 – 30 minutes. While still warm and in the pan, glaze with the following sauce.

*1 Cup Sugar
½ Cup Water
Extract of Choice*

Boil sugar and water for 2 minutes. When removed from the stove, add 2 teaspoons extract (orange, lemon, vanilla or rum) and pour over cake while still in the pan.

HANK WILSON

"Catch and release is not an a-r-e-a; it's a state of mind."

Hank Wilson is a fly tyer, fly fishing instructor and writer operating out of Gaston's Resort in Lakeview, Arkansas.

Hank instructed the first fly fishing school in the Ozark region at Gaston's Resort. He is one of the region's first full time fly fishing guides and has been a consistent promoter of the understanding and use of dry flies in Ozark tailwaters.

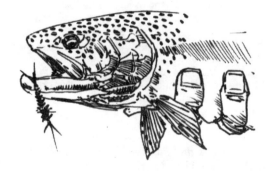

Years Fly Fishing
Forty-six

Favorite Rod
5 wt 8' Glass

Rods Owned
Twelve

Favorite Flies
Dry – Brown Bivisible
Wet – Red Butt #14
Nymph – Tan Scud #14
Streamer – Woolly Bugger
Terrestrial – Bulbous
Bivisible #12

Fly Invented
Bulbous Bivisible

Favorite US River
White (AR)

Home River
White (AR)

Favorite Stream
Crooked Creek (AR)

Home Stream
Crooked Creek (AR)

RIVERBANK BEANS

2 Cans (16 Ounces Each) Pork n' Beans
1 Medium Green Pepper
1 Medium Yellow Onion
1 Heaping Tablespoon Chili Powder
2 – 3 Tablespoons Brown Sugar
3 – 4 Clugs Catsup
2 – 3 Tablespoons Margarine

Dice onion, pepper, and place into a bean pot. Add margarine. Place the pan on hot coals to sauté the veggies until translucent. Add brown sugar and heat the mixture until it boils rapidly. Stir frequently. Add 3 – 4 glugs catsup and stir. Add chili powder and stir. Add beans and stir. Let pot simmer, stirring occasionally until just thick enough to shake off a spoon.

Serve with a hearty sourdough bread and boiled coffee from an enameled steel pot.

Serves: 2 – 4

"Royalty doesn't eat better than this." – Hank

DANIELLE WITT

"I am more hooked than any fish I catch."

Danielle Witt is a Catholic Sister and Director of Bethany Spring Retreat House near New Haven, Kentucky. She didn't get involved in fly fishing until she was fifty.

Witt now fly fishes regularly at Kentucky ponds. Her catch on a trip to Pennsylvania included two 14-inch trout. She has fished in the Smoky Mountains and on Kentucky's premier trout waters, the Cumberland River.

She calls fly fishing the poetry of fishing. *"You have to be focused, quiet, attentive,"* she says. *"I find it very reflective, very quieting."*

"The first couple of fly fishing lessons, I thought I was going to be a failure," said Witt. She couldn't quite get her casting straight for the first two lessons. *"Then, all of a sudden,"* Witt said, *"one night, it just came. The rhythm of it. Like dancing."*

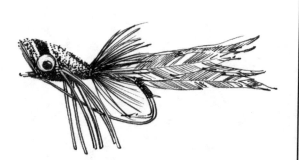

Years Fly Fishing
Three

Favorite Rod
6 wt 9' Graphite

Rods Owned
One

Favorite Flies
Dry – Pale Evening Dun (Trout) and Poppers (Bass)
Nymph – Prince
Wet – Not Provided
Streamers – Black Nose Dace and Woolly Bugger
Terrestrial – Spider for bass and bluegill.

Fly Invented
None, yet

Favorite US River
Yellow Breeches (PA)

Home River
Cumberland (KY)

Favorite Stream
Sweet Springs Creek (VA)

Home Stream
Rock Creek (KY)

PASTA PRIMAVERA

1 Box Angel Hair Pasta
4 Cloves Garlic
Fresh Broccoli – Fresh Mushrooms
Parmesan Cheese
1 ¼ Stick Margarine
8 – 10 Sun-dried Tomatoes

Sauté minced garlic in 2 tablespoons margarine. Add fresh mushrooms and sauté a few more minutes. Set aside. Re-hydrate sun-dried tomatoes by covering them with boiling water for 5 – 10 minutes. Pour off water, cut tomatoes into smaller pieces and set aside. Steam broccoli and set aside.

Melt 1 stick margarine in large glass baking dish. Cook angel hair pasta in boiling water for 2 minutes. Drain and toss with melted margarine. Season with salt, pepper and Parmesan cheese. Add sautéed mushrooms, garlic, tomatoes and broccoli. Reheat in oven for a few minutes, if necessary.

Serve with salad and Italian bread. Total preparation time is about 30 minutes.

Serves: 6

"A delicious and quick meal after a full day of fishing!" – Danielle

HARTT WIXOM

"You can't catch them twice if you kill them the first time."

Hartt Wixom is an editor, outdoors freelance writer and the author of *Utah Fishing and Hunting Guide; Elk and Elk Hunting: Your Practical Guide to Fundamentals and Fine Points;* and *Improve the World—Go Fishing.*

Hartt is based in Provo, Utah. For two and a half years he held the 1994 fly fishing world record for catching a 31" northern pike on a 6-pound test leader. The fish was caught in Canada and released.

Wixom loves to fish the high lakes of central Utah's Manti Mountains (also called the Wasatch Plateau) which contain tiger trout, a cross between brook trout and brown trout.

Hartt's fly pattern inventions include an unnamed mayfly larvae that he has to make himself.

According to Hartt, *"If everyone approached fly fishing with the idea of mastering it, there would be no such thing as crime or mischief."*

Years Fly Fishing
Fifty-three

Favorite Rod
6 wt 8' Graphite

Rods Owned
Seven

Favorite Flies
Dry – Elk Hair Caddis
Wet – Siberian Wood Ant
Nymph – Any Bead Head
Streamer – Black Leech
Terrestrial – Elk Hair Hopper

Fly Invented
See Comments

Favorite US River
San Juan (NM)

Home River
Provo (UT)

Favorite Stream
Stark (Canada)

Home Lake
See Comments

FRUIT COCKTAIL SALAD

1 Can Fruit Cocktail
1 Can Mandarin Oranges
1 Package (3 Ounces) Instant Pudding Mix
Marshmallows

Dump both cans of fruit, juice and all, in a large bowl. Stir in dry pudding mix of choice (vanilla, coconut, lemon) and marshmallows. Chill and serve.

DAVY WOTTON

WELSH STYLE KEBABS

"I live for fly fishing, the friends both old and new, the passion for all that fly fishing can offer, and the waters that salmonoids habit."

Davy Wotton was born in Wales, but currently resides in Palatine, Illinois. He is internationally known as a professional fly fisher, guide, writer, manufacturer and distributor.

Davy became the first to qualify as a National Anglers Council Instructor in 1978. He is also a Grade 1 Advanced with S.T.A.N.I.C., which covers all aspects of trout and salmon, casting, fishing, entomology, and fly tying. Wotton is the U. S. national fly fishing coach for TEAM USA.

Davy has contributed a vast amount of literature to publications such as *American Angler, Trout & Salmon, Trout Fisherman, Salmon-Trout & Seatrout, Shooting Times* and many others, but due to time restraints and a hectic worldwide travel schedule, he only recently started on his first book.

With the demise of natural seal fur, Davy developed what he calls a Synthetic Living Fiber that offers far more life than seal fur.

During the 70s and 80s, Davy performed internationally as a professional bluegrass banjo picker. He owns a 1935 Gibson Mastertone five-string banjo.

Years Fly Fishing
Forty

Favorite Rod
3 wt 8' 9" Graphite

Rods Owned
Forty-two

Favorite Flies
*Dry – Royal Wulff
Wet – Silver Invicta
Nymph – Hare's Ear
Streamer – Mickey Finn
Terrestrial – Crane Fly*

Flies Invented
SLF Emergers, Caddis, Mayfly and many others too numerous to list.

Favorite US River
Norfolk (AK)

Home River
USK (South Wales)

Favorite Stream
Wolf (WI)

Home Stream
Afon Lywyd (Wales)

*1 Pound Pork Spareribs from the Upper Shoulder, Not the Belly
1 Pound Young Lamb, 6 – 9 Months Old, from the Shoulder or Middle Loin*

Cut the meat into 1" cubes. Remove excess fat. Make a herb marinade from:

*½ Cup Olive Oil
2 Large Desert Spoons Each of Oregano, Rosemary, Thyme, and Sweet Basil
Pinch Cinnamon
Small Spoon Garlic Powder
Pinch Each of Salt and Paprika
2 Large Spoons Clear Honey*

Beat all ingredients and mix into a marinade. Still all meat into the marinade and leave for 2 – 3 days, occasionally stir.

Arrange meat on skewers with assorted orders of mushrooms, green and red peppers and onions. Cook on barbecue for approximately 5 minutes, turning while cooking. You may also stir-fry the meat until cooked.

Serve with a salad or vegetables.

Serves: 4

LEONARD M. WRIGHT JR.

"One of the few smart things I have ever done was to lay in a last-minute supply of Perfects that will last me my lifetime no matter how cleanly I live."

Leonard Wright led the movement away from short fly rods and recommended a slightly twitched caddis dry fly back in the early 70s. He currently resides in Claryville, New York and is retired.

Books written by Wright include *Fishing the Dry Fly as a Living Insect; The Fly Fisher's Reader; Trout Maverick: Fly-fishing Heresies; The Ways of Trout;* and *Superior Flies.* His most recent book releases include *The Field & Stream Fish-Finding Handbook* and *The Field & Stream Fly-Fishing Handbook.*

Years Fly Fishing
Sixty Plus

Favorite Rod
5 wt 10' 6" Graphite

Rods Owned
Thirty-five

Favorite Flies
Dry – Gray Fox Variant
Wet – Light Cahill
Nymph – Cream Seal's Fur
#6 3x Long, Weighted
Streamer – Gray Ghost
Terrestrial – Black Ant

Flies Invented
Fluttering Caddis Series

Favorite US River
Neversink (NY)

Home River
Neversink (NY)

Favorite Stream
Neversink (NY)

Home Stream
Neversink (NY)

TRUITE SAUTÉ MEUNIERE

2 Wild 8" – 11" Wild Brook Trout
Flour
Bacon Fat
Butter
Lemon Wedge

Moisten trout. Dredge in flour, and then fry in 1/8" of pure bacon fat. Keep heat high, just below smoking. Cook until dark brown, about 24 minutes or until fish is stiff.

Serve with a dab of butter and wedge of lemon.

Serves: 1 well

JOAN SALVATO WULFF

ROAST TENDERLOIN OF VENISON

"A good game fish is too valuable to be caught only once." From her late husband, Lee Wulff (1939)

Joan Salvato Wulff describes herself as a writer, lecturer, and fly fishing instructor. She is the owner of Wulff's School of Fly Fishing in Lew Beach, New York. She says she is most proud of her title of teacher.

Joan's accomplishments include being 17-time winner of National Casting Championships from 1943 through 1960. She has cast a fly 161 feet. Joan is the recipient of the Federation of Fly Fishers' *Honor of Lapis Lazuli Award.*

Joan is the first person to analyze fly casting and explain the mechanics; giving names to parts of the cast. An accomplished writer, Joan has written several books including *Joan Wulff's Fly Casting Techniques, Joan Wulff's Fly Casting Accuracy* and *Joan Wulff's Fly Fishing: Expert Advice from a Woman's Perspective.* Her most recent video (1997) is entitled *Joan Wulff's Dynamics of Fly Casting.* Joan has written a fly casting column for *Fly Rod & Reel* magazine since 1981.

Joan says, *"I can look back now and say I was born to fly cast. While it wasn't easy, I was drawn to it."* Joan is the First Lady of Fly Fishing.

Years Fly Fishing
Sixty-two
Favorite Rod
5 wt 8' 6" Winston Graphite
Rods Owned
Too Many
Favorite Flies
Dry – Royal Wulff
Wet – Hare's Ear
Nymph – Zug Bug
Streamer – Mickey Finn
Terrestrial – Hopper
Fly Invented
None, yet
Favorite US River
Gallatin (MT)
Home River
Delaware (NY)
Favorite Stream
Beaverkill (NY)
Home Stream
Beaverkill (NY)

(From "Shooter's Bible Cookbook" by Geraldine Steindler)

Rack of Venison
Bacon Strips to Cover Roast
Flour
Pepper
Rosemary Leaves
1 Cup Beef Stock

Preheat oven to 450 degrees. Lay bacon strips over the roast. Sprinkle the bottom of the roasting pan with flour. Season the roast with pepper and rosemary leaves.

Brown at 450 degrees for 15 minutes. Add 1 cup of game or beef stock and roast 12 – 15 minutes per pound at 325 degrees, basting several times. Cook to 140 degrees—no more—for medium rare. Make gravy from the pan sauces.

Serve with wild rice, cranberry sauce and other good things.

"This is the Wulff household's traditional Christmas dinner." – Joan

TODD O. YOUNG

BAKONED RICEY FISH

"The most dangerous place in the world lies somewhere between myself and a hatch."

Todd Young is a craftsman and the owner of Paul H. Young Rod Company. He resides in Traverse City, Michigan.

One of Todd's accomplishments includes making substantial improvements in all the machinery and processes involved in his rod building operations.

An avid fly fisher, Todd founded the Adams Chapter of Trout Unlimited.

Years Fly Fishing
Thirty-five

Favorite Rod
5 wt 8' Bamboo

Rods Owned
Twenty-six

Favorite Flies
Dry – Para Drake
Wet – Blue Charm
Nymph – Hex Wiggle
Streamer – Gray Ghost
Terrestrial – Turk's Tarantula

Flies Invented
Many

Favorite US River
Au Sable (MI)

Home River
Boardman (MI)

Favorite Stream
A Surprise

Home Stream
Crystal (MI)

1 Steelhead Fish or Your Favorite
Wild Rice or Favored Flavor
Bacon or Canadian Ham for Fat Free
Lemon

Fish should be cleaned as typical (not filleted) with head and tail on (optional) for presentation. Skin to be scaled. Slit skin at gill plates and tail areas.

Stuff fish with partially cooked rice and position dorsal up on a self-draining boiler pan covered with slitted foil. Season fish to taste and cover with bacon strips or smoked, moist ham. Bake for 1 hour, depending upon size of fish, at 375 degrees. When done, carefully remove skin, which usually comes off in one piece. Remove fish meat from skeleton (falls off). Remove skeleton from rice. Bacon or ham may be diced and blended with the rice and seasoned to taste.

"Best fish and rice I have ever had." – Todd

STEVE ABEL

STUART C. APTE

~ 290 ~

Steve Abel is at work in his test laboratory.

Les Adams landed a steelhead caught on the Dean River (1998).

Farrow Allen lost his Bonita to a shark.

Stu Apte is a legendary angler.

Chris Atkins and his daughter, Beryl, each caught a fish.

LESLIE ADAMS

FARROW ALLEN

CHRISTOPHER ATKINS

AL BEATTY

~ 291 ~

Al Beatty ponders his Yummy Low Fat Meatloaf.

Gretchen Beatty teaches fly tying.

Barry Beck tries to make the correct fly selection.

Cathy Beck proves she made the right fly selection.

Robert Behnke has a pet donkey named Poncho.

CATHY BECK

GRETCHEN BEATTY

BARRY BECK

ROBERT BEHNKE

FRANCIS E. BETTERS

DEANNA LEE BIRKHOLM

~ 292 ~

Fran Betters invented the Mini-Muddler fly series.

Deanna Birkholm dreams about her Chocolate Sin Cake.

Dan Blanton lands another fish.

Gary Borger's photograph is copyrighted © by Gary A. Borger.

Jason Borger "shadow casted" in "A River Runs Through It."

GARY A. BORGER

DAN BLANTON

JASON BORGER

TIM BORSKI

MAC BROWN

Tim Borski is a wildlife artist.

Mac Brown is an Associate Professor of Fly Casting.

Jim Butler's photograph is by Paul Guernsey.

Paul Cañada invented the Spanish Fly Streamer.

Jim Casada has authored over 2,500 magazine articles.

JAMES BUTLER

PAUL A. CAÑADA

JIM CASADA

HAROLD CASEY

Harold Casey owns four F. E. Thomas Rods.

Bill Catherwood invented this hair headed streamer, the Pogy.

Al Caucci's photograph is copyrighted © by Bill Smith.

Jon Cave invented the Wobbler.

Conrad CdeBaca is a member of the Middle Tennessee FFF.

JON B. CAVE

WILLIAM CATHERWOOD

AL CAUCCI

CONRAD CDEBACA

J. Leon Chandler

Bob Clouser

~ 295 ~

Leon Chandler was a 50-½ year Cortland Line Company employee.

Bob Clouser is a master at catching smallmouth bass.

Peter Corbin is a landscape artist.

Ed Craft is shown near his "Curtis Creek."

Byron Crawford's Filter Fly is made with a fluffed cigarette filter.

Peter Corbin

Ed Craft

Byron Crawford

MIKE CROCKETT

Mike Crockett is a fishing writer, attorney and investor.

Roger Cruwys is a wildlife-sporting artist.

Ralph Cutter likes snakes.

Larry Dahlberg invented the Dahlberg Diver.

Corbett Davis Jr. likes to fish for snook.

LARRY DAHLBERG

ROGER CRUWYS

RALPH CUTTER

CORBETT DAVIS JR.

JACK DENNIS

Jack Dennis taught Harrison Ford how to fly fish.

Tom Earnhardt's photograph is copyrighted © by Tom Earnhardt.

Jeff Edvalds and his "Puffer" fish photograph is copyrighted ©.

Ray Ellis is an artist.

Rob Fightmaster is shown with a Cumberland River (KY) brown.

RAY ELLIS

THOMAS W. EARNHARDT

JEFF EDVALDS

ROB FIGHTMASTER

JON FISHER

Jon Fisher holds a false albacore caught in Watch Hill (RI).

Nick Forrester caught a rainbow.

David Foster is Editor-in-Chief for "Gray's Sporting Journal."

Luke Frazier caught this fish in Alaska's Goodnews River (1994).

Peter Fromm won the first Traver Award.

LUKE FRAZIER

NICK C. FORRESTER

DAVID C. FOSTER

PETER FROMM

JAY "FISHY" FULLUM

Fishy Fullum is at his tying bench.

Ben Furminsky caught a striper.

Dan Gapen is shown with a smallmouth bass caught in 1988.

Hugh Gardner (left) and his guide, Matt Potter, released a native bull trout caught in Montana's Big Blackfoot River (1998).

Rusty Gates is tending shop.

HUGH GARDNER

BEN FURMINSKY

DAN GAPEN SR.

RUSTY GATES

PHIL GENOVA

~ 300 ~

Phil Genova teaches another youth how to fly fish.

Ken Glenn catches a Cumberland River (KY) striper.

Joe Grobarek caught this permit.

David Hall is shown testing another Umpqua fly pattern.

Eldridge Hardie is at work in his studio.

DAVID C. HALL

KEN GLENN

JOSEPH V. GROBAREK

ELDRIDGE HARDIE

GEORGE W. HARVEY

George Harvey taught 45,000 students how to fly fish.

Tom Hawthorne enjoys smoking a good cigar while fly fishing.

Chris Helm is an expert fly tyer.

Anthony Hipps is a chemist.

Tom Boyer's photograph shows Henry Hoffman's 26 ½" cutthroat that he caught in 1995.

ANTHONY HIPPS

TOM HAWTHORNE

CHRISTOPHER HELM

HENRY HOFFMAN

BRUCE HOLT

Bruce Holt adds another notch to his Loomis rod.

Susan Hopper heads to the water.

Lefty Kreh took Joe Humphreys' photograph.

Richard Izmirian (and his cute butt) is shown on a secret eastern Sierra stream. Sheree Kajiwara took the photograph.

JOE HUMPHREYS

RUSSELL HOPPER

SUSAN HOPPER

RICHARD IZMIRIAN

TOM JOHNSON

Tom Johnson is shown away from his home waters.

Ron Sorrenson took Randall Kaufmann's photograph.

Malcolm Knopp is shown with his infamous hat.

Doug Kulick is resting after fishing with two rods.

Al Kyte strikes a satisfied pose.

DOUGLAS F. KULICK

RANDALL KAUFMANN

MALCOLM KNOPP

AL KYTE

H. LEA LAWRENCE

JOHN LINDEN

Lea Lawrence wrote "Prowling Papa's Waters."

Kris Lee took Art Lee's picture.

Matt Libby runs Libby Camps.

John Linden's photograph shows him spending quality time with his daughter, Callie.

Tim Linehan is the host of "Trout Unlimited Television."

ART LEE

MATT LIBBY

TIM LINEHAN

GARY LOOMIS

~ 305 ~

Gary Loomis wears a grin.

Tracie Maler was twice voted as "Woman of the Year."

Al Marlowe is owned by his golden retriever, Skipper.

Bob Marriott is caught sneaking away from his fly fishing store.

Darrel Martin's photograph is copyrighted © by Darrel Martin.

BOB MARRIOTT

TRACIE MALER

AL MARLOWE

DARREL MARTIN

CRAIG MATHEWS

Craig Mathews is shown with his bonefish.

Rick Matthews is a pharmacist.

Todd Matthews caught another Cumberland River (KY) brown.

Darlene McManus took Pat McManus's photograph.

Ken Medling is shown performing a magic trick.

PATRICK F. McMANUS

RICK L. MATTHEWS

TODD MATTHEWS

KENNY MEDLING

MAGGIE MERRIMAN

~ 307 ~

Maggie Merriman designed the first women's fly fishing vest.

Deke Meyer started tying flies when he was 13 years old.

Mike Michalak owns The Fly Shop® in Redding, California.

Jack Miller aka One Weight Jack.

Anna Minicucci's photograph is copyrighted © by Bart Buckley.

JACK E. MILLER

DEKE MEYER

MIKE MICHALAK

ANNA MINICUCCI

SKIP MORRIS

BOB NAUHEIM

~ 308 ~

Skip Morris's photograph, taken by Carol Morris, is copyrighted ©.

Laurie Morrow's photograph is copyrighted © by Don Hoffman.

Harry Murray is a pharmacist.

Bob Nauheim invented the Crazy Charlie fly pattern.

Jon Ford took Bob Newman's photograph.

LAURIE MORROW

HARRY W. MURRAY

BOB NEWMAN

BRIAN O'KEEFE

Brian O'Keefe is a photographer.

Tom Owen paints trout and other game fish in their natural settings.

Margot Page is the grand-daughter of Sparse Grey Hackle.

Diane Pallot's photograph is copyrighted © by Flip Pallot.

Flip Pallot is in a non-fly-fishing-mode.

DIANE B. PALLOT

TOM OWEN

MARGOT PAGE

FLIP PALLOT

JON W. PARKER

R.M. "PETE" PARKER

Jon Parker is a rod maker.

Pete Parker is a ballroom dancer.

Rick Spence photographed Billy Pate's 188-pound tarpon (1982).

Jodi Pate shows off her world record 116.9-pound black marlin.

Howard Patterson's 18-pound silver salmon was caught in Alaska's Wild Man River (1998).

BILLY PATE

Stretching to equal a record

Billy Pate of Isla Morada had to stretch to show the length of 188-pound tarpon he caught Thursday using fly tackle off Homasassa in the Gulf of Mexico. The fish, believed to be a world record for tarpon on fly tackle, measured 7-feet-5 in length and was 43 inches in girth.

JODI PATE

HOWARD E. PATTERSON

C. BOYD PFEIFFER

Boyd Pfeiffer is a prolific writer.

Tom Piccolo's photograph was taken in October 1998 at The Pen.

Dick Pobst wrote "Trout Stream Insects."

Steve Probasco is Editor-in-Chief of "Northwest Fly Fishing."

Datus Proper invented the Perfect Dun fly pattern.

STEVE PROBASCO

TOM PICCOLO

DICK POBST

DATUS C. PROPER

JAMES PROSEK

~ 312 ~

James Prosek caught a non-trout.

Jamie Puckett is shown on his secret home waters.

Paul Quinnett is caught in a self-analyzing pose.

Howell Raines is shown working at his newspaper job.

Steve Rajeff's photograph is copyrighted © by G. Loomis, Inc.

HOWELL RAINES

JAMES PUCKETT

PAUL QUINNETT

STEVE RAJEFF

GEORGE W. REIGER

George Reiger was a friend of the late A. J. McClane.

Bob Richards makes Corvettes.

Bob Rodgers is a fishing guide and writer.

Craig Rogers is a freelance artist.

Neal and Linda Rogers always dress up when they fish. Their photograph is copyrighted ©.

CRAIG ROGERS

BOB RICHARDS

BOB RODGERS

NEAL & LINDA ROGERS

RICK RUOFF

JACK SAMSON

~ 314 ~

Rick Ruoff is ready for a high-speed kind of day.

Jack Samson pioneered salt water catch and release fishing.

Jim Schollmeyer is a photographer and writer.

Dorothy Schramm teaches fly tying after eating TTRJ.

Ed Shenk is a legendary angler.

JIM SCHOLLMEYER

DOROTHY SCHRAMM

ED SHENK

MARTY SHERMAN

GARY SOUCIE

Marty Sherman's dad, Martin R. Sherman, took his photograph.

Cam Sigler ties another killer fly.

Harry Slone says that unless he breaks a rod a year, he hasn't really fished his best.

Gary Soucie's next book is entitled "Woolly Wisdom."

Neale Streeks ends another day.

CAM SIGLER

HARRY LEE SLONE

NEALE E. STREEKS

LOU TABORY

WILLIAM G. TAPPLY

Lou Tabory invented the Snake Fly pattern.

Sam Talarico's photograph is copyrighted ©.

Dick Talleur is a master fly tyer.

Bill Tapply invented the Mongrel Bugger fly pattern.

Wanda Taylor was the FFF's first woman certified instructor.

SAM TALARICO

DICK TALLEUR

WANDA TAYLOR

JIM TEENY

~ 317 ~

Jim Teeny is known as The Submarine Man.

Al Troth invented the Elk Hair Caddis fly pattern.

John Troy is shown in a photograph sans Ben.

Gene Trump is a cartoonist.

Dan Turner invented the Hot Dog Chili Mac.

GENE TRUMP

AL TROTH

JOHN R. TROY

DANIEL D. TURNER

R.P. VAN GYTENBEEK

Peter Van Gytenbeek publishes "Fly Fishing in Salt Water."

Mark Van Patten's photograph is copyrighted © 1998 by T. J. Beck.

Kitty Pearson-Vincent copyrighted © Jim Vincent's photo.

The photograph of Joe Warren is copyrighted © by Melissa Warren.

Charles Waterman is a writer.

JOE J. WARREN

MARK VAN PATTEN

JAMES D. VINCENT

CHARLES F. WATERMAN

JIM WATT

Jim Watt is the one his wife, Kelly, didn't release.

Kelly Watt is shown with the one she did release.

Ray White is a wild fish expert.

Ron Hyde took the photograph of Ted Williams and his Goodnews River king salmon.

Mark Williams prefers his books.

EDWARD "TED" WILLIAMS

KELLY WATT

RAY J. WHITE

MARK D. WILLIAMS

HANK WILSON

Hank Wilson is shown with an Arkansas rainbow.

Some of Davy Wotton's hand tied flies sell for $500 each.

Leonard Wright invented the Fluttering Caddis series of flies.

Glen Lau took Joan Wulff's photograph.

JOAN SALVATO WULFF

DAVY WOTTON

LEONARD M. WRIGHT, JR.

APPETIZERS

Bluegill Cocktail, 44
Bream Italian, 248
Chile Rellanos, 136
Country Ham Balls, 167
Death Defying Chicken Livers, 178
Goose Nuggets, 239
Mango Tomatillo Pescador Salsa, 157
Oysters Wandaful, 207
Patte Monterey, 221
Pedros Cheviche, 188
Politically Correct Seviche, 254
Potato Chips & Beer, 116
Spinach Dip, 277
Steamed Mussels in a Crock, 128
Trip Food, 56

BARBECUES

Barbecued Chicken, 33
Barbecued Elk Ribs, 99
Barbecued Salmon Fillets, 252
Barbecue Spare Ribs, 7
Butler's Brilliant Barbecue Marinade, 34
Flame Thrower Barbecue Sauce, 8
Grilled Salmon ala Dave, 68
Jim's Oriental Barbecue Fish, 266

~ 321 ~

John Shewey's Cilantro
    Steelhead Barbecue, 230
Rib Tickling Barbecue Ribs, 134
Venison/Beef Barbecue, 129
Virginia's Spare Ribs, 260
Welsh Style Kebabs, 286

BEVERAGES

Bourbon Slush, 6
Chilled Olive Snack, 80
Christmas Ladies Sundowner, 241
Vodka Sorbet, 163

BREADS

Allenberry Sweet Rolls, 115
Banana Nut Bread, 258
Banoc Bread, 139
Ben's Tex-Mex Cornbread, 19
Honey Almond Bread, 24
Mom's Favorite Potato Pancakes, 187
Pratie Oaten, 275

BREAKFAST

Breakfast Burrito by Conrad, 43
"Cracker" Eggs, 240
Crepes Baba, 209
Irish Country Breakfast, 173
Mom's Favorite Potato Pancakes, 187
Pfanenkuchen (German Pancakes), 105
TTRJ Breakfast, 226

CASSEROLES

California Casserole, 48
Camp Fire Dinner, 155
Chicken-Broccoli Casserole, 65
Evelyn's Sauerkraut & Pork, 130
Eyre Hall Clam Casserole, 158
Hamburger ala Tomahawk, 164
Hash Brown Casserole, 146
Highway Stew, 162
Hobo Feast, 250
Hungry Jack Casserole, 223
Lunch-in-a-Bowl Special #1, 51
Martha's Bean Casserole, 210
Opening Day Noodles, 16
Red Beans and Rice, 62
Red Enchiladas, 45
Tater Tot Casserole, 98, 108
Tim's Mom's Never Fail Tuna, 26

DESSERTS

Apple Pie, 92
Chocolate Mousse Tart, 124
Chocolate Sin Cake, 22
Doc's Ponil Feast Pumpkin
    Cheesecake, 255
Easton Connecticut Apple Pie, 202
Hot Fudge Sunday, 161
Key Lime Pie, 42
Lori-Ann's Best Apple Pie, 172
New York Cheesecake, 279
Oatmeal Cake, 63
Old Irish Fudge Pie, 269
Orange Jell-O Cake, 282
Peanut Butter Pie, 190
Pecan Pie, 189
Pineapple Pie, 38
Rosalynn's Strawberry Cake, 36
Sally Summer's Cheesecake, 274
Spiced Sour Cream Coffeecake, 135
Tamarind Sorbet, 220
Turtle Cake, 149
Vodka Sorbet, 163

FISH, FRIED & OTHER

A. D.'s Fried Fish, 143
Bakoned Ricey Fish, 289

Big Island Pond Perch Fillets, 281
Bluegill Cocktail, 44
Boned & Broiled Shad, 61
Bream Ensalada, 165
Bream Italian, 248
Catfish & Black Bean Sauce, 75
Catfish in Mushroom Cream Sauce, 101
Dan Gapen's Shore Lunch Fish, 86
Deep Fried Trout, 159
Fish on a Stick, 87
Fried Fish, 191
Fried Fish Meal, 206
Fried Trout, 103
Gourmet Channel Catfish, 66
Grouper Fingers, 212
Probasco's Fish Stew, 200
Rancho La Puerta, 53
Roasted Brookies, 83
Salmon – *See Separate Listing*
Seafood – *See Separate Listing*
Spanish Style Breaded Fish, 71
Steamed Catfish & Black Bean Sauce, 75
Steamed Mussels in a Crock, 128
Teriyaki Crappie, 204
Trout – *See Separate Listing*

FOWL

Barbecued Chicken, 33
Broiled Wild Duck, 198
Camp Fire Dinner, 155
Casuela de Ave, 114
Chicken-Broccoli Casserole, 65
Creamy Blue Grouse Pequin Pasta, 153
Curried Quail with Sausage &
    Couscous, 205
Death Defying Chicken Livers, 178
Dutch Oven Fried Chicken, 233
Dutch Oven Grouse, 32
Edible Sea Duck, 249
Fried Chicken, Mashed Potatoes
    & Gravy, 238
Game Birds & Chokecherry Sauce, 77
Goose Nuggets, 239
Grilled Duck or Goose Breast, 102
Hot-Chengtu Chicken, 245
Joanne's Grouse, Wild Rice, Leeks
    & Morel Chowder, 141
Kaskattama Goose, 30
Lemon-Tarragon Pheasant, 55
Low Fat Glazed Chicken in Crockpot, 15
Madam M's Roast Chicken, 57
Marinated Chicken Breasts, 193

FOWL – CONTINUED

Minnesota Duck, 218
Mustard Surprise Chicken, 236
Pheasant Divan, 180
Pollo Rodriquez with Green
    Chili Quesadillas, 214
Quail Bonneau , 137
Roast Duck, 222
Roast Goose, 237
Ruffed Grouse, 192
Sauna Roast Duck, 89
Secret Sauce for Waterfowl, 46
Steve Price's Chicken Pale Evening
    Well-Done, 199
Stuffed Free Range Chicken, 272
Tangy Grilled Chicken, 253
Turkey Fried Rice, 176
Woodcock with Cranberry-
    Cassias Sauce, 90

MEATS, BEEF, LAMB & PORK

Backstrap Bonanza, 185
Barbecue Spare Ribs, 7
Beef Curry Over Steamed Rice &
    Fried Eggs, 270
Čevapčiči (Che-bop-che-chee), 152
Chili Verde Burritos, 203

Elk – See Venison, Moose & Elk
Evelyn's Sauerkraut & Pork, 130
Goulash, 175
Hamburger ala Tomahawk, 164
Hobo Feast, 250
Hungry Jack Casserole, 223
Moose – See Venison, Moose & Elk
Pan Steak, 97
Red Enchiladas, 45
Rib Tickling Barbecue Ribs, 134
Round Steak in Mushroom Sauce, 96
Steak, 133, 195
Steak & Onions, 160
Stuffed Pork Loin –
    Smith River Style, 242
Tater Tot Casserole, 98, 108
Veal Piccata, 243
Venison – See Venison, Moose & Elk
Virginia's Spare Ribs, 260
Welsh Style Kebabs, 286
Yummy Low Fat Meatloaf, 14

PASTA & RICE

Artichoke/Feta Fusilli, 183
Baked Pasta & Vegetables, 182
Bakoned Ricey Fish, 289

PASTA & RICE – CONTINUED

Basmati Rice, 181
Beef Curry Over Steamed Rice
    & Fried Eggs, 270
Cajun Beans & Rice, 79
Cohutta Mountain Crawdad Creole, 117
Creamy Blue Grouse Pequin Pasta, 153
Curried Rice Salad, 4
Denise's Shrimp Pasta, 247
Extra Garlic Lemon Pesto, 64
Fettuccini Alfredo, 54
Goulash, 175
Lasagna, 28, 156
Noodles Whatever, 168
Opening Day Noodles, 16
Pasta Amato, 5
Pasta Primavera, 284
Penne Pasta with Parsley
    & Artichoke, 104
Red Beans & Rice, 62
Rio Grande Pizza, 150
Rock Shrimp Capellini, 273
Sauces – See Sauces and Gravys
Shrimp with Rigatoni, 256
Spaghetti with Scallops, 215
Stuff n' Shells, 122
Turkey Fried Rice, 176
White Clam Sauce ala Caucci, 40

SALADS & FRUITS

Ambrosia, 1
Bream Ensalada, 165
Caesar Salad , 211
Curried Rice Salad, 4
Fruit Cocktail Salad, 285
Pedros Ceviche, 188
Politically Correct Seviche, 254
Spinach Stuff ala Coykendall, 50
Striped Bass Salad, 121

SALMON

Barbecued Salmon Fillets, 252
Garlic-Basil Salmon, 82
Gravlax, 197, 232
Gravlax in Viking Sauce, 138
Grilled Atlantic Salmon, 13
Grilled Salmon, 60
Grilled Salmon ala Dave, 68
Grilled Salmon & Mustard Glaze, 120
Grilled Thai Salmon, 59
Jim's Oriental Barbecue Fish, 266
Mustard Salmon Glaze, 120
Pressed Salmon, 197, 232
Salmon & Roasted Red Pepper, 85
Salmon Gold Coast, 263

Salmon Pescador with Blackberry Sage
    Sauce & Sweet Potato Hash, 186
Smoked Salmon, 229
Stuffed Atlantic Salmon with Shrimp
    & Crabmeat, 49

SANDWICHES

Black Bean Burritos, 126
Breakfast Burrito by Conrad, 43
Cevapcici (Che-bop-che-chee), 152
Chili Dog, 259
Chili Verde Burritos, 203
Hot Dog Chili Mac, 262
Mother-In-Law Sandwich, 268
Patte Monterey, 221
Pollo Rodriquez with Green
    Chili Quesadillas, 214
Red Enchiladas, 45
Stream Side Meal, 228
Trip Food, 56
Tuna Sandwich, 76
Val's Cheese Sandwich, 10
Venison/Beef Barbecue, 129

SAUCES & GRAVYS

Artichoke & Caper Sauce for Pasta, 27
Bear Bait Spaghetti Sauce, 261
Butler's Brilliant Barbecue Marinade, 34
Calamari in Marinara Sauce, 18
Extra Garlic Lemon Pesto, 64
Fish Dope, 219
Flame Thrower Barbecue Sauce, 8
Gazpacho, 18
Mango Tomatillo Pescador Salsa, 157
Mom's Raw Chili Sauce, 140
Mustard Sauce for Gravlax, 197
Secret Sauce for Waterfowl, 46
Simple Tomato Sauce, 216
Spicy Tomatillo Sauce, 95
Tomato Gravy, 3
Viking Sauce for Gravlax, 138
White Clam Sauce ala Caucci, 40

SEAFOOD

Arctic Char, 17
Baja Sauté, 29
Baked Bluefish, 94
Baked Bonito, 39
Baked Stuffed Spiny Lobster, 244
Blue Kabobs, 9
Boiled Shrimp, 70
Bouillabaisse, 131
Broiled Dorado (Dolphinfish), 224
Broiled Flounder & Ginger, 174
Broiled Yellowtail Snapper, 235
Calamari in Marinara Sauce, 118
Chowders – *See Soups & Chowders*
Codfish & Gravy, 21
Conch Fritters, 31
Courtbouillon ala Creole, 196
Denise's Shrimp Pasta, 247
Eyre Hall Clam Casserole, 158
Fish Dope, 219
Frog More Stew, 154, 251
Grouper Fingers, 212
Halibut Stew, 109
Halibut Stroganoff, 144
Hommell's 21st Century Fish Filet, 111
Jim's Oriental Barbecue Fish, 266
Mango Snapper, 58
Oysters Wandaful, 207

~ 325 ~

Parmesan Red Snapper, 184
Pedros Ceviche, 188
Politically Correct Seviche, 254
Rock Shrimp Capellini, 273
Seafood Gumbo, 271
Shrimp & Black-eyed Peas, 2
Shrimp Dillicious, 119
Shrimp with Rigatoni, 256
Snapper & Hash, 280
Soups – *See Soups, Stews & Chowders*
Spaghetti with Scallops & Sea Bass, 215
Spanish Style Breaded Fish, 71
Stews – *See Soups, Stews & Chowders*
Stripped Bass Salad, 121
Tim's Mom's Never Fail Tuna, 26
Trout – *See Separate Listing*
Tuna Sandwich, 76

SOUPS, STEWS & CHOWDERS

Au Sable White Chili, 88
Beaufort Cream of Crab Soup, 67
Black Bean Soup, 276
Bouillabaisse, 131
Cohutta Mountain Crawdad Creole, 117
Courtbouillon ala Creole, 196

SOUPS, STEWS – CONTINUED

Fire Side Stew, 112
Frog More Stew, 154, 251
Goulash, 175
Gourmet Dinty Moore, 20
Halibut Stew, 109
Highway Stew, 162
Hoppin' John Soup, 113
Joanne's Grouse, Wild Rice, Leeks
    & Morel Chowder, 141
Mark's Methane Madness, 264
Pothole Stew, 74
Probasco's Fish Stew, 200
Scott Lake Gumbo, 23
Seafood Gumbo, 271
Vineyard Quahog Chowder, 91

TROUT

Bakoned Ricey Fish, 289
Brook Trout & Chanterelles, 217
Brook Trout Camp Dinner, 147
Charcoal Trout Over Sage, 132
Deep Fried Trout, 159
Fresh Smoked Trout, 148
Fresh Trout, 169
Fried Stocked Trout, 166
Fried Trout, 103

TROUT – CONTINUED

Gaston's Trout Supreme, 81
Grilled Trout, 60, 234
Hatchery Steelhead, 179
Jim's Oriental Barbecue Fish, 266
John Shewey's Cilantro
    Steelhead Barbecue, 230
Native Spring Trout, 84
Poached Trout in Sherry Wine, 106
Proper Trout Recipe, 201
Rancho La Puerta
    (Chef Bill Wavrin's Grandpa's
    Pan Fry), 53
Roasted Brookies, 83
Sautéed Trout with Bacon, 145
Smoked Steelhead, 229
Smoked Trout, 267
Stocked Trout Disguise, 11
Traute Sauté Meunire, 287

VEGETABLES

Asparagus Oriental, 225
Baked Pasta & Vegetables, 182
Black Bean Burrito, 126
Cajun Beans & Rice, 79
Chicken-Broccoli Casserole, 65
Evelyn's Sauerkraut & Pork, 130

Fish Dope, 219
Fried Fish Meal, 206
Gazpacho, 18
Hash Brown Casserole, 146
Mama's Scalloped Cabbage, 52
Martha's Bean Casserole, 210
Mom's Favorite Potato Pancakes, 187
Montana Baked Beans, 257
Nicole's B.A. Baked Beans, 72
Potato Tortilla, 35
Pratie Oaten, 275
Provençal Grilled Beans, 25
Red Beans & Rice, 62
Riverbank Beans, 283
Spicy Crock Pot Red Beans, 107
Spinach Dip, 277
Spinach Stuff ala Coykendall, 50
Tater Tot Casserole, 98, 108

VENISON, MOOSE & ELK

Backstrap Bonanza, 185
Barbecued Elk Ribs, 99
Marinated Venison Chops, 194
Moose Steak Tarragon, 127
Pepper Venison Steak Stir-Fry, 227

VENISON – CONTINUED

Quick & Easy Venison, 47
Rekonovich Mexicali Moose, 177
Roast Tenderloin of Venison, 288
Round Steak in Mushroom Sauce, 96
Venison/Beef Barbecue, 129
Venison Loin Steak with Crab &
    Shrimp Sauce, 37
Venison Medallions, 213

XYZ

Angler Profiles, 1 – 289
Angler Photographs, 290 – 320
A Recipe for Living, 100
Gwenn Perkins Review, xi
Fisherman's Special, 73
Introduction, xiii
My Angling Friends, 327 – 334
Order Form, 335
Ted Leeson Review, xi
Trip Food, 56

My Angling Friends

Quote

Name

Profile

Years Fly Fishing

Favorite Rod

Rods Owned

Favorite Dry Fly

Favorite Wet Fly

Favorite Nymph

Favorite Streamer

Favorite Terrestrial

Fly Invented

Favorite US River

Home River

Favorite Stream

Home Stream

Angling Friends—continued

Profile - Continued

Favorite Food Recipe

Ingredients

Serves

Directions

Quote

Name

Profile

Years Fly Fishing

Favorite Rod

Rods Owned

Favorite Dry Fly

Favorite Wet Fly

Favorite Nymph

Favorite Streamer

Favorite Terrestrial

Fly Invented

Favorite US River

Home River

Favorite Stream

Home Stream

Profile - Continued

Favorite Food Recipe

Ingredients

Serves

Directions

Quote

_____

_____

_____

_____

_____

Name

_____

Profile

_____

_____

_____

_____

_____

_____

_____

_____

_____

_____

_____

Years Fly Fishing

Favorite Rod

Rods Owned

Favorite Dry Fly

Favorite Wet Fly

Favorite Nymph

Favorite Streamer

Favorite Terrestrial

Fly Invented

Favorite US River

Home River

Favorite Stream

Home Stream

Profile - Continued

_____

_____

_____

_____

_____

_____

_____

_____

_____

_____

_____

Favorite Food Recipe

_____

_____

_____

_____

_____

Ingredients

Serves

Directions

My Angling Friends

Quote

Name

Profile

Years Fly Fishing

Favorite Rod

Rods Owned

Favorite Dry Fly

Favorite Wet Fly

Favorite Nymph

Favorite Streamer

Favorite Terrestrial

Fly Invented

Favorite US River

Home River

Favorite Stream

Home Stream

Angling Friends—continued

Profile - Continued

Favorite Food Recipe

Ingredients

Serves

Directions

ORDER FORM

Mail to: The Hope Group, Inc.
510 Fairmont Avenue
P. O. Box 62
Bowling Green, KY 42102-0062

Please send me _____ copies of
ANGLER PROFILES: A Collection
Of Some Legendary Anglers' Favorite
Flies, Foods, Rods & Waters
@ $24.95 Each $_____
Postage & Handling $3.25
KY Residents Add $1.50
Sales Tax Per Book   _____

TOTAL ENCLOSED $_____

Credit Card # _____

Expires _____ MC ___ VISA ___

Ship To _____

Address _____

City _____

State _____ Zip Code _____

~ 335 ~

Mail to: The Hope Group, Inc.
510 Fairmont Avenue
P. O. Box 62
Bowling Green, KY 42102-0062

Please send me _____ copies of
ANGLER PROFILES: A Collection
Of Some Legendary Anglers' Favorite
Flies, Foods, Rods & Waters
@ $24.95 Each $_____
Postage & Handling $3.25
KY Residents Add $1.50
Sales Tax Per Book   _____

TOTAL ENCLOSED $_____

Credit Card # _____

Expires _____ MC ___ VISA ___

Ship To _____

Address _____

City _____

State _____ Zip Code _____

ORDER FORM

Mail to: The Hope Group, Inc.
510 Fairmont Avenue
P. O. Box 62
Bowling Green, KY 42102-0062

Please send me _____ copies of
ANGLER PROFILES: A Collection
Of Some Legendary Anglers' Favorite
Flies, Foods, Rods & Waters
@ $24.95 Each $_____
Postage & Handling $3.25
KY Residents Add $1.50
Sales Tax Per Book   _____

TOTAL ENCLOSED $_____

Credit Card # _____

Expires _____ MC ___ VISA ___

Ship To _____

Address _____

City _____

State _____ Zip Code _____